D1240917

OLD GODS NEW NATIONS

OLD GODS
NEW NATIONS

✦

A Memoir of War, Peace, and Nation Building

Eugene Staples

iUniverse, Inc.
New York Lincoln Shanghai

OLD GODS NEW NATIONS
A Memoir of War, Peace, and Nation Building

iUniverse books may be ordered through booksellers or by contacting:

iUniverse
2021 Pine Lake Road, Suite 100
Lincoln, NE 68512
www.iuniverse.com
1-800-Authors (1-800-288-4677)

ISBN: 978-0-595-37662-9 (pbk)
ISBN: 978-0-595-67539-5 (cloth)
ISBN: 978-0-595-82048-1 (ebk)

Printed in the United States of America

Contents

Foreword. xi

CHAPTER 1   Mule Teams and a Violin 1

Growing up in a railroad and farming family in Missouri. School, work, girls, and music in my life. Rumors of war.

CHAPTER 2   Training a Sea Hawk. 20

America goes to war. Learning to fly as a Naval Aviation Cadet and commissioning in Marine Corps. Training in fighter aircraft in Mojave Desert.

CHAPTER 3   A Passage at Arms 32

War and disaster in the Pacific as an aircraft-carrier fighter pilot.

CHAPTER 4   Into the World 55

What to do as a young man after World War II. Newspapering, university, working in Mexico as a foreign correspondent. The first Communist-sponsored "Latin American Congress for Peace."

CHAPTER 5   The Propaganda Wars 72

After joining the Foreign Service as an information specialist, assignments in Uruguay, Chile, and Guatemala. Press officer for Vice President Richard Nixon on his Latin American and British trips.

CHAPTER 6   American Flags over Moscow. 97

Deputy general manager of the first American National Exhibition in Moscow in 1959. Take intensive Russian language training and return to Moscow to serve as cultural counselor in the American embassy.

CHAPTER 7   Kievan Rus 109

The great Russian language. A Ukrainian spring.

CHAPTER 8   In the Heart of the Soviet Empire 120

Moscow, the imperial capital, in the Khrushchev-Kennedy days. The best job in the embassy: running the exchange program, taking Benny Goodman and his band to

Tashkent, celebrating George Balanchine's return to Russia for the first time since the 1920s with the New York City Ballet. Reporting on the politics of culture. The embassy on the night Kennedy was assassinated, and handling the Lee Harvey Oswald file.

CHAPTER 9   New York, New York 154

Invited to join the Ford Foundation as a policy and planning officer. What makes a great foundation tick. When McGeorge Bundy takes over as president, named head of the Asia program.

CHAPTER 10   Half of Mankind 173

The foundation's role in Asia and in Asian studies in the United States. Asian models and theories of development: what worked, what didn't work.

CHAPTER 11   On the Shores of the Shallow Sea 196

Assigned as the foundation's regional representative for Southeast Asia in 1973. Life and work in Thailand, the Philippines, and Malaysia. A new, small office in Saigon aiming to create a small-grant program focusing on the humanities fails and disappears in the general collapse of South Vietnam.

CHAPTER 12   A Farm in the Punjab 221

Living in New Delhi as the foundation's representative for India, Sri Lanka, and Nepal in 1976. The glories and miseries of India and some remarkable Indians. The foundation moves into support of non-governmental organizations and focuses on women's issues and the environment.

CHAPTER 13   Foggy Bottom 263

Return to the career Foreign Service in 1982 as deputy assistant administrator for Asia in the Agency for International Development (AID). Surviving and succeeding as a manager in the bureaucracy.

CHAPTER 14   The Great Game: An American Chapter 279

In 1985, USAID mission director in Pakistan. The culminating moments of the U.S. proxy war against the Soviet Union fought in Afghanistan with the cooperation of Pakistan. The good and bad in Pakistani society and politics. The short attention span of American foreign policy.

CHAPTER 15   Interlude with Crab Cakes and Grits 308

Retirement from the Foreign Service in 1988 and life, briefly, on Virginia's Eastern Shore. The pull of New York. Teaching a graduate seminar in development as an adjunct professor in the School of International Affairs at Columbia University.

CHAPTER 16   The Rubble of Empire. 316

> In the collapse of the Soviet Union, return to Washington to plan a privately
> managed, government-funded foundation that will make small grants in economic
> reform and democracy in the infant republics of the former Soviet Union.
> Managing the Eurasia Foundation for five years, launching field offices in Russia,
> Ukraine, Moldova, the Caucasus, and Central Asia. The psychological and
> economic consequences of the fall of the Soviet Union and America's policy role in
> that regard.

CHAPTER 17   Getting It Right. 354

> What we need to do differently and better in both domestic and foreign policy.
> What we can learn from the successes and failures of the past, particularly those in
> public diplomacy and nation building.

CHAPTER 18   My America. 366

> Settling down in New York City. The rewards of New York and the delights of a
> house on the Rhode Island shore. I resurrect my violin. A trip back to Yellow Creek
> to bury a cousin. Scenes from my youth.

Index. 369

Acknowledgements

I benefited from generous advice and encouragement from a myriad of friends in writing this memoir. I want particularly to acknowledge the help of Bill Harlow in the editing process. My daughter, Kathleen, designed the cover and the photograph sections. Mathias Oppersdorff took the back cover picture.

The encouragement, patience, and counsel of my wife, Judy, were essential.

Foreword

OLD GODS, NEW NATIONS
A Memoir of War, Peace, and Nation Building

This book is my celebration of a life spent on the far horizons of the world while America built something like an empire on the ruins of World War II and the victory of the Cold War, that half-century long struggle for domination of the world.

I was born in the American heartland into an agrarian and early industrial society that in the 1920s differed little from American life in the late nineteenth century. My father worked proudly as a conductor, his gold pocket watch always set to the correct time. He was the senior trainman on the Chief, the crack Santa Fe express that carried movie stars like Ginger Rogers and Fred Astaire between Los Angeles and Chicago. Trains like these connected Americans quickly and comfortably across the vast continent. The high, powerful whistle of their great steam locomotives, rising and fading in the wee hours of the night, carried on the wind a new sense of opportunity, adventure, and glamour in our national life.

When late-summer wheat harvest time arrived, I rode the Santa Fe from Kansas City, where we lived, up to my uncle's farm a few miles north of the Missouri River. In the early years of my youth, my farmer relatives still plowed the rolling hills and bottomlands with teams of mules. If the weather was bad and an emergency arose, they hitched up a team and buggy to get to town on the dirt road. In the 1920s, my farm uncles and their families still read by kerosene lamplight.

World War II shattered this traditional world. I went off to fight the Japanese as an aircraft carrier fighter pilot. Then, in the diaspora of the youngbloods that took place after the war, I followed my sense of adventure and curiosity and went abroad to work as a journalist, a career Foreign Service officer, and a private foundation executive. My work took me to complicated places like Moscow and New Delhi. Working with colleagues and local people in information and cultural diplomacy, and in a later stage on institution and nation building, I enjoyed and puzzled over the endless varieties of the human condition: how to understand and deal with it; how to try to improve it; and how we really mess it up from time to time. I learned a lot about what does and doesn't work in foreign policy and building indigenous institutions overseas.

For example, twenty years ago Pakistan was our ally in fighting the Soviet army in Afghanistan. I was in charge of the large U.S. economic assistance mission in Pakistan. Belatedly, we had begun to support the reform of Pakistani education and were building a few experimental schools in the North-West Frontier Province, that wild, dangerous borderland next to Afghanistan and Iran where Osama Bin Laden is commonly believed to be hiding today. But in 1989, the year after I left Pakistan and the Foreign Service, the United States, following the epochal victory over the Soviet army in Afghanistan, cut off all economic assistance to both Pakistan and Afghanistan. Islamist money, mostly Saudi Arabian, poured into the vacuum produced by the withdrawal of U.S. power to build the network of religious schools and holy warrior training camps for young men that produced thousands of anti-American jihadists. If we had stayed the course, the results in terms of Al Qaeda and the 9/11 attacks might have been different. Today, after 9/11, the renewed U.S. government assistance program in Pakistan is concentrating on—guess what—education, and the time is very late.

The government's post-September 11 response to the challenges of terrorism concentrates largely on military and security instruments. It devotes little serious high-level attention to the long-term questions of how best to go about nation building overseas and virtually none to the critical question of how to fight the new propaganda wars. The chapters that follow offer some lessons learned in public diplomacy, economic development, and nation building. At their conclusion is a short list of suggestions as to how to reorder our priorities more effectively in foreign affairs.

We really have no choice but to reform our approach to the world. The challenges in foreign policy won't go away, and the military option is clearly not the answer. Unilateral arms will not save us from terrorism, world hunger, population growth and migration, or epidemics of AIDS, SARS, or Ebola. Foresight, patience, pragmatism, and, above all, international cooperation must govern our policies. That is how we won the fifty-year struggle against communism.

A first step is to start listening to others. We have a great deal to learn about the world and much about which to be humble. Ironically, that is what George W. Bush said when he campaigned for the presidency in the year 2000—and in office promptly forgot.

1

Mule Teams and a Violin

Sometimes, in the stillness of the icy winter nights, I would awaken in the sleeping porch I shared with my brother, look out at the stars, and listen to the streetcars clanging and grinding along their solitary track to downtown Kansas City. In the summer, kingly thunderheads marched above us over the midwestern plain, the grass ocean of America. Heat lightning flickered across the sullen sky and then, breathtakingly, the real lightning bolts exploded in white, clenched incandescence. Thunder cannonaded and rolled off into the night with the sound of giant cartwheels, muttering as it went. Rain hurled itself in buckets at our windows.

The weather of my childhood seemed biblical in its extremes. The land in the river valleys was as rich as Canaan. Where the streetcar lines ended north of the city, one could stand on the bluffs and see the Missouri River snaking its way down south and east from the grass prairies and the Rockies. At Kansas City, where the Kansas River joined the Missouri, the burgeoning, muddy stream cut eastward through low hills toward its union with the Mississippi. This was the classic American route west to the promised land, from the days of Lewis and Clark to the era of the wagon trains and the railroads.

Railroad tracks spun off in all directions along the bottomlands. Many led into the enormous stockyards, where the steers, pigs, and sheep of the western plains came to be slaughtered. When the wind came out of the northwest, the smell of fear, manure, and blood in an oddly proud way reminded the city's citizens of its purpose. My father, Nathan Staples, and his brother, John, spent their working days and nights as conductors on the Santa Fe Railroad (or, as it was called in those days, the Atchison, Topeka, and Santa Fe), running between Kansas City and Fort Madison, Iowa, a division point on the Mississippi. Both of their sisters married railroad men. Railroading was how you moved up from farming in the late nineteenth and early twentieth centuries. The Staples family was thought to have moved west to Missouri from Kentucky after the Civil War, the first one appearing in a post-Civil War census as a laborer. Whether they were horse thieves, heroes, or plain farmers in the old South was never clear. Rich they were not.

My mother's folks, the Washburns, were farmers. Sue Emma, their youngest daughter, became a small-town teacher and married my father, a young man with a promising, steady job as a railroad conductor. The Washburns had migrated to the Midwest from central Canada in the mid-nineteenth century. As Tory sympathizers, they had fled from Maine to Canada after the Revolutionary War. Before crossing the Atlantic to seek their fortune in the eighteenth-century New World, they were reputed to be from Scotland and England.

Sue's brothers and sisters were corn, wheat, alfalfa, and cattle farmers, such diversity being customary before the soybean became king of the crops. They were small to medium farmers—the luckier ones with fifty acres or so—on the loamy, rolling lands north of the Missouri. My brother and I were thus born into the rare privilege of being city slickers in the winter and farmhands of a sort (our credentials as farmers were never taken seriously in the country) in the summer. I could ride a horse, milk a cow, gently lift the eggs out from under the warm breast of a hen, and drive a mule team, and I still found time to play a violin and study Latin in junior high school.

Sue Emma's oldest sister, Amelia, and Amelia's daughter, Lula, undertook my instruction in the gentler arts of farming. Lula, wearing a floppy bonnet against the sun, took me with her to learn the chores—egg collecting, orphan lamb feeding, milking the cows, and slopping the pigs. The men and their sons practiced the sterner disciplines of mule driving, plowing—first with horses and mules, and then with a tractor as the families got enough money to buy one—taking care of range cattle, castrating and butchering livestock, fence mending, planting, and harvesting. Lula was a gentle, serious young woman with a shy laugh; she treated me as though I were a young prince. I seldom saw her after World War II; she never married and spent her later years taking care of her aging and sick parents. She died in a nursing home, having been an angel long before her time.

My country aunts were fine cooks, better than my mother, who left her farm ways for the city and discovered the convenience of canned foods. (My brother and I became experts in the cookery of Campbell's soups at an early age.) Eva, the second of the three sisters between Amelia and Sue Emma, whose long, thin frame carried within it traces of the girls' Chippewa Indian grandmother, baked exquisitely light chocolate pies. Amelia's fried chicken and angel food cakes were prized, and she made red plum jam as a special treat for me. At harvest time, the families combined forces under the shade trees on the lawn to feed limitless helpings of fried chicken, ham, homemade rolls, potato salad, homemade pie, watermelon, iced tea, and lemonade to hordes of sweaty men. The men stripped off their shirts to wash away the sweat and field dirt with cold well water, their torsos startlingly white in contrast to the deep red brown of their sun-and-wind-burned faces, necks, and hands.

My aunts' culinary feats were performed on cast iron, wood-fired cooking stoves. Many of the ingredients came out of the cold cellar dug in the ground not far from the kitchen, where root crops, spices, and preserves were kept. Women not only knew how to cook, they also were expert at wringing chickens' necks, which they did mercilessly with a rapid cranking motion right outside the kitchen door, the headless corpse flopping around and spurting blood until it was dunked in boiling water to loosen the feathers for plucking.

When I was eleven, I was deemed responsible enough to ride a gentle, semi-blind pony, Nelly, with a load of water jugs strapped to the saddle, to deliver fresh water to the men working in the wheat fields. I prized this job, because I was on my own and doing something really useful. I inherited the job from an older cousin Margaret, who in her childhood had ridden Nelly to a country school. By now, Margaret had gone off to secretarial school to prepare herself for an office job in Kansas City.

As I grew older and stronger, I graduated to driving a grain wagon with a team of mules. Although I flew fighter airplanes in World War II, I never enjoyed the sensations of speed—its noises and wind—more than when I drove that mule team out of my elders' line of sight and whipped the mules to a full gallop against the hot west wind down the dirt road back to the barn, whooping all the way.

In stifling late August, when you could smell the heat rising from the straw of the newly shorn fields, my brother, Murray, our cousin Marvin, and I would ride down to Yellow Creek to swim in the cool, muddy water under the sheltering trees. Since I was the youngest of the three and (correctly) considered a pest, Murray and Marvin always claimed the two good horses, which served as both saddle and work animals. I was left with Nelly, the semi-blind pony. One day, as soon as we were out of sight of the house, they took off at a full gallop down a hill. I charged along after them until Nelly stumbled and fell. I flew ten feet through the air and landed on a grassy knoll. I screamed that I was terribly hurt. Murray and Marvin turned and rode back, eyes big and mouths tight with worry. I wasn't hurt at all but told them I would say nothing if they let me ride Dandy, the fancier stepper of the two saddle horses. This turned out to be no problem. I promptly stopped sobbing and climbed aboard Dandy.

Flying through the air was not an unusual occurrence when Murray, Marvin, and I were together. The next summer, Marvin and Murray, driving a team of horses with a loaded hay wagon at full speed through an open field to the barn, hit a small gully where it angled across the dirt track. The sudden wrench sent the ten-foot-high load of hay, on which another cousin and I were perched, flying through the air. I landed, as usual, without a scratch, but my cousin lit on a pitchfork and had a minor cut on his butt. The team and wagon, with Marvin and Murray seated on the drivers' bench and hanging on to the reins, spooked off into the distance. As this was reported and explained to the adults, I played the innocent bystander role with much satisfaction.

Farmers lived intimately with their animals, which worked for them and fed them. It was a functional relationship, not romantic. My cousins didn't look first for a horse to be beautiful, although that was desirable, but for power and stamina pulling a plow. Farmers looked at piglets and saw dollar signs, not adorable little animals. There was a hierarchy: good horses and mules were prized and well taken care of, as were good milking cows. Jerseys, with their handsome light tan coats, flapper eyes, and huge udders, were the favorite breed. Chickens were bred for egg production, and quality hens and roosters were both sold and traded. One of my childhood chores was to feed the chickens prepared food mixes, although mostly the birds roamed and ate a natural diet. Pigs were bred for weight, fed with household slops, and otherwise ranged free. Their slaughter in the autumn was bloody and noisy; pigs scream. The big barn produced a symphony of smells and sounds: sweet, fresh hay; manure; chickens clucking; horses snuffling and chuffing; an occasional bawling moo from a cow; the bleating of a lamb; and swallows jinking through the open spaces of the haying doors, twittering as they flew.

The farm dogs were there to work. They were watchdogs, herders of cows and sheep, and enthusiastic helpers in squirrel and rabbit hunts. They never entered the house. Cats also lived outside, kept the mice under control, and ate leftover scraps and milk. When their numbers got out of control, infanticide was a matter of course, with bags of kittens routinely drowned. When we were quite small, Marvin, Murray, and I one day took a surplus kitten down to the pond and tossed it into the water. We threw rocks at it, but it chose a strategic landing point on the shore and escaped like a whirlwind.

I was too busy drinking in life on the farm to realize I was witnessing a mold-breaking period of technological and social changes. My family's life had changed little from the farming and railroading of the nineteenth century. Most Americans were still farmers, and in the 1920s most farmers still plowed with horse and mule teams, although by the start of World War II the tractor was becoming universal. Country roads were dirt, or at best rock and gravel. When it rained hard or snowed, it could take a half-day to drive a buggy from my uncle Will's farm into Marceline, where I was born in 1922 and where the nearest doctor lived. Murray nearly died of a ruptured appendix, because in bad weather it took three hours to get him from the farm to a hospital in Marceline.

My country cousins had no electricity. They pumped water for the house by hand and for the cattle with windmills. They rode horses to school. They read by the light of oil lamps and candles and heated their houses with wood and coal stoves. Chamber pots and outhouses served the household sanitary requirements. A hot bath in a big iron or ceramic tub was scheduled every Saturday night. When telephone and radio arrived in the 1920s and '30s, the life of an entire rural world eased. But decent gravel and asphalt roads and electric power arrived only with Roosevelt's New Deal in the late thirties. Considering the backbreaking labor of farm life, most of my country relatives were a surprisingly long-lived crew, but many were crooked, worn down, and toothless by their fifties.

Families relied on themselves for entertainment as well as work. Most of my aunts and female relatives were good singers. A number played the piano, and some, like my mother, were proficient enough on the organ to play for the choir and hymn singing in church. My mother's favorites were "The Old Rugged Cross" and "Sing Them Over Again to Me, Wonderful Words of Life" (which many years later I heard sung by wandering groups of landless farm laborers in Chile, evangelical Christians singing in Spanish while idle sheep listened in the fields—"Cantadmelas Otra Vez a Mi, Maravillosas Palabras de Vida"). At home, Sue Emma played and sang popular old songs like "I'll Take You Home Again, Kathleen."

Sue and Nat had lost a girl child in infancy before my brother and I were born. Although they never talked about this, from hearing my mother sing about Kathleen, I grew up believing that this was my dead sister's name. When my only daughter was born, I suggested to my wife that we name her Kathleen. Our daughter was about ten, and my wife and I were back in Kansas City from a Foreign Service assignment, when my mother casually asked me why we had chosen Kathleen as a name. I said it was, of course, in honor of the earlier Kathleen. My mother regarded me coolly for a moment and said, "But her name was Margaret."

Many families had windup Victrolas, but sheet music was still a far bigger business than records. People read the *Saturday Evening Post*, *Colliers*, the Bible, and the Montgomery Ward and Sears Roebuck catalogs, the latter providing both a fascinating window to the great world outside and rough toilet paper for the privies. Skill at playing cards was a most desirable social grace. Rummy and hearts were favorite games. Poker was sinful, and bridge mildly suspect. Children played flinch, an old card game in which you build up sequences of special cards. The pleasures of such games have virtually disappeared from American life.

The most important extended family reunion revolved around Decoration Day (renamed many years later as Memorial Day), when old and young gathered at one house to honor the dead. Families loaded down with enormous picnic baskets set up blankets, card tables, chairs, and cushions on the lawns. The feast, usually accompanied by fine spring weather, was the occasion for cousins who rarely saw each other to test and compare their developing egos and knowledge of the world, their charms, athletic prowess and skill in games, and their social graces or lack thereof. The grownups sat on the porch, rocked, and talked about old friends—those extremely few who were doing well, the larger number who were all right but not doing great, and—with much head shaking but inner pleasure—about those few who had fallen into the grasp of the devil. They watched tolerantly as their offspring gamboled on the lawn, climbed trees, and played games. Men and their sons and nephews played catch.

Sometimes on the farm it was still possible to organize a game of authentic fast-pitch hardball. Croquet was popular. An added attraction for children of a certain age at these clan gatherings was the ancient game of sex as doctor and nurse or mama and papa, played with rapt attention and in silence in the bushes. This was, of course, forbidden and never openly discussed by anyone. I got caught once with two girl cousins by my Aunt Amelia, her face gray with anger. My mother and father were straight-laced and what I considered to be old-fashioned. They were never harsh with me, although I offered frequent provocation. My father called me "Sunny Jim" because I tended to look on the bright side of things, and for a while I was known within the extended family as "Tiny," not because of my size but from my performance as Tiny Tim in a grade school production of Charles Dickens's *A Christmas Carol*.

There were also entirely adult pastimes I was not aware of. Much later in life, I came across some old photographs showing my farm-side uncles and aunts and friends at a cross-dressing party. Marvin's father, Minor, a stern-faced, hard-working, raw-boned man whom I had seen on a freezing cold winter night clobber and knock a recalcitrant cow down to its knees with a mighty blow on the head from a heavy wooden milking stool, was wearing a long dress and a floppy hat with a ribbon.

The Staples–Washburn contingent was Protestant. They professed a moderately fundamentalist faith whose adherents called themselves Disciples of Christ and were also known as Campbellites after the nineteenth-century clergyman who developed this particular set of practices from his own Baptist origins. The Campbellites baptized by immersion, and I was submerged in an indoor tank in our church when I was about ten. Alcohol drinking was condemned. Interfaith marriages with either Catholics or, heaven forbid, Jews, were understood as grounds for lifelong estrangement.

My parents moved to Kansas City in 1927 from Fort Madison, Iowa, the Santa Fe railroad division point between Chicago and Kansas City, because they thought the Kansas City public schools would be better. The teachers were, in fact, extremely good. We diagrammed sentences. I studied Latin for two years in junior high school and read Caesar (with what I later learned was not very good pronunciation). I forever blessed my Latin teacher, a tiny, enthusiastic spinster named Miss Wynne, for injecting the concepts of formal grammar and knowledge of word roots into my head. My brother's solid grounding in mathematics and science served him through an entire career as a military pilot and aeronautical engineer.

Our neighbors included a steelworker and his wife and daughter, an invalid World War I widow, an Italian shoemaker who people thought a good man but found difficult to talk to because of his broken English, and an aviation mechanic and manufacturing worker. Although it was a working-class neighborhood of modest wooden houses and tiny, well-tended lawns, two uniformed deliverymen driving small trucks delivered fresh milk daily, the cream sitting on top inside the bottle, and fresh bread—my favorite was cheese bread. Everyone subscribed to the *Kansas City Times* and the *Kansas City Star,* one paper in the morning, the other in the evening. On summer evenings, families would sit in rocking chairs or swings on their porches and talk as the dusk gathered. Cicadas sang deafeningly. Lightning bugs pulsed magically in the heavy, moist air.

As dusk turned into dark, families would go inside and turn on the radio, listening to Fred Allen and his hilarious troupe, George and Gracie Allen, and Amos and Andy. From radio I first discovered the exhilarating new music of swing, coming magically through the air from East Coast ballrooms. I occasionally listened to opera on Sunday afternoons, though I thought it went on far too long. Most nights when my father was home and not working, he fell asleep sitting by the radio. Radio dramas could be spellbinding. Sherlock Holmes was a favorite, and the baying of the *Hound of the Baskervilles* never failed to raise the hair on my head.

Once a month or so, finances permitting, I was allowed to go to the local movie house. The great comedians Charlie Chaplin and Harold Lloyd were in their heyday. Tom Mix serials were not to be missed. I saw all the early Tarzan movies with Johnny Weismuller and the delicious, scantily clad Maureen Sullivan as Jane. My father was old-fashioned, preferring vaudeville, which still played at a downtown theater, to what he regarded as the artificial entertainment of the silver screen.

The city showered on my brother and me its incomparable resources of the public libraries. My favorite reading spot, one of the original libraries established by Andrew Carnegie's philanthropy, was just two blocks away in the high school building. My mother taught me how to read very early; I cannot remember ever not reading. I grew up, lived, and dreamed with Tom Swift, Zane Grey's *Riders of the Purple Sage*, and *Tarzan*. As I grew older I read Richard Halliburton's romances in the guise of travel books, and my parents subscribed to *National Geographic*, in whose pages I, along with many of my generation, gawked at the photographs of Buddhist monks with their butter lamps, and bare-breasted African women. I discovered the adventure novels of H. Rider Haggard, began to explore Dickens, and began to read Tennyson and the *Arthur* poems.

In the 1930s Buddhist monks and African women were far, far away. Europe may have been of interest back East, but in the Midwest, the eastern United States itself seemed of little consequence, and Asia and Africa were virtually other planets. True, the father of one of my best friends was slowly gasping his life away fifteen years after being mustard-gassed in World War I. But my father had not gone off to that war nor had any of his relatives, who were all railway men and farmers. There was a magnificent memorial monument to the veterans of World War I on a hill above Union Station, full of battle flags, old weapons, uniforms, and gas masks. But those events meant little to my friends and me. One day we watched the German dirigible, the *Graf Zeppelin*, so big it seemed to fill the sky, cruise slowly above us past the monument and the station. The notion that we ourselves would ever fight the Germans again never entered my head, and in Kansas City we hardly knew who the Japanese were.

In my mid-teens my father taught me how to drive on the parade drive of the memorial. When I got my license at sixteen, I took over the job of meeting him at the station when he came in from his trips. Nathan Staples was a charming, cautious, and steady man. He was good-looking, regular-featured, of medium stature, and had fair, freckled skin and red hair, which I helped turn to gray as my teen years advanced. An early sufferer from skin cancer, Nat proudly came home one day from the doctor's office with a tiny pellet of radium tucked away behind a lesion on his right ear. Nathan was a fine left-handed pitcher; he had wanted to play semipro baseball but had to make a better living. He loved to fish, which he did without much luck, and liked an occasional beer, which was difficult in Missouri, parts of which remained dry even after Prohibition, or else limited alcohol content in beer to 3.2 percent.

Although Nathan was not a particularly fervent believer, he supported Sue in her enthusiasm for church work, which included playing the organ, singing in the choir when not playing, and conducting Bible classes and prayer groups during the week. On Sundays we would all go to church, unless I could beg off due to the need to make a social visit to my Aunt Lena Gossage, Nathan's sister, who was somewhat housebound with obesity. While I was still young enough not to be expected to pay attention to the preacher, I would pass the time by playing with my father's gold, railroad conductor's pocket watch to see how long I could hold my breath. I enjoyed going backstage after the services and drinking the leftover grape juice from the thimbles in which communion was served. I once dutifully memorized the names of all the books of the Bible, and my mother thought she might have a Bible scholar in the family, but I balked at the unequivocal belief demanded by a succession of well-intentioned clergymen. By the time I was in high school, I considered myself an agnostic. Actually, although I didn't know it then, I was probably a deist, which I later discovered was the faith of Thomas Jefferson and Thomas Paine, and which, after many years of living in Hindu, Buddhist, and Islamic as well as Christian societies, I remain.

When I was little, I thought Nat's railroad career was a great way to live. From time to time, he would take me on his half-day run up to Fort Madison on the Mississippi River, where my Uncle John, the younger brother and second Santa Fe conductor in the family, and my cousins lived. Once, we paused for a regular short stop at a small town named Carrolton. My father and I went into the Harvey House restaurant on the railroad platform to have a Coca-Cola and, so it seemed to me, for him to flirt with a cute black-haired waitress. The Harvey Houses at Santa Fe station stops were the country's first national chain of eateries, their waitresses famous for their snappy good looks. The door from the street side opened and in walked my mother, who, in response to some family crisis, had driven up from Kansas City the previous night to see my Aunt Eva, her sister, who lived just a few miles away, and thought it would be nice to surprise Nat. That she certainly did.

On the train, the news butchers (who sold not meat but candy, soft drinks, cigarettes, and magazines) made sure I got my share of free Coca-Cola. I liked the way the train crewmen worked with each other and the easy authority of my father as the conductor and senior man. In my early years traveling on the railroad, the locomotives were still steam driven, with a fireman who shoveled coal. Later, they switched to diesel, and the high shriek of the whistle changed in timbre. The sound of a train whistle still sets off poignant memories in my soul. Trains—even today's bad ones—are my favorite way to travel.

Railroad men had reason to be careful about their behavior. The Santa Fe railroad managers watched employee attendance records and performance, on and off the job, carefully. Unauthorized absence could result in what my father and his friends called "brownie points." Too many "brownie points" cost a man his job, and in the Great Depression a railroad job was a ticket to a decent life. Railroad men were among the first workers to organize to establish safety standards and defend their interests, in 1868, in the Order of Railroad Conductors and the Brotherhood of Railway Trainmen (later joined by A. Phillip Randolph's all-black Brotherhood of Sleeping Car Porters). In the 1930s, the railway unions persuaded Congress to pass legislation establishing one of the first retirement systems for working people, based on pension systems for railroad workers dating back to the nineteenth century.

In Depression America, "big capital" was feared and often hated by many working people. The name Rockefeller stood for corruption, monopoly, and mountainous accumulations of wealth going back to the original Standard Oil days. The railroad barons were equally feared. Many big corporations routinely employed goons as strike-breakers and in some cases, as with the notorious Harry Bennett at the Ford Motor Company, even made them company executives. Hardship and sometimes blood were the price periodically paid for labor protest.

Railroad men and other working people I knew took great pride in their work. The railroads were meticulously run. One really could set his watch by the arrival time of the Santa Fe Chief, the line's premium transcontinental train on which the Hollywood stars traveled east and west, and on which my father spent his senior working years. There were few places to get a better steak than in the Chief's dining car. The popular image of a railroad conductor standing with one foot on the stair of the railroad car and looking at his pocket watch to make sure the train is on time was true to life.

Regardless of how workers might view individual industrial and financial barons, the good life of the rich was seen by all as eminently desirable. On Sunday afternoons in Kansas City, a favorite pastime of many working-class folks was to drive out to the Country Club Plaza area south and west of town to admire and compare the rich folks' houses. "I like that big stucco house," my mother would say, "just look at the garden and the waterfall." In its encouragement of mass consumption and upward mobility, American capitalism broke down, with varying degrees of success, the barriers of class and inherited wealth. Years later, when I lived and worked in the Soviet Union, I argued with my Soviet acquaintances that Henry Ford was a revolutionary far more radical and influential than Lenin, Trotsky, and Stalin put together.

But having a job was essential. When in my teenage years I began working at dead-end jobs just to earn pocket money, Nat always worried when I left a job, no matter how unpromising it appeared. In later life, he could never understand how I could leave a really good, secure job to strike off in a new direction. This was the true mark of the Depression: falling off the job ladder was the way to misery and ruin. Nobody left a good job voluntarily. Leaving even a bad job was risky. With Nat's seniority at the Santa Fe railroad, my brother and I grew up largely protected from the ravages of the Great Depression. We knew there were hoboes, because these beaten-down, smelly souls came by from time to time looking for handouts.

Although crime was generally so foreign to most citizens that people left their houses unlocked, bank robbers and organized crime began to fill the news in the 1930s, some of it caused by poverty but much of it arising from the criminal activities generated by Prohibition. John Dillinger and Clyde and Bonnie Barrow were popular folk heroes operating in our part of the country. J. Edgar Hoover was about to become a household word. One night in June 1933, my mother and I arrived at Union Station in Kansas City to pick up my father, coming in from his Fort Madison run, to find five bodies covered with sheets lying in front of the station entrance. The well-known gang leader "Pretty Boy" Floyd and two accomplices had just gunned down two Kansas City policemen, an FBI agent, a police chief from Oklahoma, and a criminal named Frank "Jelly" Nash. The officers were transferring Nash to a car en route to the federal prison at Leavenworth, Kansas. Floyd was eventually caught and executed.

I wasn't much interested in politics. My parents voted Democratic and thought Franklin Roosevelt was a great leader, although a bit radical. It seemed to me as my teen years advanced that Roosevelt had been president forever, and I got tired of hearing about him, although I knew that the New Deal had helped bring roads and electricity to the farmers. I slowly became aware that Kansas City and its surrounding counties were controlled by the political machine of the notorious boss Tom Pendergast, who turned out a massive Democratic vote year after year and presided over the passing out of an inexhaustible stream of public contract money. The rising politician in the Pendergast empire was a young county judge (a misleading title since the job mostly involved administrative management of county business) named Harry Truman, who was to become probably the best president of my lifetime.

The main problem my father faced with beer was my mother, who was a prominent member of the Women's Christian Temperance Union. Sue Emma Washburn was strongly anti-booze, although not in the bar-smashing mold of Carrie Nation, since Sue had not an ounce of violence in her makeup. She was a great teacher (she liked to recall that Walt Disney had been her student in grade school at Marceline), a church organist and singer, and organizer of church and women's activities, and I realized much later in life that a number of women thought Sue Emma to be a saint. She loved social life, and she and my father would dress up in formal clothes—tuxedo and long gown—and go to Eastern Star meetings, where they marched in ritual drills and performed secret ceremonies, with nary a drop of alcohol, but a lot of iced tea, orange Jell-O, and chopped carrot salads.

As I grew further into my teens, Sue Emma's leadership in the WCTU came into conflict with her younger son's adventures with alcohol, far bolder than my father's occasional beer. I became aware of the pleasures of what the YMCA referred to as "Demon Rum" when I was fifteen or so. My best friend, Charles Davis, and I devoted ourselves enthusiastically to this new and fascinating experience. Charles was a good-looking, popular kid who lived a block away. We walked to high school together. It was his father who was slowly being suffocated by the effects of German poison gas in the First World War. In some ways, I think Charles found my family life a surrogate for what he lacked. One night, having borrowed my cousin Margaret's Ford, we lugged some ice blocks to a city park, chipped ice for our drinks, and then sat on the ice blocks and gulped down a pint-plus of bourbon with Coca-Cola, giggling with delight at the changing sensations.

By the time I was sixteen and leaving high school, I was a devotee of Kansas City's great jazz clubs along Twelfth Street. One Saturday afternoon, I walked unsteadily out of a club where my then-girlfriend and I had been listening to Jay McShann and his band, which included the virtually unknown Charlie Parker, and nearly fell into the arms of our church pastor, who was downtown shopping and who was at least as mortified as I was by the encounter.

My brother, Murray, older by three years, was less troublesome to my parents. He studied hard and well. He was a meticulous and imaginative builder of balsa wood and paper-doped model airplanes, which in those days were powered by rubber bands, and won endurance contests for model planes flown above the hills and lawns of Swope Park on the outskirts of town. Although I didn't know it then, Murray was the very prototype of the responsible older brother in European culture, while I fitted the typology of the rebellious younger son.

I had begun to play the violin at the age of ten after hearing classical music on the radio. My teacher was a passionate, mouse-poor violinist named Norma Troja Miller. Along with most classically trained musicians of the time, Miller squeezed a precarious living out of giving lessons to the occasional weird kids whose parents encouraged or humored them in embarking on such an unpromising enterprise. I displayed some talent and became concertmaster of the high school orchestra, which is to say I was the least out of tune of the many. I loved to play but hated to practice. In my early years, I was easily tempted to run off to the vacant lot across from our house to play basketball, touch football, or simply run around and yell. Later, the blandishments became more compelling: girls, high school social life, roadhouses, and beer drinking.

On good-weather weekends, I often rode my bicycle, fiddle strapped to the luggage rack, out to the house of a piano-playing schoolmate, Melvin Zack, who went on to a career as a professional musician. We would spend an hour or so playing Handel and Schubert violin and piano sonatas; when our music making was finished, we would play handball against the Zacks' garage door, or ride our bicycles out to Swope Park and eat peanut butter sandwiches on the great lawn, and maybe go to the zoo to see if we could make the lions roar. Sometimes we would speculate about what naked girls really looked like. Melvin claimed to know, but time proved him wrong.

Melvin, whose parents had come from Eastern Europe, was one of my two good Jewish friends. As I learned in high school, these friendships marked me as mildly out of the mainstream. Jews and Italians were regarded with suspicion and little tolerance by the Protestant Anglo-German majority of the working people I grew up with. Negroes were completely outside white society, lived in cheap housing, worked in menial jobs, and perforce sent their children to segregated schools. My father knew and respected a few black men who worked as Pullman porters on the long-distance trains, but that relationship ended when the train rolled into the station. The black musicians who played the jazz and swing I heard on Twelfth Street and in the ballrooms were like magicians, but I never met a black person socially until after World War II.

In my early teens, at my violin teacher's urging and with my mother's encouragement, I enrolled in an orchestral training school organized by an Italian double bass player and conductor named Derubertis. The class, some twenty of us, met once a week to play through the simpler orchestral repertory. Mr. D. was probably forty-five, about the same size as his double bass, rotund and sartorially mussed. But his eyes snapped and lit up with music. With much patience and a good deal of humming, he led us through the easier works of Mendelssohn, Dvořak, and Sibelius. My chair in the violin section was strategically located so as to follow the Derubertis baton but also keep an eye on the lead cello player, a poetically beautiful girl named Norma.

After I had played with Mr. Derubertis for a while, he invited me to join a small group of instrumentalists who drove once a week to Johnson County across the state border in Kansas to work with an advanced class of student musicians in a Catholic convent school. The group was Mr. D. plus his son, a tall, handsome professional cellist; a young, skinny trumpet player who loved classical music but basically earned his living playing jazz and swing; and me. The four of us would drive across the flat plains, the old Ford car's heater laboring against the cold of the winter nights, to play simple Schubert and Bach with mostly not very accomplished girl students. In keeping with my romantic temperament, I developed a mild crush on the young presiding nun, an angelic creature in every sense. Back in Kansas City, we would unwind with a late spaghetti and sausage dinner at the Derubertis house, fixed and served by Mrs. D., who looked exactly as an Italian mother should look—plump, animated, and a veritable fount of delicious food and drink. They served wine as a matter of course. Everyone smoked and talked incessantly. This struck me as much more interesting than the plain and orderly lives of my straight-laced, Protestant world.

As I approached the end of high school, my childhood reputation as an outstanding student and dutiful son began to crumble. The blandishments of girls, beer drinking, and going out to dance halls and roadhouses to hear and dance to the music of the electrifying jazz and swing bands that were touring through the Midwest were far too overpowering for schoolbooks. Count Basie, Duke Ellington, Charlie Barnett, Andy Kirk (and his Clouds of Joy), Jimmy Dorsey, Tommy Dorsey and his vocalist, the skinny, young Frank Sinatra, Jimmy Lunceford, Woody Herman, Benny Goodman, and Artie Shaw all played Kansas City in the late 1930s in its heyday as a center of great jazz and swing. I heard them all. They usually performed in ballrooms, indoor or outdoors depending on the season. The floor was packed with dancers. A crush of listeners congregated in front of the bandstand. The whole building space, floor and air, would swing with the driving beat of the ecstatic faster pieces and solos. Then the lights would dim. A spotlight wandered around the floor. Young lovers swayed in musical, physical embrace.

I was frequently in love, with girls named Judy, Alicia, and Norma. The phrase "calf love" best describes most of my affairs, which frequently produced a lot of necking and petting, some of it fairly heavy. A few lasted some months. An old popular song, which band leader Hal Kemp used to sing in his whispery voice, captured the way I often felt: "Got a date with an angel, got to meet her at seven, got a date with an angel, and I'm on my way to heaven." Another Kemp song of the day, "A Heart of Stone," sums up the other side of the coin.

I was vain and much concerned with my looks. A year or more younger than virtually all my peers at school (I was barely sixteen when I graduated), I was skinny and relatively undeveloped physically and worried constantly about freckles and pimples. I read in a magazine about a freckle cream and badgered my mother to send off and get me some. She said it didn't work, and that with my complexion, which I inherited from my father, whose skin even in middle age was well freckled, I could do nothing unless I stayed entirely out of the sun. The pimples, she said, would eventually go away on their own. That was little consolation when I observed young athletes with smooth, tan complexions and muscular builds. In fact, I was actually quite well coordinated. I ran the fifty-yard dash on my junior high track team. I taught myself to play tennis from a library book that analyzed the strokes of the stars of the day—Fred Perry, Rene Lacosta, and Don Budge. Murray and I would get up at dawn on summer mornings and play on grit courts at a local park. That did not help with the freckles.

When my parents went out to Eastern Star meetings in the evenings, I would don a red bathrobe with white piping on the lapels which I had gotten as a Christmas present, borrow a white silk scarf from my mother's closet, put on black slippers, and sit in front of a mirror with my pipe clenched in my mouth trying to look as much as possible like any one of a half dozen Hollywood stars, men like George Brent, Basil Rathbone, and Vincent Price, who were frequent wearers of outfits like this (although their robes were silk, and mine was cheap cotton flannel). I didn't smoke the pipe in the house, of course, since I was not supposed to smoke at all. On our social outings, my friends and I all puffed away constantly—Camels, Lucky Strikes, or Chesterfields—lighting up with cupped hands like the movie stars. These were the days when doctors recommended smoking for good health, and no really sophisticated love affair was carried to success without a cigarette or two. The final touch in my virile charm was a good splash of Aqua Velva. And if one really wanted to make a deep, romantic impression on a date, pinning a gardenia up above the rider's seat of whichever car one could get his hands on was a virtual guarantee of at least a kiss.

When family cars were unavailable, I occasionally had to go out on double dates with a trumpet-playing friend whose father ran a fish market. Their family truck didn't smell like gardenias, but our socially adaptable dates never complained about the addition of this new smell of dead fish into their romantic activities. My father and mother were generous in allowing me to use the family car, particularly so since they must have had at least an inkling of what it might be subjected to. My cousin, Margaret, who lived with us in Kansas City for a few months while she looked for a job (and found both a job and a husband), was equally well disposed with her Ford. My father would buy the best car he thought we could afford. We went up the ladder for a while from Chevrolets to Dodges and DeSotos. At one point, we owned a Nash. I loved them all—their rounded lines, the way they smelled when new, their colors, the sound and power of the motors, the way they drove. Washing and waxing the car was a weekly family ritual. After I learned to drive, when winter storms came, I would sometimes take the family car presumably to run an errand late at night. Instead, with a couple of friends who had access to their family cars, we would spend a half hour practicing controlled skids in circles along the ice-coated Benton Boulevard.

My brother left home to attend the University of Missouri at Columbia, halfway across the state, in 1935, and I graduated from high school in 1938. It was taken for granted that the family could not afford to send both sons away to school. If I wanted to go to college, I should apply to Kansas City Junior College, a two-year institution, and then go to work. The original junior college movement, predecessor to the modern community college, was tuition-free and offered, at least in its Kansas City example, a respectable academic education to boys and girls who could not afford a four-year college. So I said good-bye to most of my high school friends, many of whom went straight to work out of high school, and took the streetcar downtown to the junior college. But I was rebellious about studying and wanted money in my pocket. I left after the first semester and went to work for Montgomery Ward, the big mail-order company founded in Chicago, purveyor of long underwear for generations of working families and provider of scratchy toilet paper torn from their catalogs for countless outhouses across rural America.

I was a pit-scaler, which meant that I sorted and weighed outgoing parcel post packages on a conveyor belt that never stopped. Some of these weighed up to forty pounds. Every now and then a disgruntled employee farther up the belt would strew a few nails or pins on the belt to make the job more interesting. I despised the floor manager, a fat, red-faced, slick-haired career employee who wore a white shirt and loud necktie. He kept a time watch on employee visits to the bathrooms, shouted and swore at the help when crushes and pileups occurred, and hung around and pressed his belly up against the younger women employees. I liked my coworkers, some of whom had already spent twenty years of their lives slaving away in this Dickensian institution. My wages were thirty cents an hour—not much but enough to buy an occasional new suit and to keep me in beer, cigarettes, and date money.

My career with "Monkey" Ward, as the company was sometimes called, came to an early end during the Christmas rush, when I told the fat foreman, who had yelled at me for smoking in the bathroom, to perform a sexual act on himself. I had become proficient in the art of profanity as a kid, picking up the rudiments from more worldly friends and muttering swear words to myself as I walked around the family yard doing chores, and my colleagues at the mail-order warehouse, men and women, were no slouches. My mother asked me once what I was talking to myself about and why I didn't speak up. When my career as a pit-scaler ended, I took pride in the thought that I was probably the only person in the long history of Montgomery Ward to be fired in the middle of the Christmas rush.

I went back to junior college, this time a bit more seriously, although I still cut classes from time to time to play pool and snooker in the local YMCA and other less reputable parlors up and down Twelfth and Thirteenth Streets in downtown Kansas City, where the old college building was located. My pool teacher in earlier years was the husband of one of my mother's favorite church ladies; like me, a reluctant churchgoer, he was, unlike me, a cigar-smoking pool addict with a fine professional-size table in his basement. A pleasant, kindly gentleman, he taught me a lot about the game and its angles and occasionally slipped me a cigar on the sly. While I made moderate amounts of pocket money playing snooker and enjoyed life in the downtown pool parlors, this interfered sufficiently with my academic performance to cause a letter to be sent from the principal of the junior college to my parents saying that my attendance and grades were headed for the bottom. I did finish the semester and went off to the world of work again.

Over the next two years, I worked as a clerk in a big insurance office and then with the help of Margaret's boyfriend, who worked in the local employment office, got a clerical job at the big new ordnance plant Remington Arms was building outside Kansas City. It was impossible by then to ignore the rising beat of the drums from across the Atlantic: the Europeans were seriously going to war. Even in the middle of an isolationist America, with its—and my—general lack of interest in affairs foreign, it was apparent that Hitler intended to take over Europe, and that the way for the United States to help, and profit at the same time, was to ship arms to England. That is where some of the ammunition Remington produced was headed; the rest was going into U.S. Army stockpiles. I was excited by the work at the plant. The engineers were hard-charging men, walking around rapidly with their blueprints and notebooks, chain smoking, and talking about production changes and problem solving in rapid, intense conversations. I was too innocent in economics at the time to realize that war production was finally going to jolt the United States out of its long depression.

In 1940 I decided that the United States might itself, after all, get involved in a war. If that happened, I wanted a chance to become an officer. I quit the bullet-producing plant, went back once more to junior college, and signed up for all the mathematics and science courses I would usually try to avoid. I also rejoined the YMCA, this time to lift weights and run on the indoor track, ignoring my old haunts in the poolroom. My weight-lifting instructor, Jess, was a short, muscle-bound, mostly toothless bar and bell athlete, delighted to get his hands on a willing subject. With his help I finally began to look—and feel—like the tough guy I always thought was in me somewhere. I even started drinking and smoking less. My violin playing became occasional and then rare.

We were sitting around our house on December 7, 1941, digesting a Sunday dinner of fried chicken and mashed potatoes, when news of the Japanese bombing of Pearl Harbor came on the radio. At first, this seemed to me both extremely strange and not very important. No one I knew had ever thought the Japanese, whoever they were, bore us ill will. In any case, the big game was in Europe. The Japanese were not up to really challenging the Americans.

But the war that began that day took my brother off to the Marine Corps and the Pacific War almost immediately, and I subsequently joined him in both. The war exploded the traditional American family like the original Big Bang into a constantly expanding universe, and opened a huge gate to the world. Neither my brother nor I ever went back home. The cousins and friends we grew up with in the city, or in the country driving mules, swimming in creeks, or playing long hours of Monopoly, were themselves swept up and away by the winds of war. When it ended, the Staples–Washburn clan was scattered all over the country—indeed, in my brother's and my case, the world.

Sometime in 1942, my parents quietly bought a four-grave family funeral plot at a cemetery on a grassy hill overlooking Kansas City. Two places were for them; that is where they are buried. The other two were for their two sons, who they thought might be killed in the war. Murray and I never used them, although we both came close. My Aunt Lena, my father's sister, who used to curl my hair and put lipstick on me when I was a small boy spending an occasional Sunday morning with her, her beautician cousin, and her songbirds and parrot, is in one of those two slots. Her husband, Joe Gossage, a rough, bullying brakeman whom my father could not abide, is in the other. My brother and I try to get there once a year to lay flowers on the graves, but it is mostly our cousin Margaret, who still lives just outside Kansas City, who cares for the plot.

2

Training a Sea Hawk

Young men went off to the gathering storm of the war, as doubtless they always have, out of patriotism (or tribal loyalties), compulsion, the opportunity to break a dissatisfying routine, a spirit of adventure, and mass psychology. Everyone was going. Why not me? And if I didn't go voluntarily, they would make me go anyway.

In my case, I was not to be outdone by my brother. In the first months of the war, he left a promising job as a junior chemist working for the government to enlist as an officer candidate in the Marine Corps, having completed the requisite college degree a year earlier. It took the Marines, well skilled in the arts of killing, just ninety days to turn him into a second lieutenant, teach him how to haul and shoot field artillery guns and command an artillery unit (which in those days still included knowing how to ride a horse), and ship him off to the already bleeding islands of the Pacific, from which he returned three long years later with bad malaria and a head wound.

When my brother left home, I decided I must continue the just-established family tradition and also become a Marine Corps officer. But I wanted to fly. It was far more dashing than slogging through mud. I had seen enough movies about World War I to know that aviators in their Spads and Fokkers were much sexier than the tired-looking, helmeted foot soldiers typified by Lew Ayres in *What Price Glory*. Aviators even earned extra flight pay for doing what one would think everyone would want to do anyway.

The way to become a Marine Corps flier was to enlist in the Naval Aviation Cadet training program. In July 1942, which symbolically seemed the appropriate month for such a historic occasion, I went to the Navy recruiting office in downtown Kansas City and enlisted as a Naval Aviation Cadet. I had finished two years at the junior college and, thanks to my YMCA training, I was muscled and fit. Given the fact that my brother had just gone off to war, my parents wanted me to wait and see if in fact I would be drafted. I was not to be held back.

A week later, after passing some relatively easy written tests and a tough physical examination, I took the oath of service and was ready to go off and learn how to be a hero. That, it turned out, was going to take a while. (My brother, who had been a virtuoso model airplane builder, paradoxically became a military pilot only after World War II.)

In the early months of the war, the Navy recruited a lot of young men to train as pilots. But its training capacities were still being built up. There weren't enough trained Navy pilots to serve as instructors, or enough flight base facilities. In addition, the Navy had decided to create a new network of preflight schools for its cadets at a number of American universities to eliminate flab and sharpen up practical math and physics for aerial navigation and related flight tasks. I could not even be immediately scheduled for an active-duty call to one of these schools.

In the meantime, I could start flight training at government expense as a civilian under an existing program subsidized by the Commerce Department and operated by aviation academies in various parts of the United States. A small private flight school at the Kansas City Municipal Airport across a bend of the Missouri River from the stockyards was eligible for the civilian pilot training (CPT) program and there, in the bright and beautiful days of the late summer of 1942 above the ripening corn fields of the river bottomlands, I began a love affair with flying. My first master was a young, relaxed flier named Ray Baker who, like many pilots in those romantic days, wore a leather jacket and a white silk scarf.

Flying, particularly in the tiny airplanes I began with, is, in its sense of feel and tactile rewards, sort of like making love with the air, the winds, the clouds, and the sky. One can always tell a fine flying airplane and a good pilot by the way the pilot gently holds off coming in for a landing, pulling back, holding, feeling for, and finally touching the ground. We frequently flew out of grass strips and farm fields. You can land like silk on grass. Like a bird, in a light plane you must master the air and the wind and soar in its updrafts and spiral like a hawk. Pilots are poets of touch. It has nothing to do with the physical appearance of coordination in walking or sports, although coordination is the essence of good flying. One of the best wingmen who ever flew with me, unshakable in any maneuver, could hardly climb a stairway without stumbling and spluttered when he talked. With the mastery of touch comes the ability to be hard and firm when the moment demands violent maneuver—pushing over into a bombing run; steadily pulling the controls back but not stalling out in an impossibly tight, gravity-multiplying turn in a dogfight; or making an emergency landing where you must thrust the plane down hard on a short runway or a pitching deck in a rough sea.

I soloed in a tiny Porterfield monoplane, powered by a fifty-horsepower engine which barely got two people off the ground, cruised at seventy miles an hour, and landed at a speed of maybe forty miles per hour. We learned how to fly perfect circles in which, having held your altitude constant as you come around through the 360-degree point, you bump into your own prop-wash. We did lazy S-turns above a road to learn how to compensate for the effects of the wind, that giant tide moving around the earth, on your pattern over the ground. We learned spins—pull up slowly and steadily into the stall, feel the tremble, plunge and flutter down, spinning around and around, feel the powerless stick, count your turns, reverse the rudder at two-and-a-half turns, pop stick forward, come out into a dive, and ease up slowly into normal flight.

When I finished my training at the Kansas City Municipal Airport, the Navy said I would not be called up for active-duty training before the end of the year. But there was a two-month, secondary civilian flight program I might be interested in at the University of Wyoming at Laramie. This training would involve larger airplanes and acrobatics. It would be my first time living away from home. In 1942, Laramie, lying at the eastern end of the high western plain before the first ranges of the Rockies begin to rise, was a cow town. Its business was livestock, ranch-connected businesses, and in more recent years the state university. Our flight school was outside the city and used its own grass strip fields. My two months there could hardly have been closer to heaven.

We flew open cockpit Waco biplanes, the instructor sitting forward and the student aft. Our group of fifteen cadets had rooms assigned in a university dormitory. The status of our group was quite mysterious to most other members of the university community. We were neither students nor active-duty military. We did nothing to dispel the mystery, and in fact tried to increase it by designing makeshift uniforms of our own consisting of khaki trousers and shirts, leather jackets, and white silk scarves.

The Wacos were direct descendents of the classic fighters of World War I, although with much-increased power. They were designed for acrobatic training, which also derived its maneuvers from the early days of flying. For two months above the plains and low ranges of eastern Wyoming, we learned and practiced loops, chandelles, that graceful climbing turn that owes its name to early French aviators, and the Immelman turn, a maneuver invented by German flier Max Immelman in World War I, which is a half loop going up, a half roll at the top, and come out headed in the opposite direction. We would dive down and waggle our wings at the cowboys and sheepherders and, if none were in sight, chase cows and sheep across the fields. At our main practice field we gathered at the landing end and watched each other whistling in for landings on the worn-down grass strip, scarves flying in the wind, and say: "There goes Paul. Not bad," or, "Boy, Jim really screwed that one up." On weekend nights, wearing our self-designed flight outfits, we hung out in the Laramie bars with cowhands and occasional university students. Some of the cowhands knew us from our flights over their ranches and said our acrobatics were a welcome break in their routine. By late October, even with our blanket-lined flying suits and leather helmets, it was freezing and becoming far too cold to fly open-cockpit airplanes. We finished our course and prepared to head either back home or off to active duty. By then, counting both primary and secondary training, we had accumulated seventy-five hours or so of flight time and deemed ourselves ready to become aces.

The Navy ordered me to active duty as an Aviation Cadet in December 1942 at the University of Iowa preflight school. This was one of four locations the Navy established when the war began to start sorting out who was bright and tough enough to become a Navy or Marine Corps pilot (the Marines being a wholly owned subsidiary of the Navy, a fact all Marines periodically try unsuccessfully to put out of their heads). To staff and run these schools, where a major part of the curriculum consisted of extremely demanding, incessant physical training, the Navy commissioned as officers a truly menacing collection of ex-college athletic coaches and athletes. The commanding officer of the physical training side of the Iowa preflight school, for example, was U.S. Marine Corps Col. Bernie Bierman, a famous football coach at the University of Minnesota. Younger, more junior jocks presided in person over the three-hour daily physical training sessions. These Navy preflight schools were a dream assignment for ex-college coaches: for the first time in their lives, they had a captive audience of generally smart young men under military discipline who would do virtually anything to avoid flunking out of the Navy flight program. Flunking out meant you said goodbye to wings and officer status and started at the bottom as an enlisted man.

Doing "anything" was often required in the three-month immersion. Midwestern farm and city boys, many of whom could barely swim, floundered around, slowly sinking in the Olympic-size university swimming pool, while officer/instructors dangled rescue poles just out of reach. Swimming was designed for survival, not style or speed. For years after the war, I could identify strange men of more or less my age in hotel swimming pools who had obviously been cadets at the Navy preflight schools by the way they swam the head-out-of-the-water, frog-kick breast stroke. Boxing and wrestling programs were designed so that competitions, rather than eliminating losers, allowed the winner of a couple of matches to stand aside: the more you lost the more you had to fight, and after a while in the losing bracket you were ready to kill your roommate in desperation.

At 6:00 AM (0600 hours) a bosun's whistle and a recorded voice came echoing through the loudspeaker: "Hit the decks, cadets. It's ten below zero." We would muster outside in the ice and snow of the disheartening Iowa midwinter landscape and then file in for breakfast. After eating, part of the cadet corps went off for military drill outside or for a forced-march hike, trailed by an ambulance. The other half went to class: practical physics, math, navigation, meteorology, drills in hostile aircraft identification using photographs flashed for split seconds on a wall screen, and Navy history and practices.

The Navy fed and clothed us well. We dressed in officer's clothing—usually Navy green, although on ceremonial occasions we wore dress blues—without any emblem of rank. My favorite Navy article of clothing was the marvelous Navy North Atlantic storm coat (I still wear mine sixty years later). Since we were all burning calories like miniature stoves, the Navy fed us like prize animals being fattened for market, which in a way we were. We ate limitless quantities of bacon or ham and eggs, pancakes, steaks, ice cream, and candy bars, which were provided free in containers in the dorms.

Cadets soon formed into small groups of friends. My best friend at Iowa, Billy Anderson, was a short, ruddy, quiet-spoken boy from a small town in Illinois, whose humor and steady philosophical approach to the indignities of cadet life helped keep my rebellious side under control. I thought some of the jock officers went way too far in their hazing. The chief swimming coach, a handsome blond fellow with the beautiful smooth musculature of a champion swimmer, was notorious. He liked to strut up and down the side of the pool yelling threats of expulsion at unfortunate cadets who thought they were drowning. "Now, now," Anderson would say, "keep your mouth shut. Keep your eye on those wings."

On graduation in early spring, I was ordered for primary flight training to the Hutchinson, Kansas, Naval Air Station. Hutchinson is a typical small farm town in the heart of the vast Kansas wheat plains. The Navy built an enormous circular asphalt landing field there—so that you could take off and land into the wind regardless of its direction—and set up a number of auxiliary grass strips and farmer fields for small-field landing practice. I was elated at the prospect of starting flying again, although the first truth I learned from my first instructor on the first day at Hutchinson was that whatever I thought I had learned about flying in civilian pilot training in Kansas City and Laramie didn't count as far as the Navy was concerned. There is only one way to fly: that is the Navy way. The Navy was different in one major respect: it demanded absolute precision in the small-field procedures required for aircraft carrier landings and takeoffs and for flying out of invasion beach air strips.

Over the next six months, first at Hutchinson and later at the sprawling Naval Aviation complex at Corpus Christi, Texas, the Navy systematically turned us into military pilots. To the work in small-field procedures and formation training, the Navy added navigation, gunnery, and instrument flying. Primary cadets flew the open cockpit Stearman biplane, a thing of beauty, responsive in flight, lovely sweptback wings, a delicate tail, and an alarming tendency to ground loop. At Corpus for advanced training, cadets graduated to the famous SNJ (the Army Air Corps version was known as the AT-6), a low-wing, two-seater monoplane with a six-hundred-horsepower motor and retractable landing gear. They were a joy to fly—handsome, maneuverable, and durable for the gunner and bombing training, formation flying, and acrobatics that comprised the curriculum. The SNJ in silhouette bore a vague resemblance to the Japanese Zero fighter and for many years most of the Zeros depicted in movies about World War II were none other than the good old SNJ.

The flying domain of NAS Corpus Christi with its super-size main field and numbers of auxiliaries spread out over thousands of acres of scrub brush, most of it the property of the enormous King Ranch, and waterfront land along the Gulf of Mexico. It was a fabulous location for pilot training: there wasn't a hill for hundreds of miles. An occasional hurricane might roar in from the Gulf, but typical flying weather was a hot, sunny day with a mild wind blowing in from the sea bearing white, fluffy cumulus clouds. It was a perfect playground for young pilots to roll and dive and chase each other's tails around the cloud peaks and valleys in the sky.

Our instructors were Navy flight officers, in most cases only a few years older than the cadets, who had been unfortunate or fortunate enough, depending on one's point of view, to be assigned to training rather than combat duties. I thought they had terrible assignments but managed not to say so. In spite of the fact that instructors weren't much older than us, we were enormously respectful. After all they were commissioned pilots, and our fate depended on them. And what tough jobs they had, particularly in primary training, condemned to sit in the front seat of the open-cockpit Stearman biplanes while the planes, cadets handling the dual controls, staggered over trees bordering the small fields or skidded perilously close to each other in formation training.

A half-century later, one of my few surviving squadron mates wrote me that the Navy was about to dispose of old flight training records that it had retained in storage since World War II. Former cadets could write in and get their records. A midcourse comment July 25, 1943, by Lt. (j.g.) U. E. Orvis, an instrument flying instructor at Corpus Christi, noted: "Cadet Staples has a quiet and even disposition. He has the industrious and persevering spirit which makes him capable at all times. He has been conscientious in handling all of his duties. He has demonstrated above average officer-like qualities." The final comment in the file dated September 1, 1943, from Ensign R. James, just before I graduated: "Cadet Staples exercises sound judgment and is sensible and cool-headed but is somewhat cocky and opinionated. I believe he will make a good officer."

One day, Ensign James led a flight of six of us out to a tiny auxiliary strip in the middle of nowhere in the scrub brush to practice landings. We parked our planes and sat under a wing to talk about flying. I looked around at these beautiful machines and my companions dressed in their khaki flight coveralls and helmets and thought we were the finest fellows in the world. We were absolutely, as Tolstoy as a youth said about his aristocratic coterie, "*comme il faut*"—"all correct, as it should be."

On weekends at Corpus, we cruised and drank in the bars and picked up local girls and an occasional WAVE (the Navy's female component, in those days completely land-based). One night, after a long drinking and nude swimming party on a beach outside Corpus, I awakened on the sand, buck naked, with the sun boring into my eyes and a naked girl next to me. After a minute, I placed her as a WAVE left over from the night's partying, although I wasn't sure of her name. We wandered back down the beach, found our clothes, hitched a ride into Corpus, and never saw each other again.

Hard drinking on weekend leave became a routine for me and a good many other cadets. A favorite partner was Don Boyd, a husky, red-haired, bright-eyed, and totally engaging cadet from Flint, Michigan, who decided he liked to party with me. I was a willing recruit. Boyd's other best friend, a tough Chicago boy named Joe Bohlen, had developed a morphine addiction while undergoing hospitalization for a serious operation and was rumored to be an occasional drug user. Drugs were, of course, totally prohibited. The Navy tolerated alcohol use as a common weakness, although never on duty. Virtually everyone smoked tobacco. Marijuana was known but not widely used. Joe Bohlen decided one day that I was so fond of talking about my flying prowess I should be dubbed a "Hot Rock." That metamorphosed into "The Rock" and then to "Rocky," which has remained my nickname until today. One of my favorite ladies, my first wife's cousin, dryly commented years later that she knew a number of men named Eugene. They all preferred their nicknames, she said.

Boyd and I, along with about 10 percent of our class, were notified a few weeks before graduation that our requests to be commissioned as Marine Corps aviators, which meant in most cases flying either from small aircraft carriers or ground bases in support of Marine ground troops in invasions and land battles, had been granted. Thus on September 4, 1943, I put on the Marine Corps working green officer's uniform, with a single gold bar on each shoulder, and took the oath of office. I was twenty-one years old, beautifully trained, and sure of myself in the air. Although I was less confident and certain than I tried to appear in my official and social life, I found that other young officers usually accepted me as someone who knew where he was going and was therefore to be followed.

After a short detour in Jacksonville, Florida, flying torpedo planes, which I thought would get me into combat sooner, I reported to a Marine Corps fighter training unit in El Toro, California, and was almost immediately assigned to join a new squadron, VMF 452 (the VMF stands for Marine Fighter Squadron) at the Marine Corps Air Station in Mojave. Mojave was a road stop in the vast scrub bush and sand desert that starts east of the coastal hills in California and extends far past Las Vegas. It was the kind of town that actually had a greasy spoon restaurant called the Silver Dollar Café. The desert's inhabitants were snakes, lizards, birds, wildcats, and an occasional prospector pursuing his dream of finding gold in the middle of military bombing and gunnery ranges, which was what much of the desert had been turned into. The Marine Corps built a modern flying field and aircraft hangars at Mojave, erected some simple wooden barracks for officers and men, around and through which the wind howled day and night, burning hot in the summer and cold in the winter, two small but well-stocked officers' and non-commissioned officers' clubs, and the requisite mess halls, ordnance, and equipment buildings.

One could fly at Mojave day and night virtually every day of the year, since it practically never rained. Vast open tracts of desert and mountain were marked off for gunnery and bombing training. An Army Air Corps field was located nearby at Muroc Dry Lake (now known as the Edwards Air Force base, famous in later years as the advanced flight test base where Chuck Yeager broke the sound barrier and then as the West Coast landing strip for the space shuttle). The Army Air Corps trained B-24, heavy bomber pilots at Muroc.

Our squadron had been assigned the still relatively new Chance Vought Corsair, a sleek, powerful, inverted gull-wing fighter that looked like an aerial torpedo with wings. It was the Marine Corps fighter of choice for invasion support, increasingly replacing some of the Navy Grumman Hellcat fighter squadrons aboard the big aircraft carriers. The Corsair was a hustling, heavy but sensitive machine, lovely to fly and tricky to land. (Dozens of pilots were killed in the early version before engineers figured out how to prevent premature stalling and rolling on final landing approaches.) It was faster than the Japanese Zero, although less maneuverable, tougher, and more versatile.

So we flew and flew, and trained and flew. I always sought the early morning flights, rocketing off over the fragrant sage in the still relatively cool air before closing the cockpit bubble and climbing steadily into the fathomless blue sky. In addition to the daily training routine, a few of us would sign up for extra flying time in available aircraft and go off dogfighting on our own over the mountains. A formal aerial dogfight started when the two fighters crossed courses on 180-degree opposing courses, one a thousand feet higher than the other (the height advantage was either agreed to or won by the toss of a coin). The goal was to get on your opponent's tail where a fighter plane is unprotected (like a dog's rear) and shoot him down (in these fights, of course, this act was recorded only with a triumphal whoop on the radio and occasionally a camera). The trick was to maneuver one's plane with such a delicate touch in impossibly tight turns and at high G (gravity) forces so as not to stall out until finally sliding into the hawk's position behind the enemy. My favorite opponent was an impassioned youngster named Hanson, who after the war became a philosophy professor at Yale University. He died in the 1960s flying his personally owned World War II fighter when it crashed in a snowstorm.

The Corsair mounted six fifty-caliber machine guns and carried up to five hundred pounds of bombs or rockets. We flew gunnery runs over the mountains in four-plane formations thousands of feet above the white target sleeve pulled by a utility plane, rolling over to dive down for the kill and leading the target to compensate for the relative speeds and courses of target and shooter. It was bird hunting on a grand scale. The Muroc heavy bomber airfield, some fifty miles away, was an irresistible, off-limits magnet for the more venturesome of us, who would come flat-hatting in across the sagebrush to rocket down the camp streets ten feet above the ground, waggling our wings at startled Army Air Corps troops and fliers, or occasionally swoop down in mock gunnery runs on B-24 formations lumbering along in the desert sky. Most of the time we got away scot-free, but my wingman and I finally got a sulfurous dressing down from the un-amused Mojave base commander and a ten-day confinement to quarters.

Training was frequently dangerous. Early on at Mojave, when I was flying as the two-plane section leader in a four-plane division, the flight commander, an experienced Guadalcanal veteran, announced that we were going to perform individual slow rolls in formation. This required each plane to carry out a complete, totally precise roll around its own axis while remaining in a tight formation. Under the best of circumstances, this would be an extremely difficult maneuver. The first attempt ended immediately with planes splitting off in all directions. The captain insisted that we try it again. I had a momentary glimpse of a plane rolling into my path, pulled away, and seconds later saw the captain's plane dive straight into the desert, a puff of smoke and dust rising on impact. The court of enquiry ruled that he was in error, which didn't help since he was dead.

Some months later Don Boyd, who had become my principal partner in bar hopping and skirt chasing in Los Angeles, spun in on a landing approach and was killed at the Mojave air field. Boyd had arrived back at the base at about 3:00 AM the night before after two days of partying in Los Angeles. We assumed he was either still tight or so hung over he had no business flying. I was assigned the unenviable job of escorting his remains back to Michigan and consoling the heartbroken family and Boyd's beautiful girlfriend, who clearly had regarded her relationship with Boyd as long-term and serious. I told them Boyd had been caught in unexpectedly high and treacherous desert winds in the landing pattern.

My closest friend at Mojave was a young lieutenant named Tom Pace. Like me, Pace was from a railroad family. He grew up in the Nebraska plains. Unprepossessing physically, with a big nose and scraggly hair, Pace had an enormous gift for friendship and great personal charm. Most of his squadron mates loved him, as did a number of young women in Los Angeles. Pace lost control in a landing one day. The Corsair ran off the runway and turned turtle. Pace suffered a sizable gash on the top of his head. Ever after, he flew with the seat in its lowest possible position. Since he was short anyway, Pace could hardly be seen in the cockpit. Hanson, the squadron artist and caricaturist, posted a drawing on the squadron bulletin board of Pace, the country boy, flying with only his large nose visible in the cockpit searching for the smells of the home farm.

Los Angeles was two hours by car across the desert and over the low mountains into the orange-blossom scented air of the San Fernando Valley and then on to Beverly Hills and Hollywood. The LA bars jumped with joyful music—in the war years one could walk in off the street and hear Nat King Cole and his trio or Fats Waller. I soon developed a circle of favorite bars and a collection of lady friends. I was somewhat in love with Alicia, whom I spotted in a bar, her black hair in a pageboy, wearing a trench coat in the *Casablanca*, Ingrid Bergman style. I carried on a sporadic but physically satisfying sex life with an older woman, a waitress, whom Boyd had introduced me to, whose interests were young men in bed, not bar hopping. My favorite lady was a stylish, square-faced divorcee named Roberta, who had been married to a millionaire vaguely connected with the movie business and lived with her two tow-headed twin boys off Mulholland Drive in a big house complete with swimming pool and well-stocked bar. Roberta was funny, brave, and totally unflappable. I thought her by far the classiest woman I met in the war; after the war ended, I moved in with her briefly. Bert, as Roberta's friends called her, and I drove back once to Missouri right after the war to visit her sister, who was living with a badly wounded Marine Corps flier undergoing plastic surgery in a Navy hospital in Springfield. Passing through Kansas City, we spent the night in my brother's and my old sleeping porch; my mother and Bert got along just fine.

I had met Roberta through Tom Duggan, an LA-based TWA public relations representative, whom I had been introduced to by another Marine Corps pilot. Duggan was accommodating, full of gossip about Hollywood, charming, and very helpful in finding hotel rooms, interesting bars, and good-looking women. He was a homosexual, a term seldom used in those days when homosexuals were usually referred to as "queer," "fairies," or "fags." Toward the end of our friendship, Duggan, who lived with his mother, offered to put me up for the night after a long evening of drinking and bar hopping. When I was in the bathroom peeing, the door opened, Duggan came in, dropped to his knees, reached out, and took my penis and began to suck it. The door opened suddenly, and his tiny Irish mother stood there, shouting at Paul: "You are an evil man. You are bad, bad, bad!" The bathroom episode ended our friendship; I wasn't interested in homosexual sex.

The Marines and the other armed forces expected that their young men were going to follow their sex drives and encouraged the use of condoms to prevent disease. A famous World War II cartoon strip shows Sad Sack, an Army enlisted man, watching an Army training film about the horrors of genital disease and then walking down the street with a buddy. The buddy introduces Sad Sack to a girl friend. Sad Sack whips out and pulls on a pair of rubber gloves before shaking her hand.

In the summer of 1944, our squadron moved up to an unused Army Air Corps landing strip at Bishop in the high Sierras to test its ability to sustain operations away from a major base. During the month we were there, I regularly flew a two-seater dive-bomber assigned to the squadron as a utility aircraft down to Mojave and back to carry mail. Frequently I carried an enlisted man in the rear gunner's seat, being sent by the squadron doctor down to our main base for treatment of gonorrhea acquired in Bishop. I prized this assignment, which became known as "the clap run": skimming along the valley floor in the cool of the morning to drop off that day's patient, a good lunch at the officers' club, and back in the afternoon with the squadron mail and the man I had taken down the day before, his butt full of injections of penicillin.

My one experience with VD was an infection in my right eye, promptly treated by our squadron doctor whom I had seen because the eye was watering excessively. When the doctor gave me his alarming diagnosis that this was gonorrhea, I traced the only likely cause back to an evening of drinking at Roberta's house, which terminated in bed with a red-haired girl who sang with Charlie Barnett's orchestra. My more ribald squadron mates accused me of "winking her off."

As our time at Mojave stretched out, the Marine Corps brass became so concerned about the presumably flabby state of the junior officers' bodies, out of condition due to too much liberty in Los Angeles and comparable recreation spots, that they sent us lieutenants, one squadron after another, for two weeks of "combat conditioning" at Camp Pendleton near San Diego. We were put in the tender care of a crew of senior Marine NCOs, who took us out in small landing craft and dumped us, carrying full combat gear, into rubber boats a mile off shore in the chilly Pacific to practice landings in the surf. They shouted cadence and selected profanities on our forced night marches, and taught us the latest techniques in modern bayonet fighting. Always eager, I volunteered to participate in a mock fight and nearly got my throat cut by a burly sergeant delighted to play at combat with a juicy, naïve, young second lieutenant.

3

A Passage at Arms

Finally, in the winter of 1944, the news we had awaited for so long came. Maj. Pat Weiland, the commanding officer, called us to the squadron ready room to announce our immediate assignment to the Naval Air Station at Santa Rosa, north of San Francisco on the Pacific coast, for carrier training and qualification. That completed, we were to board the aircraft carrier *Franklin* to join the Pacific Fleet. The *Franklin*, we were told, had been seriously damaged in the fall of 1944 by a Japanese suicide attack in the battle of Leyte off the Philippines and had just finished repairs in the Navy shipyard at Bremerton, Washington.

As the power equation tilted slowly and inevitably against them, the Japanese tide in the Pacific was draining away. But they still held Okinawa and much of China. The Japanese home islands were widely believed to be a formidable, if not impregnable, redoubt. The Japanese had earned a reputation for suicidal courage as they fought to hold island after island. In Europe, where virtually no Marines were assigned, the Allies had landed in Normandy and were fighting their way eastward toward Berlin.

In its pattern of naval fighting and island assaults, the Pacific war was very different from that in Europe. John Gregory Dunne, writing in the *New York Review of Books* to review three Pacific war memoirs and histories, remarked that in addition to these dissimilar strategic challenges, the Pacific war was characterized by "the uncompromising hatred between the Japanese military and the forces—American, British, and Australian—arrayed against them…Some of it was undoubtedly racial." In the Pacific, soldiers on both sides routinely hacked body parts—heads, sex organs, fingers, gold teeth—off the dead bodies of enemy soldiers to be used as souvenirs. To be taken prisoner in Europe was bad but survivable. To be captured in the Pacific fighting was unlikely, because battle casualties were so high. If it happened, it was considered a fate possibly worse than death. The Marines were not unfamiliar with what most Americans regarded as the lesser races: one of their famous marching songs contains the rousing stanza,

"Oh, the monkeys have no tails in Zamboanga," recalling the Marines fighting the Muslim rebels against American colonial rule in the Philippines in the early twentieth century.

We said good-bye to the drafty barracks and sunny, windy desert days of Mojave and went up to the fogs, rain, and mists of Northern California to fly endless carrier landing practice patterns around the Santa Rosa air station. These "bounce" drills taught the pilot how to fly at slow speeds and low altitudes while he came into the final legs of the landing pattern and picked up the fluorescent paddles of the Landing Signal Officer (LSO), himself a qualified naval pilot, who then employed a simple set of arm and body signals to help the pilot fly the airplane onto the deck.

When the LSO leaned his body and paddles in one direction, the pilot tilted the airplane to respond. When the LSO brought the two paddles rapidly together in a gathering motion, indicating the plane was coming in too slowly and might stall and crash, the pilot pushed on more throttle, adding power and speed. When the LSO cut the right-hand paddle across his chest, the pilot cut his throttle, dropped the nose for a second, then pulled the stick back and landed in a full stall. When the LSO waved and crossed his paddle arms vigorously in front of his head, either because the approach was unsatisfactory or the flight deck or runway wasn't clear, that constituted the famous "wave off," and the pilot had to go around the entire landing pattern again. In contemporary carrier flying, the LSO has disappeared and this is all done with mirrors and lights, which old-timers find sad. Good LSOs and their brilliantly clad deck crews were the dance masters of a unique technological ballet: the interplay between the signal officer and the pilot, the never-still sea, the looming massive deck of the ship, the final, always shocking moment of the touchdown—or slam down if the deck was dropping away in the swell—the plane catching its landing hook in the restraining cable, which slowed and stopped it within a second or so after hitting the deck, rolling backwards for another brief second to disengage the tail-hook from the cable, and then charging forward to clear the momentarily lowered crash barrier at middeck.

The flight deck of a carrier looks impossibly small from the air, but in two important aspects landing at sea is easier than landing on a land runway, unless the sea is really boisterous and the swells are running high and rough. The carrier turns precisely into the wind both to launch and receive aircraft. Planes, like birds, land into the wind. The pilot at sea thus enjoys the advantage of both the speed of the prevailing wind plus the speed of the carrier itself—World War II carriers could steam at up to thirty-plus knots—which deduct from the true landing speed at stall out and touchdown. In addition, since the carrier is steaming directly into the wind, the pilot does not have to be concerned about quirky crosswinds that can complicate landings on shore. The first touchdown on land after a long spell at sea always seems very fast and sometimes tricky.

During two chilly, foggy days off the California coast, we went through this rite of passage on an old battle and accident-scarred carrier, the USS *Ranger*. Most of us managed the eight required landings without serious problems. But we lost one Navy pilot whose fighter skidded on the oil-soaked wooden deck of the old Ranger and went over the side into the ocean. I found parking on the deck, following the hand and arm signals of the flight-deck crew, dressed in an array of bright colors like courtiers at a Renaissance court and leaning into the thirty-knot wind, more alarming than the landing itself. I followed the deck crewman's hand and head signals to park right up at the very edge of the deck with my plane's wings folded, staring straight down at the ocean fifty feet below while the great ship rolled and tossed under us.

On February 7, VMF 452, the "Sky Raiders" as we had chosen to call ourselves, boarded the USS *Franklin* at the Alameda Naval Air Station in the San Francisco Bay. The *Franklin* was a monster: 27,000 tons, 872 feet long, 150,000 horsepower. It could steam at thirty-three knots carrying a crew of 3,400 men. The ship was fresh from the navy yards at Bremerton, Washington, where large hunks of its flight and hangar decks, blown up in Japanese suicide attacks off the Philippines in October 1944, had been repaired and replaced. It was, everyone noted, CV-13, which meant simply that it was the thirteenth big attack carrier listed in the Navy arsenal. We steamed out under the Golden Gate Bridge, taking a last look at the fabulous city, and plunged into the mighty Pacific swell. Our first stop was Honolulu to carry out night landing drills, beginning with night bounce practice sessions around the Marine Corps field at Barbers Point.

VMF 452 was to fly off the *Franklin* as a Marine Corps squadron as part of Navy Air Group Five, which consisted of two fighter squadrons, each of thirty-six aircraft, plus a twelve-plane torpedo squadron, and a dive-bomber squadron of twelve aircraft. It was not an easy relationship. We were there in a Navy-run and staffed operation because of our presumed competence with the Corsair, which was proving increasingly valuable in the air war with Japan. But our commanding officer, who was a gentle man, had to report to the Navy Air Group commander, who of course outranked him and was a Naval Academy graduate as well, while our Major Weiland came into the Marine Corps out of South Dakota and civilian pilot training at the University of Miami. We made some friends among the Navy pilots, but generally we stuck to each other.

In Hawaii, we became creatures of the sea and the air. By night, we flew landing patterns, dragging slowly at dangerously low altitudes around the Barbers Point MCAS (Marine Corps Air Station) field, picking up the fluorescent paddles of the LSO and dropping down hard onto the asphalt runway, then hitting full throttle and going around again to repeat. In the free time in the mornings, we took a couple of jeeps, loaded with beer, out to the northern beaches and swam and dozed in the sun. World War II Honolulu belonged to the Navy and Dole pineapple. Its honky-tonk bars were crowded with sailors. The Royal Hawaiian Hotel was the only luxury hotel in all the islands.

I never did make a night carrier landing. Our departure was moved up before the night I was scheduled to fly aboard. When we left the dock to steam out to join the fleet in the western Pacific, the LSO we had trained with, who had been with the *Franklin* since its earlier Pacific actions in which it was severely damaged, was there, visibly intoxicated, to see us off. "I got off," he shouted, laughing. "You should get off. Get off, get off! It's an unlucky ship. Thirteen is unlucky. The ship is unlucky."

We sailed west for what seemed forever toward the war, the great ship rising and falling slowly as it sliced through the Pacific swell. I discovered a catwalk hanging below the flight deck at the furthest forward point of the flight deck where one could sit or lie and watch the prow of the carrier scything through the water, flying fish exploding out of the sea below us and skittering along flashing in the sunlight. We flew occasional training drills as we went, including a formation south of our route to see if there was any aerial activity in the general direction of the island of Truk, where a tiny Japanese contingent was dying on the vine of a once strategic Japanese redoubt, isolated and cut off from supplies as the war spun westward.

Our immediate destination was Ulithi. The Navy had captured this extraordinary geological formation from the Japanese in September 1944. The Ulithi atoll is an enormous, circular, coral reef-ringed, deep natural anchorage five hundred miles east by north from the eastern tip of the Philippines. Ulithi had become the principal forward marshalling point for the endgame with Japan. Navy engineers blasted entrance channels into the atoll for the outsize capital ships of the fleet and reinforced a tiny island in the middle of the atoll and put a landing strip on it. We steamed silently into the anchorage just before sunset in early March 1945. In every direction, all the eye could see was American fighting ships: fifteen big carriers (our arrival made it sixteen), four battleships, eight heavy and light cruisers, sixty-plus destroyers, and hundreds of transport and utility ships—oilers, munition carriers, freighters, and landing craft of all sizes and shapes. This was

Task Force 58, alternately known as Task Force 38, the designation depending on its commanding officer. Two tough, risk taking admirals, Mark Mitscher (Task Force 58) and Bull Halsey (Task Force 38), took turns commanding this awesome machine, the greatest naval fighting force the world had ever known. I thought to myself, "I am glad I am not a Japanese."

Outside Ulithi, coming into the harbor passage, we passed a long line of landing ships and smaller landing craft, heavily loaded and low in the water, heading north. We were close enough to wave down to the men on some of them. I found out much later that my brother, Murray, was on one of these landing craft with his Marine artillery unit, headed north for the Okinawa invasion, the blood-soaked semifinal chapter of the Pacific war before the anticipated final assault on mainland Japan. I had not seen Murray since the war started.

In Ulithi, we finally learned our specific assignment: to attack Japanese airfields and military bases, interdicting the movement of Japanese troops and aircraft from the main islands down to reinforce Okinawa. We loaded additional crew, fuel, and munitions including a brand new large aerial rocket called "Tiny Tim." The *Franklin* was to be Task Force 58's flagship with an admiral and his staff. In addition, a special photography crew had come aboard to shoot a propaganda film on "Tiny Tim." The ship was jammed; we totaled some 3,400 men. The junior officer quarters was so crowded that I begged a sleeping space on a luggage shelf built into the wall of a cabin occupied by two first lieutenants who were willing to put me up. The only really comfortable place was the squadron ready room, just below the flight deck with which it was connected by a short stairway, equipped with air conditioning and leather lounge chairs. It was there that pilots were briefed and debriefed and awaited the order over the public address system: "Pilots, man your planes!"

In mid-March, the fleet lifted anchor and steamed out. At sea, in battle formation, the fleet was even more awesome than at anchor. The task force divided into four carrier divisions of four carriers each, each division with its own cast of supporting cruisers and destroyers. The four divisions changed course frequently day and night in maneuvers designed to avoid submarine attacks, although by early 1945 most of the Japanese submarine fleet lay at the bottom of the ocean. The entire task force covered a thousand square-mile area of water, steaming day and night at speeds of up to thirty-three knots. It was a marvel of American military planning and training and a triumph of military technology. Most of the men running and manning the ships and aircraft, like me, had probably never set foot on a ship before the war or dreamed of flying an airplane.

As we bore north toward Japan, the sunny skies and blue seas of the equatorial Pacific disappeared. Low-lying gray clouds covered the sky. The sea turned gray-black. The air grew chilly. Our moods turned pensive. Those of us—the great majority—who had never been in combat were nervous, although trying not to show it. Along with many others, I went to a chapel service, thinking it wouldn't hurt and might even help. Our commanders told us that if we were hit by Japanese fire or had engine trouble over Japan we should try to reach the Chinese mainland where, with luck, we would be picked up by the Chinese Nationalists rather than by the Japanese.

As we pressed toward the main islands, combat air patrols found no significant Japanese contacts. The first heavy fighting was expected to start March 18 with attacks to destroy airfields, harbor facilities, and Japanese aircraft on the island of Kyushu, the southernmost of the major Japanese islands. I was assigned to fly as the two-plane section leader in a flight of four Corsairs covering two Navy Hellcat photo aircraft taking aerial photographs of Nagasaki. The division leader was Maj. John Stack, a decorated veteran of the Guadalcanal fighting who had shot down three Japanese fighters in that earlier campaign. Stack was a short, muscular, reddish-haired man with a bushy mustache, not much of one for talking but respected as a purposeful, hard-driving flier. Flying on Stack's wing was Tom Pace. On my wing was a first lieutenant named Bo Little, a gentle, small-town boy from Oklahoma who didn't drink, didn't smoke, and went to Los Angeles on liberty to see movies.

We launched shortly after daybreak, climbed up through the cloud cover to twenty thousand feet, donning our oxygen masks as we gained altitude, and picked up the two Navy Hellcat photo planes. It was bitterly cold. We had no gun heaters, which had failed to arrive in time to be installed, and had been told our fifty-caliber wing-mounted machine guns would freeze up if we didn't clear them occasionally by firing a few rounds. The jumpiness I felt was compounded by watching lines of tracer bullets zip past below me or off to one side from other groups as pilots cleared their guns in the larger formation heading for Kyushu.

At launching, we were only fifty miles off the coast of Japan, closer than any major American ship had ever gone in the war. Within less than half an hour, the clouds began to break up as we approached the coast. As we came into Japanese air space, Tom Pace radioed Major Stack that he was having both engine and radio problems and must return to the ship. Stack asked if Pace was sure he could make it back. Pace said he could and peeled off to head back. Stack motioned to me to join up in formation on his wing.

Unrolling below us as we flew northward above the two Hellcat photo planes were the wooded green hills, ocean bays, coastal towns, rice paddies, and industrial plants of Japan. We kept a constant scan of the skies around us for Japanese fighter planes, flying an interconnected side-to-side weave of slow turns from right to left and back to cover the whole sky with our vision and protect against attack from the rear. (This maneuver was known as the "Thach" weave after the Navy pilot who invented it.)

We made two passes over Nagasaki at the northwest tip of Kyushu Island. The photo planes headed south back toward the *Franklin*. Flying south down the island we suddenly heard a pilot shouting excitedly on the radio that he was under attack by Japanese planes above a "smoking mountain." That "smoking mountain" had to be the active volcano in the hills above the bay at Kagoshima, a big industrial and port city at the southern tip of Kyushu. Major Stack waved good-bye to the photo planes. Our three-man formation headed for Kagoshima.

Within minutes, flying on Stack's right wing, out of the corner of my right eye I saw a Japanese Zero curving in toward us. He was heading slightly below us, and Stack immediately turned hard right and then left to drop in behind him. Stack fired several rounds, then pulled off above. I slid in for a few seconds behind the Zero and fired two machine gun bursts at him before the Zero suddenly rolled over and in an abrupt dive disappeared straight down. For a minute or so the sky around us was a great ball of Corsairs and an occasional Japanese fighter. At least one Japanese plane was on fire, spiraling steeply down to the ground. A couple of Japanese parachutes were floating further down to the paddy fields. Then, as suddenly as it had started, it was over. No Japanese planes, no Major Stack, no wingman Bo Little. I began a slow circular turn to see what was going on. Within a minute or so, four Corsairs joined up to fly formation on my lead. I was low on gas, so I headed back for the fleet with my newly acquired formation of pilots, even more confused than I was, following me. By the time I found the *Franklin* with my flock I had five minutes of fuel left.

The ready room was full of exhilarated pilots. A number of Japanese planes had been shot down. Stack was convinced he had killed the Japanese we had been after. I thought I had hit the same plane with my firing. We were never to know. The sobering question came up immediately: Where was Tom Pace? Stack explained the circumstances under which Pace decided to return to the ship. Standing orders were that planes in trouble must be accompanied back to base. But Stack had issued no such order. Pace had not landed on the *Franklin*. First Lt. Pete Schaefer, a close friend of Pace's and mine, indignantly challenged Stack's failure to act. At first it was thought possible that Pace had landed on another carrier, or that he ditched in the sea and had been picked up by a destroyer. We eventually found out that he had been shot down and killed that morning by antiaircraft fire from a U.S. destroyer whose crew mistook him for an incoming Japanese plane when he failed to identify himself.

The next day, March 19, not scheduled to fly an early mission, I was half-asleep on my luggage-rack bunk shortly after 7:00 AM, listening to the racket of a dive-bomber flight taking off immediately above my head on the flight deck. I heard a loud explosion and then for a minute nothing. I thought immediately that a dive-bomber must have crashed over the bow on takeoff and exploded in the water. Then two tremendous explosions shook the ship along with a fierce rattle and pounding of what I thought were the ship's antiaircraft guns. I jumped out of my bunk in my shorts and went out into the narrow corridor. The rattling and explosions were growing in their intensity. I thought we were under attack and firing at enemy planes. A ship's officer whom I knew slightly came running up the corridor from amidships. I asked him what was going on. "We've been hit by a bomb, and we're blowing up," he shouted at me. "That's our own ammunition blowing up."

I ducked back into my room and hurriedly dressed as the banging and rattling and explosions continued. When I came back to the corridor, officers and men were milling around in all directions. Up along the narrow corridor from the hangar deck, stygian figures of men burned black were staggering forward toward the fo'c'sle deck area. Black smoke was pouring in from the rear. Frightening explosions, reverberating in the steel walls and ceilings, rocked the ship. Another ship's officer shouted that we should all head as far forward as possible and get out into the open fo'c'sle deck at the prow just below the flight deck. Within minutes about a hundred men, some so badly burned they were barely conscious, shivering in the cold, moist wind, had assembled on the open deck. The ship was losing speed and beginning to list. As the explosions continued, a ship's officer shouted at us to assume a pushup position on the deck using our fingers and toes to avoid ankle and leg fracture because of the pounding, hammering action of the deck under our feet.

After about an hour, the explosions abated momentarily. I followed a ship's officer up a catwalk to the flight deck to help fight the fires consuming the entire rear half of the ship behind the multistory island where the ship's command post was located. As we went back to lend a hand with the fire hoses, a horrifyingly loud explosion blew the outboard elevator, which carried planes up and down to and from the flight and hangar decks, several hundred feet into the air. All over the forward portion of the deck wounded men were limping and being carried forward away from the fires and explosions that were ripping the aft third of the ship apart. I came across a friend and squadron-mate, Lt. Jim Ormond, lying on the flight deck in pain, his leg shattered at various points from the concussions. Ormond had been in the pilots' ready room with Lts. Pete Schaefer, Joe Warren, Bill Rogalski and Wallace Mattsfield awaiting an aircraft launch. Schaefer had momentarily gone out on the catwalk outside the ready room just as the first bomb penetrated the flight deck fifteen feet away from him. He immediately dove into the water. Warren also jumped over the side into the frigid sea. Both men were eventually picked up by destroyers. Rogalski managed to climb up to the flight deck with Ormond and through the tremendous concussions, fires, and explosions helped him forward toward the bow. I encountered Ormond later in the morning and stayed with him for half an hour until two navy crew members appeared out of the confusion to help Ormond onto an improvised breeches buoy to be passed over to the Navy light cruiser, the USS *Santa Fe*, which had signaled that it was coming alongside to pick up survivors.

By midmorning, the *Franklin* was dead and low in the water, listing increasingly to starboard. Explosions and fires raged through its entire rear half. The deck was not only tilting at a fifteen-degree angle but was slippery with firefighting foam. In spite of the great danger from fires and explosions, the *Santa Fe* slowly crept in toward the *Franklin's* starboard side. A narrow gulf separated the two ships, which were pounding up and down dangerously in a fifteen foot swell, as wounded men were passed over to the cruiser. Finally, in a feat of extraordinary seamanship, the *Santa Fe* threw caution to the winds and headed in even closer to tie up directly alongside the Franklin.

Shortly after noon, an order was passed around orally—the public address system was an early casualty of the day—that all officers and hands in the air group should abandon ship, leaving only the ship's crew aboard to try to salvage the Franklin. Jim Ormond had been hauled over to the *Santa Fe* an hour earlier. I decided it was time to go myself. I judged the rise and fall of the *Santa Fe* in the swell, waited for the exact moment when the top of the *Santa Fe's* left gun turret came level for a second or two on the rise of the swell with the right edge of the *Franklin's* slippery flight deck, and took a running jump across the six-foot gap. I landed on my feet just below the cruiser's command post, stumbled for a second, and then they pulled me up. "I'm glad to be aboard, sir," I said. It was corny, but I never spoke truer words.

By late afternoon, the *Santa Fe* had completed its Good Samaritan mission and pulled slowly away from the shambles. The *Santa Fe* had taken more than eight hundred survivors aboard. A second, larger cruiser, the USS *Pittsburgh*, and the *Franklin's* salvage crew had managed in another display of amazing seamanship and strength to rig a heavy towing cable between the two great gray ships. As dusk gathered under the low gray clouds, the *Pittsburgh* began very slowly to tow the *Franklin* south away from the Japanese coast. The *Santa Fe* and a handful of destroyers circled silently in a wide arc around the crippled hulk. The *Franklin* rode low in the water, listing perilously to starboard. The glow of its fires lit up the twilight. An occasional explosion rumbled across the water.

For the next four days we steamed south, very slowly at first but then picking up a bit of speed when the *Franklin* salvage crew managed to produce some power from the ship's own engines. The *Santa Fe* steamed behind in a line astern of the *Franklin*. Those of us from the *Franklin* contingent lined the rails to watch the bodies bobbing along past us, held up by their lifejackets, in the wake of the *Franklin* as the salvage crew began to dig into and cut away the damaged rear of the ship. Occasionally we thought we could recognize someone. Many of the bodies were burned beyond recognition.

The *Santa Fe* went through several battle alerts as we slowly steamed south back to Ulithi as Japanese planes sought to find and sink the damaged *Franklin*, which would have been their last and one of their greatest aerial/naval victories of the war. When we arrived in the atoll, the small group of Navy and Marine pilots from the *Franklin* was transferred to a Navy hospital ship. The Marines then boarded a transport ship to be taken to Guam, where an attempt would be made to reassemble the squadron from the surviving pilots and men. These included those like me, who had gone over the side to the *Santa Fe* or had been picked up out of the ocean by destroyers, and those pilots who landed on other carriers returning from their early morning mission over Japan to find their ship a mass of smoke and flames.

At Ulithi, before heading back to Guam, we were allowed to board the wreck of the *Franklin* to salvage personal effects that might have survived the fires and explosions. The entire back half of the ship was twisted steel and burned decks full of gaping holes. It smelled of fire, gunpowder, and the death that some eight hundred men met on that cloudy, cold morning of March 19. Thirty-three of the dead belonged to my squadron. Most were enlisted men. They were killed almost immediately in the fires and explosions that destroyed the hangar deck when the two Japanese bombs penetrated the heavy wooden flight deck and exploded among the fully armed airplanes awaiting launch on the hangar deck. The always long enlisted mess hall line started on the hangar deck; it was breakfast time, and hundreds died in a flash.

Two *Franklin* crew members received Congressional Medals of Honor for outstanding bravery and leadership. The Catholic chaplain, Lt. Commander Joseph T. O'Callahan, had gone time after time into the bowels of the exploding ship to help find men. He seemed everywhere on the ship; I saw him kneeling to administer extreme unction and pray with several dying men on the flight deck. Another ship's officer, Lt. (j.g.) Donald Gary, found three hundred men trapped in a smoke-filled mess compartment and led them to safety through the ventilation system. Courage and skill, particularly on the part of the ship's crew, had saved lives throughout the day and night. The hulk of the *Franklin* eventually made it back to the Brooklyn Navy Yard under its own power, where after the war ended it was broken up for scrap.

As the remnants of the squadron reassembled on Guam, a flight board interviewed each of us to see what could be done with us. The board's basic decision was that VMF 452 as a squadron no longer existed. I told the board I was prepared and indeed eager to be reassigned in the field to a combat unit. But none of us was. Within three weeks, after being transferred from one transport ship to another, I was back in California at the Navy Air Station Alameda, across the bay from San Francisco. I was told I could telephone my family in Kansas City but cautioned that for security reasons I was to say nothing about the *Franklin* disaster. When the long distance operator got through to my parents, they thought it must be my brother calling. They had not heard Murray's voice for years, and they knew I had departed the States a bare two months before.

The government maintained tight security on the *Franklin* calamity until May 17, when the saga was released to the public with great fanfare and beating of patriotic drums. This was my first lesson in politics and the art of propaganda. The *Franklin* was dubbed "the ship that wouldn't sink," the bravery of its crew praised in newspapers and radio station broadcasts across the country, and Washington launched a big new war bond drive. A reporter from the *Kansas City Star* had been aboard the *Franklin*, invited on the war cruise to report on the virtues of the new Tiny Tim rockets (whose warheads were a major contributor to the dreadful damage to the *Franklin*'s guts on March 19). My parents found his story, with my picture, on the front page of their newspaper May 17.

Gabriel Heatter, by far the country's most popular wartime radio broadcaster, said in a famous, dramatic newscast:

> This ship is gone, said Japan. This ship will live, said her gallant men. Back she came with her charred and battered hull. This ship had lost a greater number of men and sustained more battle damage than any ship which ever came

in New York Harbor under her own power. Yet back she came—her flag high—her story an epic of raw courage.

Within sixty miles of Japan's coastline she received what the Jap thought was her mortal wound—as he thought all ships he damaged at Pearl Harbor would never come back to claim their retribution. As he thought his treachery would find us weak and confused only to find us now a little more than three hundred miles from his home islands...With the sky over those pagan islands blood red with flames of his war machine disappearing into smoke and rubble and ashes.... One by one the Jap cities will turn to ashes—each will feel the wrath and power of a free people...A brute and barbarian brought to his knees. And there will be peace on earth, and boys will be home again and you and I and millions of Americans will say whether this sacrifice and death and all this heroism is to be lost or won and held fast and honored with the kind of world in which men will never again be asked to suffer all that these men on the great carrier *Franklin* endured—for us.

I felt anything but heroic. The bones of my best friend, Tom Pace, lay somewhere far out in the Pacific, along with those of three dozen or so men in our squadron, including Wally Mattsfield, the best wingman who ever flew at my side—and, of course, long before that there was the death of Don Boyd, who spun into the ground at Mojave. My own view was that the *Franklin*'s commanding officer should have been reprimanded or possibly even court-martialed. Although he had ordered the crew to their battle stations several times during the night following the first raids on Japan, he lifted the order at 6 a.m. so that the crew could catch a breather. We were hit at 7:07 a.m., only fifty or so miles off the coast of Japan. If we had been at battle stations, there might have been greater attention at the antiaircraft stations; more importantly the ship would have been "buttoned up"—that is, all its watertight compartments would have been closed off and locked, and the ventilation system turned off to prevent smoke and fire from racing through the ship. Instead, because it fit the scenario of heroism, or so it seemed to me, the commanding officer received not a reprimand but the Navy Cross.

I was assigned to the Marine Corps Air Station in El Centro, California, and then almost immediately back to Mojave and a new squadron that was being formed. I felt totally uninspired by the prospect, even slightly guilty in some way, as though I would go through the rest of my life under false pretenses. The war ended in Europe on May 7, 1945. On August sixth and ninth, 1945, we dropped atomic bombs on Hiroshima and Nagasaki. Japan agreed to surrender on August fourteenth. A couple of friends and I drove into Los Angeles for the celebration.

We drank a lot and wandered around the streets yelling with the crowds, but it wasn't much fun.

Within a couple of months, after changing my mind at least twice, I decided to leave the Marine Corps, although I loved to fly, and to enter the world I knew nothing about: adult, civilian life. Several of my squadron mates signed up to stay. My brother, Murray, whom I saw briefly in California after he returned from the island campaigns late that summer, his face yellow with the atabrine he was taking for the malaria endemic in Pacific islands, elected to stay in the Marine Corps, finally got into flight training, became a pilot, and married a Navy nurse. He fought again in both Korea and Vietnam.

I was twenty-three. I put aside my familiar, comfortable green uniform and donned civilian clothing for the first time in three and a half years. I didn't really know what I wanted to do. I could fly—with great skill—but I did not want to fly a commercial airliner after the excitement of fighter flying. I had once played the violin at a near-professional level, but I hadn't touched a fiddle for almost four years. I knew I should go back to college and get a degree, but I didn't know in what. The prospect of student life was uninspiring. But the gates to the world were wide open, and I walked through them into the bright sunlight and rising tide of postwar America.

Nathan Murray Staples and Sue Emma Washburn Staples

Eugene and Murray Staples, Marceline, Missouri

Feeding the lambs on the Yellow Creek farm.
Left to right: Margaret Stanley, the author, Murray Staples, Marvin Stanley

Young Heifetz: The author and his violin,
photographed behind the Kansas City house.

September, 1943: The author, a
newly commissioned Marine Corps pilot.

Six hot pilots.
Marine Corps Air Station, Mojave, 1944. Author is third from right.

The aircraft carrier Franklin exploding after being hit by bomber. March 19, 1945

Carrier Franklin, March 19, 1945. Photo taken from Light Cruiser Santa Fe.

Author, flying the Corsair fighter.
Mojave Marine Corps Air Station, California. 1944

Major Murray Staples, returning from bombing mission. Korea, 1951

Eugene and Murray Staples, Newport Rhode Island, 1993.

4

Into the World

A striking Giacometti sculpture depicts elongated human figures striding across an anonymous square in different directions, each with its own sense of purpose. In 1945, a year whose joys at the end of the killing were tempered with grief, Americans and people across the world set out in many directions, but with an uncommon degree of unanimity in their desire to improve their individual and common lots. In the process they began to establish a new order in the world.

It was time for a new order. President Franklin D. Roosevelt, who had almost certainly saved the American capitalist system and led the war effort, died April 12, 1945. The British electorate had unceremoniously voted their indomitable wartime leader, Winston Churchill, out of office. Of the great war leaders, only Joseph Stalin remained. The Soviet Union had suffered stunning casualties, higher than any of the other participants in the war, winners or losers. (Soviet battle deaths were estimated at more than seven million; the United States suffered around three hundred thousand battle dead; Japan counted a million and a half military dead; and Germany almost three million.) Stalin, who killed more Russians in his long rule than the Germans did, still had almost a decade of life left in which to inflict his cruel and capricious will on the subjects of the Soviet Union: Russians, Ukrainians, Central Asians, and the Caucasians, now to be joined by the newly gobbled-up Eastern European and Baltic peoples. The Cold War for domination of the world, which was to become a central theme in my life, began the moment World War II ended (some historians argue it began long before). Asia, where I would spend many years of my life, and Africa were moving toward independence from their colonial masters. China was about to fall under the spell—and the fist—of Mao Tse-tung.

Until the war ended, I had paid but little attention to most of this. In the Giacometti sculpture, I would be a small figure, which on close examination would reveal a singular lack of certainty in its direction. My parents welcomed me home to Kansas City warmly if nervously in the late summer of 1945, and I found a few old friends. Charles Davis had been in the Army and was back home and soon to become a television announcer, the video camera and recording mikes having recognized the strength of his profile, his wavy hair, and mellifluous voice. Some had gotten married elsewhere and weren't coming back. Some were dead. My cousin Marvin, who fought through Europe as a combat rifleman, was back on the farm. His sister Margaret, who had provided me as a youth with both much affection and a frequent loaner car, had married a small-town banker who served during the war as a naval officer and they were living outside Kansas City.

I immediately missed flying, so much so that I ached when I saw a fighter plane in the sky. Instead of going to the officers' club to drink and brag about flying, I found myself going to bars alone (something I had never done before) and drinking morosely for hours on end. I knew I should go back to college; the new GI bill would cover most of the costs if I chose to do so. But I was reluctant to become a student again at the age of twenty-three and sit in classrooms listening to a professor drone on about some required topic I was not interested in. So I read the help-wanted columns in the *Kansas City Star* every day. Most of the jobs I might be qualified for—banking, insurance, sales—didn't interest me. Then, in the early fall of 1945, I saw an advertisement that set the course of my life.

The *Chanute Daily Tribune*, a daily newspaper in the southeastern corner of Kansas, advertised in the *Star* for a reporter trainee. They were looking for someone enterprising, with some college but not necessarily a degree, and facility in writing. Veterans would be given preference. I responded to the advertisement immediately. Within a week, Ernie Johnson, the editor, was in a Kansas City hotel to conduct interviews with applicants. Within two weeks, I drove down to Chanute to find a room and start to work.

The *Tribune* was the daily newspaper in Chanute, a town of twelve thousand people, the regional center of a prosperous farming region that in its southeastern reaches began to merge into the wooded hills and lead-mining economy that characterized the neighboring southwestern corner of Missouri. The newspaper belonged to a small chain owned by the Harris family of Kansas, who started their newspaper dynasty in Hutchinson (where I had flown in my Navy primary flight training, which may have been why they hired me). The Chanute newspaper, and the chain in general, prospered because they covered local news like a blanket.

If I had read Flaubert or Sherwood Anderson before going to Chanute, I would have been better prepared for the passions, prejudices, and hatreds that lay below the surface of this seemingly peaceful small town. I lived in a small room in a boarding house and ate mostly in coffee shops and small restaurants. The waitresses and customers were an unending source of gossip, and from time to time some of it was worth looking into. A few wealthy families quietly occupied the top tier of the social structure, their big wood and brick houses with their beautiful gardens sitting comfortably and coolly in the autumnal heat on quiet streets. The men owned banks, flourmills, grain elevators, and land. Their ladies shopped in Kansas City. They went to New York occasionally and even to Paris, and their children went to Ivy League schools. Some of their original wealth came from the land their families began to accumulate back in the days of "bleeding Kansas," the period of fighting between pro-and anti-slavery factions before and during the Civil War. Most businesses were small—hardware stores, agricultural supplies, drug stores, and haberdasheries (as they used to be called when Harry Truman owned one). From the ranks of these families came the civic leaders, boosters, and church deacons. They were good, reliable sources of information for a young reporter to cultivate. Most of them had gone to small colleges or the University of Kansas for their higher education. The men and women who worked in the mills and grain elevators, or as clerks in the stores, rarely went past high school, as was the case for the farmers.

The first lesson in journalism Johnson and his colleagues taught me was that people want to read about themselves and their communities. In Chanute, that meant that if the news was slow, a reporter was expected to saunter over to the train station, where the trains to or from Kansas City stopped two or three times a day, and ask passengers, whether a white-haired old lady or a happy young couple in the flush of love, who they were and where they were going. A one-line note in a local news column that Mrs. Mary Burton had gone off to visit her married daughter in Topeka, who had graduated from Chanute High School in 1940, constituted news in its purest form.

The *Tribune* news and editorial staff was small and efficient. Johnson, the editor, was a pleasant, smart, judicious, and even-tempered man, wore glasses, always dressed in a white shirt, tie and suit, and had an unerring sense of what constituted news in Chanute. The general assignment reporter, Duke Wallingford, was a lean journalist with a deeply lined, aquiline face who had worked around the Midwest for years and was to be my guide. A young woman wrote the society page. An advertising manager occasionally helped to report business news.

Wallingford took me under his wing, and I went to work. As summer ended and the school year began, the hot local news question was how the high school football and basketball teams would fare in the coming regional league competitions. Kansas, like all of the Midwest, was crazy about high school basketball, and every game provided the community the spectacle of heroic and breathtaking feats performed by young warriors and magicians, who just happened to be family members or friends. It was also the end of the summer season for the Chanute Class C baseball team. Wallingford not only covered the local games but served as official scorer as well, a task that I performed once when Wallingford couldn't make the game. I promptly got into a tremendous argument over my ruling that the local team's shortstop had committed an error fumbling a hard-hit ball he should have snared.

Writing sports is not only fun, if you like sports, it is also, like the police beat, a traditional training ground for journalistic skills. To write sports well demands concentration and economy in words, imagination in metaphor, and a style and pace that inject the movement and excitement of the game into the narrative. Local news also meant a lot of reporting on the farm economy, much of it relating to weather, trends in production and prices, and farmer and extension service scientists' views. Business generally, the churches, the school system and school activities, state government affairs, state and local politics, and local social and community activities were all part of the regular news diet. Big national issues were reported using the wire services but not with much persistence; international affairs were hardly mentioned at all.

Occasionally an event ripped the fabric off the sunny façade of life in the small town and made news so big that it went well beyond Chanute's boundaries. I had made it a point to have coffee once a week or so with the town police chief, who called me one morning to say I should come to a house on the shabby outskirts of town. I arrived to find a couple of police cars and a group of men and women, obviously neighbors, talking in hushed tones outside. The police chief told me to come in and walked me back to the kitchen. I had never seen so much blood in my life. The man of the house had killed his wife with a hammer and then shot himself. The wife's head was unrecognizable. Clothed in a cheap dressing gown, her body lay sprawled on a kitchen chair. The husband lay on the floor, his head half blown off by a blast from the shotgun he had used. The story I wrote after talking with neighbors, who said the man was a sullen, troubled fellow with a neighborhood reputation as a wife beater, made it onto the state Associated Press wire, and a paragraph was actually published in the Kansas City papers.

I liked my work and my colleagues in Chanute. But as the spring of 1946 began to turn into summer I decided I needed to learn a lot more about the world, which meant getting some more organized knowledge into my head. That meant I probably should go back to college. I was beginning to think I wanted to go overseas. A Marine Corps friend, Jack Rothweiler, who had flown in another squadron at Mojave and helped me keep the officers' club bar profitable, called to say he was planning to go to the University of Missouri at Columbia in the fall. Rothweiler suggested we share expenses for an apartment.

I told Ernie Johnson, the *Tribune* editor, I wanted to leave. He said the Harris family thought I had a bright future with the chain and could become an editor of one of their growing family of newspapers in a few years. I told Johnson I was eternally grateful to him and Duke Wallingford for what they had taught me, but that I couldn't stay. There was too much out there in the big world I wanted to find out about.

By the autumn of 1946 the contours of the postwar world were beginning to appear from the ruins of war. The American economy, untouched on its own soil and fed by the demands of war production for itself and its allies, was growing vigorously in spite of an alarming amount of labor unrest, which culminated in national coal and railroad workers' strikes in the spring. Harry Truman, who, on assuming the presidency after Roosevelt's death the year before, was derided by the country's leading political commentator, Walter Lippman, as uneducated and weak and jeered by Republican leaders as a country bumpkin, broke the back of the rail strike by threatening to draft all railroad workers into the Army. The national coal worker strike was then also settled promptly.

In Europe and Japan, as reconstruction began, it was becoming alarmingly clear that the Soviet Union, heaviest of the sledge hammers that had broken the back of Hitler's Germany, had a very different vision of the postwar world from ours. In March 1946, Winston Churchill, now a private citizen, speaking in Truman's presence at Westminster College in Fulton, Missouri, paid tribute to the Russian people and to his wartime comrade Stalin. Then he said he must present "certain facts," chief of which was that "From Stettin in the Baltic to Trieste in the Adriatic, an iron curtain had descended across the Continent." Lippman thought the speech an "almost catastrophic blunder." In Moscow, Stalin said it was a "call to war." Truman waffled and went so far as to say what was possibly not true—that he hadn't known what Churchill was going to talk about.

Life at the University of Missouri fulfilled both my best and worst expectations. A few teachers exhilarated and inspired me; I was bored by and resentful of others. I decided to major in English, because I wanted to learn how to write as well as my talents would allow. On my own at first, then encouraged by teachers and occasional fellow students, I had begun to devour great books by the dozens, at the start mostly American writers. I lived with Hemingway, Fitzgerald, Faulkner, Katherine Anne Porter, John O'Hara, John dos Passos, John Steinbeck, Irwin Shaw, and Sherwood Anderson. I discovered James Joyce and began to wander into the magic forests of Proust and the great Russian fiction writers.

My mentor was Professor William Peden, who invited me to join his small creative writing seminar. Peden had just come to the University of Missouri as a relatively young full professor from Virginia, where he had begun to build a small but distinguished reputation as a teacher, literary critic, and short-story writer. In a quiet way, he was a good-looking, casually elegant young aristocrat; he looked in his tweed jackets the way I always wanted to look. He was serious about writing, an inexhaustible fount of knowledge about writers and their working habits and techniques. About half of us in the seminar were veterans. One was William Manchester, the historian, who bore deep physical and emotional scars from his World War II combat service in the Marines, about which he later wrote a small masterpiece of a memoir. Peden insisted we read mountains of good writing and then read some more, and study and analyze what made it good. And if we wanted to be writers, we must establish and stick to a daily regime of writing.

The apartment Jack Rothweiler and I shared was in the basement of a big, wooden house occupied by us, a couple of other students, and the family of the landlady, a buxom widow of faded beauty, with a cackle of a laugh and a quick hand for the rent. She was raising a sizable number of children and was the worst housekeeper I had ever encountered. Rothweiler and I had access to her kitchen for certain kinds of supplies, although we mostly ate out and only occasionally cooked a meal on a two-burner stove in our basement dungeon. I regularly had to shoo fat, contented cats, members of a large feline tribe, out of the dirty gravy dishes and plates on the landlady's kitchen table and in the sink.

Rothweiler intended to become a lawyer and make money. He was a small, delicately built, sallow-faced, charming young man, well read and spoken. We had not been great friends in the Marine Corps but became so now. Our social companions at the university were mostly veterans, including a lean, dour, good-hearted former Marine pilot from a Kansas farm whom I had known in both flight school and at Mojave, Howard Stankey, who loved to correct my occasionally embellished accounts of past feats in the major Marine Corps occupational specializations of flying, drinking, and womanizing. Drinking beer with a group of vets and ladies one night at our favorite beer and hamburger joint, I commented that I was beginning to get a small potbelly. Stankey looked at me with amusement and said loudly for the benefit of the group, "Staples, you've always had a potbelly."

Stankey, Rothweiler, and I in this, the second year after the end of the war, began to fly in a reserve Marine fighter squadron based at the Naval Air Station at Olathe, Kansas, a couple of hundred miles west of Columbia across the state border. Twice a month, a pilot from the reserve squadron picked us up at the

Columbia, Missouri, field in a small, twin-engine Beechcraft, took us to the Olathe base, where we flew Corsairs on routine maneuvers, and returned us to Columbia in time for classes every Monday morning.

Reserve flying was a mixed blessing: we got paid for it and maintained a modicum of flying skill, but it also took time away from studying—not that I was doing much of that. I was doing well in my writing and history classes; mostly getting by in everything else. I had started playing the violin again after four years, practicing by myself in the basement apartment, and wondering if maybe I should try to become a professional musician. At the end of the school year, I talked to the head of the music department at the university, who was himself a violinist, about the possibility of switching my major to music. After listening to me play through a few exercises and performance pieces, he said he would be pleased to have me in the university music school and to be my violin instructor. He suggested I think about doing a music degree and then possibly going east to one of the professional conservatories.

If it is possible for a twenty-four-year-old man to regard a twenty-year-old woman as immature, that is how I felt about most of the girl students I met, virtually all of whom had come straight to the university from high school. I was in love mildly a couple of times at the university, but it was not until a month or so before I left that I met a girl I thought actually combined physical good looks, brains, and charm. She chose me over a basketball star who was courting her, which confirmed my belief in her intelligence. If I had stayed at the university, we might have gone far together.

Rothweiler and I had talked for months about the possibility of going to a university overseas for a year or two. I wrote away for catalogs to the universities in Edinburgh and Stockholm. I was restless and thirsty for new places, different people and ideas, feeling somehow shortchanged in my postwar life in the Midwest, which was right back where I started. The university at Columbia was an hour's drive from where I was born in Marceline. We finally agreed our primary priority was Edinburgh and agreed to pursue that. First, though, as the summer vacation began, we decided to drive out to Los Angeles for a week to see how the old bars and fun spots had withstood our absence. It was a bad trip: we drank too much; the town seemed somehow tawdry; and the air of war-time romance and excitement had disappeared.

After our return to the Midwest, I called Rothweiler at his home in Hannibal, across the state, to talk further about Edinburgh. To my irritation, Rothweiler had changed his mind. He had decided he was in love with a red-haired girl named Lou at the University of Missouri. Lou had begun to join our beer-drinking evenings over the past year, mostly sitting and looking at Rothweiler with adoration. Rothweiler said that in any case he wanted to stay with his pre-law school agenda and then start a serious career in law.

I decided to go somewhere abroad on my own while I made up my mind what to do over the longer term. I packed a small bag, said goodbye to my parents in Kansas City, and headed south in my old, prewar Ford, planning to spend two weeks in Mexico. I stayed, it turned out, for four years, during which time Rothweiler and I corresponded sporadically—he wrote literate, amusing letters. He and Lou became engaged. His law studies went well. I had been in Mexico City for about a year when I got a letter from Stankey back at the University of Missouri. He wrote that Rothweiler and two other Marine reserve pilots had been killed in a crash of the small Marine Corps transport airplane flying them from their reserve duties at Olathe back to school in Columbia.

When I first drove into Mexico at the border crossing at Laredo, I had a tourist card and not much else. I had read some Mexican history and before the war I had studied high school Spanish for a year but couldn't speak or understand it. I was totally unprepared to become passionately addicted to life in Mexico, which is what promptly happened to me. The road down from the border led across desert and mountain country to Monterrey, in those days still a small city. On my first night there I wandered down to the town square, had a beer in a sidewalk café, strolled around the square with the young men and women enjoying the custom of the place, and sat and talked for a while with a girl who spoke some English. I was enchanted.

Within a few days after arriving in Mexico City I found myself in a circle of veterans who, like me, had come to Mexico to have a look around. Many had decided to stay for a while and urged me to do the same. The best way, they said without hesitation, was to become a student at Mexico City College, a small, private four-year college that qualified under the GI Bill requirements. One could live comfortably in Mexico on the $75-a-month GI stipend. Mexico City, sitting under the great volcano Popocatépetl, was spectacular with its great squares and public buildings. It throbbed with street life and music. The restaurants were cheap—and I liked the food, which tasted nothing like any Mexican food I had eaten in the States. A lot of the women were very beautiful. The Mexico of 1947 was, of course, a far cry from the Mexico of the twenty-first century. The population of Mexico City in 1947 was a couple of million; today it is more than sixteen million. The fifty-year-old demographic explosion has made Mexico City unrecognizable and the country itself nearly ungovernable.

I registered at Mexico City College in a degree program in Spanish language and literature, and found a room in a Mexican boarding house for medical students, where I began to learn Spanish very rapidly as a matter of daily survival. Through a casual bar conversation, and thanks to my *Chanute Tribune* experience, I then found a part-time job as night editor of the city's only English-language newspaper, the *Mexico City Herald*. Considering my duties, the title "night editor" erred on the side of grandiosity, but I liked the ring of it.

The *Herald's* publisher and editor was Pepe Romero, a man about town of dubious antecedents, who wrote a gossip column for the paper. The editorial staff essentially consisted of him, another editorial person working the day shift, and me alone at night, presiding over the final corrections and makeup of the copy, most of it wire service news and features, as it came up from the ancient linotypes operated by non-English reading operators. The *Herald* was famous for its typos. When the pope prohibited the saying of masses for dead Nazi war criminals, the *Herald* proclaimed in its main headline: "No Ass for Dead Nazis." Pepe strolled in from time to time on his nightclub rounds, wearing a black topcoat, white silk scarf, and gray fedora and usually sporting a toothsome young lady on his arm.

At the boarding house, the landlords welcomed me into the bosom of their family. Señor and Señora Zazueta were landowners in the northern town of Culiacan, Sinaloa, who had come down to the capital years earlier to start a boarding house and to send their son to university. The Zazuetas were short, brown, mostly built like fireplugs, and obviously on the Indian side of mestizo. Señor Zazueta wore a white shirt, black vest, and suit trousers with no necktie. He was not much of a talker but excelled at clearing the dinner table of food. Señora Zazueta was a dear, tiny, gray-haired woman with a visible mustache, who invariably looked worried, wore funereal black, and was a sensational cook. When I was not out working, I ate with the family and the resident students. No one spoke much English.

The Zazueta son and heir, Roberto, was a fresh-faced, mild, eager young man, an excellent student, and the apple of his parents' eyes. The daughter, Luz Dora, was a fair-skinned young princess, the possessor of a straight, lean body with all the curves in the right places, big dark eyes, and black hair which she wore in a braid down her back. I shared a room with Rafael Perez, son of a family friend from Sinaloa, a vain young fellow with a big nose and long, well-oiled, frequently combed black hair. Roberto Zazueta, Perez, and I went out every couple of weeks or so to drive around, drink beer, and eat the delicious tacos prepared by the Indian women on street corners or to drive out to the open-air restaurants near the mountains for barbecue goat and tacos (the less scrupulous barbecues were suspected of serving barbecue dog). Luz Dora was allowed to go out with me a few times, and once, with one of her friends serving as chaperone, we even spent a weekend at the beach in Acapulco, where in the main village the streets were still unpaved and pigs ran free. I was treated as a favored member of the Zazueta community, not only because I was a gringo, which was a rarity, but because I had the only car in the house.

Late that summer, at a party given by a veteran friend of mine, I met and immediately got into a passionate, if somewhat alcoholic, argument about writing and writers with an American girl who sparkled with wit and style. Her name was Charlotte Stern. She had come down to Mexico from Pomona College in California to study at the National University, decided to stay, and went to work at the U.S. embassy library. Charlotte had read everything, spoke impeccable Spanish, and was the smartest woman I had ever met. She was the daughter of a librarian from California named Jeannette Barry, a genuine intellectual and one of the most charming and irritating women I ever knew, and a married, well-to-do businessman named Stern, with whom Barry had had an unhappy affair. Stern never recognized his paternity, or indeed Charlotte's existence. She was raised in San Diego in a cottage near the beach, partly by her mother and stepfather, an unsuccessful writer who worked for the Matson Line, a steamship company. Her stepfather drowned himself in the Pacific Ocean when Charlotte was thirteen. Jeannette Barry, a theosophist of the school of Madame Blavatsky, sent her only child to what Charlotte remembered as a fine school run by the Theosophical Society on the hills above Point Loma. I still prize the photographs of Charlotte and her classmates dancing in Grecian tunics in the columned garden of the school with the ocean in the background.

Within weeks, I moved into Charlotte's one-room penthouse apartment on the rooftop of a nightclub. When Charlotte got pregnant, we decided to get married, did so in great solemnity in a civil ceremony with a Mexican government clerk, and threw a small champagne, rum, and beer party for our friends, mostly Mexican and American journalists and students, and a French language teacher, Madame Bouchard, who had taken Charlotte under her wing when Charlotte arrived in Mexico. Madame Bouchard treated Charlotte like the daughter she never had. The two of them chattered away in French, which Charlotte learned as a child living with her beloved French-speaking grandmother, Jean Cyr, when her mother's life got too complicated. Madame Bouchard gave French lessons, ran a small rooming house in the capital, and owned a tiny house surrounded by flowers and shade trees in Cuernavaca, the heavenly town in the valley in the mountains south of Mexico City where Cortez relaxed with his Indian lover,

Malinche, when he was not destroying the Aztec Empire and imposing the long, disastrous Spanish rule on such Indians as didn't succumb to Spanish arms and the true conqueror of Mexico, European disease. Charlotte and I spent an abbreviated honeymoon there.

I graduated from Mexico City College in the spring of 1948. I no longer had the GI Bill of Rights. The *Mexico City Herald* job paid a pittance. We could live, but barely, on Charlotte's salary. The arrival of our first son, John, in March accentuated my need to get a real job, and I started to look around for possibilities in Mexico. Neither Charlotte nor I wanted to go back to the States.

Almost immediately, Frank Tremaine, the United Press (UP) bureau chief, asked me if I would like to join the UP bureau in Mexico City, which covered Mexico and managed UP's stringer correspondents in Central America. One of their three American correspondents was leaving. I accepted with alacrity, even though I immediately found out that the main reason I was hired was that I was already on the scene in Mexico. UP, a notoriously cheap outfit, would thus not have to pay the relocation costs of sending a new correspondent and family down from the States. Tremaine was a thin-faced, hard-driving UP career man with a fine news sense who taught me a great deal about reporting and writing. New York headquarters liked him, because he also was a tireless, successful salesman of the UP wire, feature, and photo services, the real ladder to success in the UP management hierarchy.

The United Press was still in its glory days in the postwar world, long before it started a long, slow slide into the depths of bankruptcy and eventual ownership by the Reverend Moon. UP was born in the early years of the twentieth century and grew to a boisterous adulthood as the brainchild of Roy Howard, the flamboyant half of the duo who founded the original Scripps Howard newspaper empire. He thought that a new wire service agency could make money by outcompeting against the staid, well-established Associated Press, which was owned by its subscribers and thus had both guaranteed readership and preferential access to the news reported by its member newspapers. Against all odds, the United Press succeeded for a long time. It earned a reputation for digging for news (not deeply enough, its critics said), adventurous reporting (hyped-up, its critics said), a lively style (breathless, its critics said), and a large stable of highly competitive reporters who produced clear, punchy news stories and features. Helen Thomas, the tiny, solid, sardonic reporter on the White House beat, who began covering Washington in 1941 and knew every president from Harry Truman to George W. Bush, is possibly the most famous, and certainly the longest lived, of the UP stars.

The UP occupied a rat-infested attic floor of one of its major client newspapers, *El Universal*, in downtown Mexico City. In addition to covering the news events of the day, the staff ran a four-man translation bureau that took English-language copy coming in by teletype from New York and turned the edited version into Spanish-language copy for transmission to Mexican clients on the local wires. We also sent Mexican news generated in both English and Spanish to New York for retransmission to UP clients around the world. UP had a gold-plated list of clients in Latin America—Argentina's best newspaper, *La Prensa*, for example favored UP news over AP—and the bureau kept a close watch for stories with special Latin interest, which included far more Mexican politics and economic news than any North American newspaper would ever absorb, and detailed coverage of soccer and bullfights. When I had an exclusive interview with the president, Miguel Aleman, for example, the story was front-page news all over Latin America, merited a few paragraphs in UP client newspapers in Texas and California, and struck out completely in New York.

We could really be sure of making it big in the American papers only when hurricanes struck, particularly ones heading north up the Gulf Coast toward Texas and Louisiana. We got our storm coverage over highly fragile telephone lines from Mexican police chiefs and local stringers in towns like Veracruz and Tampico. Invariably, at some point while these mighty storms rampaged northward, the UP New York office would send us an urgent message saying "Rox (the UP term for the Associated Press) reporting forty dead. Can you match?" Of course we could match, and we would call enough sources until we not only matched but surpassed. We knew the same process was taking place in the AP office a few blocks away.

Another big, continuing story of interest to UP clients in the southwestern United States was the war on hoof-and-mouth disease—in Spanish, *aftosa*. The U.S. and Mexican governments had established a joint commission to eradicate hoof-and-mouth disease, which cripples and kills cattle. The objective was to keep the disease out of the United States, which historically, thanks to its draconian eradication policies, has been largely free of it. The eradication campaign in Mexico produced a virtual civil war between Mexican troops and Mexican ranchers and farmers, and from time to time there was violent fighting and a lot of human blood to add to that of the cattle.

Guns were an intimate part of Mexican culture. Aztec culture worshipped blood and death; the Spaniards conquistadors were equally bloody-minded and thoughtfully brought gunpowder with them. El Dia de Los Muertos, the Day of the Dead, is a uniquely moving and deep celebration, symbolizing the Mexican fascination with death. One never sees a photograph of Pancho Villa or Francisco Zapata without a gun. Mexicans several times told me the story about an army general known popularly as "Mi General Cuarenta y Cinco." One night, he stood drinking at a bar next to a man who loudly and incessantly complained about a headache. As the complaints went on, the general asked if the man would like a remedy. When the man said yes, the general pulled out his forty-five and shot him. He never served a day in jail. President Aleman, who wanted Mexico to become a more modern, presentable society, proclaimed a "National Campaign to Depistolize (*Depistolizar*) Mexico." When the director of the campaign, a prominent young lawyer, rose to address a dinner gathering on the subject in Veracruz, his own pistol went off accidentally, wounding him in the right leg.

In spite of all the guns, Mexico in the late 1940s was a generally safe place for foreigners. The police were corrupt but efficient, and generally kept foreigners out of trouble. I usually worked as the UP night editor on the 4:00 PM to midnight shift and often unwound with Mexican newspaper friends at the famous Waikiki cabaret, a dance hall a block away on the Paseo de la Reforma. The Waikiki featured two salsa bands, a floor show, clouds of hostesses to dance with (or take out for a price), and the best organized squads of bouncers I have ever seen, who responded with tiger-like speed to the whistles that the staff used to signal the start of a fight. I never gave a thought to safety. I would drive home to our small adobe house at 4:00 AM or so and tumble into bed, smelling of rum, with Charlotte and sometimes our new infant son.

Charlotte and I took a long weekend from time to time and drove to the dream-like mountain towns and small cities: Patzcuaro, Guanajuato, San Miguel, Puebla, Taxco, Cuernavaca, Guadalajara, and Oaxaca, with their exquisite baroque churches, white colonial houses with tiled patios, and shaded, welcoming public plazas. Latin American Indian civilizations and the Spaniards shared a great sense of public space and architectonics, and their gunpoint marriage produced one of the world's most aesthetically satisfying public environments.

The collision of cultures also produced a bureaucratic and political system that, after five hundred years, still serves its citizens poorly. A detailed answer to the question of why the Spanish conquest left such a generally disastrous heritage of political, bureaucratic, and social systems in the Latin American states would require an analysis that could fill tomes of politics, economics, anthropology, and sociology, with special studies in religion and linguistics thrown in as well. Put with extreme brevity and over-simplification, the Spanish model of autocracy, hierarchy, and conservatism in politics, government, religion, and social life was imposed on top of hierarchical and conservative Indian cultures throughout most of Latin America. It has proved inefficient in both political discourse and practical governance and highly resistant to change. To this day, the dice of life are loaded in favor of the lighter-skinned, professionally trained elites. Even where there were few Indians, usually because most of or all of them were killed by the European settlers—as in the cases of Uruguay and Argentina—the results in terms of functioning political system have been generally unsatisfactory. Neither Spain nor the Indian civilizations produced a Rousseau, Saint Simon, Montesqieu, John Locke, or Edmund Burke. There have been many revolutions, in Mexico embodied in the figures of Benito Juarez and Emiliano Zapata. There has never been a true reformation, and the figure of the great man—the *caudillo*—has dominated most of Latin American history.

The historic failure to deal with the Indian question, as the Spaniards called it, continues today. In Mexico in the 1950s, probably a third of the Indian population did not speak Spanish and lived essentially outside the Mexican economy. Many still remain outside, and as the twenty-first century begins, the old, wearying civil rebellion against landlords and social injustice simmers away in the predominantly Indian states of Oaxaca and Chiapas. Migration to the United States is the main answer to the failure of the Mexican political heritage, an ironic if possibly historically just solution in light of the American annexation of half of Mexico's territory in the nineteenth century. In Guatemala, the country is staggering out of five decades of a near-genocidal civil war against its majority Indian population, which started with the CIA intervention against Arbenz in 1954.

Novelists, poets, and painters, and now moviemakers, have best captured the essence of the Latin American human condition—its cruelties and black humor, the centrality of death in life, the strain of the magical, the importance of front and ostentation, the grip of religion and family, the persistence of the all-powerful leader, the caudillo, the weakness of political and legal institutions, and the deadweight of the bureaucracies. Joseph Conrad, William White, Graham Greene, V. S. Naipaul, Gabriel Garcia Márquez, Isabel Allende, Pablo Neruda and Cantinflas: these are our best teachers about Latin America, as are Diego Rivera and his contemporaries who laid it all out in their powerful murals.

In the postwar Mexico I lived in for four years, the Partido Revolucionaria Institucional (Revolutionary Institutional Party or PRI), a ubiquitous, corrupt political machine, had run Mexico since it first coalesced as a political party in the 1911 revolution against Porfirio Diaz. Its succession to power with new presidents designated by the party leaders was taken for granted on every election day. The ineffectual Catholic party (PAN, the Party of National Action) presented candidates but seldom won. A small but influential Communist party had gained strength in the victory of the Soviet Union against the forces of fascism, as they were customarily described. As the Cold War intensified, Mexico and Latin America, as neighbors and formal allies of the United States, became major targets of Communist propaganda and subversion. In a United States where powerful voices were beginning to suggest Americans look under their beds for Communists every night, this began to be newsworthy.

The major purpose of Communist propaganda was simple: to identify the United States as the warmongering enemy of peace while the Soviet Union and Communists everywhere were hailed as lovers of peace and its fierce defenders. The target audience was the world. In 1950, to much applause and support from the Paris-based Cominform (the international Communist information organization), a Mexican committee announced the convening of the "First Latin American Congress for Peace" in a Mexico City arena. The chief organizer was Mexican labor leader Vicente Lombardo Toledano who claimed never to have joined the Communist party. Lombardo Toledano was president of the pro-Communist national labor union that competed for membership and dues with the PRI-sponsored, essentially government-run labor union. In addition, he was president of the pro-Communist Confederation of Latin American Workers, which competed throughout the hemisphere with another international group allied with the American Federation of Labor (AFL) and the Congress of Industrial Organizations (CIO).

Lombardo Toledano was a handsome, dark-skinned demagogue, a fine orator and supple in debate. He always wore a simple, well-cut dark gray suit (he was rumored to have twenty, all of them identical), and affected a pipe. I had gotten to know him slightly through calling on him from time to time in my reportorial rounds. He rather liked me, because I was the only American reporter to come around at all.

As expected, the peace conference immediately turned into a raucous, joyous festival of hatred for the United States. I sat with a small group of foreign correspondents at the back of the hall and watched a parade of political and intellectual leaders from the Americas and Europe compete in praising the peace-loving Soviet Union and damning the American imperialists for their oppression of people everywhere, particularly in Latin America. It was easy enough to make the case that the United States had often acted as an imperialist power in Latin America. It certainly had used political and economic muscle brutally in Mexico itself. To the south, the United Fruit Company record in Central America (from which stems the contemptuous term "banana republic") and the dominance of the giant American oil and mining companies in South America constituted notorious chapters in Latin American history—at least to most Latinos. But the conference was a totally one-sided show. The United States was evil incarnate—in spite of its supposedly peace-loving working class. The Soviet Union was a benevolent paradise on the march throughout the world to defend the cause of working people.

The stars of the pageant were the intellectuals, writers, and artists whom the Communists courted so successfully in Latin America and Europe, the arena hall dominated by a stage-wide blue banner with Picasso's drawing of the dove of peace hanging above the speakers. Pablo Neruda spoke to wild applause. The French poet, Paul Eluard, was greeted with enthusiasm although nobody understood him except through translation, and even then not well. A few Americans provided window dressing: Linus Pauling, the great scientist who loved the adulation he received at these affairs (he eventually received two Nobel prizes—a scientific one for chemistry and, surprisingly enough, a few years later, a peace prize for his campaign against nuclear arms), and a retired U.S. Army general, Herbert Walker, another frequent participant in these Communist circuses, who spoke to moderate applause about the sins of American foreign policy.

United Press filed a lot of copy about the Congress on the U.S. newswire, and much of it got published. Privately, I found the invective and hatred on the stage and in the hall alarming. Although I had paid little attention to politics before the war, by the time I got to Mexico after the war I immersed myself in reading and arguing about politics and history. I regarded myself as a fairly left-wing Democrat, with strong sympathies for labor unions and much skepticism about the benevolence of large corporations and their connections to government. But the America I knew, whatever its faults, bore no resemblance to the picture presented by the speakers. In the brief years since the end of the war, it seemed to me unquestionable that the Soviet Union had installed a true imperialist system of rule in Eastern Europe, while the United States was seriously trying to rebuild a free and democratic Western Europe. Lombardo Toledano told me I just didn't get it. The Soviet Union was the wave of the future. The capitalist system was finished.

Shortly after the Congress ended, a State Department officer, Forney Rankin, a big, red-haired go-getter of a man whom I had met at a U.S. embassy party and who was a high official in the U.S. government's cultural and information service, called and offered me a job as an information specialist in the U.S. Foreign Service. I was torn. Charlotte and I loved Mexico, she almost certainly more than I, but I had begun to think I wanted my world to be larger than Mexico. Nonetheless, I had many doubts about government work. The U.S. embassy in Mexico City seemed overly large, not very well informed, and quite inefficient. I also had just been offered a job by a Frenchman, a tiny, white-bearded food chemist who was a friend of Madame Bouchard, as manager of a beer factory he was setting up in Puebla (where he was later murdered in a labor dispute). But a career with the United Press as a wire service reporter seemed less attractive the more I knew about the company. Also, if I joined the Foreign Service, I could find enough free time to start to write fiction (or so I thought), and I would see a lot of the world.

I accepted Rankin's offer. In July 1951, Charlotte and I loaded our two children, John, who was three, and Kathleen, not yet a year old, into our yellow Ford convertible and headed north for the border and eventually Washington DC to report for duty. When we stopped for a coffee at the Tamuzanchale truck stop on the highway north of Mexico City, I saw a red-haired young woman sitting with a man at a nearby table. It was Lou, whom Jack Rothweiler had loved so much he would not leave Missouri. I went over. Lou introduced me to her new husband, and I introduced Charlotte and the kids to them. Lou and her husband were en route to Mexico City on their honeymoon, and then returning to a small town in Missouri. We talked a bit, awkwardly. I told her how sorry I was about Rothweiler, and that was the end of that.

5

The Propaganda Wars

I left Charlotte and the children with my parents in Kansas City and drove on east to Washington DC. My father had just retired from the Santa Fe railroad and wondered why I was once again leaving what seemed to be a good job. He *did* admit, though, that government jobs seemed to be stable. My parents were not pleased that Charlotte, the family, and I would be going abroad again.

My overwhelming first impressions of Washington in late summer 1951 were of enormous government buildings, faceless men wearing suits and ties, sweating and trying to survive in smothering heat, and how serious and humorless everyone seemed to be. Air conditioning had yet to arrive in most government buildings and private houses. I was too poor to afford an air-conditioned hotel room, because our travel up from Mexico was on our own account. I rented a stifling third-story attic room in a rooming house near the State Department and reported to the training and assignment office at State.

As the propaganda side of the Cold War picked up momentum, the State Department was building up its spindly information and cultural services, a still frail successor to the robust old Office of War Information. The assistant secretary in charge was William Benton, a legendary ad man from Chicago and a big figure in Democratic Party politics. In time, these information and cultural services were to become the United States Information Agency (USIA), a separate, semiautonomous agency under the policy control of State (although as of 2001 they were once again reabsorbed as an integral part of the State Department). Headquarters was in what was called "New State," off Virginia Avenue, to differentiate it from "Old State," originally built for the War Department, which is next to the White House and now serves as the Executive Office Building and extra office space for the White House staff.

The State Department appointed me as a commissioned Foreign Service reserve officer, class six, as a press and information specialist on an initial assignment theoretically limited to five years. The one-month training consisted mostly of lectures about the organization, objectives, and responsibilities of the Foreign Service. Of my classmates, thirty or so lively young men and women, including both officer and secretarial recruits, I seemed to be the only one with journalism experience. A few came from advertising and a few from the academic world. Scarcely any had lived or worked overseas. Most had no serious foreign language competence, and some of these were to be assigned to language training. When assignments were announced at the end of training, a wave of gasps and "wows" swept across the room when my name and assignment to Montevideo were called out. No one there had ever been to Montevideo, the capital of Uruguay, but it sounded romantic, far away on the South Atlantic ocean beaches and across the great Rio de la Plata from Buenos Aires.

Charlotte, our two children, and I sailed from New York for Montevideo in September 1951. It was the starting point of a Foreign Service career of nineteen years, divided into two widely separated periods and two different specializations. It led me into a long, intimate involvement with our Cold War enemy, the Soviet Union: in the 1960s, living in Moscow at the height of its power and confidence; two decades later, serving in Pakistan during the final, disastrous Soviet imperial adventure in Afghanistan; and finally as a private citizen helping to build democracy in the chaotic, heady 1990s in the republics that arose from the wreckage of the former Soviet Union, stripped finally of its satrapies and military glory, its economy in shambles, but its people free at last.

At first glance, Uruguay appeared to be small potatoes in the great contest of East and West. A tiny, militarily insignificant country which had once been the eastern province of Argentina (and is still sometimes called the República Oriental), it raised cattle and processed beef for sale to the European market, mostly through the local branches of the big American packing houses, Armour and Swift. The essence of the Cold War between the two great empires, however, was that no place was small potatoes. As both Moscow and Washington viewed the world, danger lurked everywhere. The domino theory of international politics reigned supreme.

In the early years of the twentieth century, Uruguay began to establish a socialist democratic tradition unique in Latin America—and much envied by many Latin Americans still living under caudillos. Political life rather resembled a debating society. When we arrived, Uruguay had two major political parties, one liberal and socialist-leaning, the second conservative and rooted in the countryside, which historically tended to alternate in power. It also had a small but noisy Communist party that played a role far bigger in intellectual debate than its actual size might suggest. The labor unions were powerful, the press was free, and the Uruguayan economy was beginning to strain under the burden of its excessively costly, feather-bedded state corporations, based on European socialist models. Like its far more powerful neighbor, Argentina, an overnight steamer trip across the vast estuary of the Rio de la Plata, Uruguay had virtually no surviving Indians and a strong Italian component in its population. Montevideños went to the opera, danced the tango, drank red wine, ate staggering amounts of beef and sausage and tons of pasta, played *pelota* (a local version of jai alai) and world-class soccer, spent as much of the day as possible in espresso bars, and thronged the magnificent beaches that ran eastward from Montevideo up to and past Punta del Este, where the waters of the Rio de la Plata finally turn into the Atlantic Ocean. By the early 1950s, the wealthy Argentines who had built the marvelous early beach mansions in Punta del Este were all bankrupt or locked up by Juan Domingo Peron, the populist dictator who strutted like a peacock across the Latin American stage, and you could rent a luxurious house in Punta for virtually nothing. This fairytale democracy lasted until the 1970s, when its overweight social services and bloated government bureaucracies, increasingly ineffective politicians, and the failure of its international markets led to its collapse into a maelstrom of violence and civil strife in the 1970s, a period from whose consequences Uruguay still struggles to recover.

I started my education in the art of Cold War diplomacy. My first boss, Frank Herron, a politically smart, prematurely white-haired man with snapping, intensely blue eyes, had, like me, once been a small-town newspaper reporter in the Midwest. He had then gone to Argentina on a foundation travel grant and written a perceptive book about his year there before entering the Foreign Service. Herron started with the essentials. The first lesson for an embassy press officer, he said, was that all ambassadors, big businessmen, and (especially) U.S. senators like to have their photographs taken all the time. So when I traveled with such types, it was essential never to be without a staff photographer on quick call. Indeed, my staff photographers learned (without me telling them) that getting me in the picture frequently, doing something presumably important like interpreting while everyone else listened, was an excellent idea. Occasionally they also caught me carrying a bag for a big shot—not a great pose for an ambitious, rising young officer.

We took a lot of photographs of my first ambassador, who happened to be extremely photogenic. He was a career officer, tall, good-looking, and a man of great personal charm who had served mostly in Europe, where he had married an aristocratic Austrian woman, a bit of a shrew. He loved to escape from the capital, where the American ambassador was a big social lion, and travel around the tiny provincial capitals of the dusty Uruguayan cow country visiting mayors, schoolmarms, and local dignitaries. At the end of our school visits, the ambassador would put his right arm around the shoulder of the principal in a gesture of companionship as they walked toward the exit. If the principal was a woman, the ambassador would slide his hand down and give her breast a gentle squeeze. The speech for these occasions, written by our senior USIS local employee and me, was *"El Hombre de Bronce"* ("The Man of Bronze"), referring to the statue of Uruguay's founding father, José Gervasio Artigas, which stands not far from the State Department in Washington. The speech paid tribute to the devotion to democracy our two countries shared and got in a few licks on the dangers represented by Communism. The ambassador pretty much knew it by heart and delivered it in acceptable Spanish even when he was tipsy, which he sometimes was by the time we got to the Chamber of Commerce banquets. His military attaché, a sober, straight-laced Army colonel, and I, his favorite drinking companion, would help push him up to his feet and he would rhapsodize, with great feeling, to invariably warm applause.

More seriously, I worked with Frank Herron learning how to focus and concentrate the limited but useful official resources we had on the targets we needed to reach. The Communists and fellow travelers controlled most of the intellectual debate throughout Latin America. The battleground was the minds of intellectuals, the students, and labor. I thought it essential for us to get far more involved in that debate, and in both Uruguay and a subsequent assignment in Chile I made it my business to get to know, almost as though it were a reportorial beat, the influential leftist intellectuals and writers whom others had thought to be beyond the pale. In most cases, these men—and an occasional woman—had never had a serious discussion with an American about anything, much less the pros and cons of the American and Soviet cases. It helped that I had fought in World War II (which Latin American leftists referred to as the War against Fascism), had been a journalist, was genuinely interested in ideas, and was virtually bilingual in Spanish.

Other agencies and forces were at work in the fight against Communism as well. I became a close friend of the CIA station chief at the embassy in Montevideo, talked with him about strategies, and we partied together with our wives (he suggested one evening we might consider a wife-swapping party, to which I demurred). He asked me a number of times why I didn't join the CIA. As a Cold War growth stock and source of employment opportunities and access to larger budgets, the CIA certainly was a better bet than USIA. But I didn't like what I thought I knew about my friend's working circles, which included both the police and much less savory types, and the years immediately ahead confirmed my misapprehensions.

In 1954, returning to Washington for consultations and leave between my transfer from the Montevideo embassy to my new assignment in Santiago, Chile, my chiefs informed me that my new posting to Chile was canceled, and that I must proceed immediately, without finishing our home leave, to Guatemala to become the embassy press officer. I agreed with great reluctance. I had visited Guatemala twice on assignment from the United Press office in Mexico City and regarded a tour of duty there, no matter how beautiful the lakes, mountains, and Mayan Indian culture were, as essentially serving in a small-time, southern extension of the Indian civilization of Mexico. Chile was a far more exciting prospect.

The atmosphere in the American embassy in Guatemala City was weird. Everyone was hushed, waiting for something to happen. The ambassador, a political appointee named Jack Peurifoy who had powerful friends in Congress, was totally uninterested in most things Guatemalan and sat in his office reading American newspapers most of the day. My immediate boss, the public affairs officer, was jumpy as a cat. A few American correspondents wandered through smelling something in the wind. But when weeks and months went by and nothing seemed about to happen, I finally persuaded my bosses in Washington that I should be allowed to rejoin my family in the States, finish home leave, and then return. While I was back in the States, the "something in the wind" blew in. The CIA paid for and directed a comic opera invasion of Guatemala, drove President Jacobo Arbenz, who was undoubtedly sympathetic to Communism but had been legitimately elected, into exile. Arbenz's ultimate sin was the expropriation of two hundred thousand acres of banana plantations belonging to United Fruit. The CIA installed the monumentally stupid Castillo Armas in the presidential palace, and Guatemala began a long slide into decades of terror and war against its Indian population, a history whose scars may never heal.

I finished my leave time with Charlotte and our three children (John and Kathleen, born in Mexico, had been joined by Peter, born in Montevideo) and we flew down to Chile, that long, skinny, spectacular land of Andean peaks, mountain lakes, deserts, fertile valleys, and glaciers, running a thousand miles down the Pacific coast from Peru to Cape Horn. Like Uruguay, Chile in the 1950s was a functioning, lively democracy, with a few menacing clouds beginning to form on the horizon.

Charlotte found us a small farmhouse ten miles north of the capital, Santiago, where the floor of the valley begins to tilt upward toward the Andes. Drinking martinis on our balcony, we could watch the evening sun turn the high snowfields on the western slopes into glowing pink. The farm occupied seven acres, with a small stream and its own irrigation ditches. Walking or riding a horse along the dirt roads in these high stretches of the valley, one was never out of earshot of the sound of water gurgling and rushing down through the field channels. The farm was planted with cherry, peach, apricot, almond, fig, nectarine, orange, and lemon trees and a grove of eucalyptus and acacia trees noisy with birds, and our road was lined with red roses and wild violets. I bought a couple of horses and started learning how to jump at a local riding club. On weekends, an embassy friend and I rode up into the foothills of the Andes and took jumping and dressage lessons with an ancient German baroness, who years earlier rode a string of horses across the Andes from Argentina and now lived alone on her small horse farm. Alberto, our farm laborer from the far south of Chile, fed and brushed the horses, milked the two cows which produced the milk we pasteurized for our children, and fed and scratched the ears of an enormous pet pig named Penelope, who responded with wiggles and grunts of sheer pleasure. As a charming piglet, Penelope was the gift of a young lady rider I bought one of my jumping horses from. Penelope turned out to have a much better disposition than my expensive jumping horse, a gelding with a short earlier career on the racing track, whose behavior frequently reflected his name, *Encono* (Irritated). Alberto hired a truck and took Penelope back south with him when we left Chile. His amply built wife, Adelita, cooked and cleaned, performing both functions unskillfully.

Our neighbors, with rare exceptions, were rich, conservative landowners. One of their favorite guests at social occasions was a young blond Catholic priest from Spain, handsome as a movie star, who had answered the pope's call to save the church and fight Communism by going to the Americas. He presided over the local church; his sister had come with him from Spain and cooked and ran the household. Their bête noire was a Yugoslav tavern owner, whose establishment just across the street from the church served other needs of the desperately poor agricultural laborers who worked on the big *fundos*. Coming home late at night from parties or work in the city, one had to be careful not to run over a farm worker passed out on the road. Chileans called these agricultural peasants *rotos* (broken ones) from the frequently torn clothing they wore.

The misery of the *rotos* was symptomatic of Chile's failure to produce genuine reform. Despite Chile's democratic heritage, Chilean politics had splintered into a bewildering array of political parties over the past century, without producing much equality of opportunity. From the original Conservative Party, which for all practical purposes was the political organ of the powerful Catholic church and the great landowners, a faction split off that called itself the Liberals, who weren't liberal at all except in their desire to reduce the influence of the church. As European political thought spread throughout Latin America in the nineteenth century, a moderate Socialist party split off from the Liberals, and it eventually gave birth to a powerful, genuinely radical variant (known as the Popular Socialist Party), and ultimately the Communists, small in numbers but powerful in their finances and outreach. A rising new contender, the Christian Democrats, modeled itself after the postwar European liberal/centrist Christian parties, in order to compete with the Communists and Socialists for the organized labor vote. The Chilean press was free and lively, although heavily influenced by party and class affiliations.

The *rotos* had their origin as workers in Chilean agriculture in the sunny, irrigated central valleys between the mountains and the sea, which was dominated by the *latifundio* (large landholdings dating in many cases from Spanish royal land grants). The great estates produced the fine, densely flavored wines for which Chile is famous and most of the superb Chilean fruit. A small fishing industry brought in delicious fish from the ice-cold waters of the Humboldt Current running north up the Pacific coast. Chile's non-farm economy was distorted by an almost total reliance on production and foreign exchange from the huge copper mines run by two American companies, Kennecott and Anaconda, in the Andes. The small domestic manufacturing sector was badly managed and uneconomic. The labor unions were a political battleground between the Communists, the radical Socialists, and the newcomer Christian Democrats.

The ancient, amiable Chilean president, Gen. Carlos Ibañez del Campo, popularly known as *El Caballo* (the Horse), both from his long service as a cavalry officer and his horse-like stubbornness, had been popularly elected after having once previously seized the presidency and governing as a generally benign military dictator. The old man was slowly losing his grip on the country. He had great difficulty in understanding modern economic problems. Inflation was running at fever pitch; labor strife was endemic and increasingly violent. Cabinets fell and rose almost monthly. My middle-class Chilean friends in the business world feared a return to an army dictatorship, but they worried far more about a takeover by the radical Marxist Socialists or the Communists than a coup by Ibañez. They tended to dismiss Senator Salvador Allende as a parlor Marxist. Eduardo Frei, the new and coming Christian Democratic leader, had just been elected to the Chilean Senate. Many Chileans hoped that Christian Democracy might save democracy from the extremists of both the left and the right, as it had in Italy and Germany.

My boss, a distinguished historian named Albert Harkness, and I set out to increase American involvement with the writers and intellectuals who both generated and commented on much of the political debate rocking the country. The Staples farmhouse north of the city became a popular venue for wine and barbecue picnics for editors and writers. I sought out and became a friend of the country's most popular political commentator, Luis Hernández Parker, a former Communist whom no one in the U.S. embassy had met before. Harkness and I encouraged the launching of a new independent literary review to compete with the existing Communist-dominated journal, where Pablo Neruda's influence was omnipresent. We used travel grants for people who previously would never have been admitted to the United States because of their past Communist connections, like Hernández Parker. I argued for six months, first with the ambassador himself and then with Washington, to get an exception to the visa rules for Hernández Parker. He finally went to the United States on a travel grant to see for himself the good as well as the bad. He was an honest man, was impressed with the lot of American working men, the freedom of American life, and the strength of its institutions, and his commentaries reflected what he had seen and learned. We also stepped up labor leader exchange programs. I even wrote the first episode of a radio soap opera series about the life of an American working family that won commercial sponsorship and ran with considerable success for a year.

I decided that I wanted to stay in the Foreign Service as a career officer in the State Department, although one of my original reasons—having leisure time to write fiction—had long ago gone by the boards. At least in my case, the Foreign Service seemed to demand hard work during the days and many nights as well. After spending three months boning up on American history, I took and passed the written examination, which at that time was a three-and-a-half-day endurance test of questions about history, international politics, economics, and culture, and which required a number of written essays. Eighteen months later, on home leave, I passed the oral examinations in Washington, whereupon the department offered me a career appointment, but only at the entrance-level Foreign Service rank and salary. I turned it down. I later entered the career service laterally at my then existing rank and salary through the examination processes created in the late 1950s for the unified Foreign Service which covered State, the U.S. Information Agency, and the Agency for International Development (AID).

When I could take a break to disappear from the capital for a few days, Charlotte and I explored the long country: the copper port Antofagasta, and the Atacama desert in the north; the wine valleys of central Chile; and the glacial lakes and pine forests of the south, all the way down to Punta Arenas, the chilly southernmost city of the continent near Cape Horn, where the winds blew gale force day and night. We spent quiet weekends in little towns on the central coast watching the broad swells roll in from the Pacific, occasionally sprinting into the freezing waters of the Humboldt current and immediately out. At night, we feasted on the sea urchins, sea bass, conger eels, and abalone that thrive in these waters and drank the heady Chilean white wines.

If I was happy at work and in my personal life, the country by and large was not. As the Ibañez presidency entered its final year, our Chilean friends grew glummer. The international price of copper fell, and so did the peso. I had never seen firsthand the ravages that inflation inflicts on an economy. Consumer prices in pesos went up by 100 percent in less than a year. People visibly grew more worn looking. Foreigners, and the relatively few wealthy Chileans with access to dollars, were unaffected, or indeed benefited, as price increases in pesos lagged well behind the purchasing power of the dollar in the exchange rate. Charlotte bought (in pesos) a beautiful antique chest for half the dollar cost we originally considered. The political situation grew chaotic. Students rioted to protest increases in bus fares. Much of the nation was on strike.

In 1957, Washington ordered me back to the States for an assignment at headquarters. When the family and I departed Santiago, we drove through empty downtown streets reeking of the teargas employed against student demonstrators. The port at Valparaíso, where we boarded a ship for the trip up the west coast and through the Panama Canal to New York, was under Chilean navy and army patrol.

In the years after I left Chile, Eduardo Frei, the Christian Democrat, and Salvador Allende, the Socialist Party candidate, won successive elections to the presidency. Frei became president in 1964 and governed with some distinction until 1970. Allende was elected and installed as president that year. He left the presidential palace as a corpse in September 1973 when the Chilean army under Gen. Agustin Pinochet seized power, ostensibly to prevent a Communist coup. That the White House and the CIA encouraged and funded Allende's enemies has long been beyond dispute. The exact circumstances of his death in the National Palace are not.

In the late 1970s, long after General Pinochet installed both torture chambers and the young Chilean University of Chicago-trained, free market economic advisers whom many Chileans and Americans credit for the reform and subsequent growth of the Chilean economy, I was living and working in New Delhi as the representative of the Ford Foundation. An Indian friend asked me to organize a small reception for a group of international "wise men" visiting Asia on a human rights mission. Frei, at that time living in Europe in exile, was a member of the group. During the evening, I went over to him and said in Spanish, "Yo conozco su país, y lo quiero mucho" ("I know your country, and I love it very much"). We talked for a few minutes. The old man's long face grew even longer, and finally he put his head down and began to weep. "How much we have lost," Frei said. "I still cannot believe it. So much we have lost. And I always ask myself: How could we have done differently?"

My new Washington assignment in the U.S. Information Agency headquarters was to be the policy officer for the Latin American program division. In essence, I was responsible for interpreting and putting into programmatic terms a host of policy directives flowing mostly from State and occasionally from the White House, which ran the gamut from basic long-term policies to short daily dicta and bulletins. I met daily with agency policy colleagues and frequently with officers in the relevant geographic bureaus in State. No better spot could have been found for an introduction to the tortuous relationships between policy and program implementation among the various foreign affairs agencies and between the executive branch and Congress. A major task was to help prepare written materials for and to brief senior USIA directors on their testimony before congressional authorizing and appropriations committees.

The move to Washington brought me, for the first time with a wife and children, back into the mainstream of American life. I had not lived in a major American city for fifteen years: after leaving Kansas City I had spent three-plus years living at Marine Corps air stations and on Navy ships; two years working as a newspaperman and student in Midwestern small towns; four years as a student and foreign correspondent in Mexico; and the six most recent years as a Foreign Service officer in Latin America. I got married in Mexico, and two of our children were born there, the third in Uruguay. All three spoke Spanish as fluently as English. They had never lived in the States at all, of course, and their adjustment to U.S. living was a matter of particular concern.

We rented a pleasant, modest old wooden house in Chevy Chase, Maryland, right across the border from the District of Columbia. The kids enrolled in a well-regarded public school, did well academically, began to lose their Spanish (deliberately and almost immediately, since they didn't want to be different from their peers), and appeared to handle the workload, the friendships, the indifference, and the occasional cruelties of their fellow students and their teachers with reasonable equanimity (although what parents don't know is always a lot). They found playmates among the children of our neighbors, a typical profile of Washington middle-class families: the heads of household, mostly men, were lawyers, bureaucrats, psychologists, teachers, lobbyists, and an occasional doctor. Our older son, John, became a Boy Scout. Several of the troop's fathers, a most unscoutish collection, were asked to organize an overnight hike, camping in tents. It turned out none of us knew how to make a fire without matches, particularly in the rain that greeted us. I used a cigarette lighter to start the fire and groused about missing my evening martini. Like good Washingtonians, when the Turkish bath days and nights of the Washington summer wrapped the swampy city around us, we escaped for two weeks to a Rehoboth Beach cottage on the Atlantic, swam in the cool ocean, savored the fresh tomatoes and sweet corn of the Delmarva Peninsula, and thought how blessed we were.

President Eisenhower was in the second term of his administration, still enjoying great popularity. The American economy, stimulated by Cold War defense spending, provided a good life to most Americans (although by the end of his term, Eisenhower was warning about the influence of the "military-industrial complex"; by 1960 the military budget constituted nearly half of total federal budget expenditures). Eisenhower had handled the nasty challenge of Senator Joe McCarthy with caution verging on cowardice. He failed to say a word to defend Gen. George Marshall, who in the Second World War was the single most influential voice arguing for Eisenhower's promotion to supreme command. McCarthy charged Marshall, who had been Harry Truman's secretary of state, with being soft on Communism and presiding over "a conspiracy of shame," but Ike said nary a public word. McCarthy, a drunk, finally destroyed himself in 1954 when he attacked the U.S. Army directly as being soft on Communism and died a nonentity in 1957.

The smell of McCarthyism still hung in the air of Washington when I went to work there, affecting the hiring practices and substantive work of all the foreign affairs agencies. State and USIA were particularly affected, as McCarthy's two infamous staffers, Roy Cohn and David Schein, roamed the world harassing USIS libraries and investigating the Voice of America. John Foster Dulles, Eisenhower's lugubrious secretary of state, went along supinely with all of this, showing his own brand of patriotism by firing the best China experts in the Foreign Service, the ones who had correctly reported the advancing internal decay of the Chinese Nationalist government and the growing strength of Mao and his Communists. (A half-century later, the basic concept of McCarthyism—the public questioning of the loyalty and patriotism of one's opponents—remains a favorite tool in the American Far Right's arsenal of political rhetoric, as witnessed by President George W. Bush's offhand comment in the early discussions about domestic security after the 9/11 attack that the Democrats value union rights more than the security of the homeland.)

I was not to enjoy my job as the Latin American division policy officer for long. One day in 1958, Henry Loomis, the special assistant to the USIA director, Ambassador George V. Allen, dropped by my modest office, ostensibly to chat about matters Latin American. The next day, I was called down to the director's suite for the first time, where Loomis introduced me to a ruddy-faced, soft-spoken man named Bill Key, a former journalist who turned out to be an administrative assistant to Vice President Richard Nixon. President Eisenhower had suffered a stroke in November of the previous year. He therefore had asked Nixon to make a South American good-will tour in his stead, primarily to signal American approval of Arturo Frondizi, just elected as the successor to the anti-American dictator, Peron, in Argentina. The Nixon staff wanted a professional press officer to handle the logistics of the trip, since dozens of journalists were expected to accompany the delegation. Nixon was the obvious heir apparent to the presidency, and this would be an excellent opportunity for the American press to see how Nixon looked as a statesman in a role very different from his earlier, red-baiting days in the U.S. Congress.

Loomis called the next morning to say that I should report to Key and start working with him on the trip. I protested that as a liberal Democrat I was hardly the man for the job. Loomis laughed and said this was a professional, not a political, assignment, and that my combination of competency in Spanish, journalistic experience, and on-the-ground knowledge of Latin American made me the obvious choice. Plus which, he said, Key liked me. This turned out to be mutual, and I liked various other members of the vice presidential staff as I got to know them over the coming months. I became particularly fond of Rose Mary Woods, Nixon's secretary. Once Rose made up her mind you were a good guy, she was a warm and invariably helpful friend. Nixon's Navy attaché, a Marine Corps colonel named Robert Cushman, thought I would be fine, doubtless in part because I was an ex-Marine.

Key showed me the schedule the State Department had proposed. It was routine to a fault: calls on presidents, laying wreaths at national monuments, embassy receptions, and press conferences. Clearly the State Department wanted no trouble on the trip. I asked Key if he and his boss wanted real press interest. He said, "Of course." I told him, "You'll never make news with this schedule." "What do you suggest?" Key asked. "You've got to get the vice president out of these official circles to talk with some real people," I replied. "Visit some universities and talk with teachers and students. Maybe talk with some labor leaders. See more of the press."

Key consulted with Nixon, whom I did not meet personally until just before the trip began, and told me to prepare a new schedule with the Latin American division at State. These officers, all people I knew from my regular duties, were in fact concerned that because of his strong public anti-Communist posture, and particularly because of his record as a member of the House Un-American Activities Committee and subsequently the Senate Internal Security Subcommittee, Nixon would become a lightning rod for street demonstrations. I told Key this was certainly a possibility. But if they wanted headlines, they needed a different, more open schedule. Key said to go ahead, and State proceeded to produce a new trip outline incorporating visits to universities and a much wider range of discussions with private citizens.

American reporters signed up in large numbers (some thirty in all), and with accompanying photographers and staff we had to charter a separate DC-6 (the largest, propeller-driven airliner then flying), which the sponsoring news media paid for. The reporters included Tad Szulc of the *New York Times*, whom I had known when we worked on opposite ends of the United Press night wire between New York and Mexico City, Earl Mazo, who later became Nixon's biographer, and Bob Hoffman, a prominent journalist with a strong conservative bias. They were a rambunctious and demanding group. A few drank too much, but I generally enjoyed my role of housemother.

The first part of the South American trip—Uruguay, Argentina, Paraguay, and Bolivia—went smoothly. At the La Paz airport, thirteen thousand feet high, the embassy suggested the airplane be met with portable oxygen tanks. One heavy-drinking news agency photographer passed out promptly when we deplaned. We clapped an oxygen mask on his face, and within hours he was dancing "La Bamba" with barrel-shaped Bolivian Indian ladies wearing their rainbow shawls and marvelous fedora hats.

After that, the trip rapidly got interesting from a news point of view. At San Marcos University in Lima, a solid wall of a thousand or so protestors, led by about a hundred agitators, blocked Nixon's access to the university gates. Nixon got out of his convertible and walked toward the crowd, accompanied only by his interpreter, Col. Vernon Walters, and his senior secret service agent, Jack Sherwood. He shouted: "I want to talk to you. Why are you afraid of the truth?" The crowd started throwing rocks. A rock hit Sherwood in the mouth and broke a tooth. The three men got back in the car, and as they drove away, Nixon shouted back: "You are cowards. You are afraid of the truth." The rest of the brief Lima visit went off peacefully, with much genuine Peruvian admiration expressed for the vice president's show of courage. The headlines in the States were big, Eisenhower sent a telegram of support and admiration, and the Nixon party was delighted.

The final stop, Caracas, produced the near disaster my State Department friends had feared—and headlines back home and abroad. When we deplaned in front of the airport terminal in the blazing tropical sun (this was long before jetways came into use and passengers still walked or rode across the tarmac from their planes to the terminal), we could hear and see a big crowd waiting. The roar of the crowd, it soon became clear, was not to welcome our party. The vice president and his wife, accompanied by the Venezuelan foreign minister, were hurried out under an open-air observation deck just in front of the terminal to get to their cars, but they had to stop to stand at attention while an army band played the Venezuelan national anthem. Members of the mob, hanging over the rails of the deck overhead and screaming curses and anti-American slogans, spat on the vice president and his wife. The rest of us, following right behind, hurried through a continuing shower of spit and imprecations. The Venezuelan government's security had broken down completely.

Nixon's limousine took off with tires squealing for the first scheduled official call, a wreath-laying ceremony at the Panteón Nacional. I headed for the U.S. embassy residence to make sure that arrangements for the first press conference were in hand. I found out shortly after arriving at the embassy that the Nixon limousine had run into a mob of angry demonstrators on the streets far short of the national monument. The crowd stopped the car, rocked it back and forth for ten minutes or so, pounding on and breaking the reinforced window glass with clubs and iron pipes, and screaming at the occupants. Nixon, his interpreter, Vernon Walters, the senior secret service agent, Jack Sherwood, and the Venezuelan foreign minister were all hit with flying slivers of glass. The crowd concentrated on the Nixon limousine, ignoring Pat Nixon and her escort alone in the limousine to the rear. Both cars finally broke through the mob and drove to the embassy residence.

By morning, after a night of street violence, the government finally clamped down. Armed troops and armored vehicles patrolled the entire downtown area. When our caravan, accompanied by armored cars, drove to the airport, the city was practically deserted. Szulc said that his Venezuelan sources told him there had been a serious Communist plot to use the Nixon visit to try to take over the government. Later, I learned that Nixon had been told at our brief earlier stop in Bogotá, Colombia, that the CIA had informed the FBI of reports it had received of a possible Communist assassination plot against him in Venezuela. When the violence occurred, Eisenhower—without informing Nixon—ordered a U.S. Navy battle group to move into a position off the coast of Venezuela to be ready to use military force if necessary to get the Nixon party out.

On our arrival in Washington, after a brief stop in Puerto Rico where numbers of my press group knelt and kissed American soil, Nixon was basking in a rare spotlight of virtually unanimous, warm public and press approval. Eisenhower met the plane and embraced Nixon. For the first time in Gallup trial heat presidential polling, Nixon drew even with John F. Kennedy. His courage under attack gave his personal reputation and political fortunes an enormous boost.

In a minor way, I found myself a celebrity at USIA headquarters. The agency was an institution more accustomed to being pilloried for screwing up than praised for participating in a successful, even dangerous, mission. The USIA director, Ambassador Allen, and his deputy, Abbott Washburn, received me with big smiles and pats on the back, and within weeks, Allen, who behind a façade of a kindly Southern gentleman was a canny, power-wise Washington operator, asked me to move into the executive suite to become his special assistant. Henry Loomis, who had found me for the Nixon Latin American sojourn, had just been appointed chief of USIA's research and intelligence division, and Allen clearly thought an assistant with friends in high places could be useful. I installed myself happily in a bright, comfortable office in the executive suite, with a elegant, extremely competent secretary, and began to learn and enjoy the intrigues and games of front-office Washington bureaucratic politics.

The Nixons invited me to a couple of cocktail parties that summer in honor of the press corps and staff that accompanied the vice president on the Latin American journey. At parties, Nixon drank too much (a habit I had not known about earlier) to the point of slurring his speech. At occasions like these, he was cordial in a jolly, "hail fellow well met" kind of way, but I never thought him really very comfortable with anyone.

In the fall, Eisenhower asked Nixon to represent the United States in London at the dedication of the American chapel in Saint Paul's Cathedral, honoring the American World War II dead. Bill Key called and said Nixon wanted me to serve as the delegation press officer again. I went to London in advance to set up the press arrangements, traveling with a couple of Secret Service agents assigned to scout out the terrain with colleagues from Scotland Yard and other British security agencies. As guests of Her Brittanic Majesty, we stayed at the Connaught, enjoying England's finest hotel beds, best hotel service, and juiciest lamb chops, and the delights of Dover sole and English bacon and eggs for ten days. The London trip was a quiet success, even in the eyes of a not very friendly British press, as Nixon spoke eloquently at the dedication of the chapel in St. Paul's about the British and American sacrifices in the war. He himself, of course, had served as a U.S. Navy officer in the Pacific. We spent part of a day at Oxford, which, having welcomed centuries of big shots, was quite relaxed about our visit. I was highly amused when the limousine assigned to two Scotland Yard officers, two U.S. Secret Service agents, and me got lost on country roads when the Scotland Yard driver decided to take back roads to Oxford to avoid heavy traffic on the super-highway. The Secret Service agents didn't think it was funny at all. We finally got to Oxford just in time.

I found it difficult to make up my mind about Nixon. He was a very strange man. His head was too big; his nose, which cartoonists adored, was large, hairy, and shaped like a ski jump; his voice was deep and mellifluous; and his physical movements oddly uncoordinated and jerky. Nixon was smart, although I did not think him brilliant, and his interest in and understanding of foreign affairs was far superior to the Washington average, which is not high. Nixon prided himself on cutting to the heart of the matter. His overwhelming characteristic was his driving passion for power. The flaw in his character—which ultimately ruined him—was his profound suspicion of the world outside a tight circle of friends and trusted staff members. Even in the middle years of his career when I knew him—though only slightly in my role as an outside staff man—he sometimes seemed close to the brink of paranoia. In *The Memoirs of Richard Nixon*, referring to Watergate and his presidency, Nixon writes, "If we often made the mistake of acting like an administration under siege, it was because we were an administration under siege." But he had always thought that he was under siege and must attack back.

On the other hand, Nixon sometimes approached greatness. The China open-ing was a genuinely historic step, and Nixon carried it off with skill, a great sense of timing, and panache; probably only Nixon could have done it. As president, he displayed more leadership in social and economic justice than anyone expected. He was far ahead of the times in his efforts to reform the welfare system by including the working poor. He put into practice and enforced a policy of affir-mative action for minority firms in government contracts and pushed hard for school desegregation under the Supreme Court ruling of 1969. Nixon was, in fact, somewhat of a liberal, and he would have been contemptuous of the domi-nant wing of today's Republican party, with its proud ignorance of foreign affairs, its kowtowing to the Christian Far Right, and its ideological reluctance to use big governmental power to tackle big national issues.

After the London trip, Bill Key inquired if I would be interested in joining the Nixon staff. I politely declined. I valued my life in the Foreign Service, I said, and in any case I didn't think my political views were right for a job with Nixon. I lost track of Key in later years, but I was happy to see he was not a member of the Nixon White House's inner circle of scoundrels when it all fell apart. While I declined the informal invitation, my future was to hold yet one more encounter with Nixon in completely unforeseen circumstances.

I settled into the heady life of a special assistant in the USIA director's executive suite with great gusto. I represented and reported back to Ambassador Allen in a lot of high-level policy and personnel meetings, including the agency's senior assignment board deliberations (which I found fascinating as senior officers' strengths and weaknesses were discussed as plum assignments were decided), and sat in with the director for meetings with visiting dignitaries. The only time I lost my newly cultivated, high-level cool manners was during a visit from a Protestant evangelical leader, accompanied by a goggle-eyed young assistant who sat leaning forward in his chair, glaring at me. They came in to complain that USIA libraries overseas had too many books by Catholic authors (shades of the McCarthyites) and to insist that the agency remove from its library shelves a long list of books, which they promptly produced. I thought the preacher and his young protégé were badgering Allen far more than acceptable. I dived into the discussion, thereby violating the cardinal rule of conduct for special assistants, which is never to open your mouth unless you're asked to. I finally lost my temper and told the preacher firmly that we selected books for quality and how well they reflected the diversity and strength of American life and views, and that we didn't give a damn about the religion of their authors. The evangelist and his glaring assistant leaped to their feet. The man of God said they were shocked by my use of profanity, and out they strode. The evangelist raised a minor fuss with a couple of congressmen, but it didn't amount to much.

Chanute, Kansas, Spring 1946.
Duke Wallingford, news reporter and author's mentor in journalism.

Author as the night editor, <u>Mexico City Herald</u>, 1948

Charlotte Stern Staples and Eugene Staples, 1950.

Life in the Foreign Service. Author and his jumper, Encono, Santiago, Chile, 1956.

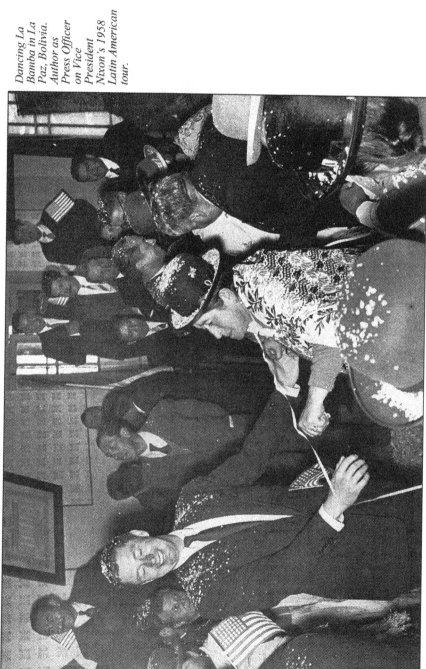

Dancing La Banba in La Paz, Bolivia. Author as Press Officer on Vice President Nixon's 1958 Latin American tour.

Preparation for 1959 U.S. National Exhibition Moscow. Manager Harold "Chad" McClellan, third from left, and author try to blow down experimental plastic umbrellas on Long Island airfield.

Designer Jack Masey and author:
mounting the first U.S. traveling exhibit in Kiev, Ukraine, 1961.

The Staples family, Moscow, 1964.
Author, Charlotte, John, Peter, Kathleen.

6

American Flags over Moscow

In late 1958, Ambassador Allen and his deputy, Abbott Washburn, became immersed in the planning of a major American exhibition to be held in Moscow in the summer of 1959 at Sokolniki Park. The Soviet premier and party boss, Nikita Khrushchev, then at the height of his power and confidence, felt strong enough to proclaim a new Soviet policy of "peaceful competition" with the United States. This by no means signified a reduction of Soviet military and political pressure anywhere in the world, but Khrushchev thought that Soviet life and culture would come out well in a limited, highly controlled set of comparisons with America.

The Eisenhower administration and the Soviet government painstakingly negotiated an agreement to carry out a number of new cultural and information exchange programs, of which the most visible single piece was to be an exchange of major national exhibitions. The Soviets would mount a large exhibition in New York, while the Americans would put on a comparably sized American show in Moscow. President Eisenhower named Allen as the official coordinator of the American effort. The State Department would provide policy guidance and help, USIA would have the lead role in exhibit planning and preparation, and the Department of Commerce would oversee construction of the exhibit and management of operations in Moscow. Abbott Washburn (in private life a highly successful public relations executive) served as the de facto conduit to the American private sector, which was expected to supply much of the materials for the exhibit. All of this had to be fitted into an extremely tight timetable with a July 1959 opening date scheduled for Moscow. Nobody had ever done anything like this, although USIA regularly sent out small exhibits to overseas posts and an office in Commerce sponsored overseas trade shows of American products. In its trifurcation of tasks, it was, as any student of bureaucracy would recognize immediately, a virtual blueprint for disaster.

To command this unwieldy operation, Eisenhower appointed a prominent California businessman and Republican activist, Harold "Chad" McClellan, to be the general manager (a title McClellan chose) with the rank of ambassador. McClellan had two deputy general managers: a senior officer from USIA to help run policy, planning, and preparation, and a senior officer from the Department of Commerce International Trade Fair office to oversee exhibition construction in Moscow and to manage the on-ground staff and operations. This was no small show: the Soviets had promised a multi-acre open space in Sokolniki Park which lay on the outskirts of Moscow but was easily reachable on the famous Moscow subway system. Early planning called for a series of large pavilions and outside exhibits, with a staff of two hundred, almost entirely from the private sector and including some eighty Russian-speaking American guides.

McClellan, Washburn, and Allen conferred at least twice a week on the early progress of exhibit preparation, or the lack thereof. Usually, I was not asked to sit in on these meetings, and that suited me fine. I had read a lot of Russian literature and some of the country's history, and on my own had studied the rise and practice of Communist power and the international Communist movement, but I certainly was not an expert on the Soviet Union. Privately, I thought the exhibit project so complicated and time-restricted that it could easily turn into a disaster. McClellan's USIA-designated deputy general manager, a senior officer whom I knew slightly, sometimes attended these planning and review meetings in Allen's office, as did McClellan's deputy from the Commerce Department, a tough old international trade-show operator named Howard Messmore.

I began to pick up rumors in agency senior officer circles that McClellan was dissatisfied with his USIA deputy. My first reaction was to wonder which unfortunate soul might be snatched out of senior officer ranks to be thrown into the breach, if it came to that. One morning, walking through the reception room of the executive suite, I met McClellan and Washburn bustling in for their regular meeting with Allen, and McClellan, whose professional manner featured a lot of smiling, gave me a particularly sparkling smile as they said good morning. In about twenty minutes, Allen called on the interoffice phone and asked me to come in. In his best Southern gentleman, diplomatic style, as McClellan and Washburn beamed at me, Allen said, "Rocky, I've got a very important job which I want you to take on." Then he went on to drop the bomb. McClellan wanted a new number two, and he wanted me. In some shock, I mumbled that I was neither a Soviet expert nor knew much about organizing exhibits. Then, of course, I accepted and said I would do my best. McClellan said he'd see me the next morning.

Indeed, the very next morning, I said good-bye to my comfortable suite and elegant secretary in the director's office and reported for duty down at the Washington Mall in one of a long line of shabby, anonymous, noisy and drafty Quonset huts where the exhibit headquarters office was located. The Quonsets, now long and happily gone from the Washington landscape, were first designed and built by the U.S. military in World War II for use overseas and on new bases in the United States. A whole small city of these huts sprouted on the Washington mall during the war to accommodate the burgeoning civil bureaucracy. Although they were never intended for long-term use, they were still there fourteen years after the war. They had toilets and heat, but that was the extent of their amenities, and they were to be my home, virtually every day and frequently late into the night, for the next several months.

I met my new working colleagues and plunged into the chaotic planning process. McClellan worked like a machine boring through rock. He spent about half his time traveling, frequently with Abbott Washburn, to line up private-sector exhibits and support. I ran the office. I made my highest priority the preparation, circulation, and strict follow-up of a simple chronological calendar of deadlines and staff responsibilities. If one had existed before my arrival, it had long disappeared, and the schedule was in disarray. In addition to the exhibit content tasks, the calendar included the major checkpoints for exhibition construction and operating staff hiring (this was the Commerce Department's job under Howard Messmore). I emphasized that I must know immediately about bottlenecks and implementation problems as they developed. I said I would listen carefully, try to understand what, where or who the problem was, and help to marshal the staff, money, or outside resources to deal with it on time. No matter what it took, we were going to get all the components of the exhibit to Moscow and open the big show by July 24. We had a satisfactory budget. And because of the priority of the exhibition and President Eisenhower's personal interest, we could get immediate attention from any branch of the federal government.

As an example, in mid-spring, we were about to sign a contract for the construction of a forest of interconnecting, fifteen-foot-high plastic umbrellas to function both as outside exhibit space and shelter for the crowds during Moscow's frequent summer rain showers. I discovered that no one knew how much wind was customary during the summer in Moscow, or how stable the umbrellas would be in a windstorm. While the manufacturer assured us the umbrellas were strong, they were brand new and had never been tested, and I thought it would be disastrous if a bunch of newfangled American umbrellas fell down on a Moscow crowd. The answer to the first question was easy: over a hundred-year cycle of recorded wind-speeds in the Moscow summer, winds were historically gentle. To answer the question about the umbrellas' strength and stability, I called the Pentagon and asked if the U.S. Air Force could generate some big wind for us by using parked bombers at an airfield to try to blow down a group of umbrellas. Within ten days, we had erected a cluster of umbrellas on the tarmac at the old MacArthur airfield on Long Island. McClellan and I flew up on a rainy morning and, accompanied by an amused Air Force colonel, watched two old B-25 twin-engine propeller-driven bombers huff and puff and try to blow the umbrellas down. The umbrellas were as steady as oak trees.

The two key USIA Foreign Service officers already assigned to the staff were exceptionally talented and experienced young men. Jack Masey, the agency's chief expert on overseas exhibits, was a graduate of Yale's School of Art and Architecture and a veteran of the U.S. Army's remarkable camouflage regiment in World War II, which landed at Normandy and—under combat conditions—installed fake tanks, gun emplacements, and airplanes all across Europe for the Nazis to expend their scarce ordnance attacking. He also had worked as a designer in New York before joining the Foreign Service. Masey was electrically passionate about design, modern art, and architecture. He walked and spoke in a rush of thought, often loudly and frequently profanely, and could not tolerate fools. McClellan, the big boss, was no fool—very far from it, I thought—but McClellan and Masey represented totally different approaches to life, and their relationship was uncomfortable.

The staff policy expert on the Soviet Union was Wallace "Pic" Littell, a stocky, gentle, good-looking country boy who in his youth had developed an abiding interest in Russia. Littell graduated from the topnotch Middlebury College Russian language and area studies program, spoke beautiful Russian, and had just finished a two-year assignment at the U.S. embassy in Moscow as the first cultural attaché assigned there as the new period of peaceful competition got under way. Littell commanded an enormous fund of knowledge about things Russian—history, the Russian and Soviet empires, the Communist party and how it ruled, and the way the Soviet people lived and thought. One could not have invented a better counselor on exhibit content. The Soviet specialists at State and in the Moscow embassy liked and respected Littell. That set of relationships produced a lot of helpful ideas.

On the centrally important question of design, Masey had been instrumental in the early decision to hire George Nelson as the chief exhibition designer. Nelson, trained originally as an architect, was one of the half-dozen Americans who shaped modern design theory and practice, and his work was already well represented at the Museum of Modern Art. He was a man who walked around with startling and beautiful shapes in his head. Masey and Nelson together were, I thought, a national asset. Nelson was marvelously charming when he wanted to be, sardonic and very funny. He smoked constantly, had a sallow complexion, and usually looked half dead. Women loved him—and he returned their affection generously. (During the course of the exhibition, he had an affair with Jack Masey's USIA assistant, divorced his wife, and married the assistant, as it turned out happily and for life.)

Nelson was responsible for overall design and layout: the buildings, the subject and nature of the interior exhibits, and the flow of traffic. Masey had already enlisted Buckminster Fuller to design the biggest geodesic dome ever constructed as the main exhibition building. This would serve as the theater for a giant-size, multi-screen movie about a day in the life of America and also introduce the Russian crowds to the layout of the overall exhibition. Nelson enthusiastically approved of Fuller. With equal fervor, he disapproved of the West Coast architectural firm chosen, largely under pressure from McClellan, to design a second group of major exhibit buildings. Nelson thought them at best pedestrian.

The exhibit subject matter included American daily life, culture, sports, fashion, automobiles, science, and technology. IBM was to install a big computer on site (and in those days they were so big they looked like railroad box cars), since the Soviets were fascinated by computers and well behind us in computer technology. General Motors was to send a couple of dozen automobiles. General Electric agreed to build a model American kitchen in a small house, provided by a Long Island builder, to be erected on site. Pepsi would provide free drinks. The renowned designers, Charles and Ray Eames, were working on the multi-screen movie. Edward Steichen had agreed to mount a large version of his photographic exhibition, "The Family of Man," and there would even be an exhibit of modern American art long anathema to Soviet ideologists, including a Jackson Pollock. In addition, Shirley Goodman of the Fashion Institute of Technology was putting together a style show complete with fashion models and cosmetics demonstrations for Soviet women.

As problems and pressures built up during the spring, it became clear that my most important management task was to serve as a buffer and interpreter working to keep McClellan and Nelson from a ruinous break in their relationship. I made sure I knew in advance of any unpleasant surprises that might be sprung by either man and intervened on my own to straighten out misunderstandings before they got out of control. The two men truly were antithetic: McClellan, the hard-driving, conservative, California Republican executive, usually dressed in a dark blue suit and necktie, who would be at home in any Chamber of Commerce meeting; and Nelson, the liberal New York intellectual, who wore a frayed sports jacket and managed a creative design team located near the Flatiron building in downtown Manhattan. McClellan, greeted in the morning, would reply smiling, "I'm great, just great! And how are you?" The Nelson response was, "Terrible." They held different views about virtually every aspect of the exhibition. McClellan loved the plans for the automobile exhibit; Nelson thought the cars had been given far too much space, and that most of them were poorly designed anyway. McClellan never really understood why the art exhibit contained so much abstract art, and particularly why we must show a Jackson Pollock. But out of their disagreements came a remarkably appealing show. The Chevrolets and the Pollock were both crowd favorites.

Every crisis that arose on the exhibit content and preparation side could be matched—and more—on the construction half of the ledger. The Soviets gave Messmore and his colleagues a tough time in Moscow, insisting that all construction plans conform to Soviet standards (which very few Soviet buildings did). There were endless hassles about labor costs. Masey had hired a Finnish construction firm to build the exhibits and to supervise their installation in Moscow, but the Soviets refused to allow them to work as supervisors. The Italian firm providing the anodized aluminum panels for Buckminister Fuller's domed roof misread the blueprints, and their first shipment was unusable. Replacements were delivered behind schedule, and at one point got lost in Eastern Europe. But the hiring and abbreviated training of the Russian-speaking guides went swimmingly. There had been an enormous response to the advertisements for guide positions. Most of the guides chosen were young college students of Russian. A good many were young men and women of Russian and East European extraction who spoke Russian at home.

In late June, almost miraculously, it all began to come together in a rush. We were like jockeys whipping their horses to the finish. In early July, carrying still unresolved problems in our heads and in our briefcases, McClellan, the tiny senior headquarters staff, and I set up an operating base in Moscow. The Sokolniki site still looked like a big construction project that, with luck, might get finished sometime in the fall. Soviet workers were installing the last of the gold-anodized panels on the geodesic dome. The other major exhibition building complex, because of blueprint confusion and the delays in the arrival of steel from

Italy, was way behind schedule. Eames had still not finished the vitally important multi-screen movie on a day in the life of America.

McClellan plunged into discussions with Messmore, the operations deputy, and his senior Soviet counterparts, a thick-bodied, gray-suited, gray-shoed set of Soviet bureaucrats from the Soviet Chamber of Commerce. Of course, the Soviets blamed us for all the problems plaguing the site construction because of relatively minor design changes and lateness in arrival of some materials. They were, of course, partly right. But they had compounded the problems by failing to provide the right engineering specialists at the right time and place and by using miserably shoddy construction materials. Messmore had ordered early tests of the Soviet-produced concrete that was to be used and had rejected it as insufficiently strong. The poor quality of the concrete floors, which began to disintegrate on opening day of the exhibition, plagued us from start to finish.

The senior exhibition staff was housed at the Hotel Ukraina, a vast horror of a hotel situated in a Stalin-period skyscraper in downtown Moscow, where it was virtually impossible to get breakfast—if a waitress finally deigned to notice your presence—in less than two hours or so. Most mornings, McClellan, Messmore, a few other staff members, and I got up at sunrise. I would pick up enough black bread, sausage, and cheese at the small all-night hotel buffet—when that was open—to feed at least a few of us, and we would head out to the site. I was wretchedly frustrated by my inability to communicate. I was accustomed to living in Spanish-speaking countries where I was virtually bilingual. I could get along adequately in Europe in self-taught French. But Russian was a complete mystery, and I found few Soviet citizens who spoke much English. Our guide staff, on the other hand, was delighted; they were going to speak Russian with more Russians in three weeks than they could have met in a lifetime if they hadn't been selected for the show.

With a few days left until the July 24 opening, even though construction was still going on and exhibit material was still arriving by rail and air, the site finally began to glow like the jewel its designers dreamed of. We heard on July 23 that Vice President Nixon, who had just arrived in Moscow to represent President Eisenhower at the exhibition inaugural, was going to visit the site that afternoon for a pre-opening tour with Nikita Khrushchev, the Soviet premiere and party boss. Their arrival produced a great stir of newspaper people and curious workers.

Neither of the two men was the least bit shy about arguing in public. (Khrushchev, who in a second could shift from real charm to outrageous bullying, became notorious during his first U.S. visit in 1960 for taking a shoe off at the United Nations and pounding it on his desk to protest against a speaker with whom he disagreed.) Nixon, in spite of his painful private shyness, always liked a good public argument and had seen the political benefits of standing up to protestors in public during his Latin American tour. The two crossed swords almost immediately in the exhibition's model color television studio. Khrushchev jumped onto the platform and started talking to the camera, aiming his remarks at a group of Soviet workers. "How long has America existed?" he asked Nixon. "Three hundred years?"

"One hundred and eighty years," Nixon replied.

"Well, then," Khruschev said, "we will say America has been in existence for one hundred and eighty years, and this is the level she has reached. We have existed not quite forty-two years, and in another seven years we will be on the same level as America." As Nixon notes in his memoirs, the audience was obviously enjoying Khrushchev's boasting. "When we catch up with you, in passing you by, we will wave to you," Khrushchev said, waving good-bye to an imaginary America. He then pointed to a Russian worker and said: "Does this man look like a slave laborer? With men of such spirit, how can we lose?"

Not to be outdone, Nixon pointed to an American worker and said: "With men like that we are strong. But these men, Soviet and American, work together well for peace, even as they have worked together in building this exhibition...If this competition in which you plan to outstrip us is to do the best for both our peoples and for peoples everywhere, there must be a free exchange of ideas. You must not be afraid of ideas. After all, you don't know everything."

A furious Khrushchev shouted, "If I don't know everything, you don't know anything about Communism except fear of it."

The two men moved on to the model house (built to replicate a $14,000 middle-class American home) and continued their verbal sparring in the kitchen (in what became known as "the kitchen debate"). When Nixon suggested it was better to argue about the relative merits of washing machines than military rockets, Khrushchev shouted: "Your generals say we must compete in rockets. Your generals say they are so powerful they can destroy us. We can also show you something so that you will know the Russian spirit. We are strong. We can beat you."

Nixon replied: "No one should ever use his strength to put another in the position where he in effect has an ultimatum. For us to argue who is the stronger misses the point. If war comes we both lose."

"We, too, are giants," Khrushchev said. "You want to threaten—we will answer threats with threats." Nixon said the Americans would never engage in threats. "You wanted indirectly to threaten me," Khrushchev shouted. "But we have the means to threaten too." Finally, the two agreed that they wanted peace. The press loved it.

On the eve of the exhibition opening, as Jack Masey describes the scene in a piece written for a book about the Eames, "In (the) 250-foot-diameter golden anodized aluminum geodesic dome designed by Bucky Fuller sat seven inter-locked 35mm projectors aimed upward at seven giant 20-by-30 foot screens, each ready to receive simultaneous film images. Together, these images would tell the story of America at work and play. Into the dome burst Charles and Ray Eames who had just flown in from the States. They were clutching seven cans of 35 mm film…Word spread in the Park and a crowd began gathering in the dome: there were Russian construction workers, Finnish carpenters and American designers and exhibition staffers, all eager to see what magic would appear on the seven screens. Soon the projectors were synchronized and the 13-minute multi-screen film got under way. The combination of moving and still images, accompanied by a powerful musical score by Elmer Bernstein, was fantastic. Here were early morning scenes of milk bottles in front of doors across America; aerial views of deserts, mountains and plains; clover leaf highways jammed with automobiles; skyscrapers glistening at night; and the final closing scene: a bunch of 'forget-me-nots'—the universal symbol of friendship—depicted as a single image on the central screen. The Russians whispered 'nezabutki' (forget-me-nots in Russian) and there were tears all around."

The next morning, shortly before the exhibition opened its doors to the public, I stood at the entrance to the great dome and looked down the long, wide entrance walkway that led from the Sokolniki Park entrance and the subway stop. At first, we thought no one was coming. Then we realized that in the distance a solid line of men, women, and children was marching toward us, filling the walk-way from side to side and extending back as far as we could see. Within minutes, we were overwhelmed with visitors. It went on like that for forty-two days. It was estimated that from two-and-a-half to three million Soviets saw the exhibit (the discrepancy reflecting the widespread gate-crashing that occurred on particularly crowded days). It was the hottest ticket in Moscow.

The Soviets had literally never seen anything like the Sokolniki exhibition, not American modern art, American cars (although some of the older Soviets remem-bered American military trucks from the days of World War II), American kitch-ens, or American fashions. The Eames multi-screen movie and its depiction of Americans in their homes, at work, at school, at worship, and at play was a great crowd favorite from the start. The massive IBM computer responded to ques-tions typed in the Cyrillic alphabet with data and information in Russian about

American life. Sweating crowds pushed and shoved to get into the small art exhibit hall to argue with the guides and each other about the modern art on display, particularly the Pollock painting, which had to be protected with a special metal railing to prevent curious or angry visitors from scratching off swirls of paint. Our Russian-speaking guides in the art exhibit were so besieged that we had to put them on half-hour rotational schedules. I became familiar here with the practice of the Soviet system of "agitation," a technique originally invented by Lenin, in which the Party chooses and trains party cadres to serve as "agitators" to spark and guide public debate into channels and themes chosen by Party ideologists. Agitators were assigned full time at the art show to make sure the Soviet public understood that much of the art was "obscene" and "decadent" and at places like the automobile show, where the message was that most of these cars were made only for display at this exhibition and that, anyway, Soviet cars were better. Some visitors claimed to be offended by the startling, larger-than-life Gaston Lachaise bronze nude statue of an extremely well-endowed woman standing outside the art exhibit, although they all wanted to have their photograph taken next to it. One guide commented to the crowds that this was what most Soviet women secretly hoped they looked like at the beaches on the Black Sea.

Within a day or so, the floors made of Soviet concrete began to crumble under the impact of first tens and then hundreds of thousands of footsteps, turning into a thick, white dust that rapidly covered every foot of exhibit material. The Soviet cleaning crews were totally inadequate, so one of my self-appointed management responsibilities became a daily, early morning appearance at the site with brooms, mops, and cleaning equipment to work with willing volunteer guides to clean up the worst of the dust spots. Dust or not, the exhibition was jammed with visitors daily, and most of them appeared to be having a great time. (Thirty-plus years later, visiting Moscow after the fall of Communism, I found numbers of Russians with fond memories of the exhibition.)

In addition to the fact that the American national exhibition in Sokolniki park was a fabulous show, there was very little novel for Soviet citizens to do in Moscow in the summer and certainly nothing offering a taste of the usually forbidden seductions of life in America. The Bolshoi ballet, the symphony orchestras, and the opera closed down for the season, as did most of the theaters. That left only a few movie houses showing films liberally laced with propaganda, Lenin's tomb, and the art museums, where even the picture titles were written to provide strong doses of socialist education. The exceedingly few decent restaurants were impossible for most Russians to get into. Public service everywhere was skimpy and rough. The big, state-run department stores offered an almost laughable collection of badly designed, ill-fitting clothes. The people one encountered on the streets (with whom, of course, I could not talk unless I found someone who spoke some English) were mostly friendly, helpful, and curious but as hard as barrels. I got the impression in Moscow of a land of immense power and total control; there were militia and police everywhere and a lot of men in military uniform.

(The counterpart Soviet national exhibition at the Coliseum on Columbus Circle in New York was, by contrast, a dud. The Soviets chose to emphasize industrial and technological progress, and the exhibition was mostly memorable for the number and size of its scale models of factories, industrial complexes, hydroelectric dams, and machines. It paid little attention to Russian accomplishments in culture. And since, unlike Moscow, New York offered a great deal to do and see for virtually any combination of interests and tastes, New Yorkers mostly ignored the Soviet show.)

The night the American exhibition closed in Moscow, I went around until near dawn partying in assorted hotel rooms with Shirley Goodman, the director of the fashion show, and a few of her staff. I drank far too much Armenian cognac and ate too much caviar and heavily buttered bread. When I awakened the next morning in my stiflingly hot hotel room, I got violently sick. The next day, after saying good-bye to my staff friends and colleagues, I headed back to Washington. Jack Masey, the designer, and I were to work together again in the future and became close, lifelong friends. Pic Littell, the Russian expert, remains a friend after four decades. I also saw a lot of George Nelson and his new wife, Jackie, for years after I left the Foreign Service and went to work in New York.

I flew out of Moscow for Copenhagen with a small group of embassy staffers going on leave, feeling a bit like I was escaping from Alcatraz. There was not a hotel room to be found in Copenhagen, so the embassy staff man who met the plane had booked us into a small resort hotel near Elsinore, a short drive up the Øresund strait between Denmark and Sweden. When we walked into the hotel, bedraggled, and still full of the dust of the Moscow streets, I thought I had landed in paradise. The bar and restaurant just beyond the lobby were full of tanned, gorgeous women and good-looking blond men, a small jazz group was playing softly, and the food looked—and was—delicious.

On the way back to Washington, I began to think hard about what USIA might have in store for me. McClellan and I agreed that I needed about two weeks to clean up and close down any pending exhibition business. My job as special assistant to the USIA director had been filled months earlier. During the exhibition, I had visited the U.S. embassy on Tchaikowsky Street to discuss exhibition business with Ambassador Lewellyn Thompson and his staff, and I had talked a number of times with the two USIA officers assigned to work in the cultural and information field in this new period of "peaceful competition." They handled press relations, monitored short-wave radio broadcasts (in the U.S. case, the Russian-language broadcasts of the Voice of America, which USIA ran, and the CIA-owned Radio Liberty), and negotiated and managed the exchange visits of cultural attractions like symphony orchestras, a limited number of academic exchanges of students and scientists, and a just-agreed-to program of small, traveling exhibits. Each side was also allowed to distribute a magazine. The Americans produced and sold through SovPechat, the official Soviet publishing monopoly, the handsome and very popular magazine *Amerika*, which mostly picked up articles and photographs from American magazines. The Soviets distributed a heavily propagandistic periodical called *Soviet Life* in the States. The Moscow embassy slots all required fluent Russian.

I talked to USIA Director Allen as soon as I returned to Washington to give him my impressions of the exhibition. Allen was generous in his comments and asked me for my thoughts about a future assignment. I said that I thought the Soviet Union was a dreadful place, but that it represented the most important foreign policy challenge the United States faced. The still new and developing cultural and information programs were important instruments in trying to improve Soviet understanding of American life in a relationship dominated by nuclear weapons, missiles, espionage, closed borders, and hostile rhetoric. I said I would like to take the intensive Russian language course at the State Department's Foreign Service Institute (FSI) across the Potomac in Arlington, Virginia, and return to Moscow in a year to occupy the senior cultural counselor slot in the embassy. Allen said simply, "That's great," and with his help in the bureaucracy within a matter of days I was assigned to intensive Russian-language training. The fall course at the institute began almost immediately, and the institute agreed to allow Charlotte to take the classes with me on the grounds that her Russian-language abilities would be highly useful in Moscow.

7

Kievan Rus

The intensive learning of a moderately difficult language like Russian requires a monkish regime. One wakes up early, spends the entire day learning, and goes to sleep chanting the sounds and rhythms of the scripture, which in our case was the Russian language. Philological estimates vary widely, but Russian and English are probably about the same size in terms of numbers of usable words, somewhere around a half million words each.

Like English, Russian historically has swallowed up and uses words from many languages. The Russians borrowed words from the Byzantine Empire's Greek Orthodox missionaries, sent to convert them and record their language in the Cyrillic alphabet, from the Turkic and Mongolian conquerors of the Golden Horde, and from the Vikings, who more than a thousand years ago sailed and rowed down the rivers and mingled with Slavs and Finnic peoples to produce Kievan Russian civilization. As they came into contact with Europe, they helped themselves to vocabulary from German and French (and now, increasingly, English).

Russian is marvelously onomatopoetic, reflecting its roots among peoples who lived close to nature, and its sounds have helped produce great poets and writers. Thunder, for example, is *grom*, and to speak loudly is to speak *gromko*. Stillness, or quiet, is *tishina*. To tell someone to be quiet, you simply say, "*Tixo*" (pronounced "teeha," with an accent on the first syllable). Alexander Herzen, the nineteenth-century political philosopher and man of letters, wrote, "The leading characteristic of our language is the extraordinary ease with which everything is expressed in it—abstract ideas, the lyrical emotions of the heart...the cry of indignation, sparkling mischief, and shaking passion." In writers like Pushkin, Tolstoy, Turgenev, Dostoyevsky, Gogol, Chekhov, Mandelstam, and Akhmatova, the power and subtlety of the language become evident. However, Russian is also, as new students find out immediately, structurally complex. Nouns and adjectives are divided into three genders—masculine, feminine and neuter. They also decline into six cases, and correct case endings must be used in speech and writing for an expression to make any sense. Verbs not only conjugate rigorously by number and person, but their past tenses must also be declined to identify the gender of the person or object referred to.

The Foreign Service Institute used a teaching method called total immersion (widely employed by the U.S. military in World War II to teach Japanese), first developed in language learning research carried out at Cornell University. Total immersion requires three hours of classroom conversation every day, plus three hours or so of individual drill using recorded tapes, plus additional tape work at home at night. The student of Russian immediately becomes heartily sick of the old Russian saying: "Poftoreniye, Mat Ucheniya" ("Repetition is the Mother of Learning"). Don't think. Just listen and repeat. The student must worry about grammar only much later. Basically, the method aims to replicate the way a child learns a language. When one of us would complain, "You can't really expect us to remember all those different endings," the invariable response was that *any* child in Russia can do it!

The other secret of immersion learning is small classes. Our class started its nine-month journey with three State Department officers, two mid-level military officers, and Charlotte and me. We worked with three native Russian speakers, all refugees from one period or another of Communist repression, who were forbidden to speak English with us. The informants, as they are known, worked in turn under the supervision of a professional linguist (who, it turned out, was a Japanese specialist and didn't really speak much Russian at all), who began to answer our many questions about grammar as the months went on. By mid-course, both military officers and one State Department officer had dropped out. For those of us who survived, as the months passed it was as though a fog slowly began to lift through which we could begin to see the outlines of an enormous new continent.

At the end of the year, I received a probably over-generous evaluation of my test performance (before a separate group of native Russian speakers and a linguist I had not met before) with a four-four rating on the FSI language competence rating scale (zero being the lowest rating, five the highest). This met the FSI definition of "ability to read and speak with fluency and accuracy on all levels pertinent to professional needs." I could converse fluently about a host of topics, including politics and culture. My private goal was to become fluent enough to speak extemporaneously to an audience of students at Moscow State University. I achieved that (and was never, of course, invited to speak). But as we prepared to depart, I was troubled by one gaping hole in my Russian language preparation. I didn't know how to swear. Obscenity, in which Russian is rich, was totally absent from our course work.

When I pointed out this deficiency to our supervising linguist, she laughed and said I was probably right. She asked Vladimir Stepanovich, one of the native informants, to give me a few hours of private instruction. Stepanovich, or "Step" as he liked us to call him, was a former motion picture director who had fled the Soviet Union after World War II to escape one of Stalin's periodic, terrifying purges of Soviet intellectuals. While he loved to talk about things cultural, Step was extremely embarrassed to be asked to utter obscenities in Russian and, as might be expected, didn't know any in English. I was in somewhat the opposite condition, although I didn't in the least mind swearing in English. We spent many a difficult moment trying to come up with the right way to translate "screw you"—and far more colorful phrases—from English into something roughly comparable in Russian. In the teaching of obscenities, sign language is of little help.

Just before the FSI training ended, I was informed that the officer I was to replace in the Moscow cultural counselor position had asked to extend his assignment for another year. If I wished, therefore, I could continue training as a student and take the final year of the U.S. Army's four-year Russian language and area training course at their school in Oberammergau, Germany. The school annually accepted two or three State Department officers headed for assignments in the Soviet Union, who would then go on to Moscow from there. Charlotte and I jumped at the opportunity.

In the chaotic days at the end of World War II in Europe, the Army, anticipating the need for trained Russian-language officers, took over a small former SS base in Oberammergau and recruited a staff of teachers from the ranks of Russians who desperately did not want to return to the Soviet Union. Russians returning to Stalin's Soviet Union—many were forcibly turned over to the Soviets by the Allies—faced immediate shipment to a forced-labor camp or immediate execution (as so vividly and horrifyingly recounted in Alexander Solzhenitsyn's *Gulag Archipelago*). The language and area studies school, known as Detachment "R," was openly run by Army intelligence. Its major purpose was to train mid-level military officers—Army, Navy, Air Force, and Marines—for service as military attaches behind the Iron Curtain. The training represented the third and fourth years of a program that began with two years of language training in Monterey, California. Classes in subjects like advanced Russian language, history, geography, the Soviet military, the Soviet economy, and the Communist Party were taught in Russian by Soviet refugees, most of whom had served in the

Soviet armed forces or in a few cases the KGB (the notorious State Security Committee). They were a tragic, if lucky, group. Some of the earlier instructors had been officers in the Vlasovite army, so-called after the Soviet Army General Andrey Vlasov, captured by the Germans in 1942. Vlasov recruited a small army of Soviet war prisoners as an anti-Stalinist force to fight with the Germans to liberate Russia from the communists. In 1945, Vlasov surrendered to the Western Allies, who turned him over to the Soviets, who promptly hanged him. The teachers I knew best loved and yearned for Russia, hated Communism, disliked Germans, and were stuck with German life for the rest of their days. My best friend among the teachers, Sasha Krylov, who had been a major in the Soviet army, took some small solace in the excellent quality and variety of the mushrooms he found in the hills around Oberammergau, but he still said they couldn't compare with those in the Russian forests.

Our family lived in a comfortable modern chalet in Garmisch-Partenkirchen, a resort town in the foothills of the Bavarian Alps where the U.S. Army had set up a large rest and recreation base. I commuted to and from Oberammergau by bus. The children enjoyed a memorable year going to a good school, learning how to ice-skate and ski, and reveling in the joys of Army commissaries and free movies. Charlotte and I hired a German teacher and started to study German seriously on our own but gave up in two months when it became apparent that my mind, at least, was incapable of digesting both Russian and German grammar simultaneously.

In the early spring of 1961, I got a telephone call from Washington. The manager of the first traveling exhibit the United States was sending to the Soviet Union under the new cultural agreement had suffered a nervous breakdown. The exhibit was scheduled to open in June in Kiev, capital of the Ukraine, and I was ordered to fly back to Washington to take over as exhibit director, get it and the staff to Kiev, open it, and run the operation until mid-summer, at which time I would move into the cultural counselor job at the Moscow embassy.

U.S.–Soviet negotiations for the exchange of six traveling exhibits over a two-year period of "peaceful competition" had produced an oddly assorted list of exhibit topics. The two sides agreed they did not have to agree on the same topic for each one-to-one exchange, and the United States didn't really care very much about the subjects the Soviets might present in our country. For their part, the Americans would have been delighted to present topics like books, art, or consumer products, in which interesting materials with a strong intrinsic message of freedom and opportunity could easily be shown. The Soviets dug in their heels against anything as freewheeling as that. They insisted that only they knew the kinds of topics Soviet citizens would be interested in, which usually meant something with an industrial or scientific angle. In the final agreement, it was agreed that plastics, graphic art and design, and health would be the subjects of the first three exhibits to be sent by the Americans. Each exhibit would travel to three cities, and in the case of the plastics exhibit, these were to be Kiev, Moscow, and Leningrad.

On my arrival in Washington, the irrepressible Jack Masey, who welcomed me with a broad grin, was in charge of putting this first series of traveling exhibits together. Each exhibit was to have a staff of twenty-plus Russian-speaking guides, would occupy a space of not more than ten thousand square yards, and must be easily mountable and transportable. The staff for the plastics exhibit, in the process of recruitment, included a few young men and women whom I remembered from the Sokolniki exhibition two years earlier, their ranks swelled by new additions from graduate schools. They were a fresh-faced, eager crew, delighted to test their language skills and their toughness in this new adventure in the totally uncharted territory of Kiev. Our traveling engineer, a man who could fix virtually anything with a screwdriver and hammer, was a Russian-American named Boris Nepo, who with his sun-tanned bald head, eagle nose, and mustache looked like the Caucasian mountain warriors he descended from. Our technical adviser was an amiable, bespectacled engineer named Armand Winstead, who had been hired directly out of a plastics factory and could hardly stop talking about plastics. We put him to work lecturing the guides on his favorite topic.

In 1961, plastics constituted a relatively new industrial and consumer-use material in the world. The Soviet Union was far behind the United States in understanding its production and virtually endless potential uses. In that sense, the topic fitted the Soviet argument that American exhibits should fulfill a pragmatic, educational purpose and avoid anything political or propagandistic. What Soviet citizens wanted, the Soviet negotiators said, was to be educated. The Americans were not opposed to the scientific or industrial education of a Soviet audience—quite the contrary. But the American side wanted our exhibits, even if narrowly focused by topic, to yield a broad, not a limited view, of American life. Even if the subject was technical, the message of freedom, creative opportunities, and excitement had to come through.

When I heard the word "plastics," I thought, "What a dull subject for an exhibit." But I had not reckoned with the imagination and ingenuity of Masey and his colleagues. Masey had turned once again to his old friend Buckminister Fuller to obtain a small, portable plastic geodesic dome, a new design then just going into production to serve as storage sheds and small temporary housing structures. General Motors lent us a gorgeous red 1961 Chevrolet Corvette convertible (that model is still famous today as a landmark in modern design, the first plastic car to be mass-produced anywhere). Winstead found a small industrial stamping machine that used powdered resin and water to produce small sheets of hard plastic as an exhibit demonstration. No one had yet decided what design to press into these eighteen-square-inch sheets as they came out of the stamping machine, and then, at one of our first brainstorming sessions, someone suggested the machine should stamp out lion-head masks in various colors for visitors to take home as souvenirs. These lion masks were to become legendary in Kiev.

In late spring, I flew to Moscow to talk with the embassy staff about the logistics of getting the exhibit into Kiev, out to the exhibit park on the outskirts of the city, and mounted and inaugurated by early June. (Such exhibit parks, used primarily to show off "Achievements of the Peoples' Economy," were a standard party instrument for public education and indoctrination in virtually all Soviet cities.) I met the chief figures on the Soviet side assigned to facilitate—or hinder, as more often was the case—the mounting and operation of the show. The main actors were three heavy-handed bureaucrats from the All-Union Chamber of Commerce, two of whom were assigned to work with me in Kiev as liaison officers. The real power, though, clearly resided with a handsome young officer, Valentin Kamenev, from the high-ranking State Committee for Cultural Relations with Foreign Countries, the Soviet counterpart to the U.S. Embassy and State Department in the overall cultural exchange negotiations. Both Masey and I thought Kamenev was KGB. He had great freedom in talking with foreigners. Ordinary Soviet bureaucrats almost visibly shivered and deferred to him when he appeared on the scene. We, of course, represented a risky assignment for any Soviet official, but since we bore the stamp of approval of the inter-government cultural agreement, the exhibit presumably had to take place. There was an inherent tension, however. The Soviet officials wanted us only to talk about plastics as an industrial material. We were prepared to talk about that, but we also wanted to talk about American science and technology, American workers' rights, wages and benefits—and the consumer goods workers could buy with their wages, and how the American capitalist system encouraged the development of new industries. We wanted huge crowds. The Soviets would have preferred a much more restrained popular response.

These Moscow meetings were the first opportunity for me to put my newly acquired fluency in Russian to the test in the ring of ideological combat. It proved to be a formidable tool in managing my kind of diplomacy and understanding the enormous, house-of-mirrors universe of Soviet life. I needed it immediately in Kiev, where my exhibit staff colleagues and I daily went through a minefield of problems and objections with the chief Chamber of Commerce liaison officer. They insisted on the right to approve the texts of the pamphlets we intended to distribute. We refused and won our point. Then the chief liaison officer told me the traveling exhibit cases, which had just arrived by rail in Kiev, were too big when loaded on Soviet trucks to fit under the trolleybus lines out to the exhibit park. I said they would either have to find lower profile trucks or raise the trolleybus lines. They finally found suitable trucks, but we fell days behind schedule. When matters got really heated, I would warn them that if necessary I would close the exhibit down, and they could explain that to Khrushchev.

We opened on schedule to big crowds of mostly blond, beefy, pink-cheeked, happily sweating Ukrainians and Russians eager to see the hottest attraction in town. The women wore the atrociously designed printed cotton dresses that then constituted leisure wear, the men wore white shirts and baggy dark trousers, and all were shod in the standard gray plastic sandals (a plastics item we did not have in the American exhibit). Within days you could spot lion-head masks and red, white, and blue exhibit buttons on the streets of the historic city.

Settling into the daily schedule of managing crowds and arguing with the Moscow liaison crew, I discovered an unexpected and welcome ally, the director of the Kiev exhibit park, a tall, gray-haired, ramrod straight Ukrainian woman who wore severe dark dresses and skirts and regarded the park as her personal domain. The director fought in the Soviet Army against the Nazis in World War II, was decorated for her bravery, and was, of course, given her position, a party member. She had little use for Russian bureaucrats from Moscow and went out of her way to make that clear the second night of the exhibit by inviting me to her office for cognac while ignoring the Moscow contingent standing next to me. We became fast friends and allies. One day, as daily attendance continued to run at capacity or more, the chief liaison officer told the director that Moscow wanted the exhibit to be closed a half-hour earlier each evening for crowds to clear out of the park by closing time. The director stood even straighter, fixed him with a steely gaze, and said, "Ya nye khochu" ("I don't want that"), accenting and giving the broad vowel sound to the first syllable of the verb "want." That is the way Ukrainians talked when they wanted to emphasize their difference from Moscow, since Muscovites, as the director well knew, accent the last syllable. The hours stayed the same.

That was my first taste of Ukrainian nationalism, although my best friend among the Oberammergau teachers was a Ukrainian Russian, and we had sometimes discussed the complicated love-hate relationship between Great Russians and Ukrainians. Much later, in the mid-1990s, working with an American foundation whose programs supported democratization and economic reform in the former Soviet republics, I visited a small town on the Ukrainian side of the Carpathian mountains, which separate Ukraine from Moldova and Rumania. One afternoon, on a solitary walk through mountain meadows up into the forest, I came across a small, cultivated enclosure. A low iron fence surrounded a stone cross with a photograph of a young man and an inscription in Ukrainian. Roses grew on the fence, and there were fresh-cut flowers below the cross. The youth had been a fighter in the Ukrainian National Army, which led a rebellion against Moscow in the latter part of World War II. He died in a gun battle with Soviet KGB troops at that spot in the late 1950s not long before we went to Kiev with the exhibit. Today, of course, Ukraine is independent and, if you are a young person seeking to prosper there in the new country, you must speak Ukrainian, not Russian.

The very name of Ukraine bears within it the sense of distance from the Russian center, since the word *krai* denotes a far-away, border place. Yet its capital, Kiev, was the first great trading city and center of military might of the Russian people, a city situated on the southern reaches of the north-south river routes between Scandinavia and the Byzantine Empire at a time when these waterways were the only real highways through the vastness of the steppes and forests. The Vikings had been raiding and trading down the Dniester, the Dnieper, and the Volga since at least the ninth century, and the word *Rus* itself is thought to be of Scandinavian origin, from *rothsmen* (seafarers), a term corrupted to *Ruotsi* by the Finns and Slavs whom the Vikings first encountered. These Rus traded in furs, wax, honey, and slaves.

In the tenth century, Vladimir, a Viking warrior described by historians as "a savage and zealous heathen," defeated his rivals and became the Great Prince of Kiev, celebrating his triumph with the sacrifice of a thousand human lives to his pagan gods. In 989, clearly deciding that it was not politically correct for a modern man to be a pagan, Vladimir embraced Orthodox Christianity and ordered his people to convert as well, with the help of a sword if necessary. According to the *Russian Chronicle*, Vladimir first considered Judaism, which had been adopted by the Khazar tribal kingdom to the east, on the southern reaches of the Volga, but decided against that, because Jews were scattered all over the world. He looked at Islam, but Vladimir loved to drink, and Islam was too restrictive. Latin Catholicism required acceptance of the authority of the pope, and Vladimir intended to be master of his own house. Orthodox Christianity accepted princely authority, was relaxed about personal behavior, and Vladimir's envoys had waxed eloquent about the magnificence of the Byzantine cathedrals and the Orthodox rituals. (By this time, sizable communities of Viking and Slavs lived and traded in Constantinople, where a Viking "Varangian Guard" served as the emperor's bodyguards.)

Vladimir's son, Yaroslav, built a cathedral called Saint Sophia in Kiev, and the famous Golden Gates to the city (memorialized in Mussorgsky's musical suite, *Pictures at an Exhibition*) both in emulation of the originals in Constantinople. Yaroslav also established a library to copy Greek documents, and, in the famous cave monasteries built into the bluffs running down to the Dnieper, monks began to collect and write the historical materials that became known as the *Russian Chronicles*. British historian Bernard Pares notes that in these chronicles, recorded locally by monks in various great cities, "each individual district developed its own psychology: Kiev, radiant and many-colored, Novgorod, short and drastic, Suzdal, dry and plain."

In the full bloom of summer, I indeed found Kiev radiant and many-colored particularly when compared to Moscow, even under the drabness of Soviet rule. Saint Sophia had been destroyed in the war, blown up by the Soviets, and what remained of the Golden Gates was mostly rubble. But some of the houses of the old city still stood, and in the newer parts the Stalinist architecture mandated by Moscow had been dressed up with baroque flourishes and cadenzas in an unmistakably Ukrainian fashion. When I could escape from the exhibition for a few hours I wandered the streets and handsome parks downtown. We would take small launches out to the sandy islands to swim in the river, or, on an occasional free evening, board an excursion boat up the river to drink vodka and sweet Soviet champagne and eat sturgeon and black bread. Every few days, Boris Nepo started up the red Corvette, and we drove out in the early evening through the solitary back roads of the exhibit park. The black earth was bursting with life, the sky suffused with pink light. The smell and bird-sounds of the fields reminded me of summer on the farm in Missouri, and peace descended on our souls.

I liked to walk along the bluffs on the high, western bank of the Dnieper looking far, far out at the steppes stretching to the infinite horizon and wondering what it must have felt like to watch the Tartars flood that vast plain with their wild horses and the sounds of war drums and battle cries. Kievan Rus fought Central Asian and Caucasian nomadic tribes for three centuries with fair success, but finally in 1240, after the Tartars had ravaged the newly developing towns of the north, Khan Batu, the great-nephew of Genghis Khan, marched on Kiev. Pares describes the scene: "The city was deafened with the rattle of wagons, the neighing of horses, and the noise of camels. Battering rams pounded the walls day and night. The inhabitants, who under the boyar Dmitry made a stout defense, built new walls of wood in the center of the town; but on December 6 these too were stormed and there was the usual wholesale extermination, especially in the crowded churches." A monk visiting Kiev six years after the sack of the city found only two hundred houses left. Everywhere in the country, he saw skulls and bones.

As the star of Kiev paled, that of Muscovy, far to the north in the forests and rivers, slowly began to rise. Pares writes: "The new Great Russia of the Middle Volga was crushed almost at its birth. It was not merely that great numbers of Russians were killed and the rest terrified and abased. This new Russia was taken out of the orbit of Europe. A growing culture and civilization was practically extinguished except for one saving force, the national church, which remained one in a Russia hopelessly sundered."

The Tartar yoke left a permanent scar in the Russian psyche. Pares writes: "The (Tartars) carried on their horses baskets in which to kidnap Russian children, particularly girls. They took with them leather thongs, with which to drag away with them Russian men-prisoners. These they sold...to all parts of Asia Minor, to Africa, and even to some parts of Europe...In one of the Tartar raids on Moscow in the reign of Ivan the Terrible, 130,000 prisoners were carried away. A Jewish merchant who sat at the entrance of Perekop had seen so many pass through that he asked whether there were any more people left in Russia."

The stunning Eisenstein film, *Alexander Nevsky*, made as anti-German propaganda at the outset of World War II to celebrate Nevsky's triumph over the invading Catholic Teutonic Knights, opens with a scene of the tall, blond, beautiful Nevsky, Prince of Novgorod, helping peasants with great scythes to harvest grain in the countryside. A squat, swarthy Tartar commander passes with his entourage, a long line of Russian slaves with their hands bound being dragged along behind. The commander stops and dismounts, using the back of a subaltern as a footstool. Nevsky and the commander talk briefly; then the caravan goes on to the east. When an angry Russian peasant wants to attack the convoy, Nevsky says, "No, we'll deal with them afterwards (after the Teutonic Knights)." The major part of the film then deals with the Russian victory over the Germans on the frozen waters of a northern lake. The parallels between the Teutonic Knights and the Nazis would have been apparent to any Russian in the late 1930s. As concerned the Tartars, Nevsky and all the early Russian princes and czars made periodic visits to Kazan, the Tartar capital on the Volga, abased themselves by kissing the ground, and paid tribute to the Tartar Khans (the Russian word for money, *dyengi*, comes from the Tartar *tyengi*). Finally, Muscovy, the strongest principality in the rising great Russia of the north, repudiated its allegiance to the Tartars, and Czar Ivan the Terrible in 1552 destroyed the Tartar capital. There are Tartar genes in many Russians; "Scratch a Russian, find a Tartar," is a trite but true saying. The father of the Bolshevik revolution, Vladimir Lenin, born in a family of the minor aristocracy, had the eyes of a Tartar.

The Kiev plastics exhibit closed its doors in late June. It had been a success—swarms of visitors and no disasters. The guide staff handled the party "agitators" working the crowds with aplomb and good humor. The favorite target of the agitators in the exhibit was the Chevrolet Corvette, sneeringly referred to as not a real production car but made only *na pakaz* (for show). But we had plenty of information to refute that charge, and Soviet citizens were known to be congenitally, and correctly, skeptical of the agit-prop line about anything. It was time for me to move to Moscow to join the embassy staff. We threw a party for the park director, to which I invited the Soviet liaison crew—generously on my part, I thought, since they had spent more time hindering us than helping. I spent a day or so briefing the new exhibit director, who had just arrived from Washington, and flew up to Moscow.

8

In the Heart of the Soviet Empire

At the height of the Cold War, the Moscow embassy was probably the most important diplomatic assignment in the world. It was certainly one of the most difficult. The staff was small, isolated, controlled, and spied on, and dealing with Soviet officialdom was wearing. But the embassy was the vital American observation and negotiating outpost in the titanic military, economic, and psychological confrontation that split the world for nearly a half century. Working there stretched the mind.

I thought I had the best job in the embassy. To be the counselor for cultural affairs bore with it a special cachet. The contemporary British historian Orlando Figes wrote:

> For the past two hundred years the arts in Russia have served as an arena for political, philosophical and religious debate…The (novels) were huge poetic structures for symbolic contemplation, not unlike icons, laboratories in which to test ideas; and, like a science or religion, they were animated by the search for truth. The overarching subject of all these works was Russia—its character, its history, its customs and conventions, its spiritual essence and its destiny…Nowhere has the artist been more burdened with the task of moral leadership and national prophecy, nor more feared and persecuted by the state. What did it mean to be a Russian? What was Russia's place and mission in the world?…These were the "accursed questions" that occupied the mind of every serious writer, literary critic and historian, painter and composer, theologian and philosopher in the golden age of Russian culture from Pushkin to Pasternak.

When the Bolsheviks came to power, these "accursed questions" immediately became matters of life and death. In the early 1930s, the poet Osip Mandelstam remarked to his friends: "Poetry is uniquely respected in this country. There's no place where more people are killed for it." Mandelstam later wrote a short, secret poem about Stalin—never published, and read only to friends. An informer reported this to the secret police. Stalin sent the poet into internal exile and eventually to a forced-labor camp in Siberia, where Mandelstam died of heart failure in 1938. Of the seven hundred writers who attended the First Writers' Congress in 1934, Nina Berberova, the fine writer who lived most of her life in Paris exile, estimated that only fifty survived to attend the second in 1954.

In the late summer of 1961, Charlotte drove our red Volkswagen Beetle with the children up from Garmisch-Partenkirchen to Stockholm, where I joined them for the ferry trip across the Baltic Sea to Helsinki and the drive through birch groves and pine forests to the Soviet border and then down to Moscow via Leningrad. The Soviet side of the border with Finland was a ten-mile-long killing zone of barbed wire, watchtowers, and minefields. We became well acquainted with this landscape out of hell, protecting the tiny Soviet Union from mighty Finland, over our three-year Moscow residence. Three times in our assignment, we rode the international train (consisting of a single car detached from the Moscow express after it arrived in Leningrad and then pulled in solitary splendor by a Soviet locomotive to the border, where Soviet frontier guards would go through the car from top to bottom) out for decompression trips to the clean, comfortable hotels and restaurants of Helsinki and the riches of the Western world at Stokman's. This famous Finnish department store, which continues to prosper, assigned Moscow-based diplomats a personal shopper, packed your purchases, and delivered them to your Moscow-bound train car on departure. When we first drove in by car, my weight, added to the contents of the VW, with its luggage rack already piled high with luggage and with suit bags draped on the sides, meant that we couldn't generate enough power in fourth gear to maintain speed, and so we chugged bravely in third gear down the Leningrad highway to Moscow, dwarfed by Soviet trucks belching black smoke, and looking rather like a scene out of a Jacques Tati film.

In the finest Foreign Service tradition, Charlotte set up a functioning, comfortable apartment household within days. Our apartment immediately became a favorite dining spot (much canned, corned-beef hash plus local potatoes) for visiting exchange professors, students, performing artists, and an occasional Soviet guest brave enough or well-enough connected to pass through the militia guards at the archway entrance to the embassy compound. One of the attractions of the Moscow cultural counselor assignment was having exchange program participants like John Steinbeck and Robert Frost or ordinary American students and professors over for supper. In our apartment, George Balanchine informed a group of Soviet journalists that the home of the classical ballet no longer was Moscow or Leningrad but New York. When we went out on special occasions, it might be to have supper with Marlene Dietrich on her first Soviet tour, or for drinks at the Metropole Hotel with someone like Igor Stravinsky, his marvelous wife, Vera, and his traveling companion and biographer, the composer Robert Craft, while Soviet cultural commissars swarmed around trying to convince Stravinsky to leave Los Angeles and come back to Russia.

We enrolled John (then thirteen years old), Kathleen (eleven) and Peter (ten) in the tiny embassy school, which promptly proved unsatisfactory on virtually every count of teaching and discipline. We decided, after much discussion with the kids, to take them out and enroll them in a Soviet public school. We had considerable first-hand positive testimony from Soviet refugee instructors and friends at the Army intelligence school in Oberammergau as to the quality of the system of education in mathematics and science. There was some reason to be concerned about indoctrination, but we thought this would be manageable. At first, the Ministry of Foreign Affairs said enrolling our children was impossible, but when we argued that the Soviets boasted that their educational system was the best in the world, and that they should not deprive our children of such an opportunity, the ministry changed its mind. John, Kathleen, and Peter were promptly enrolled in Public School Sixty-Nine, a large, sprawling building within walking distance of the embassy. This, of course, required crash, private intensive lessons in Russian. Even with these, for a period of several months the children were largely clueless in class. But they survived, their Russian became fluent, their teachers proved to be excellent, they made good friends (who couldn't visit the embassy compound for fear of the KGB uniformed militia guards at the entrance), and the school principal handled their unique status with great common sense and sympathy. They were excused from activities involving the Pioneers, the Communist political organization for schoolchildren (followed as Soviet children became of high-school age by the Komsomol). Within months, the daughters of an American Air Force attaché and the American and Norwegian ambassadors and their wives followed suit and joined our children at Public School Sixty-Nine. The quality of education was high; when we went back to the States three years later our children were at least a year ahead of their American classmates in mathematics and science.

A succession of America's finest diplomats had represented the United States in Moscow. George Kennan, diplomat, historian, and political philosopher, served there twice and wrote the basic policy paper on which the United States planned and carried out its containment policy for fifty years. Charles "Chip"

Bohlen had managed the U.S. outpost with distinction and elegance. Lewellyn "Tommy" Thompson, to whom I reported on my arrival, was in the mainstream of this great tradition. A lean, soft-spoken gentleman possessing an admirable mixture of common sense and equanimity, Thompson looked at the long sweep of history and politics and refused to be flapped by everyday events. Thompson thought culture and history, broadly defined, were fundamental to understanding the psychology and political motivations of nations, and he urged his officers to break out of the circle of Pravda diviners and cocktail party gossipers and to think more about the long-term evolution of Soviet policy. Thompson was an enthusiastic supporter of the exchange programs whose management I was about to undertake.

Considering the enormity of the challenges presented by the Soviet Union, the embassy diplomatic staff was tiny—thirty-five-plus American employees counting a couple of dozen civilian officers and secretaries, six military attaches and their staff, and a few code clerks, all Americans. Embedded in the staff structure in various State Department or military slots were three or four CIA officers. The Moscow staff as a whole constituted an elite group inside the already elite Foreign Service. Most of the Foreign Service officers spoke fluent Russian and had studied Russian history and politics. At least one was also an assiduous student of the Vatican, which appeared to him, as he studied the Communist Party, to be a relevant model of decision-making and career paths in a secretive, ideologically inspired elite institution with universal aspirations. Some were on their second assignments in Moscow. Virtually all hoped to dedicate their careers to the subject. (Many I worked with in Moscow went on to become ambassadors to Moscow or elsewhere in the Communist bloc countries: Walter Stoessel, Malcolm Toon, Richard Davies, Herbert Okun, Jack Matlock, and William Luers.) The diplomatic staff worked on the presumably secure seventh, eighth, and ninth floor of the U.S. embassy building on Tchaikowsky Street, the entrance to these floors guarded by U.S. Marines.

A small consular office functioned on the ground floor. Separately on that floor, several dozen Soviet citizens worked in administrative and service jobs as clerks and as embassy chauffeurs, all provided by the infamous UPDK, the Soviet administration for service of the diplomatic corps, and all assumed to be in varying degrees Soviet informers. (In Washington, the Soviet embassy diplomatic staff was about the same size on paper—if one counted only officers. But Washington allowed the Soviets to bring in Soviet citizens as drivers, clerks, and even plumbers, so it was in fact much larger. The American government, primarily for reasons of cost, had chosen not to pursue this alternative for its own support staff.

The Soviet government consistently rejected suggestions that the embassy be allowed to assign additional officers, although in the early years of the Khrushchev "thaw" both sides had added a handful of information and cultural officers.)

The embassy's traditional roles in the tightly controlled Soviet state were political and economic reporting, representation, and negotiation, although in negotiations Washington maintained a tight rein. The small consular section issued visas to those chosen few Soviet citizens allowed by the Soviets to visit the United States and handled citizenship questions and related enquiries for the extremely small number of Americans who lived in, or were passing through, the Soviet Union. In that number, as we all came to know in 1963, was a young American named Lee Harvey Oswald.

The embassy's work was hobbled in every direction by difficulties arising from the totalitarian control systems that Lenin invented and Stalin and his successors perfected during four decades of practice. The party controlled all media—newspapers, magazines, book publishing, and radio, television, and film production. (This was, it should be noted, long before e-mail, fax machines, and printers.) To produce a significant number of copies of anything required a press, or at least a mimeograph machine, and possessing such equipment could land a Soviet citizen in a concentration camp. Catastrophes occurred—a nuclear accident, a famine, or an occasional local riot or insurrection—without a word being published in the Soviet media. Airplane and train crashes occurred frequently, but one knew of them only by hearsay and rumor. The press told the people only what the party wanted them to hear. It was useful occasionally for the hints it would drop about the pecking order in the Central Committee or for the first mention of the rise of a new star in the party heavens, usually a one-or two-line reference to a new figure who had done something exceptional enough to warrant mention in *Pravda* (Truth) or *Izvestia* (News). (Ordinary Soviets joked that, "There is no truth in *Pravda* and no news in *Izvestia*.") Even though reading the Soviet press was about as satisfactory as reading tea leaves, the embassy zealously read every word of every newspaper, and then they were all mailed off and pored over back in Washington as well.

Travel controls were rigorous. U.S. embassy personnel were forbidden to travel outside a twenty-five mile radius from the center of Moscow without specific permission. The embassy must present a diplomatic note to the Ministry of Foreign Affairs notifying the ministry that Eugene Staples, counselor for cultural affairs, proposed to travel from Moscow to Leningrad (or another city not permanently closed to Americans) on such and such a date. In the absence of a negative reply, it was, in theory, possible to book passage on the Soviet airline, Aeroflot, and hotel accommodations, but none of these could be reserved or purchased directly. Rather, they must be handled by the hard-faced UPDK ladies who sat downstairs in their office in the embassy building. From time to time, they would inform us that although there appeared to be no Foreign Ministry objection, for reasons of "a temporary nature" or because space was allegedly not available, the trip could not take place. When an embassy officer did get on a flight, the seat assigned frequently was windowless. Travel was, of course, vitally important to us. From time to time, in addition to sniffing the feel of a different city or region, one might fall into a real conversation with a real person or see something unintended. My colleagues and I in the relatively new cultural and information section were important additions to the embassy staff. Beyond the intrinsic value, fun, and excitement of our work, we had an indisputable reason to travel to escort exchange groups and to arrange for student and scientific exchanges. We talked with more real Soviet citizens than anyone else in the embassy.

I also found myself nominally responsible for supervising the publications and procurement section of the embassy, which consisted of two Russian-speaking officers who bought books and other documents in Moscow and, as travel permitted, in the provincial capitals for the Library of Congress and a consortium of American universities interested in Slavic and Soviet studies (and, of course, for the CIA). I refused to write performance evaluation reports on these two officers unless I actually observed their work and spent some real time with them, so from time to time I would head out with them for book-buying expeditions in the hinterlands. Moscow had a number of large Russian bookstores, and one foreign language book center, all selling the standard Soviet political texts, approved national and foreign classics, and contemporary fiction and non-fiction. The reason to make an occasional round of provincial capitals open to foreign travel was that the regional publishing houses, in addition to publishing in the local languages—e.g. Estonian, Ukrainian, Georgian, for example—from time to time also published in Russian books about regional affairs and subjects unavailable in Moscow. We once found, for example, a number of openly anti-Semitic books in Vilnius, the capital of the Lithuanian republic. Our trips were a source of frequent merriment. The three of us would walk into a provincial bookstore, obviously foreigners although speaking excellent Russian, find an interesting shelf, and say to a clerk, "We want all the books on this shelf." A flustered manager would often respond that the store had just closed, but we always got our books. Sometimes if we found a local telephone book—they were exceedingly rare—we would swipe it.

Embassy officers exchanged information and rumors with other friendly Moscow embassies. The Canadian and British embassies were particularly well informed and useful. The embassy also talked a lot with the Western journalist corps. A small band of top-flight American reporters worked the Moscow beat, including among them Seymour Topping of the *New York Times*, Whit Bassow of *Newsweek* (whose book, *The Moscow Correspondents*, provides an excellent portrait of that period), Henry Shapiro of United Press, Dave Miller of the Tribune, and Sam Jaffee of ABC. They dug hard in the inhospitable soil of the Soviet system and produced, given the circumstances, surprisingly accurate and perceptive reporting. One of the best-informed American journalists and a good friend of mine, Ed Stevens of *Time* magazine, had covered the Soviet Union as far back as the late 1930s and World War II. Stevens first knew Khrushchev as the hard-driving party political commissar during the great and victorious Russian battle against the Nazis at Stalingrad. When party and KGB files opened up slightly after the collapse of the Soviet Union in the early 1990s, they listed Stevens as a longtime member of the Communist Party, recruited as a student in New York.

In addition to uniformed KGB guards at the entrance to the embassy compound, who stopped all obvious non-Americans coming in and inquired as to their business, it was assumed that the embassy and all the apartments its employees occupied were bugged. In 1963, a major debugging operation at the embassy revealed that the walls of all the supposedly secure offices were riddled with old-fashioned but still functioning bugs, which looked rather like small pieces of a Lego set, presumably installed before the building was turned over to the embassy many years earlier. After this debugging, the department installed at the embassy one of the first overseas plastic-enclosed, secure meeting rooms where conversations could not be electronically monitored. My office, originally occupied by the senior military attaché, yielded a particularly high number of bugs. The embassy residence apartments were not debugged. We lived with the psychological consequences of knowing that our apartment was bugged, and that the most intimate details of family life were therefore regularly listened to and analyzed. Of course, you could turn up the radio full blast. But you couldn't sleep that way, or talk for very long. The only way to talk privately with your spouse was to go for a walk, and on many a snowy, deep frozen night Charlotte and I would head down into the old quarter behind the embassy building to walk and catch up on our private affairs, talking as the Russians did, in low voices, and glancing from time to time over our shoulders.

The KGB occupied the large building directly across Tchaikowsky Street in order to observe the flow of traffic at the embassy, to listen in on conversations as available, and also, it was later discovered, to microwave the entire embassy building day and night, presumably to interfere with communications. When that low-level radiation was discovered and news about it finally leaked out, it turned out that a tiny number of U.S. government officers, including the national security staff at the White House, had known about this situation for years but held the information very tightly, and staff assigned to Moscow were never informed. When the knowledge became public, the Foreign Service Association, a professional association of active and retired diplomatic personnel, concluded that what appeared to be an unusually high incidence of cancer and heart problems among the employees of the Moscow embassy was a result of this continuous radiation. A Johns Hopkins research study found no solid evidence this was so. I was never certain. I developed a serious heart murmur and eventual arrhythmia while serving in Moscow. My wife, Charlotte, died of cancer, which first manifested itself seven years after we left Moscow. Walter Stoessel, who served as deputy chief of mission during my tour, died at a relatively early age of leukemia.

Some embassy officers were routinely and openly tailed, particularly the military attachés. I usually was not, but by this time in the Soviet state, totalitarian control was so thoroughly imprinted on the general population that any foreigner walking into a Soviet apartment block or office would be spotted immediately, and the event would be reported to the chief local vigilante. Americans traveling alone were warned that they were enticing targets for sexual entrapment by the KGB, and I knew of two such cases. One was an exhibit guide, the other an embassy officer. Both were clandestinely photographed in sexual congress with beautiful Soviet agents, serving as presumably irresistible bait, and pressured to become Soviet agents. Both had the good sense to report their problems to the U.S. authorities.

In the early 1960s the U.S.–Soviet cultural and information exchange program was in a growth period, although it was never a large operation considering the size and resources of the two rival societies. From the U.S. point of view, a formal, controlled exchange program between two major nations was unprecedented and basically undesirable. With the Western European nations, for example, the U.S. government played only a small part in the free flow of ideas and people in both directions, whether of books, movies, artists, scientists, students, or just ordinary citizens out to enjoy the sights. In addition to this vastly larger universe of private activities, the U.S. government might sponsor information libraries, an occasional exhibit, and leadership and student exchange programs like the Fulbright scholarships.

With the Soviet Union (and the rest of the Communist bloc) this kind of free, private movement of people and ideas was impossible. In the absence of a formal government-to-government agreement, Moscow would have sought unlimited access to American scientific and technological institutions for its scientists and engineers while using its multiple techniques of control to limit any real American access to the Soviet people. Since Stalin's time, there had been virtually no non-governmental contacts between American private citizens and the people of the Soviet Union, not even during World War II when the two countries were allies. When in the late 1950s Khrushchev unseated Malenkov, the remaining survivor of the incompetent triumvirate of party leaders that inherited the empire at the time of Stalin's death, the climate slowly began to change.

Although his own career had prospered mightily under the dictator, Khrushchev believed that the Soviet Union and worldwide communism could not achieve their full potential under the stranglehold of Stalinist methods. In his famous "secret speech" on the crimes of Stalin made before the Twentieth Party Congress in 1956, Khrushchev told the delegates that Stalin had murdered senior Party officials and military leaders and that the staggering Soviet losses in World War II were in large part due to Stalin's paranoia and incompetence. The speech became public in the West when the CIA released a transcript of it in Europe in 1956 (the text, which the CIA got from Polish communist sources, wasn't recognized by Russia as authentic until the final years of Gorbachev, and was never published in the Soviet period). Khrushchev's speech was a seminal event in Russian history. Alexander Yakovlev, later a close adviser to Mikhail Gorbachev, was a young party official sitting in the balcony. He recalled in a conversation with the American journalist Hedrick Smith that, "I had thought of Stalin as a great man, a great intellectual, a profound thinker, and so on—and all that was destroyed."

In the early days of his rule, Khrushchev achieved some degree of popular acceptance among the intellectuals as he ceased to use mass terror as the automatic, primary instrument of state policy—although the citizenry knew the KGB fist was always there in reserve. He became convinced that over the long term Soviet power would prevail in the world. "Peaceful competition" with the United States and the West was thus more in the interests of the Soviet Union than nuclear war. Khrushchev thought such peaceful competition, under the controls and rules of a formal exchange program, could yield real benefits to the Soviet side, partly for propaganda purposes but primarily in the limited but useful access to American science and technology that it would provide to Soviet scientists and institutions. To achieve that end, he was prepared to accept a certain number of

American performing arts groups and exhibitions and limited numbers of students and scholars studying and working in Soviet institutions. President Eisenhower and most Americans welcomed the opportunity, even though the opening into Soviet society was limited and controlled.

To manage this unique exercise in public diplomacy, the State Department created—separately from the Soviet political affairs desk—an office of Soviet exchanges, headed by a tough, Russian-speaking lawyer and ex-FBI agent turned senior Foreign Service officer named Frank Sisco. Sisco and I spent many days over the next three years planning and conducting negotiations with a host of Soviet counterparts. Sisco, dressed impeccably in a black pinstripe suit, carried himself with the authority of a Mafia don, which was a good way to approach a negotiation with the Soviets, and the Soviets clearly respected him. Once a year, Sisco and I and our staffs sat down for the major, always contentious negotiations with the high-level Soviet State Committee on Cultural Relations with Foreign Countries on the direction and content of the coming year's program. The formal umbrella agreements specified the subjects, the number, and the names of the performing arts groups and exhibits that were to be exchanged, and the numbers and specializations of the scientists, scholars, and students who would be authorized. The American sponsors of particular parts of the program—the Social Science Research Council, the American Council of Learned Societies, and an inter-university committee on academic exchanges—carried out separate negotiations on their parts of the overall program with our assistance, and participated as appropriate in the annual overall negotiation.

In the broadest terms, the arguments had to do with access: granting it and limiting it. Generally, the Soviets wanted to limit American access, allowing U.S. groups to visit only the same small list of cities and prohibiting any subject or participation that by the very broad Soviet definition might be controversial. The Americans generally wanted to expand access, adding cities and institutions. Controlling Soviet scientific and technological access to American institutions was the ace negotiating card that the Americans held.

When it came to implementation, reciprocity was the name of the game. We demanded reciprocity in fact as well as on paper and usually got it, but getting it required constant attention. For example, the agreement might specify that the Soviets would accept American professor X to do research on some obscure period of Russian history at Y university. But when Professor X arrived, he was not permitted access to the books and archival materials he had asked to use. It was an unending task to unlock these small doors and to keep the overall program from drowning in Soviet red tape. GosKontsert, the State Concert Bureau, usually tried—with little success—to control the content of the musical programs to be presented by American groups. The control of the subject matter and specific content of American exhibits generated endless arguments.

Halfway through my tour, for example, an American traveling exhibit on technical books arrived in Moscow (we had been trying unsuccessfully for years to get an agreement to bring in a general, comprehensive book exhibit, to which the invariable reply was that the Soviet people would find the contents of many American books objectionable and unacceptable). Late in the night after its arrival, the exhibit staff and hired workers began to open the packing cases. Without warning, two-dozen grim-faced Soviet ladies disembarked from a bus, marched into the hall, and without further ado started to leaf through every one of the several thousand technical books that constituted the exhibition. Pandemonium broke out. We had agreed with USIA and State in Washington that the exhibit must really concentrate on technical subjects—science, medicine, engineering, architecture, and similar topics—although the choice and content should reflect the intellectual vigor and freedom of the American system. But Washington had added a number of general encyclopedias and reference books with articles on Lenin and Stalin and the purges, famines, and terror of the Soviet system that had nothing to do with technical subjects at all. When I called Washington and asked if someone back there had read these passages, the reply was, "Do you think we're crazy? We're not going to try to read all those books." I replied, "Well, they're reading them here. Every word!" After two long, heated arguments with the senior State Committee officer, who said flatly that the Soviet authorities could not and would not allow the exhibit to open, I decided that we had in fact crossed the line of our understandings about this book exhibit, and that discretion was preferable to valor. I said nothing further to the State Committee but removed a dozen or so general reference books, justifying this to the American correspondents—who were drooling with the prospect of a story about American capitulation to Soviet power—as the embassy's routine final review as agreed to with Washington. The exhibit was mobbed day and night—and said a great deal positively about American life.

My immediate embassy colleagues were Terry Catherman and Bill Watts, young, smart, vigorous, and personable career officers who spoke impeccable Russian. (Watts later achieved a degree of deserved fame when he resigned from Henry Kissinger's staff in the Nixon White House in protest against the invasion of Cambodia—in the process telling Kissinger's deputy, Al Haig, to go screw himself.) In addition to the State Committee for Cultural Relations, we dealt with problems arising in the implementation of the vitally important performing arts section of the agreement through the Ministry of Culture, headed by the poisonously handsome hatchet lady, Madame Irina Furtseva, a favorite of Nikita Khrushchev, and the ministry's implementing agency, GosKontsert, the Soviet concert bureau monopoly on music and ballet exchanges. On exhibits, we dealt with the All-Union Chamber of Commerce, my old sparring partners from the 1959 Sokolniki and 1961 Kiev exhibitions. We regularly talked with the Soviet Academy of Sciences, mostly with the president, who was always a senior scientist and party member, and with the head of the Foreign Relations Section, invariably a senior KGB officer although not publicly identified as such. We had only rare contacts with the Ministry of Foreign Affairs, which the political side of the embassy saw on an almost daily basis.

We divided up the nocturnal task of monitoring the English-and Russian-language broadcasts of the Voice of America and the Russian-language programs of Radio Liberty, the CIA-supported station in Munich. As a matter of policy, the Voice generally foreswore comment on Soviet domestic affairs. Radio Liberty, in contrast, concentrated on Soviet domestic news and politics, using whatever sources it could find, and employed Soviet refugees as broadcasters. By far the most popular VOA program—not only in the Soviet Union but worldwide—was the Willis Conover jazz hour, which came drifting into our Moscow receivers late at night, fading in and out like music from another, happier planet, which in a way it was. Both VOA and Radio Liberty transmissions were heavily jammed by signals—a snarling, grinding static—emanating from jamming towers scattered around Moscow (and elsewhere as needed throughout the Soviet bloc). We knew the locations of the jammers in the city, and an expert listener could even tell one from another. The jamming was selective in the case of English-language programs. You could be listening to a newscast and hear the beginning of a story about an international question in which Soviet policy might be involved, and then on came the jammer. The Voice's Russian-language programs were jammed most of the time; Radio Lib, as we called it, was jammed constantly. We regularly sent jamming reports back to Washington, along with comments and suggestions about programming. In spite of the jamming, a lot got through, though, particularly in the smaller provincial cities and in rural areas. The BBC, which some Soviet citizens regarded as more objective than the American programs, was widely listened to.

Although the imperial Russia of the nineteenth and early twentieth century was not even a living memory for most Soviet citizens, the table of rank for civil service (in Russian, *chin*; thus an official is called a *chinovnik*), first created by Peter the Great in the eighteenth century and modified by successor czars, continued to survive in spirit. The Soviets were highly conscious of bureaucratic rank and privilege, and office heads dealt substantively only with diplomats of suitable rank (although they might deign to receive a verbal message from someone of lesser rank). These representatives of the proletariat loved engraved cards with the complete, resonant titles of their jobs, and high rank brought with it plush office space, complete with green baize-covered conference tables and bottles of Georgian mineral water and Armenian cognac plus, of course, a proper-sized apartment, preferably in one of the old Stalin-era skyscrapers, which the party built for comfort. The czarist regimes classified people by their official rank, social and economic class, and their ethnicity, and those practices carried over into the Soviet period. A Russian Jew's identify card officially identified him as a Jew; an Armenian as an Armenian (no matter where in the Soviet Union he was born or lived); workers and peasants were identified as such, and identify cards served as internal passports for the control of internal travel and place of domicile. The Soviets took over the czarist hierarchical systems of rank and categories and expanded them.

Reading the accounts of nineteenth-century Russian intellectuals and writers about their brushes with the bureaucrats and secret police of their day was like hearing ancient voices in a modern echo chamber. Like the czars who exiled Dostoyevsky to hard labor in Siberia (where he wrote the notes for *The House of the Dead*), the Communists sent Andrei Sakharov, the physicist who more than anyone else helped the Soviet government build its first atomic bomb but then became a dissident leader, into house arrest and internal exile. The czarist police suggested to the young Alexander Herzen that he was crazy because he participated in a Moscow university protest against a professor and sent Herzen first to a psychologist and then into internal exile. The Communists regularly sent dissidents like the Nobel Prize winning poet Joseph Brodsky to internal exile in labor camps or to their dreadful state psychiatric hospitals.

While the police and secret services originated in the centuries of czarist rule, they had become infinitely deadlier and more pervasive in the Soviet empire. By the 1880s, writes Harvard historian Richard Pipes, "The police institutions of later imperial Russia (were) the forerunner, and, through the intermediacy of corresponding communist institutions, the prototype of all political police organs of the twentieth century." Even so, Pipes concludes, "It would be difficult to maintain that imperial Russia was a full-blown police state; it was rather a forerunner…which fell far short of its full potential." It had too many loopholes: private property, foreign travel, and the liberal, westernizing attitudes of a significant section of the aristocracy and gentry. The Communists effectively closed these loop-holes.

Solzhenitsyn put the comparison more brutally:

> If the intellectuals in the plays of Chekhov who spent all their time guessing what would happen in twenty, thirty, or forty years had been told that in forty years interrogation by torture would be practiced in Russia; that prisoners would have their skulls squeezed within iron rings; that a human being would be lowered into an acid bath; that they would be trussed up naked to be bitten by ants and bedbugs; that a ramrod heated over a primus stove would be thrust up their anal canal (the "secret brand"); that a man's genitals would be slowly crushed beneath the toe of a jackboot; and that, in the luckiest possible circumstances, prisoners would be tortured by being kept from sleeping for a week, by thirst, and by being beaten to a bloody pulp, not one of Chekhov's plays would have gotten to its end because all the heroes would have gone off to insane asylums.

The KGB was a police and espionage empire with virtually limitless authority over Soviet citizens and a vast overseas espionage and subversion apparatus. It and its predecessor agencies killed millions over their seventy-year-plus existence. (The 1940 Katyn forest massacre, in which the NKVD—a predecessor of the KGB—murdered fifteen thousand Polish army officers as Stalin prepared to divide Poland with the Nazis, is but one of many great mass murder events. The gulag system [in Russian, Gosudarstveniy Upravnitelniy Lager, which translates as "State Corrections Camp"], the forced-labor camps where Alexander Solzhenitsyn toiled, at any given time contained, by his estimate, twelve million men and women, at least half of whom were political prisoners.) When more labor was needed and the regional branches of the KGB failed to deliver their expected quotas of prisoners to the camp system, the KGB simply imposed a levy on the local population and picked up people at random. Solzhenitsyn noted bitterly, and correctly, that, "Hitler was only an amateur and he was stupid enough to leave proof of his crimes," while the Soviets not only hid their crimes from sight but had more than enough utopian intellectuals, like-minded dupes, acolytes, apologists, and fellow travelers in the West to help them in their cover-up.

In the cultural exchange program, those Soviet intellectuals and artists who for reasons of state interest were permitted some contact with foreigners were particular objects of suspicion. A senior KGB officer (never openly identified as such) sat as director of the foreign relations section of every important Soviet cultural institution. Performing artists not only were required to turn over the foreign exchange their tours might earn, but to inform on fellow artists as well, and denounce them if state policy required (a European documentary film on the life of Russian violinist David Oistrakh contains an example of this, related by Oistrakh's son, when Oistrakh denounced his friend and fellow musician, the great pianist Svyatoslav Richter, on instructions from the KGB). KGB officers accompanied all performing arts groups going abroad to prevent defections. Yet these embarrassing dashes to freedom occurred regularly nonetheless, possibly the most notorious being those of the ballet stars Rudolf Nuryev and Mikhail Baryshnikov.

Under such circumstances, real friendships between an American diplomat and a Soviet citizen were virtually impossible. Because of my assignment, I met and knew a lot of Soviet officials, and from time to time met writers and musicians, but we were never invited to their homes. I went frequently to banquets in honor of visiting American musicians at the Union of Composers, which people like Rostropovich and his striking wife, the fine soprano Galina Vishnyevskaya, would attend. The KGB foreign relations section head would usually try to drink me under the table with round after round of vodka toasts—the Russian toast challenge *na dno* (to the bottom)—little realizing that he was dealing with a U.S. Marine Corps drinker trained in the bars of Los Angeles. I underwent comparable trials of fire at the Union of Writers when American novelists and poets came through town. Jack Masey and his wife, Mary Lou, and my wife, Charlotte, and I, one night in the grip of a mighty winter freeze, drove out with the poet Yevgyenni Yevtushenko to his dacha in the birch forests for a night of gargantuan eating and drinking. Yevtushenko had written a good deal of poetry critical of the Soviet state but had gotten away with it, both because he was as popular as a matinee idol through his theatrical poetry readings, and because Khrushchev liked his patriotic poetry. He was a rare exception to the rule that out of fear, Soviet citizens, all of whom—Russians, Ukrainians, Georgians, Armenians, or Central Asians—came from cultures with ancient traditions of warm, generous hospitality and friendships, avoided any kind of open relationships with American officials.

The frankest conversations, paradoxically, took place with total strangers. Once in Yalta, accompanying an exhibit, I took a lone walk in a city park, untailed, and sat down for a moment to enjoy the air. A rough-looking man sat down next to me and began to talk. He was a miner, on holiday from a Ukrainian coal mine at one of the dozens of labor union sanitariums and rest homes the Soviets built in resort areas along the Black Sea coast. After we passed the time of day, I told him I was an American from the Moscow embassy and that talking with me might get him in trouble. He said he wasn't worried about that. He thought from the way I looked and spoke Russian that I was from Latvia. We talked for a half hour or so. He complained bitterly that working people never got a chance to go abroad and see the real world, that the union bosses were corrupt and reserved the good life and all the overseas trips for themselves, that workers couldn't buy cars, and that life as a miner was tough and dangerous. In Leningrad on another occasion, in a casual conversation about life in America with a group of Russian students at an exhibit reception I remarked that the greatest barrier to understanding was the Soviet government's foreign travel restrictions on its citizens. Out of a combination of politeness and caution, I said I thought if these restrictions were removed most Russians would probably go out and enjoy their travels, see and learn a lot, and then return because of their love of their country. "What makes you think that?" said one of the students. "We would all leave and never come back."

The Communist system imposed an ideological construct for everything, and the party ideologists accorded particular importance to the role of culture in Russian history and political life. The primary rule was that all art, under the party's direction, must educate the masses, be uplifting in its content, and in form and shape be completely realistic. In painting, decades of "socialist realism" produced thousands of large, flat, overblown canvases of happy peasants, sturdy workers, and brave soldiers. The Khrushchev "thaw" revealed the existence of a small underground in painting and sculpture, some of whose bolder members, led by the sculptor Ernst Neizvestny (who later was exiled and lived and worked in New York), actually succeeded in organizing an exhibition at the Manezh exhibition hall near the Kremlin. Khrushchev himself went to see the show, pronounced the paintings and sculptures "shit," and the exhibit doors were promptly closed and locked. The rich holdings of French impressionists and experimental Russian painters from pre-revolutionary and early Communist days in the Hermitage and the Russian Museum in Leningrad were kept under lock and key, shown occasionally to a selected few foreign guests but never to the masses. In music, "socialist realism" frowned on experimentation in tonal systems and produced endless troubles for Prokofiev and Shostakovich. In ballet, all dances must have a stated theme and story line. In writing, the author was at his own risk: some left voluntarily or were thrown out—Solzhenitsyn, Joseph Brodsky, and Vasily Aksyonov. Others stayed and suffered: poets like Anna Akhmatova and the many (like Osip Mandelstam and Isaac Babel) who perished in the KGB prisons and camps.

In the years from 1961 to 1964, at the height of the cultural exchange program, the United States unfolded the panoply of a rich, free-spirited, and very different kind of cultural life to the Soviet people: Benny Goodman and the first swing/jazz band ever to perform in a country whose leaders called jazz "degenerate"; the New York City Ballet, for which George Balanchine had created an entirely new school of startlingly moving and beautiful abstract ballets; the Robert Shaw chorale singing Bach masses before Moscow audiences that had not heard them for many years; and a score of individual artists and performers like Jan Peerce, the great Metropolitan tenor, whose spontaneous addition of traditional Jewish songs as encores to his performance at the Conservatory, brought the audience to tears—and enraged the Soviet authorities. Igor Stravinsky, looking rather like a pterodactyl as he waved his arms, conducted a concert of his seldom-heard music at the Conservatory, opening it with his own spectacular arrangement of "The Star-Spangled Banner."

When Benny Goodman and his band played Kansas City in the late 1930s, I cut classes at junior college for two days in a row to hear every performance. By the 1960s, when Goodman and a different band (but still with Teddy Wilson) came to Moscow, Goodman had long and deservedly been recognized as the "King of Swing" (starting with his Carnegie Hall jazz concert of 1938). Not only was Goodman a superb musician in both jazz and classical music, he was the first white jazz star to recognize and include in his band some of the great black jazz artists of the day. By 1960 he had been around for a long time, and as the Beatles emerged from Liverpool onto the international stage, a few Americans thought Goodman, and jazz itself, were becoming old hat. But in the Soviet Union, this modern, dynamic, hard-driving, powerful, beautifully orchestrated and coordinated music, which still managed to be free and joyous, was largely unknown to the mass of the public (although thousands of mostly young fans listened to jazz on the Willis Conover VOA programs). Jazz had long been in disfavor in the world of Communist ideology, but in the late 1950s, an occasional article in the Soviet press suggested that the official position might be softening. George Avakian, the musicologist, who helped negotiate the Goodman trip and accompanied the band on its 1962 tour, writes in his jacket notes for the *Benny Goodman in Moscow* album that it was even suggested "there was such a thing as Russian jazz played on the riverboats going up the Dnieper river from Odessa at the turn of the century—an obvious play on the old legends of how jazz spread northward from New Orleans." The Soviet acceptance of the group in the official exchange program was a mark of the extent of the Khrushchev "thaw."

That didn't mean that Khrushchev himself liked jazz. He came to the opening concert in July 1962 along with much of the party hierarchy, large beefy men with their equally voluminous wives, and ostentatiously sat on his hands. He also attended the official July 4 reception at Spaso House, the American embassy residence, and engaged in badinage with Goodman himself. I helped steer the enormously broad and round Soviet leader, who resembled nothing so much as the Michelin tire man, around the big reception hall, admiring, as we went through the crowd, his renowned talents for spontaneous politicking and the art of baloney. (Stalin is reported to have liked to get Khrushchev drunk at Kremlin social evenings and make him dance—"like a cow on ice," Stalin said.) The band toured five more cities in addition to Moscow, and outside Moscow the concerts were sold out and enthusiastically applauded.

The internal dynamics of the band were fascinating. The Goodman band for the Soviet tour included a number of jazz greats—tenor saxophonist Zoot Sims, alto Phil Woods, trumpeter Joe Newman, and pianists Teddy Wilson and John Bunch. Goodman also brought along some younger, lesser-known musicians and some new arrangements, including his own electrifying version of the Soviet Red Army song, "Meadowland," which invariably brought down the house. Goodman traveled first class, the band members in the back. He was jealous of his primacy. The senior band members got their share of solos, but when one of the young trombone players started getting too much applause for his solo breaks, Goodman promptly sat him down for much of the tour.

An even more revolutionary presentation of a different concept of art, one whose presiding genius was himself a Russian trained in the Russian classical school of ballet, was the October 1962 visit of the New York City Ballet. It was the first time that George Balanchine, an ethnic Georgian trained at the renowned Marinsky Ballet in Leningrad, had returned to Russia since he left the Soviet Union for Paris in the 1930s to dance and learn choreography with Sergei Diaghilev. In Europe, Balanchine met Lincoln Kirstein, an American poet, littérateur, philosopher, aesthete, amateur boxer, and wealthy visionary, who persuaded him to come to America to create a new vision of dance. Their long collaboration in New York created a great ballet company and the best ballet school in the world. The New York troupe, whose soloists included such superb dancers as Jacques D'Amboise, Arthur Mitchell, Allegra Kent, and Kay Mazo, and the plotless, abstract ballets they danced in Moscow and Leningrad—"Symphony in C," "Agon," "Bugaku," and "Apollo"—created a huge stir in the world of Soviet ballet, theater, and music. The official line in the press was that these ballets lacked meaning, and that some of the dancing was ugly and contorted, but the private word and the reaction of night after night of full houses in both Moscow and Leningrad reflected enthusiasm and interest. When the Soviets asked why Balanchine did not return to the land of his birth, the Georgian genius responded that New York was now the true home of Russian classical ballet, which had stagnated in the Soviet Union since the Bolshevik Revolution.

In October 1962, at the midpoint of the New York City Ballet's Moscow engagement, the two superpowers came close to going to war when the Cuban missile crisis reached its boiling point. President John F. Kennedy told Prime Minister Khrushchev on October 22 that the United States would not tolerate the deployment of nuclear weapons in Cuba. When Khrushchev refused to acknowledge that Soviet missile launching sites were under construction in Cuba, and medium-range missiles already in place, President Kennedy sent Adlai Stevenson to the UN Security Council to show U-2 aerial photographs of the sites to the Soviet ambassador and the other members of the council. Soviet freighters were photographed en route to Cuba with missile containers clearly visible on their decks. Kennedy declared a naval blockade of Cuba. The ambassador and the embassy political counselor spent hours every day and night shuttling to and from the Soviet Foreign Ministry. (This was well before the establishment of the "hot line" between Washington and Moscow, the need for which was demonstrated by the Cuban missile crisis. Ironically, earlier critics of the idea had thought that misunderstandings and unpredictable behavior in direct telephone conversations between leaders might actually bring about war. The "hot line" concept, after many years of use, is now standard in high-level crisis diplomacy.)

In that golden autumn, Moscow overnight became a very scary place to be. It was an obvious prime target in the crosshairs of any American nuclear attack, whose fireball would certainly not differentiate between Soviet and American citizens. Public School Sixty-Nine sent our children home with instructions not to return until they were called back; carefully organized but noisy daily demonstrations began in front of the embassy. The ballet company performed on schedule with no visible public reaction in the theater to the crisis, but many of the dancers were terrified, Kirstein told me. There were, of course, no non-Soviet newspapers to be had; reception of radio broadcasts, most of which were jammed anyway, was spotty, and no one in the company understood the complexities of the great test of will that was being played out six thousand miles away in the Caribbean. I spent a lot of time drinking tea with the dancers and the administrative staff trying to make sure they understood as much as I did of what was going on. I told them that in the final analysis I thought neither side would choose to unleash the apocalypse, although my public face was calmer and braver than my private one. I personally thought we were in great danger.

During these uneasy days, Kirstein and I occasionally drove out to the old, high-towered monastery on the Moscow River at Kolomenskoye and wandered around the park talking about Russia, what it had been and why it had become what it was, or sat and talked in the cemetery gardens of the beautiful Donskoi monastery, a masterpiece of elegiac decrepitude. I had never known anyone like Kirstein. Tall, powerfully built, hawk-nosed, and with short-cropped hair, he was enormously learned in history, the arts, and literature, and fierce and passionate in his opinions. Art, he said, required the utmost in study and discipline. To prove his point he wrote poetry every day, which he had done even during the Second World War when he enlisted and served as a private in the U.S. Army in Europe (his book *Rhymes of a PFC* is a fine picture of Army life). We became good friends. After I left the Foreign Service to work for the Ford Foundation in New York, Kirstein and I continued our cultural and political conversations for many years.

During their stay, Kirstein and George Balanchine were invited to visit both the Moscow (Bolshoi) and Leningrad (the former Marinsky) ballet schools. Kirstein wrote up his notes about these visits and sent them to me as the cultural affairs officer of the embassy. Kirstein thought better of the Leningrad school (now once again called the Marinsky, its original name under the Russian Empire) than the Moscow academy, but he regarded both as markedly inferior to the School of American Ballet he and Balanchine had built in New York. A few excerpts afford a good sampling of his analytical abilities and critical style. In regard to the Moscow school Kirstein wrote:

Madame Golovkina, Director of the School, is an ex-dancer of no great reputation. She is a formidable woman, frank, hard and extremely disagreeable. She is a strong executive, I should imagine, a Party Member and by no means an intellectual. Her energies are devoted to the smooth running of her apparatus rather than its aesthetic or technical efficiency…The school currently seems to have some four hundred students, half boys and half girls…Students are accepted from the age of ten, all over the USSR. I saw one excellent class of 14–16-year-old Central Asian boys.

The teaching, in so far as we were able to judge, is adequate, but in no way remarkable. Few of the teachers are really impressive personalities. Instruction in the advanced men's class is perfunctory, and from our taste, often faulty. Toes are not pointed, hands incline to be flaccid, the abdomen is not held in tightly, and shoulders are hunched. There is some accentuation on the muscle-builder type body, capable of one-arm lifts. Elegant proportions, long bodies and small heads are no criterion here…There are a number of well-trained girls, none of whom we saw were to any degree exceptional. They have nice arms and a rather loose style. There is no great musical sensitivity, due in large part to the fact that the practice music is badly chosen and poorly played.

The single greatest fault with the Moscow School is the inadequate musical base. American children hear jazz from the time they can hear words, and this gives their analysis of movement a certain style, based on a sense of syncopation, improvised elegance and loose stricture. The simple march, polka and waltz rhythms of the Muscovite class-room limit extension of movement, as well as of manner and style. The taste, or lack of it, (in a Western sense), is the main obstacle for the vitalization of the Russian dance...Tradition is always a lie. The "tradition" of the Bolshoi repertory, and the school which supports it, is the 19th century romantic ballet in desuetude...The latest abstract-close-of-quotes ballet at the Bolshoi (*Scriabiniana*, by Kazian Goleizovsky) is a distressing mish-mash of piano pieces, unsuitable for dancing in the first place, swollen up in Metro-Goldwyn orchestrations with brass and percussion, but offering nothing more than an emotional debauch. The local version of *Les Sylphides* is also very over-extended, but at the same time tired, tatty and tasteless. These are the three Ts of Muscovite ballet.

The xenophobic neurosis of the USSR in aesthetic terms over the last fifty years has not only resulted in the rigidity of the training but also in a certain professional deformation; it is impossible to place dance-style like a fly in amber; the dancer is not dead, but artistically he starts to stink. The criterion is forgotten, the purity fades, and what is perpetuated is a pale version of a lost original.

Although Kirstein found plenty to criticize at the Leningrad school—"turns are not good...hands are weak," some of the dancers are "inelegant," and "there is no real criterion of quality of aesthetic formulation either here or in Moscow"—in general he thought the Leningrad instruction "in every way superior to that of Moscow." He also wrote that "the virus of Western possibility has been introduced into this Academy by the historic return of Balanchine. How it will be used or handled is anyone's guess. But there was absolutely no resistance to his aesthetic, as there was in Moscow. In Moscow, success was admitted due to public response. Here, it was something far deeper, the realization on the part of an informed public that this was a drastic and merited criticism of a way of instruction, indeed a way of life."

On October 28, Khrushchev finally blinked and backed down when the Soviet freighters carrying missiles encountered U.S. Navy war ships steaming in blockade formation athwart the eastern sea approaches to Cuba. The Soviet ships turned around and headed back across the Atlantic. The Soviets removed the missiles and dismantled the sites. As part of the deal, although at the time not recognized directly and publicly, the Americans agreed to remove missiles from Turkey threatening the Soviet Union from the south. The world breathed deeply. Life went on. Most historians agree today this was the closest the world has yet gotten to full-fledged nuclear war.

Life returned briefly to normal, or what passed for normal in the life of an American diplomatic family in Moscow. On November 7 (October 25 in the old Russian calendar), the party celebrated the Bolshevik victory in the Great October Revolution of 1917. The climax of this most important celebration of the year was the parade of Soviet military might through Red Square before the party leadership, which senior members of the diplomatic corps were invited to witness. For weeks we slept only fitfully, listening to the monstrous roar of the tanks and the shrouded missile carriers, as the troops went through midnight practices for the parade, observed mainly by curious foreign military attaches and foreign correspondents, all of them in turn observed by the KGB. Portraits of the party leaders, set out in super-life-size at strategic intersections throughout the city, were carefully checked by Soviets and foreigners alike for order of precedence. *Pravda* published the fraternal greetings from other parties and the recommended slogans for the holiday. Everyone noted the content of, and the order in which, greetings from the Chinese, Albanian, and Yugoslav Communist parties appeared, an important thermometer of the state of their relations with Moscow.

On the morning of the great parade, having passed through a maze of checkpoints to keep the common folk out, the elites of the enormous empire congregated in Red Square, fur-collared and muffled, to watch the rulers display their armed might. The rulers themselves—the senior politburo members, dressed in identical black overcoats and fedora hats—stood on a special reviewing platform on top of Lenin's tomb. (In 1962 Stalin's body still lay embalmed in the tomb across from Lenin. In 1964, he was unceremoniously removed and buried in the Kremlin wall, and Stalingrad, site of the greatest Russian victory over Germany in World War II, was renamed Volgograd.) When the Kremlin clock struck ten, the already assembled eight-hundred-man-strong military band began to blare out marches. The young troops of the elite regiments lining the sides of the square shouted a mighty "OOOraaaaah" in unison, echoing around the square, as the parade marshal drove in standing in a convertible. Aging colonels, their legs straining against accumulating fat and tiring muscle, goose-stepped across the red bricks at the head of their elegant young officers. The goose step grew higher in inverse proportion to age, and the boy cadets goose-stepped with a high snap, like frightening marionettes. The Kremlin guns boomed their salute, pigeons exploded in flight from the Kremlin heights, and in climax the wicked-looking tanks and missile carriers snarled across the square.

As one of the few senior embassy officers who received tickets to the parade from the Foreign Ministry, I was always asked by our military attachés to carry a camera and photograph selected pieces of military hardware. They knew the size of every brick in the great square and said they could extrapolate the dimensions of any truck or tank from the bricks shown in the photographs. When the day's newest-model intercontinental missile, as identified for me by the U.S. attachés from their midnight observations of the rehearsals, pulled by an enormous truck, came roaring into and across the red brick pavement of the square, I would leap up, focus, and snap away. It was rather like a cheering routine at a football game, since at least half the men in the senior diplomatic corps seated with me in the stands behind the party leaders also jumped up, shot photographs, and sat down in unison. The intelligence briefings at the embassies around town had obviously been thorough. Just as obviously, we all saw just what the Soviets wanted us to see.

Then in late November came the quiet time. The great Arctic air mass pressed down on the continent-sized plain that is Russia; the thermometer dropped and dropped, and one day out of a colorless sky dry snow sifted down. Suddenly, the sky cleared, the sunlight sparkled, the air fractured in one's lungs. It was ten degrees below zero centigrade, and all the Russians were gloriously happy. "*Kak Khoroscho*," said my embassy chauffeur. "How great. There is nothing like our Russian winter."

As the snow sifted down and piled up and the days grew shorter, our lives fell into winter routine. Our kids rose in the dark, put on their school uniforms—gray tunics, black coats, and fur hats for John and Peter; a brown dress and black apron for Kathleen, heavy jacket, and a fur hat—and walked in the bitter cold to Public School Sixty-Nine. Except during the really dangerous cold spells, everyone went out. One always saw little children, almost spherically bundled into imitation fur coats and hats, swaddled in rough wool shawls and scarves, and so booted and mittened that they could barely walk, accompanied by a grandmother and playing in the parks. The gardens of the ruined monasteries and the simple city parks were never lifeless. Old people walked slowly, hands clasped behind their backs, talking guardedly about ancient tragedies or present sicknesses, and glancing over their shoulders to make sure no one was listening. Young lovers leaned against trees and embraced, wishing they had a private place to go make love and, maybe some day, even find an apartment. At night, we sometimes joined the young and vigorous set who crowded into Gorky Park, across the river from downtown Moscow, where in deep winter the authorities sent trucks out to spray the miles of footpaths and roads with water, which immediately froze. Skaters flew down the glittering paths, their shouts and laughter frozen in the black air, and cut solitary arabesques on the ice above the river landing.

Charlotte, the children, and I spent an occasional weekend at the U.S. embassy dacha, just inside the twenty-five mile travel limit on the road running north from Moscow to the great monastery at Zagorsk. According to legend, it belonged to Stalin's son Vasily, the hard-drinking Red Air Force officer whose carousing and wenching were once the scandal of Moscow and who disappeared without a trace or tears after his father's death. An old stucco mansion, isolated in a pine grove and eminently suited to orgies, it now housed more proper pursuits, mainly unraveling the nerves of embassy wives escaping with or without their children from the cramped quarters of Moscow apartments. Charlotte and I would pack a knapsack of garlicky Russian sausage, Danish cheese, and Stolichnaya vodka, and ski out from the dacha into the snowy woods, pushing along silent trails to find a solitary clearing with an old log to sit on at lunchtime. The low winter sun, the delight of the lungs in the sparkling air, the taste of the sausage and cheese, the frozen jolt of the vodka—these were purest of pleasures.

With casual, summer visitors long gone, my daily life settled into a routine of negotiations and large and small crisis management in regard to the exchange program. For diversion, Charlotte and I went often to the Bolshoi Theater for ballet and opera. The ballet was magnificent, though by then getting fusty and a bit cold. By the time we left Moscow, I was declining invitations to see *Swan Lake* again. A unique pleasure was the chance to hear the operas of Glinka, Mussorgsky, and Rimsky Korsakov, most of which are rarely performed outside Russia. The performances were opulent: great basses and tenors, massed choral scenes surrounded by wooden fortresses and stone palaces, and usually an on-stage conflagration at one point or another in the plot. We attended chamber music evenings in the Maliy Zal (the small hall) of the Tchaikovsky conservatory whenever we could. We once sat up front to hear the passionate, young Mtislav Rostropovich and Dmitri Shostakovich, who looked as though he expected to be dragged off the stage any minute by KGB executioners, perform the Shostakovich cello and piano sonata.

We spent a lot of evenings at the theater, and by the time our assignment ended in 1964 we had probably attended every theater in Moscow. Seeing the Moscow Art Theater productions of Chekhov and Ostrovsky at least once was mandatory, but the staging and the performances seemed, like the ballet, frozen in time, a lifeless echo of its days under the great directors Stanislavsky and Meyerhold (the latter shot in 1940, on Stalin's orders, after publicly coming to the defense of Shostakovich's opera, *Lady MacBeth of Mtsensk*). The productions at the contemporary theaters were much more poorly written, but more interesting politically. With encouragement from Ambassador Thompson, I had organized a voluntary embassy critics' panel, which included all the Russian-speaking officers of the embassy, who could choose a contemporary work at one or another of the theaters and write a short review. (A typical review comment, by Herb Okun, on a play about life on a collective farm: "Soviet agriculture is a flop, and so is this play.") Ambassador Thompson agreed that, even if much of the theater fare was meretricious, taken as a whole it provided an important mirror of the messages the party currently wanted to imprint on the minds of the masses. There were some stirrings of experimental drama at two new theaters, the Sovremyenik, and in 1964 the Taganka, whose director Yuri Lyubimov became one of the great figures in modern Russian theater. One theater actually dared to produce the much earlier Yevgenniy Shwartz work, *Dragon*, about a mythical monster who might be thought to resemble Stalin. The State Department commended us on our theater criticism project. It was much more fun than deconstructing *Pravda* editorials.

We extended our commentaries to the movies; the once great Soviet cinema of Dovzhenko and Eisenstein was beginning to stir as directors and artists sensed that the Khrushchev thaw might permit some experimentation. One of the films produced in this period, *Clear Skies*, used as a metaphor for the political thaw probably the longest scenes ever shot anywhere of rivers of ice breaking apart and roaring downstream. (In the end, the rivers thawed far more than the party did.) Andre Tarkovsky was in the early stages of a path-breaking career that in 1966 produced *Andrey Rublyev*, and Grigory Dudintsev directed the finest film version of *Hamlet* I know with the incomparable Soviet actor Inokenty Smoktunovsky in the title role and a musical score by Shostakovich. No one understood and portrayed palace intrigue better than the Russians.

We cooked potluck suppers for exchange program visitors; went out for cocktails and dinner with friends and journalists, and occasionally were invited to dine with the British Ambassador, Sir Frank Roberts, who liked to talk about Russian history and culture. We ate infrequently at one or another of the few acceptable restaurants in Moscow. These were usually set up as "national" restaurants, serving a menu more or less reflecting the cuisine of one or another Soviet republic. There were the "Armenia," the "Aragvi" (Georgian), and the "Peking" (China was not, of course, a Soviet Republic but in those days still nominally a friend), and the shabbily elegant old National Hotel off Red Square served excellent Russian food. With dinner, it was customary to drink vodka, purchased by weight (*sto gram*, one hundred grams, was a good serving to start with) and served at room temperature in a decanter. Soviet wines were usually not very good, and the champagne was cloyingly sweet, but Armenian cognac was justifiably famous, and Russian beer not bad. The "national" restaurants were wildly popular with Soviet citizens but very hard for them to get into. Once you got in, dinner required at least three hours, which was how long it took to get a waiter's attention, order, and eventually be served and eat. Part of the evening's entertainment was watching a table or two of Russian men passing through the classic stages of intoxication: mild animation; extreme animation with much gesturing and the voice raised; lurching movements; head lolling; head on table; body collapsing on floor. Alcoholism was the major national disease.

A couple of times each winter, Charlotte and I attended parent-teacher meetings at Public School Sixty-Nine. Our fellow parents, none of whom we knew, represented a spectrum of Soviet families. A number of them, judging by the way they dressed and spoke, appeared to be professionals of one sort of another; some were clearly workers, the men decently dressed in white shirts and dark trousers, the women in dowdy dresses. We always greeted and tried to chat with the other parents, but generally they were uncomfortable with us. Parents had little to say in these meetings: most of the evening was given over to exhortations from the school management for discipline, hard work, and good behavior. The ordinarily pleasant principal and teachers whom we knew identified by name those children who were lagging behind in their class work or behavior, and publicly and sharply took their parents to task for their parental failures.

Charlotte, a talented amateur painter, began to study landscape and figure painting under the instruction of a Russian artist, Ilya Glazunov, whom she met through the wife of a European diplomat. Once a week or so, she drove to Glazunov's spacious, comfortable studio and apartment, where he worked and lived with a beautiful young wife. Glazunov, we knew, must have KGB encouragement for his contacts with foreigners and almost certainly passed on whatever gossip he picked up. He was, in spite of that, an excellent teacher and extremely talented artist in the process of becoming famous for his realistic, large-scaled canvases of Russian life, which in later years contained a strong religious and nationalistic bent. He also painted portraits of party leaders, which didn't hurt his standing in official circles, and did three perceptive charcoal portraits of our children. When time and weather permitted, Charlotte headed out in the Volkswagen and set up her easel outside one of the old churches or monastery complexes around Moscow inside the twenty-five mile limit. She produced a series of lovely watercolors of the old Moscow churches, capturing the fading reds of the brick, the white or golden domes, and the other-worldly, northern light of the skies.

We shopped in the crowded, inefficient state grocery stores (the embassy finally set up a small, basic commissary for canned goods) and went often to one of the open-air peasant markets, where *kolhoz* (collective) farm workers—sturdy, red-cheeked women and rough-looking men—sold eggs, cheese, vegetables, various Russian versions of yogurt and sour cream, pickles, mushrooms, and other delicacies produced on their own small private plots, which amazingly produced almost a third of total Soviet agricultural production. The children picked up fresh, delicious black and rye bread at the local bakery on their way home from school. In the winter of 1963, the quality of the bread deteriorated to the point of near inedibility. Although the Soviet press never said a word, we discovered, both through the taste of the bread and the long, silent lines that appeared outside those state stores that sold spaghetti and macaroni, that the fall grain harvest had failed. Our general policy on seeing lines on the main streets, as we drove or walked around Moscow, was to stop and get in line immediately. Once you got a place at the end of the line you asked what was being sold. If it was oranges or fresh fruit from the south, we stayed in line and bought as much as the vendor would sell. These sidewalk salesmen and women usually had flown up from the Caucasus with as much produce as they could load onto a Soviet passenger airplane. Once a month or so, the Soviet authorities allowed the U.S. ambassador the privilege of an American official flight, usually an Air Force DC-3 transport, in from Western Europe with diplomatic freight for the embassy. These flights whenever possible brought in a few small boxes of fresh lettuce. The kindest invitation you could offer a fellow, long-term resident was supper with a lettuce salad. Cabbage and potatoes were standard in our diet, and by winter's end even these were getting moldy.

By March and April, old Moscow grew visibly tired, gray, sullen, and malevolent. One's very skin drew back from the cold and the long, nocturnal darkness. It seemed winter would never end. Snow piled high, dirty, disgusting. People plodded, faces turned down so as not to trip on the brown, dirty sidewalks. Around the ring roads, hundreds of dirty green trucks clanked and grumbled along in second gear, puffing out nauseating black smoke and losing large metal parts.

Then, one day, a soft breeze came stealing into the capital, the ice began to break on the river, the thaw began. Pushkin, writing about his beloved Petersburg and the Neva, said, "The river threw itself like a wild beast on the city." In Moscow, the little river was banked and chained with concrete, but around Moscow the waters flooded the lowlands and turned villages into seas of icy water and mud. Strolling along the embankment of the Moscow River on a chilly, sunny day in April, shortly after the last ice floes had gone off downstream, I watched two workers strip down to their black drawers and dive into the brown stream. (The river in the city is not inviting at its summer best.) "Hey, Ivan," shouted a passerby. "*S'uma soshol ty?*" ("Have you gone off your rocker?") "Nyet," shouted Vanya, image of Russian daring. "*Vyesna prishla.*" ("Spring has come.")

Across the wide northern land, spring finally did come: marsh flowers, groves budding around the villages; the sky increasingly high, wide, and light; birds returning to the belfries of ruined churches; and the great religious celebrations of the rebirth of life—Russian Easter and Passover, and May Day for the new secular religion of Communism. The Orthodox celebrations at the few open churches were jammed, mostly with old women and men and a smaller number of the curious. The priests sang the mass, the air smelled of incense, candles, sweaty clothes, and strong Russian perfumes, and when the crowd lifted their voices in the songs of resurrection old Russia came alive. The Jews celebrated Passover quietly; there was much anti-Semitism in the population and the government, although the party denied this. May Day, in honor of the workers of the world, was a big political event with anti-capitalist and anti-American speeches and a big parade of workers and schoolchildren across Red Square. Most of all, it was a day off to enjoy the spring weather and get the family together for cucumber (if you could find them) salad, blinis, caviar (if you could afford it), and champagne.

In the spring of that fateful year, 1963, we decided to stay on for a third year. The pressures of arguing with the Soviet authorities about the exchange program were endless, but the more experience I acquired, the better I became at the job. The psychic rewards were high—to see and sense the warmth of the people's reaction to American musicians, dancers, and writers, and to watch the small number of American students and scientists at their hard work of learning and surviving in Soviet universities. Charlotte was deep into her painting. The children, whose Russian by now approached bilingual quality, were doing well in Public School Sixty-Nine and had both Russian and Western friends. They spent three weeks when summer arrived at a children's camp outside Moscow taking walks in the woods and mandatory naps in the afternoon (it being Russian childraising theory that children expend so much energy in the harsh winter that they need a lot of fresh air and rest in the summer). I have a delightful photograph of our youngest son, Peter, playing chess with a Russian friend in a forest grove at the camp, which we could not visit since it was outside the twenty-five-mile limit. In summer and into the fall, we drove out to picnic and swim at Uspenskoye, a village just at the twenty-five-mile limit, where the Moscow River curves through low, rolling hills and fields before joining the Moscow canal coming down from the Volga to the north. The hills were marked with birch and pine groves, the grassy river banks were sprinkled in May and June with wild flowers, and against the immense horizon the occasional onion-shaped dome of a ruined church marked a village of wooden peasant houses. The Uspenskoye road passed through the most elegant dacha country in the Soviet Union. Both Stalin, in his time, and Khrushchev, in ours, had dachas on the Uspenskoye road, as did many other dukes of the realm, the estates lying behind wooded entrances with red and yellow "keep out" signs. On Saturday afternoons, chauffeur-driven Chaika limousines raced out from Moscow, crowding ordinary mortals to the side of the road.

Another important reason to stay a third year was that we still had a lot to see and learn. Sometimes with exchange visitors, but occasionally on our own, Charlotte and I traveled widely to the Caucasus, Siberia, and Central Asia, where we were among the first outsiders in many years to see the fabled mosques at Samarkand, built by Tamerlane's successors, and the historic Silk Road bazaar now filled with once-fierce tribal warriors and traders squatting disconsolately, selling tin and plastic buckets instead of rugs and spices. Years later, when I first traveled to northern India and Pakistan, I felt that I had been there before, and, in a way, I had: the Mogul emperors of India came from Central Asia, and the mosque and palace shapes of Samarkand and those parts of India and Pakistan ruled by the Moguls all are rooted in the same cultural tradition. We traveled to Irkutsk and Lake Baikal, Tbilisi, and Yerevan, and I even accompanied an American scholar to Yakutsk, far in the Siberian north in the permafrost. The embassy's economic counselor, Dick Funkhouser, and I took a silver ship's bell from a maritime union in Philadelphia up to Murmansk for a rare ceremony on a powerful, luxuriously furnished Soviet Navy icebreaker (built by Finland as part of its war reparations to the Soviet Union after World War II) honoring American seamen who died in the North Atlantic delivering arms to the Soviet Union during World War II. The city and the winding fjord where the icebreaker was anchored were shrouded in fog and low clouds, and we were carefully escorted to insure that we saw as little as possible of the northern Soviet fleet. Charlotte and I drove the Volkswagen down to Tolstoy's country home at Yasnaya Polyana southeast of Moscow, wandered through the birch groves, stood at his grave, and were eaten alive by voracious bedbugs in the local hotel.

The more I observed of Russian life, the more I was struck by the perceptiveness of Richard Pipe's analysis of the fundamental difference between Russia and the West. In Western Europe, the rise of alternative centers of power to the king eventually led to rules of the game (like the Magna Carta in England): codes of law, legislatures, and constitutions. In Russia, by contrast, the czars became all powerful. Even as late as 1902, the Russian Czar Nicholas could declare, "I conceive of Russia as a landed estate, of which the proprietor is the czar, the administrator is the nobility, and the workers are the peasantry." The Russian state, to use Pipe's terminology, was patrimonial. The ruler controlled not only the state and political power, the economy and the populace were his household goods and produced for him, and in their spiritual life the czar was the head of the church. Like the czars, the Communists allowed no sources of real power other than their own—in this case the Party itself—although they created an elaborate façade of vacant institutions and rhetoric: written constitutions, endless proclamations that all power belonged to the Soviets (the councils at various levels of society that constituted what passed for parliaments), and the myth that all land belonged to the people (while in fact the collective and state farm workers of Communism were every bit as much serfs as their ancestors of two hundred years ago). The Communists also continued the patrimonial tradition of glorifying an all-powerful ruler, who interpreted the meaning of the new religion of Communism.

On the positive side, the Soviet state produced important benefits for the people under its rule: literacy, job security, and worker pensions, impressive accomplishments in science and technology (with an overwhelming emphasis on military applications), and a sense of pride in Soviet power, particularly after the titanic victory over Nazi Germany, and on such occasions as the successful launching of Sputnik. These came at great costs though: a class system that divided the rulers from the ruled, terror, censorship, and widespread ignorance of the world. Most Soviet citizens led a double life, loyal workers and regime supporters on the surface and occasional or frequent doubters privately. It was a profoundly cynical, and in many ways a schizophrenic, society. A Soviet citizen could be horrified by the brutality of Stalin and the KGB and yet be proud of the military and technological accomplishments of the regime. I used to tell my Soviet counterparts in the government that Communism could never triumph, because the central planning and control of the economy—and everything else in life—that the party demanded and practiced could not possibly meet the long-term, changing needs of a dynamic, modern society. I told them: "The system will never work because here in Moscow you never hear the truth back from the provinces. People tell you what they think you want to hear about meeting production targets. Not only can you not believe what you hear, but the targets themselves are often wrong." I was right, of course. Twenty-five years later the elaborate, sclerotic house of cards collapsed.

But as I observed Russian life through the limited field of vision we were afforded, I also became convinced that beneath the Orwellian façade of the system, the essential humanity of the Russian spirit survived. Primo Levi caught its essence in *The Reawakening*, the book he wrote to describe his survival in 1945 after Auschwitz when he wandered half-dead, sick, and hungry through southern Russia seeking a way home to Italy. Red Army soldiers picked him up, healed, and fed him. Levi described the Red Army camp as "the most picturesque example of a gypsy encampment that one could imagine…The whole troupe lived in harmony, without timetable or regulations, near the camp, lodged in the buildings of an abandoned primary school. For the most part, they lived together with friendly simplicity, like a large temporary family, without military formalism. They were cheerful, sad, and tired, and took pleasure in food and wine, like Ulysses' companions after the ships had been pulled ashore. And yet, under their slovenly and anarchical appearance, it was easy to see in them, in each of those rough and open faces, the good soldiers of the Red Army, the valiant men of the old and new Russia, gentle in peace and fierce in war.…"

At about the same time, returning to Moscow after a seven-year absence, George Kennan wrote: "Through war, through peace, through drama, through suffering, unceasingly and irresistibly, there goes on that vast organic process which we can only describe as the spiritual life of the Russian people…The Russians remain…the most unspoiled and the most curious of peoples. No other people has such a thirst for knowledge, such a zest for intellectual and artistic experience. They are as unspoiled in the immaterial things as they are in the comforts of life, and their tastes are as primitive in one sphere as in the other."

One night in November as we entered the third year of our Russian education, Charlotte and I sat in our living room enjoying a quiet evening alone. It was ten o'clock. The telephone rang. Jerry Prehn, a newly arrived information officer on my staff, came on the line. "I thought I should call you right away," he said. "I was monitoring shortwave broadcasts, and I picked up a European station quoting reports out of Dallas, Texas, that President Kennedy has been shot." I asked him to wait a second and turned on our radio. The VOA was jammed, but I found a Swedish station broadcasting in English and reporting fragmentary bulletins on the events in Dallas and Washington from various wire services and news agency sources.

I immediately called John McSweeney, the deputy chief of mission, who lived two floors above us in the residential wing of the embassy, and told him what was happening. McSweeney took a second to turn on his radio and asked me to join him as soon as possible. By the time I reached his apartment, McSweeney had called Spaso House and alerted Ambassador Foy Kohler, just in from a diplomatic dinner. We sat down and penciled out a list of tasks and embassy officers to handle them. We still had no official notification from Washington, which in those days required an urgent, coded telegram to be sent and then decoded at the receiving end. Within a half-hour or so, the shortwave broadcasts were reporting the president's death. Then, in rapid succession, bulletins began to come in reporting that the suspected assassin was a man named Lee Harvey Oswald, who was said to have lived in the Soviet Union. We were already stunned by the news of Kennedy's death; the Oswald reports seemed almost incredible, and their potential consequences frightening to conceive. I suggested to McSweeney that we immediately ask a consular officer to come in and send him, accompanied by another officer in anticipation of the almost inevitable inquiries that might take place, down to the consular office files on the first floor of the embassy to retrieve any files that might exist on Oswald and hand-carry them up to a secure safe in the top floors of the building guarded by Marines.

We were up most of the night, having moved our conversations into the secure plastic room in the embassy offices. Cable traffic finally began to flow in from Washington, and sometime after midnight McSweeney took an official note to the Foreign Ministry informing them as to what had occurred. We were getting telephone calls from journalists all over Europe, a rarity in a place where open telephone calls virtually never got through. In the dark hours of the morning, the embassy set up an official book of condolences at Spaso House. Early the next morning Anastas Mikoyan, the deputy premier, dressed in black and looking shaken, came to write an official condolence in representation of the Soviet government. Sizable numbers of Soviet citizens dared to come in off the street to sign the book at Spaso House, and numbers of Americans were stopped on the street by Russian men and women to express their sorrow. It was clear many Russians were deeply affected by the tragedy. The small American community was in a state of deep shock. No one's eyes were dry.

Over the ensuing days and months, the Soviet government went to great lengths to dissociate itself in every possible way from any involvement with Oswald or any possible plot to assassinate the president. KGB files that have become available in recent years reveal that original KGB suspicions about the assassination centered on a group of wealthy, Far Right Texas conservatives who thought Kennedy was soft on Communism.

We know today, after the exhaustive investigations that have continued almost nonstop over the four decades since the Kennedy assassination, that Oswald did go to the Soviet Union in 1959, ostensibly seeking a better way of life, and visited the U.S. embassy consular section "to dissolve my American citizenship," according to the files. Oswald left his passport at the embassy, got Soviet permission to remain in the country, and was sent by the Soviets to Minsk, where he worked in a radio factory and married a Russian woman, Marina. The KGB files make it clear that the KGB knew all about Oswald's Russia sojourn, bugged his apartment in Minsk, eventually decided that he was an unreliable, unstable nut, and wanted nothing to do with him. In 1961 Oswald wrote the embassy requesting the return of his passport, claiming that he had never renounced American citizenship. In February 1962, Oswald got his passport back, and with a repatriation loan of $500 from the consulate, departed the Soviet Union with Marina and their baby girl for the United States. The files suggest the U.S. government had decided it would be worthwhile to have him return, so that he could be questioned about Soviet life for intelligence purposes. On the most important question of all, that of Oswald's guilt, one of the most thorough of the many studies about Oswald, Norman Mailer's 791-page book, *Oswald's Tale, an American Mystery*, concludes, "He probably did it alone."

The cloud of the Kennedy assassination hung over us throughout a gray, bitter Moscow winter. In the 1960s no one in the general public, including the Foreign Service, knew of Kennedy's attitudes toward women and his sexual escapades in the White House and on his travels, or for that matter the parlous condition of his health. For most of us he really *was* the handsome young prince of Camelot, and Jackie was his princess. Regardless of the Bay of Pigs invasion failure, Kennedy handled the Cuban missile crisis with wisdom, toughness, good timing, and luck. We, who had been on the spot in Moscow during the showdown, had particular reason to admire his leadership. To be out of the United States as the nation mourned for its slain young president was like being exiled from one's family as it sorrowed for a particularly loved one.

I began to think seriously about leaving Moscow for a future assignment. When Lincoln Kirstein was in Moscow with the New York City Ballet the previous year, he asked me if I ever thought about leaving the Foreign Service and said that sometime when I was in the States, he wanted me to meet W. McNeil Lowry, the senior vice president of the Ford Foundation. Lowry conceived and ran the institution-building grant program that the foundation conducted with major symphony orchestras, ballet troupes, and regional, nonprofit repertory theater companies. Kirstein continued to push the point in our intermittent exchanges of letters, and in early 1964 I agreed that meeting Lowry was a good idea, even though my Foreign Service career seemed to be prospering. I wrote Lowry in the spring, and he invited me to visit him in New York for a talk. I was, in fact, having a serious disagreement with Washington about onward assignments. The deputy director of USIA wanted me to take over the public affairs counselor job in Mexico City and said, in essence, that since I was the most qualified person for the job I had no choice, even though I was coming out of a notorious hardship post, had expressed a strong preference for Madrid, and had already spent four years of my life in Mexico and five more in other capitals of Latin America.

We packed our scanty household goods in June, and on a perfect spring day said good-bye to this Eurasian empire, sharing toasts with friends who had brought French champagne to the Moscow airport. My psychological baggage included some regrets, memories happy and dark, and anticipation and excitement about the future. I still had not decided what to do if the Ford Foundation wanted to hire me. As the plane climbed out over the birch forests and green fields and headed west, I thought it likely I would never see Russia again. But I had only played out the first act with Russia; more was to come.

9

New York, New York

After returning from Moscow to Washington, I flew up to New York to talk with Mac Lowry at the Ford Foundation. Since our first correspondence about the possibility of my joining the foundation's arts and humanities program, Lowry had taken on an additional responsibility as vice president of a new foundation-wide Office of Policy and Planning. After talking for a while, Lowry and I agreed I should consider joining the small staff he envisioned for that new office rather than the arts program. Ford planned and funded major grant programs in overseas development, international affairs, and language and area studies. Lowry thought my Foreign Service experience would allow me, as the new office's associate director, to become its main resource in analyzing and communicating with these programs and their staffs. I could also work as needed on domestic issues, which I wanted to do. Charlotte and I discussed this big potential change in the pattern of our lives at much length. I thought very hard about what I wanted to do with my life. Then, with a lot of regrets and a few trepidations, I resigned from the Foreign Service and joined the foundation staff in New York in late summer 1964. When I told my eighty-four-year-old father, who was living in retirement in Kansas City, he thought I was crazy to leave a good government job.

For not much more than a song, a bankrupt textile manufacturer sold us his decrepit but charming old house perched on the western bluffs above the Hudson River north of New York. The kids, now in their teens and fresh from three years in a Russian-speaking school in Moscow, enrolled in the supposedly excellent, local county school system, where, as we were to discover, drugs were rapidly becoming incorporated into the unofficial curriculum. I commuted via carpool across the Tappan Zee Bridge to Tarrytown and then into New York by rail.

New York was (and is) a marvel to me—like no other city in the world. From time to time I said (and still say) a silent prayer of thanks for the privilege of living there. Walt Whitman long ago caught its excitement in his poem "Mannahatta": "An island sixteen miles long, solid-founded, numberless crowded streets, high growths of iron, slender, strong, light splendidly uprising toward clear skies, tides swift and ample…" A city of immigrants, he called it (Walt should see it today!), of strong men and women. Riding the 7:58 commuter train down the Hudson that late summer and fall, while my blasé fellow commuters buried their heads in the *New York Times* and the *Wall Street Journal*, I would spend most of the trip gazing at the majestic river stretching out its skin calm and mauve, here and there dappled by a breath of air or bathed in a morning mist. When winter came, the hard northern sun caught spikes of icy light off the fractured rocks of the Palisades, and the wind blew whitecaps briskly down to the sea. The richness and artistry of the New York store windows fed my fancy after years of living in poor countries and gray Moscow. I strolled by Cartier's and Harry Winston's on Fifth Avenue and gawked with pleasure at the sparkling baubles. The city's food counters spilled over with cheeses, meats, and fruits from all over the world; the stores reeked of chili powder, melons, and sausage, and the smell of pizzas cooking. I stood enraptured with giant strawberries. I started to walk the New York way—fast, eyes scanning (seldom making eye contact, of course) the infinite varieties of my tribe in the waves and eddies of the stream of people on the sidewalks and streets.

Both Charlotte and I believed it was important to get the family back into sync with our own country. In some respects, we found it almost unrecognizable, like looking in a crazy mirror at an amusement park. During the four years we had been away—one in Germany and three in the Soviet Union—the plates under American life had shifted. As Bob Dylan sang in his croaky voice, "For the times, they are a-changin'." A revolution in sexual mores and public tolerance was under way. Within a year after my return, a magazine called *Screw*, replete with photographs of naked vaginas, went for sale at New York newsstands. Drug use and street violence and brutality were on the upswing everywhere in the country. One fall afternoon on our first year back from Moscow, three young thugs held up Charlotte, the three children, and me at gunpoint in our house on the Hudson, tied us up in the basement, and threatened us for two hours while they ransacked the house looking for non-existent expensive jewelry. The poisons of the Vietnam War were slowly beginning to flow into the veins of American life. The passionate cadences of Martin Luther King's mellifluous voice echoed across the land, and in 1964 the Civil Rights Act was signed into law. The times indeed were a-changin'.

The institution that had hired me was the wealthiest and most powerful of the great American philanthropic institutions, whose roots go back to the early years of the twentieth century and such philanthropists as Andrew Carnegie and John D. Rockefeller. In the mid-1960s, the Ford Foundation's worth was $2.5 billion dollars (in 2004 dollars over fifteen billion). Its annual grants were averaging around $225 million (in 2004 dollars about $1.4 billion). The foundation came into existence in 1936 as a small philanthropy to make grants primarily in the state of Michigan, Henry Ford's home and the heartland of his automobile-making enterprises. The great industrialist died in 1947. His oldest son, Edsel, had died three years earlier. To preserve family control of the motor corporation, their wills provided that the majority of the company's stock, held by Henry and Edsel in the form of non-voting shares, would pass on their deaths to the foundation. When their estates were settled in 1950, the Ford Foundation received 90 percent of the stock of the motor company as non-voting shares and overnight became the world's largest private foundation. Its charter dedicated the foundation to use its income "to advance human welfare."

The modern American foundation typified by Ford is an instrument of great flexibility. By law, it must be privately incorporated, make its funds available only to nonprofit organizations or for nonprofit purposes (it can, if it wishes, make grants for such purposes to governments), and spend annually an amount roughly equal to at least 5 percent of its investment assets. A foundation board of trustees is self-sustaining and autonomous in managing the foundation's asset holdings. U.S. law does not dictate a foundation's choice of subject matter. If its governing body so decides, a foundation may enjoy a degree of experimentation and risk-taking difficult to achieve in institutions like the World Bank, the UN agencies, or governmental development agencies like U.S. AID. Unlike most non-governmental organizations—OXFAM or Save the Children, as examples, which usually work on specified and limited agendas—a foundation may work across a broad horizon of problems. On the other hand, even a large foundation like Ford possesses limited resources by comparison with governmental institutions. A foundation should be, to use an overloaded word, a catalyst.

The Ford trustees were headed by the chairman of the board, John J. McCloy, a Wall Street lawyer and former high commissioner of the American occupation regime in Germany; and figures like Henry Ford II; Eugene Black, the first president of the World Bank; and Stephen Bechtel, builder of one of the world's largest engineering and industrial service organizations. As successful Americans of their time, they regarded themselves as men of vision who could solve almost any problem. Comfortable with large sums of money, they liked the idea and sound of big grants. The trustees had delegated a high degree of authority to the foundation's officers in the United States and to its representatives overseas. The staff was encouraged to be innovative and take risks.

In its U.S. grant making, the foundation early on established a pattern of deploying its rapidly increasing resources (as the post-World War II stock market burgeoned in the 1960s in the largest economic expansion in history) in blocks of sizable grants. This decision reflected the complexities and staff demands that would be required by a plethora of small grants, plus the desire of the board to keep stock portfolio growth in hand. As part of the strategy, the foundation spun off three separately administered funds: the Fund for the Advancement of Education, the Fund for Adult Education, and the Fund of the Republic. (The latter, run by the very bright, pugnacious Robert Maynard Hutchins, and dedicated to democracy and free speech, caused endless political problems with the U.S. Congress and both the Ford Foundation and the Ford Motor Company.) In 1955 alone, the foundation board approved a special appropriation of a half-billion dollars, nearly half of it dedicated to a nationwide program to improve college and university faculty salaries with the rest earmarked for medical education and hospitals.

In its first and most significant policy decision to open an office in India in 1952, Ford became the first major American foundation to set up an international program of multipurpose, grant-making offices overseas focusing on problems and nation building rather than disciplinary subjects. (In the 1920s and 1930s, the Rockefeller Foundation had carried out admirable work in the education and health fields in China. The early Rockefeller-supported research in plant genetics in Mexico in the 1940s and 1950s prepared the ground for the high-yielding wheat varieties that revolutionized agricultural production in the 1960s.) The decision to go overseas reflected the trustees' concern about the already joined struggle for world domination with the Soviet Union and the triumph of Mao Tse-tung's Communists in China, the world's largest nation. India, the world's second most populous nation, must not be allowed to follow that path. As the Cold War spread and became more intense, it became a major factor in foundation decision-making. By the mid-1960s when I joined the staff, the foundation had established overseas development offices in every major continent, had become the largest single private supporter of language and foreign area programs designed to increase American competence in foreign affairs, and funded an active international affairs program that began with a concern for refugees from Communism and developed into a major source of assistance for non-Communist intellectuals and private leaders in Europe. Taken together, these international and overseas concerns became the single largest component of Ford Foundation grant making.

My boss, Mac Lowry, was a mild-mannered, soft-spoken, charming, extremely well-read and bright, much-admired foundation entrepreneur, in the process of becoming a towering figure in the world of the performing arts. Lowry combined scholarly excellence—he had a Ph. D. in English from the University of Illinois—with a world of practical experience and good contacts. He had joined the Ford Foundation after a career as chief Washington correspondent for the Cox newspaper group and a senior executive position in the International Press Institute in Geneva, Switzerland. He believed in careful, journalistic style, personal, on-the-ground research. Lowry and his small, tightly knit arts and humanities staff (which I had originally expected to join and came to know well) had carried out a yearlong exploration of the state of the institutions of classical culture—symphonic music, the dance, the theater, and the arts and humanities—in the United States. Its basic conclusion was that the foundation could make a lasting contribution to the stabilization and long-term growth of key institutions through a series of potentially large, developmental grants to selected institutions, requiring them not only to raise matching funds but to produce and agree to stick to individual management plans to improve institutional fundraising and financial control systems. Lincoln Kirstein's and George Balanchine's New York City Ballet and its professional school, the School of American Ballet, were recipients, as were a large number of the country's best symphony orchestras and nonprofit repertory theater groups. This program was Lowry's primary love and required most of his management time.

Lowry inherited responsibility for the new Office of Policy and Planning, which I was to join, as the just-birthed brainchild of an earlier vice president, who died unexpectedly before it began to function. The rationale was that the foundation's resources were already so large and growing so fast that the president and the board needed a small, foundation-wide office to monitor and understand better the larger universe in which the foundation operated. The foundation had become notoriously decentralized, its programs run by powerful barons called program directors who established direct lines of communication and openly lobbied board members for more autonomy and an increasing share of the annually larger pie. It was a bit like feudal Europe or the period of warring states in Chinese history. The president, Henry Heald, a tall, noble-headed figure and a man of great decency, who had been an engineering professor and then president of the Illinois Institute of Technology and subsequently New York University, found it increasingly difficult to contain these raids on his authority.

A primary responsibility of the new office was thus to establish a presumably impartial and objective overview for the president and the board. A second task was to maintain a short watch-list of potential large, new grant-making opportunities for the president and board for use as necessary to contain the growth of the capital portfolio within acceptable political limits. This was a matter of political concern, particularly to the Ford family, two of whose members, Henry Ford II and Benson Ford, still sat on the board in the mid-1960s. The foundation was midstream in the process of divesting itself of its Ford Motor Company stock and diversifying its stock holdings, a decision taken at the very beginning of the foundation's expanded role in the early 1950s (divestiture was completed in the 1960s).

My colleagues in this new endeavor were the office director, Malcolm Moos; another associate director, Richard Sheldon, a Harvard-trained anthropologist knowledgeable in the social sciences and humanities; and, after a year, Bill Watts, a Foreign Service officer who had served with me in Moscow. A distinguished political scientist and moderate Republican intellectual, Moos served in the Eisenhower White House as a principal speech writer, where he was responsible for the one Ike quote to become part of American popular history: the need to beware of the "military-industrial complex." (Quadrillions of dollars later, when he is not playing golf in heaven, the prophetic Eisenhower must be shaking his head at the follies of his beloved country.) Moos was a delightful man: lean, handsome, prematurely white-haired, intense blue eyes, possessed of an infectious sense of humor and an inexhaustible fund of knowledge and opinions about politics, politicians, and scholars. We formed a reconnaissance agenda of major foundation policy issues and outside leaders and thinkers to consult with and set off on our beneficent mission.

The great barons of the foundation welcomed us rather as if we bore the plague, although the more statesmanlike received us warmly, at least on the surface. Part of our agenda included evaluation, a lofty concept much praised but seldom practiced seriously in the foundation's vertiginous growth (as is true in most institutions). The program staff view, doubtless with some justification, generally was, "Who the hell are you to be evaluating my work?"

I spent two years as a policy planner before the board dispensed with the services of Henry Heald. I immersed myself in two of the biggest questions the foundation faced. The first was overseas development policy and the lack therein of a seemingly consistent set of understandings. The second was how the foundation's grant programs, with the big American cities on fire and the South in a virtual revolution, might better help bring African Americans (in the mid-1960s still referred to by virtually all American institutions as Negroes) into the mainstream of American life.

On the overseas development side of the house, a decade-plus of experimentation in Asia, Africa, and Latin America had produced some successes and a number of looming crashes. The approaches had been extremely varied, which in an anthropological and cultural context made some sense, usually reflecting the backgrounds and convictions of the early program developers. In Africa, for example, as essentially tribal societies achieved independence, Ford's programs gave emphasis to constitution writing and the creation of modern legal systems. Not surprisingly, a few of the early foundation managers and advisers in Africa came from the ranks of senior British colonial administrators. In South Asia, the emphasis was on improving agricultural production to feed already very large and rapidly expanding populations; unsurprisingly, the head of the India program came out of the U.S. Department of Agriculture. Where common threads existed across geographic lines, they were to be found in a concern for training indigenous economists and civil servants to help understand and formulate development policy and the creation of new patterns and institutions in higher education, including high technology and business and public management. A major issue was the relative priority to be accorded to extension activities as opposed to research and institution building. A growing concern was the degree to which the foundation was supporting government, as opposed to private, not-for-profit programs.

The main overseas theater of combat for these policy skirmishes was the India program. Biggest of the foundation's overseas operations, India was the province of the first and most senior of the barons, Douglas Ensminger, who in 1952 had opened the foundation's first overseas office in New Delhi. I therefore made the first of many trips to the fabled subcontinent (where, some years later, I was to devote a decade of my life to development work in both India and Pakistan, the two fractious, endlessly complicated offspring of Mother India born in the bloody craziness of the 1949 partition). A Ph. D. in sociology from the University of Missouri, Ensminger had been a senior official in the extension services of the U.S. Department of Agriculture. He favored large-scale, action-oriented extension approaches, invariably requiring teams of usually American specialists matched with Indian government counterparts in demonstration projects ranging from agricultural extension to establishing family planning clinics and distributing contraceptives in both rural and urban settings. A key concept was "technology transfer"—the transfer and adaptation of Western methods and models.

The central exhibit in the argument between Ensminger and New York was the ambitious, so-called Intensive Agricultural Districts Project (IADP), the largest single project the foundation had undertaken overseas. Conceived by Ensminger and a group of American and Indian agricultural experts in the late 1950s as a response to food riots and increasing rumors of famine as India's population growth outstripped its food grain production abilities, the IADP strategy was to concentrate money, additional expert staff, and agricultural inputs in a few well-endowed agricultural districts. Immediate, significant increases in national food grain production and availability were the goal: equity was not a major consideration. Almost from the start, the program had sputtered.

The chief New York critic was the senior vice president for overseas development, Francis ("Frosty") Hill, an agronomist who had served as provost at Cornell University. Hill had reluctantly approved the original project but, as it developed problems, thought the foundation should cut its losses. Ensminger pushed for program correction, continuation, and further expansion. Hill became convinced that no really important production jumps would occur in rice and wheat production, the basic food crops in most of the developing world, without a much greater investment in research—starting with basic genetics and plant breeding—and that Ford should fund this kind of work. His thesis was that farmers would themselves rapidly adopt new varieties of seeds and cultivation techniques if these could be invented and if significantly higher yields could in fact be demonstrated. Since agricultural research traditionally had been a trademark of the Rockefeller Foundation, this meant it was a touchy subject at Ford, which tended to go its own way. Heald, the foundation president, lined up uneasily with Hill, well aware that the trustees admired Ensminger's drive and vision. Hill, with Heald's authorization, was meantime in discussions with George Harrar, president of the Rockefeller Foundation and a distinguished agricultural scientist, about joining forces.

Accompanied by massively built, bearded, white-turbaned Sikh farmers in the Indian Punjab and thin, lungi-clad rice farmers in the south, I puddle-jumped and walked along the bunds and through the paddies of wheat and rice fields asking questions about these complex equations of seeds, support systems, and cultivation techniques, usually under the guidance of one of Ensminger's staff experts. Ensminger was larger than life, a buzz saw of energy and ideas, and a bluff, no-nonsense man. He saw his job as the first foundation representative in newly independent India as being both responsive to Indian ideas and leadership and as an initiator and facilitator of ideas for development programs and institutions. In the early days of his assignment, Ensminger developed a warm personal rapport with Prime Minister Jawaharlal Nehru (emulating Nehru, Ensminger frequently wore a red rosebud pinned to his coat lapel) and a host of senior civil servants, as well as with large numbers of Indian private-sector leaders and ordinary citizens, essentially placing himself and the foundation at their service in the cause of development. When India's folk art and cottage industry stores needed to be brought into the modern world in advertising, presentation, and marketing techniques, Ensminger flew out a young Macy's executive from New York who reorganized the marketing system quickly and successfully (and stayed on in New Delhi, married Ensminger's secretary, and became one of the country's leading art textile entrepreneurs). At the government's request, Ensminger sent five hundred Indian steel engineers to the States to be trained in modern technology. He commissioned Harvard and MIT to establish two modern Indian Institutes of Management (along with the great architect, Louis Kahn, to build the one in Ahmedabad), hired the famous man-and-wife design team of Charles and Ray Eames (who had done the pathbreaking movie about America for the 1959 Moscow exhibition) to set up a National Institute of Design, and in Calcutta launched a large, innovative project in regional planning for services for one of the world's densest and poorest populations.

With some justification, Ensminger viewed himself, as did many others, as the most important American in the country, not excluding the American ambassador. He presided over a staff of one hundred expatriate experts, almost entirely American and mostly from university life, who worked in agriculture, education, population, and family planning subjects, and the social sciences and management; on special occasions drove to the office in a horse-drawn carriage; kept a specially rigged jeep for deer and antelope hunting expeditions to the Punjab and Rajasthan; and followed foundation projects in the back country with the help of a small, private foundation airplane (in the early days, a single-engine Piper Cherokee, later replaced by a twin-engine, turboprop Beechcraft). On the surface, Ensminger could sound like a country-boy populist. He was in fact sophisticated and cunning (at the end of my first visit as a member of the policy and planning staff, he offered me a job in New Delhi as a new assistant representative to set up a public affairs program.), ruthless, stubborn, tirelessly persistent, and totally dedicated to India and the dreams he had shared with Nehru.

The fact of the matter was that the IADP was not working very well. After years of illness and growing national disillusionment with the slowness of economic growth, Nehru died in 1964. The Nehruvian model of government-guided development with large teams of foreign experts and technology transfer was under increasing fire; Indian nationalism and regionalism were on the rise.

None of the great Nehru's quarreling successors could deliver the local politicians and goad the vast Indian bureaucracy into action to support large-scale experimental approaches that required new thinking in relations with private citizens and reform in budgeting and personnel management—all essential to the success of the IADP approach. And the best of the then-available seeds were not, across the board, delivering markedly higher productivity.

The debate over the relative priorities of big extension projects versus research was essentially decided in the late 1960s when Hill convinced the board of trustees to meld Ford resources with those of the Rockefeller Foundation to create a network of international agricultural research institutes working on basic food crops. It was the vision and persuasiveness of Frosty Hill at Ford and George Harrar at Rockefeller, the muscle of their combined funding, and the scientists at these new institutes (people like the Nobel Prize-winning plant breeder Norman Borlaug) that in an unbelievably short time produced the Green Revolution in basic food crop production throughout the developing world, which almost certainly became the main factor in preventing mass starvation in those very large countries like India, Pakistan, and Indonesia where population growth was visibly outstripping food availability. There were other reasons as well, one being that rising nationalism made big teams of foreign experts less welcome. By the mid-1970s, large-scale, extension-type projects with big expatriate teams carrying out "technology transfer" (including the transfer of ideas about economic and public finance policy) had virtually disappeared from the foundation's overseas portfolio, although modern versions of the approach continue to characterize many AID, World Bank, and United Nations programs to this day.

On the domestic side back in New York, President Heald asked the small policy and planning staff to look at the foundation's overall programs for black Americans in light of the continuing crisis of decay and violence in the American city—where the catch phrase of the day described the situation precisely, "burn, baby, burn"—and the civil rights revolution in the South. Riots and arson swept through many of the major American cities in the late 1960s, leaving them looking like doughnuts with charred holes where their middles used to be. Lyndon Johnson, who had taken over the presidency from the murdered Jack Kennedy, had laid his presidency and reputation on the line to move the nation into a new era of social and economic justice, but the process was barely launched.

By no means had the foundation been inactive in regard to big-city problems or the role of African Americans in American life. When Bill Watts toted up the foundation's grants since 1952, the year of its inception as a national grant maker, the list showed a total of $82 million committed to various aspects of these problems. The largest components were a series of major developmental grants to traditionally black colleges and universities. In 1964, the year I joined the foundation, it committed $7 million to the National Merit Scholarship Corporation for a special scholarship program for blacks and made a $1.8 million grant to the Howard University law school to improve legal education.

The most innovative work took place in the foundation's so-called Gray Areas program of community development. Starting as a concept in the late 1950s, by 1964 the foundation had committed $23 million to address community development issues in Oakland, New Haven, Boston, Philadelphia, Washington DC, and the state of North Carolina. Its director was Paul Ylvisaker, a scholar, preacher, and charismatic intellectual, who was slowly going blind. The program Ylvisaker created and managed was one of the earliest and most important efforts to understand and do something about the mid-century, new style, predominantly ethnic and racial ghettoization of the American city. As described in a 1961 document, the program postulated that:

> 1) A set of coherent premises can be pulled together from the present jumble of community (and state and national) policies relating to the deteriorating areas of the central city. Currently, urban renewal is carried on in isolation from programs of schools, social agencies, and other service agencies. Seldom do these activities reinforce each other; rather, they usually operate independently and too often in contrary directions. 2) The stimulus of new ideas and the catalytic action of an outside force such as philanthropy are needed to activate the mass and variety of existing resources. 3) A way must be found to assure that the recent and growing interest in the renewal of American cities extends not only to real estate but to the human beings who flow through this real estate. Specifically, efforts are needed to facilitate the upward educational and economic movement of these people.

In New Haven, for example, city leaders established a private, nonprofit corporation to serve as coordinator, planner, and catalyst of the city's human renewal program. The board of directors consisted of the mayor, the redevelopment agency, a citizens action commission, the board of education, Yale University, and local business, philanthropic, and black community leaders. The director of the project was the street-smart Mitchell "Mike" Sviridoff, former president of the board of education and the Central Labor Council of Greater New Haven. The foundation grant plus local money—and eventually federal funds—established neighborhood service teams to identify local problems, a whole set of remedial school programs, a rent supplementation program to relocate large, low-income families in private rather than public housing, a variety of skill-training programs for jobs identified as available by citywide committees of businessmen, industrialists, union leaders, and educators, and community nursing teams.

America was hungry for new ideas and approaches to the explosive problems of the cities. It did not take long for the new federal Office of Economic Opportunity, with vastly larger financial resources, to take over the "Gray Areas" program concepts—and with them part of the original Ylvisaker staff. The foundation, if it wanted to be an innovator and risk taker, faced the question of what it should undertake next. Other than the "Gray Areas" program, the bulk of large grant making had been to black colleges, certainly important but hardly innovative, although more recently the foundation had begun to fund urban school reform projects primarily involving blacks.

For three months, I crisscrossed the United States, sometimes accompanied by an Ylvisaker staff member, visiting the war zones of central cities—including my old hometown, Kansas City—and the spookily quiet rural towns of the Mississippi Delta, where white men drove pickup trucks with shotgun racks, and rural black communities where the threat of violence almost literally trembled in the air. We were seeking information and ideas from African American and white private and government leaders. I talked with dozens of extraordinary people—Marion Wright Edelman of the NAACP (National Association for the Advancement of Colored People) Legal Aid and Defense Fund in Jackson, Mississippi, Aaron Henry, a pharmacist in rural Mississipi and an NAACP leader, Floyd McKissick and James Farmer of CORE (Congress of Racial Equality), and less well-known figures like two of the public school principals I talked with in Harlem, Seymour Gang and Martin Frey.

The unsurprising conclusion of the report Bill Watts and I produced for the board was that "the problem of achieving full entrance into American society for the Negro remains the major unfinished business of our domestic society in the twentieth century" and that the central theater of action was the big-city slum. (Some twenty-first century readers will comment that only the century has changed.) Since the federal government was appropriating the basic concepts and program structures of the "Gray Areas" approach pioneered by the foundation, the report recommended that Ford increasingly seek an experimental and remedial role in research and action programs that fell between the cracks of the big federal money projects—whether this required work in drug addiction, health programs, or investments in job creation. It recommended a major effort to upgrade predominantly black school systems, primarily in the South. It suggested a much more aggressive approach to job training for blacks and programs to encourage entry into business and the professions and suggested a high priority for civic education for newly qualifying black voters.

On the one really controversial issue—whether the foundation should directly support civil rights organizations like the NAACP and the more radical groups like SNCC (Student Non-Violent Coordinating Committee) and CORE—the final draft of the report took a very conservative position. In the original staff discussions, Watts and I had suggested selective support for specific projects. The report that went to the board, after long discussions involving Lowry, Heald, and a number of program directors, recommended that the foundation refrain from direct grants to civil rights organizations because, in some parts of the country, such actions might discourage moderate white support for important activities—as, for example, a major program in upgrading southern state education systems. (It might also offend Ford Motor Company auto dealers, although both Henry Ford II, whom I grew to admire for his courage and straight way of talking, and his brother, Benson, who still sat on the board, always took great pains to draw a line between company and foundation matters.)

At its autumn 1965 board meeting, the trustees found the report informative and useful. But it was a discussion paper, requiring no specific action, and their minds were focused on far more interesting business. President Henry Heald was on the way out—he had resigned in the summer and left in December—after years of an increasingly troubled and angry relationship with some of the leading trustees, headed by the chairman, John McCloy, who in spite of Heald's opposition openly encouraged staff and board fraternization. (The Heald/Lowry management philosophy for the foundation started with the separation of trustee and staff functions. Operating under broad policy outlines established by the board but with specific program and grant analysis in the hands of a large professional staff, the basic Heald/Lowry management policy was, "The staff proposes; the board disposes.")

McGeorge Bundy, it was rumored, would leave his job in Washington as President Johnson's National Security assistant to become the new Ford Foundation president, recruited personally by Chairman McCloy. "Frosty" Hill was to retire as vice president for overseas development, to be replaced by another Washington luminary, David E. Bell, who would serve as a new executive vice president for international affairs and development. Bell had worked for President Kennedy first as Director of the Bureau of the Budget and subsequently as the administrator of the U.S. Agency for International Development (AID). Bell was an economist out of Pomona College and Harvard and as a young man headed an economic policy advisory group in Pakistan under a Harvard project funded by

Ford. My boss, Mac Lowry, would serve as acting president until Bundy's arrival in April 1966.

Most of the senior staff knew Bundy only by reputation, daunting in its brilliance, and through the public prominence of his career. Forty-seven years old in 1966, Mac Bundy was a true Boston Brahmin. After following a family tradition and graduating from Yale, he went to Harvard, where he became a Junior Fellow, a university-designated small, elite group chosen for their brilliance and promise, and at a precocious age a tenured professor of government and then an extremely popular dean of the college. In World War II, as an Army officer Bundy served as a special assistant to an admiral who helped plan the Normandy invasion. He had co-authored a biography of Secretary of War Henry Stimson. As National Security assistant in President John F. Kennedy's White House, David Halberstam writes in *The Best and the Brightest*, Bundy "was the brightest star in that glittering constellation around the President." After Kennedy's assassination, he stayed on as the top foreign policy adviser to President Johnson as the U.S. stake in Vietnam grew ever larger.

By all reports, Bundy was neither a notable hawk nor a dove on Vietnam until relatively late in the game. Halberstam writes: "As the debate on bombing and escalation raged, he had been more of an adjudicator, trying to keep himself out of it to a large degree, trying to present to the President as honestly and coldly as he could the various alternatives and possibilities." But in February 1965, following a policy review visit to South Vietnam that included Pleiku, where a Communist mortar attack had just killed eight American soldiers, Bundy wrote a fateful memorandum recommending a policy of sustained and escalating military reprisal that, in essence, guided both the Johnson and Nixon administrations. The key sentences concluded that a "policy of graduated and continuing reprisal…is the most promising course available…." The memorandum recognized that: "We cannot assert that a policy of sustained reprisal will succeed in changing the course of the contest in Vietnam. It may fail and we cannot estimate the odds of success with any accuracy…What we can say is that even if it fails, the policy will be worth it. At a minimum it will damp down the charge that we did not do all that we could have done, and this charge will be important in many countries, including our own. Beyond that, a reprisal policy—to the extent that it demonstrates U.S. willingness to employ this new norm in counterinsurgency—will set a higher price for the future upon all adventures of guerrilla warfare, and it should therefore somewhat increase our ability to deter such adventures. We must recognize, however, that the ability will be gravely weakened if there is failure for any reason in Vietnam." The subject of Vietnam was to haunt the rest of Bundy's career.

For the foundation staff, the winter of 1965–66 was like Beckett's *Waiting for Godot*—a lot of standing around and asking from time to time: "Is he coming? What's to be done?" When Bundy did arrive, after a short but decent interval he made it clear he wanted a different foundation in both program direction and top management staff. The most surprising change was the departure of Paul Ylvisaker, the charismatic leader of the "Gray Areas" program, who was eventually replaced by Mitchell "Mike" Sviridoff, the quondam union boss who had attracted national attention through his leadership of the foundation-funded "Gray Areas" project in New Haven.

Bundy lost no time in staking out a new and much more courageous policy stance on the foundation's approach to problems of black Americans, specifically removing its restriction on grants to predominantly black civil rights organizations. In 1996, the foundation committed $1 million to the NAACP Legal Defense and Educational Fund to help it create a national office for the rights of the poor, the first of many such grants to comparable organizations for civil rights purposes, and during his presidency Bundy consistently sought imaginative, new ways to tackle the problems of American minorities. Writing in the foundation's annual report for 1965, Bundy said:

> The most deep-seated and destructive of all the causes of the Negro problem is still the prejudice of the white man...Prejudice must be overcome...Men *are* brothers, with all that brotherhood implies in terms of rights and claims. And if I do not feel that way, then I am guilty of an offense against the fundamental principles of the open society; in this sense there is no right to prejudice...It seems to me the plainest of facts that the destiny of the Negro in America is to be both Negro and American, and that as he makes progress he is likely to do what the rest of us do: he will take pride in his particular group at the same time that he insists on full membership in the society as a whole...Our society is going to solve this problem. The white man will outgrow his prejudices and the Negro will strengthen both his sense of identity and his membership in the whole of society.

Under Bundy's presidency, Ford invented the "program-related investment" concept, in which funds from a foundation's investment portfolio can be deployed as loans or investments to support programmatic charitable purposes, and the first of these investments and loans went to support inner-city enterprises. In the Bundy period, Ford also established, under Sviridoff's leadership, the Local Initiative Services Corporation, possibly the most consistently innovative and useful national community development instrument on the scene over the past several decades.

In management terms, from my strictly personal and parochial point of view, Bundy's most important decision was to abolish the Office of Policy and Planning, on which the paint was barely dry. Publicly, Bundy said he preferred that policy, planning, and operations be united in the structure of each of the foundation's major programs, with himself as the overall arbitrator. Privately, he would suggest that he had seen firsthand the bad consequences of separating operations from policy and planning—as, for example, in the Bay of Pigs fiasco. Those of us who worked in the policy office were free to seek employment elsewhere, in the foundation or outside. Lowry would remain as vice president of the Arts and Humanities, although his relationship with Bundy was never easy. Mac Moos moved west to become president of the University of Minnesota. Bill Watts left, eventually to join Henry Kissinger's staff in Washington. David Bell, the new executive vice president in charge of international activities, asked me to join the Asia program staff as its deputy director. I had established a cordial relationship with George Gant, the director of the Asia program, largest and oldest of the foundation's overseas operations, during my visits to India and other Asian offices—doubtless in part because George knew I shared his skepticism about the big Delhi office operation.

Before I could move into this great new job (I felt like I was receiving the gift of half of the world), Bundy asked me to help him carry out a special assignment where he thought my recent Soviet experience and Russian-language capabilities would be useful. This was to undertake staff work on an imaginative proposal in "bridge building" to the Soviet Union recently floated in President Johnson's White House, which Johnson had asked Bundy to explore in his new incarnation at Ford. The idea was to create an international center where scientists, thinkers, and managers from advanced countries with similar problems cutting across ideological and political concerns—transportation, energy, and other such public management problems, environmental questions, and educational and social issues—could compare notes and work together to understand how to employ productively the intellectual and technological power being generated by the advances in computer technology and the new discipline of systems analysis. A number of bilateral and multilateral meeting fora (the so-called Pugwash conferences were an example) dotted the Cold War landscape, where Western nongovernmental scientists and leaders met occasionally with Soviet counterparts. But no permanent center existed where scientists and thinkers from the advanced nations of the West and the Soviet Union could sit down for quiet, continuing work on common problems. It was assumed that the Soviets, hungry to glean as much as possible about Western, and particularly U.S., computer technology and systems analysis, might welcome the opportunity to join in developing such an institution. This could be done, it was thought, without compromising national or corporate security in the West. The result might be a small, new bridge across the frozen gulf of the Cold War.

Using the clout of the Bundy name to open doors in foreign ministries and scientific institutions, I went to Europe for three weeks to present the idea to senior level officials and scientists. The reactions I brought back ranged from bemusement (the Italians), skepticism (the French), to moderate enthusiasm and interest (the British and the Germans). In Washington, the U.S. government was, of course, assumed to be on board, but the question was what kind of non-governmental organization might represent the United States in such a center—and who would run it. As concerned Soviet participation, it was decided it was necessary to get the more important Western European countries lined up before making a high-level approach to the Soviets.

As this ad hoc assignment began to stretch out, George Gant, my new boss in the Asia program, began to press to have me pick up my new duties, which I was anxious to do, and Bundy obliged by assigning another staff member to carry on constructing bridges. I made one more trip to accompany Mac Bundy and Carl Kaysen, Bundy's former deputy on the National Security staff and a distinguished Harvard mathematician and economist, to Moscow for discussions with the Soviet Academy of Science and its premier computer science institute. As predicted, the Soviets were titillated by the prospect of access to American and Western systems thinking and information technology, although with classic Soviet bombast they clothed their expression of interest with assurances that Soviet technology and systems thinking were really the most advanced in the world. The Soviet Academy of Science became one of the founding members. Today, the International Institute of Applied Systems Research, housed in an old palace in Laxenburg, Austria, carries out research and educational programs in the fields of energy and technology, environment and natural resources, and population and society. It has sixteen institutional members, typically national-level scientific institutions, from Russia, the United States, China, most of the Eastern European nations, Kazakhstan, and Egypt. The U.S. member is the American Academy of Arts and Sciences in Boston.

In the midst of the hullabaloo at the foundation, Charlotte, my unflappable wife, and I thought our lives in Grandview-on-Hudson could hardly be more rewarding—although I would have to be absent a great deal while on the road in

Asia. My best friend in the carpool, Jack Keil, a creative and amusing advertising executive, whose two sons became lifelong friends of my youngest son, Peter, complained that his travel schedule consisted of endless trips to Cincinnati, where he ran the Proctor & Gamble account for his firm, while I was always flying off to or arriving from Singapore or Bangkok or Kathmandu—with a stopover in Rome or Paris. Our children seemed to be successfully surviving—so we thought—the transition from Moscow Public School Sixty-Nine into the local Rockland County school system. John, the oldest, excelled academically and in his test scores, and was about to go off to the California Institute of Technology; Kathleen was not far behind in departing for Bennington, which turned out to be not a wise choice. From cocktail party and PTA conversations, we knew teenage drinking and drugs were around. Like most parents, we thought our children immune.

One chilly, clear early winter night, closing up the downstairs part of our big old house, I heard first laughter and then a faint but distinct cry of "Help, help" coming up from the river immediately across the road below. I ran down to our dock, heard one more shout of distress as I peered out across the moonlit black expanse of the Hudson, and then all was silent except the sound of the water. I saw nothing but the moonlight. I ran to the town office building a few hundred yards upriver, where our Grandview town cop lived and worked, roused him, and helped him get started in putting a search boat in the water. The next morning, two overturned canoes and the bodies of two young high school students, both of them acquaintances of our kids, were found a few miles downstream. It was assumed, although never known and possibly unjustly, that they had gone out pot smoking on a moonlight adventure. Over the next few years, all three of our children went off to good colleges and promptly dropped out. They finally survived the sixties, and today all three are productive citizens—one a computer programmer, one an artist and teacher, the third a commercial fishing and ferryboat captain. They were lucky: the sixties were a tough time to be a teenager in the United States, and a lot didn't survive, or survived with severe psychic and physical damage—both those who fought in Vietnam and those who stayed at home.

Our social life in Grandview, a tiny village on the Hudson below Nyack where the river expands into the broad Tappan Zee, mostly revolved around friends I made in the carpool that drove across the Tappan Zee bridge every weekday morning to catch the 7:58 AM express commuter train to Manhattan. Grandview was a beautiful and desirable place to live and not bad as a commute, although in winter weather the bridge offered challenges. The village population of a few hundred souls included advertising executives, commercial artists, a few financial executives, a couple of psychiatrists, an airline pilot, and a few working-class families left over from the prewar period. Unlike the wealthy New York and Connecticut counties and the Hudson River commuting towns to the east—places like Tarrytown, where the Rockefeller family lived, Greenwich, and Westport—we had neither stockbrokers nor old family wealth. Almost everyone drank too much. And as the years went by, we all found out that alcohol and drugs rocked the lives of many of our children as they entered their teens and adulthood.

When we could find time away from work and family responsibilities, Charlotte and I feasted on the art and music of the great museums and concert halls (in the early 1960s, the Metropolitan Opera was still in its old building at Thirty-ninth and Broadway, and Lincoln Center was just beginning to rise on the Upper West Side of Broadway and opened its doors in 1966). We dined often with Lincoln Kirstein and his wife, Fidelma, in their town house in the East Twenties and would then career off in a taxi to the ballet, arriving, stuffed with roast beef or lamb and fortified with gin and good wine, just before the curtain rose. Kirstein and I lunched regularly at the Hotel Gotham off Fifth Avenue. Over the coming decades as I traveled and lived in Asia and studied the great Asian philosophies and cultures, he would probe my thinking about Asia, and we would argue and speculate about how the world could produce such marvels and devils. Kirstein had visited India twice and hated it. For me, India epitomized the dilemma of an Asia seeking to retain the greatness and the beauties of its past cultural achievements while simultaneously striving to modernize. Kirstein said simply, "I thought India was the closest thing to hell I have ever seen on earth."

10

Half of Mankind

At mid-twentieth century, the peoples of Asia, whose lives and ways for the next quarter century were to intertwine with and greatly enrich my own, represented half of mankind. (They still do: the numbers today are vastly larger; the proportion is roughly the same.) On the whole, we knew surprisingly little about them. We had defeated imperial Japan in a bitter war and, to our great credit, used our occupation regime to begin to help establish a successful, democratic state. But Japan remained a mystery for most Americans—and still does. In China, we watched helplessly as the corrupt Nationalist government of Chiang Kai-shek collapsed and the Communists took power after World War II. Secretary of State John Foster Dulles, cowering before Senator Joe McCarthy's wrath, took revenge by shooting the messengers who predicted the Nationalist debacle, firing and ruining the lives of the brilliant young China experts who had served us so well as diplomats in China before the fall. Until the end of the Second World War, our closest connection to Asia was the Philippines, America's modest, almost forgotten, and ultimately not very successful experiment in imperialism. (Professor Eric Rauch, writing in the *Financial Times* in March 2003, recalls that in 1898 when we took Cuba and the Philippines away from the collapsing Spanish empire we referred to this as "liberation." Foreshadowing a much later American president pondering an invasion and "liberation" of Iraq, Rauch quotes President William McKinley as saying, "I am not ashamed to tell you that I went down on my knees and prayed to almighty God for light and guidance." After hearing God's guidance, McKinley decided that "there was nothing left for us to do but to take them all, and to educate the Filipinos, and uplift and civilize and Christianize them, and by God's grace do the very best we could by them as our fellow men for whom Christ also died."). There was unquestionably a strong Christian impulse guiding many of the most benevolent and useful American activities in Asia. The most notable of these were the schools, colleges and hospitals founded by American missionaries, joined subsequently by the Rockefeller Foundation, in China, India and elsewhere in Asia starting in the early twentieth century.

Most Americans still claimed a European ancestry (although blacks were beginning to take open pride in their African roots). As an ethnic group, Asians represented only an infinitesimal percentage of the American population in 1945 (today they are more than 4 percent). In those post-World War II days, if one had suggested that fifty years later most of the fine young classical violinists in the United States would be of Asian origin (as contrasted to Russian Jewish origin)—*and* that the majority of these would be female—or that in New York the corner delis would usually be run by Koreans, or that a disproportionately high percentage of the finest university science and engineering graduate students would stem from Asian backgrounds, he would have been greeted with derision. The greatest World War I and II battlegrounds were in Europe, not Asia. We traded mostly with Europe, not Asia. A small war in Korea could come and go bloodily and almost stealthily in the 1950s, leaving hardly a trace in our national memory. The most striking testimonial to our ignorance of Asia was America's long, always flawed, dishonestly managed, and disastrous war in Vietnam, based from the start on misconceptions about the national and cultural histories and characters of the Vietnamese and the Chinese.

For centuries, most of Asia had belonged to the Europeans (with the exception of the Philippines, where, of course, we viewed the long American period of occupation as unselfish and educational as contrasted to the behavior of the grasping European imperialists). In the nineteenth century, we had cracked open the great abalone shell of Japan with Commodore Perry's "black ships," but for most purposes that shell closed again, and Japan remained a sleeping giant for many years. We joined the Europeans in competing for the benefits of the China trade. But the prize properties were exclusively European. The British ran a splendidly profitable enterprise in India, where the Indian maharajas entertained superlatively and the tiger shooting was unequalled, sold opium in China out of Hong Kong, and ruled the roost in Sri Lanka. The Dutch milked their big, rich colonial holding in Indonesia, treating their natives much more roughly than the British treated *their* coolies (there were, for example, virtually no Indonesian university graduates when Indonesia became independent, whereas in India a few, educated, upper-caste Indians actually began serving together with Englishmen in the elite civil service in the 1930s). The French ruled Indochina with Napoleonic law and bourgeois greed, leaving behind a tradition of sexual liaisons and good French cuisine, and not much else. Only Japan, the warrior nation, remained truly independent throughout the great wave of European colonialism in Asia, and that was possible only through its policy of rigorous, bristly isolation. When, having bested the Russian empire in battle in the early part of the century, Japan burst out of its doors to establish its suzerainty over first Korea and then much of China and ultimately to invade and occupy Southeast Asia, defeating and humiliating the English, the Dutch and the French, it shook the foundations of colonial rule throughout Asia. For the first time in modern history, an Asian nation had rubbed European noses in the dirt. Most Asians hated the Japanese for their cruelties and arrogance, but Japan's military success speeded and ensured the collapse of colonialism.

The dominant factor in the development of American relations with the new, independent Asia was the Cold War. U.S. foreign policy and governmental development assistance were openly designed and justified to keep Asia from going Communist. In spite of growing evidence to the contrary, for many years most Americans assumed—and it was certainly U.S. policy—that Soviet Russia and Red China marched in lockstep, and that their goal was the world. Every nation must be regarded as a potential domino. Although the Ford Foundation was a privately managed, privately funded organization, its board of trustees came straight out of the upper ranks of the American establishment (a sociological profile that slowly began to diversify in McGeorge Bundy's presidency and, in later years, became radically different). As a result, the foundation's Asia program, while neither planned with nor coordinated with U.S. government priorities and programs, aimed to help Asian societies develop modern democratic, governmental, and economic systems, both because that seemed to us demonstrably the right way to run things, and because we wanted to strengthen them against the temptations and subversions emanating from the Communist world conspiracy. There were, in fact, a lot of conspiracies around, Communist and otherwise, including American, real and imagined.

In addition to the powerful, and ultimately successful, Communist/Nationalist struggle against the French, and then the Americans, in Indochina, a now long-forgotten and ultimately unsuccessful jungle insurgency pitted mostly indigenous Chinese Malays against the British in Malaya in the post-World War II years. The so-called Huk rebellion in the Philippines and the rise of the Communists as a powerful threat in the strategically important nation of Indonesia under the Sukarno presidency were matters of great concern in Washington. By the mid-1950s, the Indonesian Communist Party numbered in the millions, and Sukarno, who had been the hero of the independence movement, was openly sympathetic to Mao Tse-tung's Communist China. The CIA supported an unsuccessful rebellion against Sukarno in 1958. In the still murky events of the fall of 1965, with increasing unrest in the countryside, a group of junior officers and soldiers, whose political loyalties remain unclear to this day, murdered six Indonesian army generals considered to be anti-Communist but loyal to Sukarno. General Suharto rallied the Army to defeat the plot and rapidly moved to assume power. Twenty-five years later, former State Department and CIA officers acknowledged that the U.S. embassy provided the Indonesian army leadership with Indonesian Communist Party membership lists. More than a hundred thousand suspected Communists were executed in the early months of the Suharto government and even larger numbers imprisoned. The atmosphere surrounding these events is vividly depicted in the film *The Year of Living Dangerously*, and the fine Indonesian writer Pramoedya Ananta Toer wrote a gripping account of his internal exile, imprisonment, and near starvation on a bleak island in the archipelago. When I first visited Indonesia in 1967, the country still lived on the rough edge of fear and real hardship. Power and transportation were very shaky in the capital, Jakarta; hard-faced soldiers barricaded and controlled the highways. On a visit to Sumatra, passing through a coastal town that still smelled of smoke and death, the Indonesian navy lieutenant who served as the town's mayor boasted to me that he had dealt firmly with the Chinese, whose quarter had been burned out and looted because of their suspected harboring of Communists—and also, of course, because of Malay antagonism to the overseas Chinese population regardless of their Indonesian citizenship. "We know how to handle these people," he said.

No really serviceable, indigenous models existed for a modern Asian nation state. India, China, and Indonesia had once been ruled by maharajas, sultans, and emperors. Their day in the sun had long since passed, although it is striking to note that all the leaders of the Asian independence movements were children of local elites. Jawaharlal Nehru's father, Motilal, was a wealthy, respected lawyer of the Brahmin caste, who threw his prestige behind the Indian independence movement at an early date. Mahatma Gandhi, a truly iconoclastic figure, despite his homespun loincloth and homemade sandals, was the son of a minor court functionary in a princely state in West India and trained in law in London. Mohammed Ali Jinnah, Nehru's great adversary in arguing the cause of the Muslims of India, who eventually took most of India's Muslims into a separate state of Pakistan, was a successful, London-trained lawyer from a prosperous family in Bombay. Indonesia's Sukarno was a scion of the Javanese aristocracy. Lee Kuan Yew, whose willpower and vision converted tiny Singapore into a bustling, prosperous city-state with an influence far surpassing its size, was born into a well-to-do Chinese family, graduated from the elite Raffles College, and read law at

Cambridge. The father of Malaysian independence, Tunku Abdul Rahman, was a sultan. Ho Chi Minh's father was a functionary in the court of the puppet Vietnamese emperor, and as a young man Ho went off to France as a worker to see what liberty, equality, and fraternity were all about—and became a Marxist.

When it came to nation building, while paying lip service to local traditions and institutions, with the exception of Gandhi who really believed in and wanted to build on them, the new leaders looked outside for successful models of how to build a modern state (although in the last analysis, the ability of the new Asian states to adapt and use traditional local patterns of culture and life proved to be the key to their success or failure). Studying the post-World War II world for guidance, the new Asian leaders found roughly three functioning models of how to organize and manage societies. With the fall of Germany, Italy, and Japan, fascism had, of course, been cast on the garbage heap of history. The three obvious models were capitalist democracy, as practiced by the enormously powerful United States; Communism, exemplified in the equally powerful Soviet Union and the newly victorious Communists in China; and the democratic socialism arising in Western Europe, basically another version of capitalist democracy which, its adherents claimed, struck the proper balance between social justice and economic and political freedoms.

Each model offered attractions and disadvantages. The United States was attractive for its dynamism, openness, and the sheer power of its privately driven economy. But the Asian founding fathers feared the potential political power of big business (in every Asian culture, whether it had a formal caste system or not, the mandarin bureaucrats, the priests, and the warriors outranked the merchant class). The business magnate as national hero was an exclusively American phenomenon. The Soviet Union and the new Red China represented desirable models to many because of their success in organizing large, backward, primarily peasant societies—precisely the challenge faced by the new Asia—and molding them into formidable world powers (even though achieving this in the Communist examples had required violent and bloody means). Throughout Asia, the locally organized Communist parties, supported originally by the Soviet Union (and, at a later date, with competing parties supported by both the Soviets and Chinese), sought supreme power for themselves. But none of the new Asian nations embraced the Communist route except Vietnam, and even there Ho Chi Minh owed his success primarily to his role as leader of the nationalist struggle for independence against first the French, and then the Americans. In the event, the most widely adopted—and over the long term most damaging—feature of the Communist model picked up by many of the new nations of Asia was the notion of centralized state control of economic planning and development and reliance on state enterprises for basic industrial production. The European model of democratic socialism was also attractive in a rather fuzzy way: it held out the promises of political democracy, social justice, and state planning all at the same time. Aspects of socialism became thus incorporated in national political rhetoric and doctrine throughout Asia, but socialist parties as such never prospered.

The first nation-building question for the new Asian leaders was: "Who are we?" Each of the new, independent states encompassed a bewildering mosaic of minority populations, multiple languages, religions, race, cultural patterns, eating habits, sexual styles, and different histories affecting every aspect of social, political, and economic behavior. For ten centuries, as an example, the Indian subcontinent had been torn apart by the struggle of the two most antithetical of the world's great religions, Hinduism and Islam. Diversity was everywhere: the Hindi language of the Hindus versus the Urdu preference of the Muslims; the Hindi and Punjabi-speaking wheat eaters of northern India, and the Tamil and Malayalam speaking rice eaters of the south, all entwined in a caste system that seemed impervious to change. In Southeast Asia, it was the local Chinese traders and merchants against the Malay-origin populations of the Malaysian peninsula and Indonesia. Even in the smaller states like Sri Lanka, the Buddhist Sinhalese and the Hindu Tamil minority nourished their historic enmity. In the tiniest of all, the Singaporean city-state, a Chinese majority dominated Malay and Indian minority populations. The answer to the question of "who we are" could not be sought in a common history because history disunited, rather than laying the base for a new polity. The European colonizers had used disunity for their own purposes. In Southeast Asia, the Malay majorities believed that the British and the Dutch rulers deliberately favored the local overseas Chinese populations in running the colonial civil services and financial institutions in order to keep the Malays in a subordinate position. In Sri Lanka, the struggle for power between the Sinhalese Buddhist majority and the Tamil Hindu minority, which enjoyed a favored position under the British colonial administrations, eventually erupted into a viciously cruel civil war, with the Tamil revolutionaries, alleging anti-Tamil discrimination, demanding *de facto* independence in a Tamil region on the island. In India, the British favored the northern "martial races"—the Punjabis, Sikhs, and Rajputs—as soldiers in their colonial army, while Brahmin and warrior caste families dominated the civil services.

In addition to the theoretical and practical questions of writing constitutions, creating and staffing political institutions, and deciding on national languages, a host of immediate challenges in basic human activities had to be dealt with. In the biggest of the new Asian nations—India, Pakistan, Indonesia, and China (although for many years we knew very little about what was going on inside Red China)—growing enough wheat and rice to feed the already large, rapidly increasing populations was an immediate challenge (annual growth rates reached up to 2.5 percent). Public health facilities were scarce, and their personnel ill trained. Extending access to education to the masses and establishing modern educational institutions in science and technology to support industry (and the military power all Asian leaders wanted to build) required immediate attention. And the nature of the relationship between the new civilian leaders and the new, indigenous military leaders of independent Asia, which was to prove a critical weakness in Pakistan and Indonesia, had to be defined.

The Ford Foundation overseas development programs in South and Southeast Asia, whose management I inherited from George Gant, were the oldest and largest of the foundation's overseas ventures. Within a year of my moving into the Asia program, Gant went off to open a regional office for Southeast Asia in Bangkok, responsible for increasing and coordinating grant-making in Thailand, the Philippines, Malaysia and Singapore. While a number of significant common threads ran throughout the Asia programs, decentralization ruled the roost in the international work of the foundation every whit as much as it did in the domestic programs, and the background, training, and judgments of the Ford representative on the ground usually carried the day in program decisions. The representatives were a capable, strong-headed, and hardworking crew, who came to their Asian avatars from a variety of backgrounds. Gant was a public management specialist, a one-time director of personnel for the TVA. Frank Miller, the representative in Jakarta both before and after the bloody days of the risings against Sukarno, was a lawyer steeped in the Indonesian language and culture. His replacement, Jack Bresnan, a former journalist, Foreign Service officer, and a fluent Bahasa Indonesian speaker, was to become one of America's leading experts on Indonesia. In Pakistan, Haldore Hanson, who together with the Nobel-prize winning scientist Norman Borlaug launched the green revolution in wheat by smuggling in bags full of the new high-yielding varieties and passing them out to farmers, had started as a journalist and foreign correspondent. In India, Ensminger, the most senior and powerful of the representatives, was an agricultural sociologist. As concerned their programs, at one time or another, Ensminger in his long career had tried virtually everything (when I took over the management of the Asia program, he had been in India for fifteen years). Other programs were smaller and more concentrated.

Except in Singapore, which had no agriculture except for a few truck farms, each country or regional office supported programs in agriculture and food production. Education, broadly defined, was a common, major element, although not a single office undertook a significant commitment to mass education, this being considered as simply too large a bite for even the world's richest foundation to chew and digest. The Ford programs became leaders in funding education and research related to language development (of both English and regional languages), a critical political and economic factor in building these new nation states. The foundation was a pioneer in management education, both business and public. It supported elite civil service training programs throughout Asia. Its projects in economics training and research identified and helped train many of Asia's best economists who became responsible for economic policy over the generations to come, and the foundation was the first, major financier of economic policy and planning advisory groups to Asian governments—a ticklish enterprise, as it turned out. It was a major outside sponsor of the development of modern social sciences in the Asian higher education systems, and it supported legal reforms and the development of modern law schools, where research was actually carried out and taught. The foundation helped set up graduate programs and institutes of science and technology. It was the first major outside actor in population and family planning programs in Asia, responding to the concerns of national and community leaders that the then-existent annual population growth rates of 2.5 percent or higher would double the already large populations in a quarter of a century, making real *per capita* economic growth virtually impossible to achieve.

In the sweeping Bundy reorganization of the foundation that took place starting in the late 1960s, I also took over management responsibility for the Asian area studies programs originally funded by a separate office called International Training and Research, plus some scattered activities in Japan and Korea funded by an International Affairs office. The area studies program, which put Ford's funding muscle to work to build on earlier grants by the Carnegie and Rockefeller foundations, had trained a new generation of American scholars and researchers in Asian politics, economics, and the social sciences and humanities, covering all of Asia and including as subjects of study the Northeast Asian societies—China, Vietnam, Japan, and Korea—that, for a variety of reasons, had not been touched by the early "overseas development" programs, which focused on South and Southeast Asia. Throughout the 1960s, 1970s, and 1980s, most of the best American scholars on Asia learned their trade at Ford Foundation-funded area institutes at universities or through the important Foreign Affairs fellowship program. (In the early 1970s, at the height of the anti-Vietnam War protests, invited to give a presentation on foundation plans for further support for scholarly activities at the annual meeting of the Association of Asian Studies, I found myself being loudly and angrily abused by a claque of protestors from the so-called Committee of Concerned Asian Scholars, who disagreed with both U.S. policy on Vietnam—which Ford had deliberately steered clear of—and the foundation's position as what they called "the CIA of the establishment." When the shouting died down briefly, I said, I thought rather mildly under the circumstances, that neither I nor the Ford Foundation had anything to do with the CIA. To demonstrate that our support for scholarly research was broadly based, I suggested that anyone in the room who had not received Ford Foundation grant or fellowship assistance in one form or another should raise his or her hand. Not a single hand was raised. John King Fairbank, the country's leading authority on China, was the only scholar to stand up and come to the public defense of the foundation.)

This amalgamation of all the foundation's Asian interests took place primarily for management reasons: to reduce the number of program directors reporting to top management and to find the most logical shelters for those important pieces of prior programs that had previously rated separate office categories. When accomplished, it offered starkly a fundamental paradox of the American (and Western) approach to development assistance. To illustrate: the agricultural scientists, population experts, and management professors who staffed the West's projects in overseas development in post World War II Asia (and elsewhere) were highly trained in their disciplines. They were not, however, with rare exceptions, trained in Asian history or cultures. They communicated in English and typically did not speak an Asian language. At the opposite side of the paradox were those scholars steeped in Asian languages, cultures, and history who, again with the rarest of exceptions, virtually never participated in the technical work of development—not even in such obvious topics as university development. The paradox was by no means peculiar to Ford. U.S. government programs in development displayed the same typology, as did European agencies and the powerful World Bank. The great Western universities were themselves compartmentalized. I could visit Cornell University, for example, to talk one day with a world-class agricultural scientist about rice research projects on the ground in the Philippines or the particular problems of small cultivators in India and on the next with a sociologist or anthropologist about the state of research and graduate student training in the regional institute where he carried out his specialized studies. The two worked on opposite sides of the campus, got their funding through different pipelines (in Ford's case, this changed when we brought all Asian interests under one programmatic roof, but U.S. federal funding continued the old pattern), and rarely, if ever, talked with each other. The U.S. Agency for International Development, I was to discover in a later assignment, had once made a deliberate effort to incorporate area expertise into its regional bureaus by employing sociologists, economists, and political scientists with relevant language and area skills as advisers to the managerial and technical staffs. They were generally ignored, and the effort lapsed.

This was (and remains) a great shame. The structure of neither development agencies nor universities has changed much, even though the best of social scientists trained in a particular country's language and culture are better able than almost anyone to understand and, if they have common sense and a modicum of tact, to point out flaws and weak points in development strategies. I once interviewed a young woman recommended to me in New York for possible foundation employment. She had studied anthropology and then law at Harvard and had lived in and written a PhD thesis on Iran, which I asked to see and read to get a sense of her thinking and style. Her topic was the impact of the westernizing economic reforms of the shah of Iran (then still in power) on the conservative peasantry and the *bazaris*, the powerful, traditional urban merchant class. Her conclusion was that both groups essentially resented and rejected the reforms, and that if the shah were to continue to push in these directions he faced the danger of revolt. Which is, of course, exactly what happened. (She never came to work for us but did join the staff for some years at the International Rice Research Institute in the Philippines, where she drove the agricultural scientists up the wall by telling them what the farmers really thought about their new, high-yielding varieties, and where, after her departure, the position was eliminated.)

In the early 1970s, when I lived in Bangkok and managed the foundation's regional Southeast Asia program, we decided to open a very small office in Vietnam (where the foundation had previously not operated, because the development landscape was dominated by extremely large U.S. government development assistance, intelligence, and military programs) to see if the foundation could accomplish some useful small-scale things like helping a few Vietnamese specialists in traditional culture to survive and be productive. We also wanted to be on the ground to see if we could be of help when the war finally ended (our small office was forced to close down when the Communists took Saigon in 1975, and it was not until 1996 that the foundation finally opened a grant-making office in Hanoi for unified Vietnam). One of our consultants was a young American anthropologist, who had lived and traveled much in the villages, spoke fluent Vietnamese (as did our office director, Charles Benoit, a scholar of Vietnamese classical poetry with both fluent Vietnamese and Mandarin Chinese), and had a good political head as well. When the Communists began to take over the mountain towns in 1974, the conventional American wisdom held that this was a problem, but that there were still a lot of fine fighting units in the South Vietnamese army, and they would stand and fight as the Communists moved from the hills down toward the plain and Saigon. Our anthropologist said: "The soldiers won't fight. They are sick to death of the corruption and brutality of the officer corps. The Communists will cut through them like a knife through butter." Within three months, the Communists took Saigon.

Indeed, the kind of intellectual commitment to understand national culture and social history that characterizes anthropology and the best of serious journalism is essential to development work. One of the most widespread efforts in agricultural development in postwar Asia, for example, was to replicate the model of the American agricultural university and agricultural scientific institutes in Asian circumstances, and to combine, as had been done so successfully in the United States, the scientific research work of professors with field-level adoption of new technologies on the farm through agricultural extension services. In many cases, this simply didn't work. The American model assumed a constant two-way flow of information, with professors spending a lot of time with farmers, learning from farmers' practices in the field, and designing their research programs with farmers' problems in mind. In much of Asia, professors are direct heirs of the Hindu Brahmin tradition in which the high-caste priest imparts knowledge to the working, ignorant lower castes and classes. Most farmers are small and of low—or at the most—middle caste and economic status. The continuing information loop between scientist and farmer that made the American model productive was simply not the way things were traditionally done in Asia, and the model itself was not enough to break down traditional patterns that were imbibed with the mother's milk of the actors involved. Similarly, many of the educational reforms in Asia funded by foreign agencies ran aground on the reefs of caste, ethnic, and language differences, leading one perceptive Indian scholar, Andre Beteille, to write a book called *The Indianization of the University* about how caste was ruining the western-style, post-independence Indian universities. The academic standards first established by the British and encouraged by post-independence American donors like the Ford Foundation began to slide as administrators and professors resorted to caste and religion in making new faculty appointments.

I managed this newly amalgamated Asia program in New York from 1967 to 1973, working with an extremely able staff that possessed a lot of on-the-ground experience, before moving out to Asia as a representative for another nine years, first in Southeast Asia and then in the Indian subcontinent. As I came to know Asia from this unique standpoint, I found little to fault in the foundation's early program decisions. Some had been very perceptive.

An example was the foundation's early support for research and training in critical national language problems as well as the English language, which was universally expected to be the tongue of international discourse for the new Asia. The decisions that the new elites made about language bore far-reaching consequences for building their new nations. This was where the new leaders first had to face the question of "who we are." In Indonesia, for example, long before independence, language was a major concern of the small group of patriots who met clandestinely to discuss how, when they sent the Dutch packing, to turn this vast array of islands, spectacularly diverse in ethnicity and languages, into a coherent nation. They reached the radical and politically astute decision that the national language could not be Javanese, the tongue of the historically dominant Javanese elites and the great Javanese sultans, but should be a more accessible, related language with no resentments trailing from the past. They chose Bahasa Indonesian, which essentially is the Malay idiom as spoken in Sumatra (and Indonesia's neighbor, Malaysia), as the new official idiom. English would be the major backup language, with Dutch disappearing as the older generation passed away (as Spanish did in the Philippines). In India, strong, anti-English, nationalistic pressures existed to install Hindi as the national language, but this would be resisted by the non-Hindi speaking mass of southerners. The Indian National Congress party finally and wisely established a policy of basic education in the regional language, with additional facilities for learning Hindi in the south (and a southern Indian language in the North), and *de facto* accepted that for many purposes English would continue to be the lingua franca the elites would use. I first visited Madras, the Tamil capital in the south, at a time when the Tamils still feared the imposition of Hindi. I drove into town passing mile after mile of billboards with slogans painted in red in English: "Out, Hindi dogs!" to enter a city still tense from language riots. The Tamil speakers wanted as little to do with Hindi as possible and for English to be left alone so that their most important weapon on the economic playing field—their fluency in English—would be level or better. In addition, of course, Tamils noted that their language had a millennia-long history of great poetry and grammar, far more impressive than that of Hindi. Two of the most distinguished language research institutes in India, the

Central Institute of English and the Central Institute of Indian languages, were launched with Ford support, and the foundation supported research and training in both Asian languages and English throughout the continent. In Japan, where the foundation was still working in English language training, even in the 1960s, two decades after the end of the war, it was difficult to find enough competent translators to handle a meeting of Japanese and English speakers. Each side of the table would laugh as its speaker told a joke. The other side would sit stony faced because, with rare exceptions, the interpreter had completely missed the point of the joke.

A second set of foundation innovations established what became an important part of today's Asian resources for dealing with the modern economic and political world. Although pre-modern Asian cultures produced great indigenous trading and merchant houses—the overseas Chinese settlers in Southeast Asia with family ties throughout southern China, and the family-run Parsi and Gujerati merchant caste banking, trading, and textile manufacturing houses in India— with the single exception of Japan, Asia was unprepared to enter the world of modern enterprise management. Working with Asian business leaders (people like the textile magnate and patron of the arts, Vikhram Sarabhai of Ahmedabad in India), the foundation helped to create a network of modern management education institutions that, over the years, became as prestigious and successful as their foreign partners, chief of whom were the Harvard Business School and the Sloan Institute of Management at MIT, which helped to design their programs and to train their staffs. The Indian School of Management at Ahmedabad and the Asian Institute of Management in Manila themselves are case studies of the elements that are required for successful development. These included a local will to innovate, which required both government and private sector decisions regarding funding and institutional management (in India, a hidebound University Grants Commission, inherited from the old British model, controlled all higher education and was inalterably opposed to changing the existing patterns of university-level education, so the new management schools were created outside its jurisdiction); a commitment to "technology transfer" in terms of a foreign model that was being adapted, and "institution building," which required a long (ten-year-plus) horizon for support from the funding agencies, both domestic and foreign, in this case Ford. The foundation also supported the innovations in graduate-level science and technology education in such places as the Indian Institute of Technology at Kharagpur and advanced engineering faculties in other countries that foreshadowed the development in Asia of a now-flourishing economic growth sector in computer technology and software writing.

The foundation's early encouragement of graduate-level economics training produced both a number of outstanding Asian economists, whose work as scholars and government officials became essential in modernizing the Asian economies, and a number of indigenous research institutes whose work remains central in Asian economic thought today. In Indonesia, for example, a small group of indigenous economists (headed by Widjojosastro, collectively known as the Berkeley "mafia" because they did their graduate work at the University of California), brought order and economic progress to Indonesia out of the mess left after the bloody events of 1965, which unseated Sukarno and brought General Suharto to power the following year. (In spite of the fact that Suharto's three-decade-long rule ultimately turned into a deeply troubling case in the corruption of power and the ruinous consequences of military politicians, in the early years of his rule his policies in economic reform and family planning, two essential elements in Indonesian growth, were a model of intelligent decision-making. He relied on the Berkeley-trained economists to establish sensible development policies. In the population and health field, he recognized that the only way family planning programs could succeed in slowing the rapid growth of the huge Indonesian population was by persuading the village-level power structure, including both the headmen and leading women, that population limitation was in their interests. The Indonesian program became a model of how to handle this sensitive topic: traditional Indonesian cultures gave women a very considerable role in village life, and most Indonesian women wanted a greater say in how many children they should have. But as the years went by, Suharto came to regard himself as indispensable, as indeed he was for his greedy family members, notably his wife and sons. The scale of the corruption was so unprecedented that the Indonesian language had to invent a new word to capture it, and it took another revolution in 1998 to unseat Suharto.) In India, foundation-assisted organizations like the Institute of Economic Growth at Delhi University (led in my times by the current Indian Prime Minister, Dr. Manmohan Singh) and the National Council of Applied Economic Research became important centers in economic policy research and decision-making. Unlike Indonesia, India remained democratic, except for the brief period in the 1970s when Indira Gandhi declared "emergency rule" and effectively established a dictatorship. The economic policy challenge in India was to break the spell of centralized economic planning, a concept Nehru imported from the Soviet Union and socialist models of the West, and to liberalize the functioning of the economy.

It was one thing to identify brainpower and to train first-rate economists (and other social scientists), an essential task in modernization, which the foundation generally did very competently. It was another to try to help indigenous economic policymakers on the ground make wise economic decisions. In the first two decades of its Asian work, the foundation in various places tried to do both. In the second endeavor, the funding of economic policy advisory services, the foundation became swept up in the intoxicating delusion of power that affects those sitting near the center of government decision making. This turned out ultimately to be an untenable place for a foreign funding agency to work (although to this day the World Bank and other official government development agencies continue to try to play that role in many countries around the world).

In Pakistan and Malaysia, for example, the foundation made a series of grants to the Development Advisory Service at Harvard University to provide advisers to government economic planners and to train their staffs. The Pakistan project trained some outstanding Pakistani economists, but the development plans the Pakistani and American economists produced together might as well have been written on water. It became clear over the years that the data they used was frequently bogus and invented, or guessed at, by officials eager to please. Even more important, neither the elites in the society nor the military governments that have governed Pakistan for most of its political life were ever willing to provide the funds and political muscle to carry out the reforms the plans stipulated in such aspects as genuine mass education and health services for the poor. In the late 1960s, when I managed the Asia program in New York and Ford still supported the Harvard-managed economic advisory project in Pakistan, I became a friend and admirer of Charles Benson, a leading American economist at the University of California at Berkeley, who specialized in the financing of education. Benson was working with Pakistani colleagues to help prepare the education chapter of the new five-year economic development plan then being written, which stipulated serious investment and management reforms in the mass education system. Twenty years later, when I served as director of the USAID mission in Pakistan at the time of the American-supported war against the Soviet Union in Afghanistan (a period when the United States government briefly reappeared as a major actor in Pakistani economic development, only to disappear like the Cheshire cat once again as soon as the Soviets were defeated), I asked Benson to come out to Pakistan to look at education as a potential subject for major U.S. government assistance. After a month carefully surveying the landscape, Benson said we could take the same recommendations he and his colleagues made in the 1960s, update a few figures relating to population size and funds required, and use them with no substantive change. In other words, nothing had been done for a quarter of a century. (And nothing significant ever was done, which is a major reason for the explosive growth of the *madrassa* system of radical Islamic education in post-Afghanistan-war Pakistan after the Americans left. The *madrassas* are essentially uncontrolled by the government—indeed, quietly supported by some of the senior generals in the government, funded in large part by the Saudis, and responsible for the spiritual indoctrination of the Taliban and a whole generation of anti-American activists.)

In Malaysia, the Western economic advisers supported by the Harvard project found themselves ensnared in the pro-Malay majority bias of the Malaysian government, which in its economic planning deliberately built in educational and economic advantages for the Malays—about half the population—over the Chinese—about 40 percent of the population. The rationale for these policies, preached and carried out with much conviction and success for twenty two years by Prime Minister Mahathir bin Mohamad (who first gained political prominence by his role in allegedly fomenting bloody anti-Chinese riots in 1969), was that the Malays had been deliberately held back by the British colonial administration while the Chinese were favored. The Western advisors split into supporters and opponents of the Malayanization economic development policies the government demanded, and the project ended in considerable confusion.

By the mid-1960s, when I went to work in the foundation's Asia program, strong winds of change were blowing. The first generation of post-independence leaders was passing from the scene. Their successors were, almost inevitably, of smaller stature: Indira Gandhi, in spite of the adulation she received—and cultivated—became, unlike her great father, Nehru, a nation divider and not a nation builder. In Pakistan, no outstanding leader ever rose to take the place of Jinnah. The Pakistani military (in those days, Pakistan was still united politically, West and East, which changed in 1971 when the East rebelled and Bangladesh was born) fell into the disastrous habit of taking over the government whenever it deemed it appropriate on national security grounds, a pattern which continues today. General Ayub Khan, who was elected as President of Pakistan in 1958 and then ruled until 1968 as a not very bloody dictator, practiced what he called "guided democracy." In his early period, Ayub was the darling of Western development agencies, but after the 1965 war with India his regime eventually crumbled in political chaos and corruption. In country after country across Asia, the scope and size of corruption grew steadily. Corruption became a cruel tax on the poor people of Asia as leaders and bureaucrats lined their pockets with aid money, bribes from local and foreign businessmen required for licenses, and the enormous profits of illegal natural resource exploitation. In a quarter century of flying over South and Southeast Asia in my various assignments, most of the great forests of Asia shrank and in some cases disappeared before my eyes as the combination of population growth, both human and livestock, and illegal and corrupt logging decimated the trees for firewood, cattle-grazing, or to illegally harvest and export precious tropical hardwoods to Japan and other rich countries to make plywood. The one state that managed to keep the poison bottle of corruption sealed was tiny Singapore, where Lee Kuan Yew at the start made two key decisions. The first was to pay the cabinet ministers and the senior civil service extremely good salaries and benefits—the salary of the prime minister of Singapore today is more than one million dollars per year! The second was to demand total honesty from all public servants in public transactions and to jail, with harsh sentences, the very rare bribe taker. This has been the major factor in bringing foreign investors in to support the consistent, dynamic growth of the Singaporean economy.

As the early generation of national leaders passed from the scene, the ethnic and religious passions and enmities that the enthusiasm and momentum of the first decade or so of independence papered over began to surface: Malay versus Chinese, Tamil versus Sinhalese, the Punjabis of West Pakistan against the Bengalis of East Pakistan, and Hindus versus Muslims. Development began to appear much more complicated. The earlier practice of bringing in large teams of supposedly wise expatriate experts to teach and advise Asian counterparts in extension-type activities was losing its appeal. The Asian societies now had their own experts, trained to the PhD level in American or other foreign universities in addition to those being produced in their own modern institutions like the Indian Institute of Management and the institutes of technology. There had been more than enough crashes on the road to development for Asians to question Western wisdom. In India, for example, in addition to the failure of the intensive agricultural district project to achieve its objectives, a similarly designed government-run, intensive districts project in population and family planning was plagued with political controversy and never really got off the ground. Bureaucracies, as is their nature everywhere, proved deeply resistant to change, and foundation efforts to support civil service reform throughout Asia met with only mixed success.

The most traumatic change in the Ford Foundation senior ranks was the slow, delicate, and painful process of bringing to its end the nearly two-decade long assignment of Douglas Ensminger as the Ford representative in India and Nepal. Ensminger had, after all, opened the foundation's first overseas office. He had been so sensitive and eagerly responsive to the Nehru government's pressing early needs that the foundation for years played a role in Indian national development activities far larger than its resources would have suggested, and in doing so had created a powerful body of support among the trustees, sufficient for Ensminger to challenge the president, Henry Heald, directly on a number of issues. Ensminger found it difficult to give up the old models of expatriate advisory groups and to adapt to the new politics of post-Nehru India, where outside experts were much less appreciated. The new president, Mac Bundy, and his executive vice president, David Bell, who had come to the foundation straight from establishing and managing the U.S. Agency for International Development, had no doubt that it was time for a change in New Delhi. Given the board's interest in this matter, it took three years to negotiate the terms of Ensminger's departure, which included a year for Ensminger to write a book about his experiences and to record a long, valuable oral history of his Indian odyssey before joining the staff of the University of Missouri as a sociology professor. (I played no substantive part in this process, although I was the head of the Asia program.)

I had been fascinated with India since I first set foot on its soil in 1964 and would have been happy to move there as the new representative, but Bundy and Bell thought I had not spent nearly enough time as the head of the Asia program at headquarters and named as Ensminger's successor a young public management expert, Harry Wilhelm, who had worked in the Bureau of the Budget in Washington (and had known Dave Bell there) before joining the foundation to serve as, among other things, the representative in Santiago, Chile. In Santiago, Wilhelm pulled together a bright young staff that clearly admired and respected him and built a program notable for its support of the development of the social sciences, including the graduate training at the University of Chicago of the Chilean group of economists who some years later presided over the economic restructuring of the early days of the Pinochet dictatorship, the one generally well-regarded accomplishment of a much detested regime. He then became the head of the Latin American program of the foundation in New York, a position comparable to my job as the head of the Asia operation, and we knew each other well. Wilhelm, like virtually everyone in the foundation, was a person of strong convictions. He prided himself on his logical reasoning, was, in my view, an unabashed elitist, and had little time for people who disagreed with him, which frequently included me.

In India, Wilhelm threw himself into the unpleasant task of dismantling the Ensminger *raj* (as it was often called) of one hundred or so expatriate employees plus hundreds of support staff. He displayed such zeal that a foundation colleague likened it to "Christ scourging the money changers from the temple." In the subcontinent, losing a good job is a terrible fate, almost worse than death, and even with generous separation payments the resentment among the fired Indian employees was such that Wilhelm, and some of the Indian administrative managers he retained, received anonymous death threats. On at least one occasion a foundation car's brakes were sabotaged. Having dismissed virtually all the foreign project experts, Wilhelm proceeded to build a much smaller staff advisory group of Americans, Europeans, and, for the first time, a couple of Indian experts. He terminated most of the extension-type projects that had characterized the Ensminger period and began to move the foundation into a major support role in development of the social sciences and to explore the desirability of making grants to non-governmental organizations.

I brought in two extremely capable young men for representative jobs in Pakistan and then in Bangladesh, when East Pakistan split away from West Pakistan (with powerful military help from Indira Gandhi's India) and became an independent state. Robert Edwards, a lawyer who had worked in the foundation's African program where the writing of constitutions for the new states and training of lawyers and judges were central elements, took over the difficult task of managing our affairs in Islamabad as the war clouds of the as-yet-undeclared conflict with India over East Pakistan thickened. When Bangladesh became independent in 1971, we sent George Zeidenstein to Dakha as the foundation's first representative. Zeidenstein had been a promising young corporate lawyer before going out to Asia as the first director of the Peace Corps in Nepal. Fresh from Kathmandu, Zeidenstein was, according to our personnel director in New York, the first man the foundation had ever hired wearing a tunic, with long, blond hair down to his shoulder and a gold bracelet around his wrist. (In later years, Edwards served as president of Carleton and Bowdoin Colleges, and as an adviser to the Aga Khan on education and culture. Zeidenstein, in a later avatar with a short haircut, a well-tailored pinstripe suite, and still wearing the gold bracelet, became president of John D. Rockefeller III's Population Council).

As program policies and operating styles began to shift, the most egregious anomaly in the foundation's grant making in Asia (and elsewhere in the foundation's overseas work) was the absence of any kind of support for the Asian arts and culture. Throughout developing Asia, the traditional arts and humanities were reeling under the impact of modernization. The past meant little to most of the modernizing intellectuals, civilian or military, who were interested in economic progress. The great monuments—even such internationally known treasures as Borobodur in Indonesia, Angkor Wat in Cambodia, and the great Buddhist and Hindu cave temples at Ellora and Ajanta in India—were crumbling, sporadically subjected to inexpert restoration. Much of the best of classical

Asian painting and sculpture was flowing out illegally to the markets of the West. Traditional indigenous sources of support for dance and theater, most of these private, were drying up. All this was in sharp contrast to the foundation's domestic agenda, where Mac Lowry's arts and humanities program was a powerful and generally much admired actor.

Like virtually all Western donors in Asia (and elsewhere in the world), Ford's approach to development was thoroughly technical, in Ford's case concentrating on agriculture, population growth, certain aspects of higher education systems, economics training and advisory services, and both private and public management reform and innovation. These priorities largely emulated the development planning of the Asian governments themselves. The argument was that feeding the stomach was more important than feeding the soul. The arts and humanities were a "soft" subject. (The one exception in Asia was a small program in the arts and humanities run out of New York by the JDR III fund, a personal charity of John D. Rockefeller III.) My colleagues and I in New York and Asia disagreed with that conclusion. We argued that helping Asians to preserve the best of their past traditions was an important part of building new societies, not only for Asia but the rest of the world as well. We proceeded to explore what a program might look like. We talked with experts like Harold Stern, then deputy director of the Freer Gallery in Washington and one of the country's leading lights on the subject of Oriental art, and brought aboard as consultants George Dales, one of America's leading archaeologists, who had worked extensively on the Harappan civilization of the Indian subcontinent (most of whose sites lie in present-day Pakistan), and Stan O'Connor, an art historian at Cornell and an expert on Southeast Asia. I also met and began a dialogue about Asian culture that was to last for many years with a marvelous woman, Lisa Lyons, a specialist in Buddhist art from the University Museum in Philadelphia, who later worked with me on the Ford staff in both Bangkok and New Delhi. In Asia, our representatives sought the views of indigenous specialists as to what the foundation could usefully do without ruffling feathers in this sensitive field.

In August 1970, I wrote Mac Bundy a memorandum titled, "The Case for a Modest Program in the Cultural Field" that made five brief points:

> 1. We should devote a small portion of our developmental funds to helping to preserve the great Asian cultural traditions, seeking always to encourage greater national interest and support. We believe this work fits both the foundation's substantive yardsticks as set forth by our charter and our own understanding of the increasingly complex challenge of development in increasingly nationalistic and identity-seeking societies.

2. A modest interest in working in the cultural field, primarily in the preservation of traditional Asian culture, is of high enough priority that our representatives are prepared to fit these modest requirements into their very tight budgets....

3. We do not expect this to become a field of large-scale foundation endeavor. We think large-scale investment neither necessary nor desirable—nor probably wanted....

4. We have excellent outside advice from well-qualified people on which our preliminary conclusions are based....

5. We have reason to believe that at least some of the trustees would regard our modest presence in the cultural field with favor. Alex Heard (the chairman of the board, a historian and chancellor of Vanderbilt University) has written us his views on this specifically, and John Loudon (the chairman of Royal Dutch Shell) expressed a similar favorable view this past year during his trip to Southeast Asia.

Bundy, Dave Bell, and the board approved the launching of the new program, which over subsequent decades, long after I left the foundation, expanded from an original focus on preservation and archaeological training to support work in folklore, theater, and dance. Our first forays began immediately with three small grant programs in Thailand, Indonesia, and India to fund exploratory research and training grants in the fields of art and archaeology. Comparable activities later became an Asia-wide, and then an important, worldwide component of foundation work, one that the foundation continues to point to with pride.

In 1971, our seventh year of residence in the States after returning from Moscow, Charlotte and I sold our castle in Grandview-on-Hudson and bought a cooperative apartment on the east side of Manhattan across Gracie Square from Gracie Mansion, the traditional residence of the mayors of New York. When we bought the Grandview house on the Hudson River, I had told our lawyer that we loved it so much we planned never to leave. He laughed and said, "The average time Americans live in one home is seven years." He was right on the button. After seven years, our children had all flown the nest and were alternately swimming or sinking at various universities. I was heartily sick of commuting. Charlotte, having picked up a master's degree in language teaching at Columbia University's Teacher College, had become the head of the modern language department at Briarcliff College and was teaching Spanish and Russian, driving back and forth daily in a little BMW she loved the way people used to love a thoroughbred horse. We both wanted to enjoy the city directly.

One autumn after we moved into Manhattan, gazing out our apartment window on Gracie Square, which is a lovely, quiet, small city park with a spectacular esplanade above the East River where I jogged every morning before going to work, I watched the park workers sweeping up the wet carpet of falling leaves and remembered what a chore taking care of the large old Grandview house had been. "Good move," I thought. Although I spent a lot of time in Asia, we regularly found time to have dinner and ballet evenings with Lincoln and Fidelma Kirstein, and I lunched with Kirstein once a month or so at the old Hotel Gotham on Fifth Avenue. We dined occasionally with Mac and Mary Bundy, David and Mary Bell, and a host of other friends, heard a lot of great classical music at Lincoln Center and the opera, and jazz down in the Village, and tested the endlessly varied cuisines of New York restaurants. It was a happy period. But the old folk wisdom is really true: the gods grant perpetual happiness to no one.

The following summer of 1972, Charlotte accompanied me on a trip to Southeast Asia and Australia, where I had been invited to give a series of lectures on modern American philanthropy. During a stopover in Bangkok on the way to Australia, she discovered a dimpled area in her right breast. She decided, with my support, that she needed immediate minor surgery to remove a specimen for a biopsy. Within a day, the Danish specialist who examined Charlotte told us she had breast cancer. We canceled the Australia visit, flew back to New York, and within a week Charlotte underwent a radical mastectomy, which required removal of the lymph glands under the armpit as well as the breast itself. The doctors thought they intervened in time to prevent the cancer's spread, and after radiation therapy, with Charlotte exercising faithfully, she slowly regained strength and mobility, and we began to resume our daily routines.

My boss, Dave Bell, and I had earlier discussed my possible move to Bangkok to replace George Gant as representative for Southeast Asia. Gant, who originally brought me into the Asia program as his deputy, wanted to retire. We agreed to plan for a move in the spring of 1973. Charlotte's recovery seemed to be complete. But three months before our expected departure, in the complete physical examinations required by the foundation for overseas assignments, the examining doctors discovered a small node in Charlotte's neck. It was diagnosed as cancerous. Clearly, the cancer had spread. We postponed any thought of leaving immediately. Charlotte began treatment with chemotherapy (in this case, the then new, powerful, essentially poisonous compound known as Fluorouracil).

After a couple of months, the specialists decided we could go out to Bangkok, with Charlotte continuing therapy under the weekly supervision of a young Thai doctor trained at the University of Chicago medical school and known personally to one of Charlotte's doctors. I met and talked with the Thai doctor on a swing through Asia and thought him serious and very well informed (about a subject I knew little about, of course). We decided to give it a try; Charlotte very much wanted to. Our children were by now young adults and personally doing OK, although their university careers were erratic, to say the least. So we said good-bye to family and friends, and in late summer 1973 went off to live in the enchanting, beautiful, hospitable, mystical, and cruel tropical land of Siam. With her unerring sense of style, Charlotte found us a big old wooden Chinese merchant family house with a lotus pond and an orchid arbor, plunged into Thai language study, orchid growing, and reading Buddhist texts, and started giving some of Bangkok's most sought-after parties for Thai intellectuals, big shots, and foreigners lucky enough to be invited. When we went back to New York some years later, it was only for Charlotte to die.

11

On the Shores of the Shallow Sea

Sprawling across the steaming coastal plain of the Gulf of Thailand, with its dragon-peaked, rambunctious temples and palaces, luxury hotels, high-rise office buildings, floating markets, orchid gardens, street stalls with the best pork-fried rice in Asia, massage parlors and whore houses stocked with dusky teen-agers from the northern provinces, and its air full of car, truck, and boat exhaust fumes and the over-ripe sweet smell of durian fruit, Bangkok is like a giant planet pulling the entire nation into its vortex. Ten million foreign tourists a year fly in and happily head out in sandals and straw hats on the trail of great beaches, bargain shopping (Thai silks, rubies, and emeralds are famous and cheap), well-organized and safe exoticism (temple dancing and elephant roundups), and a horizon of special tastes ranging from Buddhist meditation to teen-age girls for cheap sex (more of the latter than the former). None of this would change the inscrutable smile on the lips of Lord Buddha, who in his travels through Northern India three thousand years ago witnessed all human vanity and suffering. The small royal city of a century ago, romantically if not accurately recalled in Margaret Landon's *Anna and the King of Siam* and *The King and I*, where most of the population performed its daily rounds traveling by boat up and down the Chao Phraya River and an endless web of canals (*klongs*), has metamorphosed into a roaring, concrete monster of a city: ten million people in a country with a total population of sixty million. (On a comparable basis, if New York were the only major city in the United States, as Bangkok is in Thailand, it would have a population of forty five million).

Such giant, dominating metropolises—Bangkok, Manila, Jakarta, Hong Kong, and the cities of the south China coast—are characteristic of the post-World War II development of Southeast Asia, one of the great transitional zones and melting pots of the world. The Ford Foundation defined Southeast Asia as the region that begins with Burma on the west, continues through Thailand and Indochina, and terminates in those lands bordering what Joseph Conrad called "the shallow sea"—the Malay peninsula and the great archipelagos of Indonesia and the Philippines. By any standard, it was a vital, diverse, and potentially rich region. In its grant-making programs since the 1950s, the foundation had regarded Southeast Asia as second in priority only to the Indian subcontinent, with its vast and poverty-stricken populations. The reasons were obvious: Southeast Asia had been a major disturber of the peace (in Indonesia and, notably, in Vietnam). If moderately poor, the region was immensely promising in human and natural resources; and these were countries in which foundation assistance generally had been welcome and well used since the 1950s. With the exception of miniscule Singapore, the populations and most of the developmental problems were predominantly rural. But political and economic power resided in the great cities.

In accordance with the developmental wisdom of the day, the foundation focused its early Southeast Asian grant-making activities in five major categories: agriculture, education, economic planning, business and public administration, and population and family planning. With the help of Cornell University, its grants helped to turn the College of Agriculture in the Philippines into an international-class research center, while simultaneously with the Rockefeller Foundation it built and launched the work of the immediately useful International Rice Research Institute in the rice paddies near Manila. It sponsored research and training on language learning throughout the region. The foundation established a number of high-quality, graduate-level programs in economics, public administration, and business management (schools like the National Institute of Development Administration in Thailand and the Asian Institute of Management in Manila) whose graduates and researchers made an immediate impact on the process of modernization. It was the first major Western financier of population and family planning work in the region (the dimensions of the challenge could be seen in the growth of the region's population from 1955 to 1975 from one hundred seventy million people to three hundred twenty five million), with little success in the Catholic Philippines but better results elsewhere in Singapore and Thailand. Working with a Harvard advisory group, the foundation had funded an economic planning group of advisers in Malaysia (with comparable projects in Indonesia and Pakistan). Finally, as a contribution to regional understanding, in a part of the world where mutual ignorance and hostility reigned among neighbors, the foundation established a Southeast Asian Fellowship Program through which regional scholars received training and research grants within the region to inform themselves—and their academic communities—about their neighboring societies (virtually all other fellowship opportunities required residence in a Western country).

The management of the programs in the region was highly decentralized. The first offices were opened in the 1950s in Indonesia and Burma. In the 1960s, when the military seized power in Burma, the foundation closed its office, and it never reopened. (The once rich and peaceful land of Burma is one of the two saddest countries in Southeast Asia: its prosperity destroyed by decade after decade of greedy, incompetent, and brutal military dictators, who wage an unending war against the tribal groups along the Thai border and suppress all manifestations of political opposition; its treasures of ancient Buddhist art looted and sold all over the world; and its fabled forests depleted by illegal, corrupt logging. The second is Cambodia, still struggling to emerge from the nightmare of the torture and death chambers of the Khmer Rouge regime.) By the early 1960s, the foundation had offices with full-fledged representatives in Jakarta, Manila, and Kuala Lumpur, and then in 1968 George Gant opened the Bangkok office, which was to deal with grant-making in Thailand and handle projects of a regional nature that encompassed more than one country. When I arrived in 1973, the foundation decided to put all of Southeast Asia except Indonesia (which because of its size remained separately administered) under one regional representative in Bangkok, with small sub-offices in Manila and Kuala Lumpur. We ran our programs with a regional staff of about eight Western and Asian specialists, relying outside Bangkok for both local administrative support and substantive intellectual assistance on the resources of the sub-offices in Manila and Kuala Lumpur.

The extraordinarily diverse peoples we were concerned with—the Thai (the *muang tay*, as they call themselves), the Malays, the Vietnamese, the Filipinos, the Indonesians, the Cambodians, and the overseas Chinese and Indians of Southeast Asia—speak many languages and pray to different gods. All are rice cultivators, fierce warriors, boat builders, textile weavers of exquisite taste, consummate traders and entrepreneurs, fish eaters, and masters of rice and noodle cooking using the exotic spices that, starting in the sixteenth century, made their lands the target of Western adventurers. For centuries before the arrival of the long-nosed Westerners, these tribes and ethnic groups, sandwiched between the classical Asian civilizations of India and China, whose cultural and religious remnants remain enshrined in the life of the contemporary societies of the region, fought each other with gusto. Buddhism may be a religion and philosophy of peace and meditation, but that prevented no Buddhist king from fighting a war of conquest against another Buddhist kingdom (as Christianity did not deter the European

Christian kings from fighting each other). The Thai, Burmese, Cambodian, and Vietnamese kings took turns at conquering and enslaving each other's people. In Indochina, the Vietnamese essentially wiped out the native people, the Chams, whose ghosts still haunt the countryside. In our own time in Cambodia, the cruelty and thoroughness with which the Khmer Rouge leaders murdered their own countrymen remain without parallel.

Eating rice is almost religious. In Vietnam, one might greet a friend by asking "Have you eaten rice?" and parents do not punish children while they are eating rice in order not to disturb the spiritual relationship between the child and those who provide the rice. In Thailand, a predominantly Buddhist nation, at the start of the rice-planting season, the much-loved king presides annually over a ritual spring plowing ceremony performed by priests known as Brahmins, rooted in Indian custom. In this charming rite, the king pours sacred water on the forehead of the most senior agriculture department civil servant, who plays the role of Lord of the Ploughing Ceremony. With the help of a pair of sacred oxen, four beautiful young ladies serving as celestial maidens, and the Brahmin priests, the Lord presides over the actual plowing. (According to a report of a recent ceremony, the two oxen, named Rung and Roj, were given grass, rice, corn, beans, sesame, liquor, and water to choose from as the reward for their work. They chose corn and water, after which it was predicted that there would be abundant crops, vegetables, and rice during the crop year.) One of my favorite fast-food snacks while traveling in northern Thailand to visit our multi-cropping projects was sticky rice, bought on the roadside, carried along in the car in a banana leaf, and eaten with the fingers.

The classical dancers of Cambodia, Thailand, and Indonesia embody the poses and gestures of the Hindu temple dance; and in the ubiquitous Chinese populations of the region Confucianism influences family life and patterns of governance and commerce. The Hinayana Buddhism of Burma and Thailand, born in India and dominant in Sri Lanka, teaches that Lord Buddha was a supreme philosopher but should not be worshipped as a god. It is the most powerful religious force in much of mainland Southeast Asia. Virtually all Thai men, for example, still put on the saffron robe and enter a monastery at some point in their youth for a brief novitiate in a Buddhist temple, and many of the Thais I worked with arose before dawn for a quiet time of meditation. Taoist temples in Indochina and the Chinese quarters of the port cities throughout the region reflect the Chinese heritage. The Filipinos are Malays, predominantly Catholic Christians dating back to the Spanish conquest, although increasing numbers worship in evangelical sects; and in the southern islands the flames of a Muslim insurgency that began more than a century ago when the United States first occupied the Philippines and fought the Moros still burn, allegedly linked today to the Al Qaeda of Osama Bin Laden. Malaysia and Indonesia, the world's largest Muslim country with nearly two hundred million worshipers of Allah, practice a relatively moderate Sunni Islam brought to their shores by Arab traders starting in the tenth century.

From the time of Magellan's sixteenth-century voyage of discovery and the earliest Portuguese and Dutch expeditions, these lands drew Western explorers, traders, adventurers, and writers like a magnet. Joseph Conrad wrote some of his finest novels about the life that pulsed on and around what he called "the shallow sea...that foams and murmurs on the shores of the thousand islands, big and little, that make up the Malay archipelago...(It) has been for centuries the scene of adventurous undertakings...The race of men who had fought against the Portuguese, the Spaniards, the Dutch and the English, has not been changed by the unavoidable defeat. They have kept to this day their love of liberty, their fanatical devotion to their chiefs, their blind fidelity in friendship and hate—all their lawful and unlawful instincts."

Graham Greene writes in *Ways of Escape*: "In Indo-China I drained a magic potion...The spell was first cast, I think, by the tall elegant girls in white silk trousers, by the pewter evening light on flat paddy fields, where the water-buffaloes trudged fetlock-deep with a slow primeval gait, by the French perfumeries in the rue Catina, the Chinese gambling houses in Cholon, above all by that feeling of exhilaration which a measure of danger brings to the visitor with a return ticket...." Greene loved to smoke opium. "Of those four winters which I passed in Indo-China opium has left the happiest memory, and...it played an important part in the life of Fowler, my character in *The Quiet American*." About his debut performance smoking four pipes of opium, Greene writes, "The ambiance won my heart at once—the hard couch, the leather pillow like a brick—these stand for a certain austerity, the athleticism of pleasure, while the small lamp glowing on the face of the pipe-maker, as he kneads his little ball of brown gum over the flame until it bubbles and alters shape like a dream, the dimmed lights, the little chaste cups of unsweetened green tea, these stand for the 'luxe et volupte'...After two pipes I felt a certain drowsiness, after four my mind felt alert and calm—unhappiness and fear of the future became like something dimly remembered which I had thought important once...."

Charlotte and I spent our first weeks in Bangkok at the old Oriental Hotel on the banks of the Chao Phraya River, where Somerset Maugham lived and wrote during his Southeast Asian voyages, doubtless enjoying the handsome native boys. Maugham wrote one of the English language's finest short stories in *The Letter*, about a British rubber planter's wife in Malaysia who murdered her white lover when he spurned her for a Chinese woman (the movie version, with Bette Davis as the wife, is a marvel of ambiance). Andre Malraux, a superb writer and a bona fide adventurer and intriguer, as a young man edited an anti-colonial newspaper in Saigon (and during his stay managed to swipe some fine bas-reliefs from the Khmer temples at Angkor Wat in Cambodia), and Marguerite Duras's books celebrate the steamy joys of love among the Vietnamese and the French.

In their rather unsubtle way, Americans have long been involved in Southeast Asian power politics, starting with the American conquest of the Philippines during the Spanish-American War of 1898 and the ensuing half-century of colonial rule in Manila. A major reason the Japanese attacked the United States in the Second World War was their conviction (which was correct) that the United States was determined to keep the oil and other natural resources of Southeast Asia out of Japanese imperial hands. Two decades later, the Americans slowly and inexorably drifted into war in Vietnam believing the domino theory that a Communist triumph in Indochina inevitably would topple state after state in a region vital to U.S. policy. Today, with the region in relative peace, it remains a premise of American foreign policy that passage for merchant and military ships across these shallow seas through the straits of Malacca, Singapore, and Makassar must forever remain unrestricted, an essential element in the strategy of American naval power first expressed by Capt. Alfred Mahan in 1890.

Before moving into the old Chinese merchant family mansion on Wireless Road built on the banks of what used to be a *klong* (canal), now filled in and teeming with traffic, I seriously considered renting a beautiful, airy, old, country-style wooden house on stilts, originally constructed near Chieng Mai in the north, then after fifty years taken apart by hand, trucked to Bangkok, and rebuilt in the midst of a large jungle garden on the river about ten miles upriver from the Ford Foundation office. Given the impenetrable traffic jams on the roads, I intended to buy a small, long-tailed (outboard motor with a long shaft, designed to be tilted and used in shallow waters) river boat and hire a captain to rocket down the river to work every day, flying a Ford Foundation flag which Charlotte said she would design. But the owner of the house insisted on keeping his mostly junky antiquities in the house, and we would have had no space for our own belongings. So we went into the heart of the city to find our old merchant house and rode boats as convenient and necessary. On special occasions, we would charter a whale-like, motor-driven rice barge rigged for parties, invite sixty or seventy guests, and spend the evening eating Thai fish, pork, and noodles, drinking whisky and the excellent Thai beer, and dancing to the music of a small combo while chugging up and down the Chao Phraya. When the party ended at midnight, we always carefully checked the boat to make sure no guests were enjoying the sleep of the intoxicated under the benches. Mostly though, we entertained quietly at home in the Chinese house. Charlotte's fluency in Thai was much admired; her ear for the five-tonal language was far better than mine, and she rapidly acquired a circle of Thai friends. Her weekly chemotherapy sessions at a local hospital went generally well.

To complete our household, we bought a pair of charming little Chinese-style dogs—"Mii Noi" ("Little Bear") and his mate, "Bitsy"—at the vast weekly open market on the palace grounds, where one could buy virtually everything in the world but which we found most interesting for its rich variety of fish, game, vegetables and fruits, orchids, handicrafts including more fake antique Buddha figures than the entire world of tourists and foreigners could buy, textiles, and a veritable zoo of wildlife and pets. I traveled regularly up-country to visit Ford development projects. When Charlotte could make it, we would head off the beaten track to visit the small gems of old Thai and Khmer temples still to be found in the jungles and rice paddies of the northern and eastern provinces. The foundation had begun to fund a modest regional program in archaeology and restoration, and one of the world's rare experts in Southeast Asian art, Lisa Lyons, had joined our staff on leave from the University Museum in Philadelphia. She often guided us on these intimate picnics—with ice-cold martinis and crayfish salad—in the jungles. From time to time, they included expeditions to the recently discovered site at Ban Chiang in northeastern Thailand, where a series of small grants in cooperation with the government archaeology department supported on-site research and training. The excavations were yielding ceramic and bronze pots and household objects dating from the second millennium BC, and the local tribal people happily sold visitors fake, and occasionally authentic, pots.

A large, handsome, red-haired woman with a hearty laugh, Lyons was a famous charmer. In her earlier years, she had been a lover of Jim Thompson, the designer and promoter of Thai silk (with reputed connections with the CIA), before he disappeared mysteriously in the hills of Malaysia. She knew by heart hundreds of Buddhist folklore tales (the so-called Jataka) and the meanings of all the hand gestures. She was acquainted with dozens of senior monks throughout the backcountry and would with unfailing good nature but in all seriousness argue with them in ungrammatical but adequate Thai about their failure to take even the most elemental precautions against damaging the paintings about the life of Lord Buddha that covered the walls of the monasteries. (If the monks decided to start using a loudspeaker, more often than not they would simply pound it into a wall covered with murals.) In Bangkok, Lisa lived in a tiny, Thai-style house with a fishpond, a devoted cook, and a gardener, and entertained the really interesting people of Thailand, including journalists, scholars, artists, and a number of princes and princesses with good connections in the artistic and cultural world. She became Charlotte's closest friend, both in Thailand and on our later assignment in India. We were all gourmets of Thai and Chinese food, both at home and in our favorite restaurants. (Like New Yorkers, Bangkok dwellers maintain and compare notes on which restaurants are in. Typically, the Bangkok cycle starts with a poor but exceptional Thai or Chinese cook setting up a street stall. He or she moves up to a small, open-door and window restaurant with electric fans, and in two or three years finds a wealthy backer and opens a big, dark, freezingly air-conditioned restaurant with a loud band and a Chinese singer. This stage usually marks the end of the good cooking.)

The structure and nature of Thai society were different from anything I had experienced. It combined the gentleness and quiet inner strength of its Buddhist heritage, exquisite hospitality, and a streak of wildness and savagery perhaps most easily visible in Thai kick boxing, where with drums beating and ceremonial bows to Lord Buddha two tough young men try to kick each other's brains out with the crowd squealing and roaring with excitement. Charlotte and I knew dozens of upper-and middle-class Thai women who were liberated and often extremely successful businesswomen and professionals. At the other end of the scale, poor rural families still peddled their daughters to the Bangkok and coastal resort sex parlors. In all the city populations, one found a strong mixture of Chinese blood with Thai, and there was in all the cities a strong, totally ethnic Chinese quarter, but most Thais preferred to be regarded as pureblooded (the Tay people originally came down from southwestern China, where a sizable Tay-speaking population still exists). The king was a constitutional monarch who assumed the throne after his brother was mysteriously murdered in 1946. A half-century later, King Bhumibol is revered almost as a god by a significant portion of the population as both king and a senior figure in the Buddhist ceremonial structure of Thai life. The prime minister and a national parliament effectively governed the country, but underneath the modern, Western structures of government there still existed the traces of the days when the king was an absolute ruler, and powerful lords controlled the various regions of the kingdom in his name. The Interior Ministry, generally responsible for law and order, was, for example, the hereditary overlord of the large, poor northeastern provinces along the Mekong River bordering Cambodia and Laos, and any developmental programs in that sensitive region, where Thailand was greatly concerned about Communist infiltration, needed Interior Ministry clearance in addition to that of the bureaucracy substantively concerned. There was, in fact, a small but active Communist insurgency in the provinces along the Mekong River border with Indochina that had begun to attract student recruits from the Bangkok universities.

For decades before our arrival, in spite of a persistent and unfaltering drive toward democracy, most of Thailand's rulers had been generals and field marshals, usually relatively moderate, feckless, and invariably corrupt, and inevitably supported by the United States because they were regarded as anti-Communist at a time when a Red tide from China and Vietnam was assumed to be rising in the region. When I arrived to take up my duties, Gen. Thanom Kittikachorn had been prime minister for four years. A courtesy call was arranged for me at the National Palace, and we talked briefly, smiling for the television cameras as we sat in his ornate office. Our conversation was mostly in English, which Thanom professed to speak, although not with great fluency. I had met the general before on trips out from New York and explained that this time I had arrived in Bangkok to remain for some years as the foundation representative. Thanom smiled politely. When I rose to depart, he shook my hand, asked me if I had enjoyed my visit to Thailand, and said, "When are you leaving?" It turned out he was leaving before I did.

Within three months, I stood with my deputy, David Pfanner, looking out our office window across the city toward the government enclave on the Chao Phraya River, watching in disbelief as smoke billowed from fires and explosions in a student-led revolution that overthrew the mighty military government. For almost a year, university students had begun to organize and carry out public demonstrations against government policies. The immediate rallying cause was student anger with the increasing Japanese domination of the economy, which fed on anti-Japanese feelings in much of the population dating back to the Japanese occupation of Thailand during World War II. Underlying the student protests was dissatisfaction with the arbitrariness, corruption and inefficiency of the old system and indications that General Thanom was preparing his son, a brutal and widely despised Army colonel named Narong, to take over power on Thanom's retirement. The uprising was a bloody affair: more than four hundred people were killed and thousands wounded. King Bhumibhol intervened, persuaded Thanom, Narong and a much-feared field marshal, Prapass Charusathiara, to leave the country, and appointed Sanya Chammasakdi, the popular rector of Thammasat University, which had been the seedbed of the rebellion, to become prime minister. Thailand began unsteadily to build a genuine democracy. The times were difficult. The Indochina war was spilling out of its Vietnamese confines, and Thailand was under great pressure from the United States to provide military bases and rest and recreation access to the growing numbers of U.S. soldiers and sailors in Vietnam (giving a big boost to Thailand's already flourishing sex and bar industry, which had first blossomed when the Japanese occupied Thailand during the Second World War).

One of the early prime ministers in the unsteady new dispensation was the novelist and journalist Kukrit Pramoj, whom I knew slightly from Lisa Lyons' small dinner parties as a courageous opposition figure. For a brief period, he and his brother, Seni, who as ambassador to the United States at the beginning of World War II, refused to deliver the Thai government's declaration of war (under Japanese pressure) to the U.S. government, alternated in power as prime ministers. They typified the best of the Thai elites in combining a deep sense of nationality and Thai uniqueness with a belief in democracy and modernization. In a program report I sent to New York in 1975, I noted that Kukrit "had survived (1) the fall of Vietnam; (2) widespread and sometimes violent strikes and demonstrations on the most extraordinary variety of issues; (3) the burning and looting of his house and personal art treasures by drunken policemen; (4) the worst floods in thirty five years; and (5) even the reissue of the movie *The Ugly American*, in which Kukrit plays the part of the prime minister of a mythical Asian country undergoing a serious Communist insurgency. The common estimate is that Kukrit…has done a masterful job of reading the Thai character and the Thai political scene and in riding the storm both domestically and internationally. (His) government may be described as essentially conservative, mildly reformist, politically innovative, and staunchly dedicated to personal freedom."

All the postwar Southeast Asian societies (with the exception of the Vietnamese Communists) were in theory and rhetoric dedicated to democracy and modernization. Sukarno invented the term "guided democracy" in Indonesia, with far more emphasis on the "guiding" part than on "democracy." This accent on "guiding" tended to be the pattern in most of the region—with widely varying results. In the Philippines, where the long American occupation had produced a reasonably literate society and a surface layer of American-style institutions, the elites talked with great Filipino charm and eloquence—and, of course, in fluent English—about a new kind of democratic society. In fact, the powerful, landowning families that had dominated Filipino life from the time of the Spaniards consistently sabotaged any serious social and economic reforms. More than any other major society in Asia, although the Philippines began the postwar period with great expectations, it consistently failed to break through the centuries-old pattern of concentrated wealth, deep rural and urban poverty, and economic stagnation. (In the Asia of the late 1950s, the Philippines were regarded as a virtually certain winner in the development sweepstakes, while Korea, for example, was regarded as hopelessly strife-bound, sleepy, stagnant, corrupt, and out of contention. By the end of the century, Korea had done far better.)

Ferdinand Marcos, scion of a powerful if not prosperous family with its economic and political base in Luzon, became president in 1966, pledging to put the Philippines on a new path to economic growth and social justice. He was popular during his first term, partly because of his public works programs and partly because of his forceful personality (and that of his wife, Imelda, a former beauty queen and herself a member of a powerful family in Leyte). In his second term, it became evident that no serious reform of the land problem was taking place. Crime and random violence began to wrack Manila. In 1972, Marcos declared martial law, which produced immediate but evanescent approval as it put a short-lived lid on crime. Martial law lasted until 1981, with Marcos ruling by presidential decrees.

During his two-decade rule, Marcos and Imelda embarked on a spree of thievery of public resources that became notorious around the world: after their ouster in 1986, an inventory taken at the presidential palace found more than a thousand pairs of shoes belonging to Mrs. Marcos, nine hundred handbags, seventy-one pairs of sunglasses, and sixty-five parasols. When the Marcoses arrived in exile in New York that same year, U.S. customs seized property valued at eight million dollars. Marcos died in Hawaii in 1989 awaiting U.S. criminal charges that he plundered more than one hundred million dollars from the Philippine Treasury in his two decades in power. In the end, though, it was not the thievery that brought Marcos down, but rather Filipino and international revulsion at the assassination of Sen. Benigno Aquino, a lifelong Marcos rival, on Aquino's return in 1983 from medical treatment in the United States. Aquino was shot and killed with a bullet to the head as he was escorted off an airplane at Manila Airport by soldiers of the Aviation Security Command. His widow, Corazon Aquino, became president in 1986 after the popular revolt against Marcos sent him and Imelda into exile in the United States, ultimately in Hawaii. President Ronald Reagan's administration supported Marcos until almost the very end. In Singapore Prime Minister Lee Kuan Yew's memoirs, Lee recounts a 1985 conversation in which Secretary of State George Schulz asked him during an official visit to Washington to convince President Reagan that his old friend Ferdinand Marcos was the problem of the Philippines, not the solution.

The most far-sighted of the early leaders of Southeast Asia was Lee Kuan Yew of Singapore. Originally, because of his early, pre-independence political alliance with the Communists in the People's Action Party, some Westerners thought him a dangerous leftist. For an independent country, Singapore's population and territory were ludicrously—and perilously—tiny, encircled by neighbors with far larger populations, vastly richer natural resources in land, forests, minerals, and oil and gas, and no reason at all to love a Chinese-dominated Singapore. When Lee assumed power in Singapore in 1965 after a brief, unsuccessful merger with Malaysia came to an end, the conventional wisdom was that Singapore hadn't a chance. The British had closed down their naval bases in Singapore and were withdrawing their troops. The *Sydney Morning Herald* said: "An independent Singapore was not regarded as viable three years ago. Nothing in the current situation suggests that it is more viable today." The *Sunday Times* in London predicted the collapse of Singapore without British aid. To speed that day, Indonesia's Sukarno sent in saboteurs across the narrow ocean straits that separate the largest nation in Southeast Asia from the smallest.

But Lee Kuan Yew had a large intellect and a Confucian vision of how to modernize Singapore with hard work and respect for authority and to turn it into a prosperous, competitive society able to withstand the storms of regional and international economic and political conflict. A key element in his vision was the conviction that corruption was the poison that killed growth and development. Plus which, he played a very cool hand in the perilous game of international politics. When I first visited Singapore in 1967, I called on the then still-new prime minister and listened to his lucid exposition of how Singapore would take advantage of its unique natural position as the historically preferred entrepot and shipping port on the main east-west and north-south maritime routes through the Straits of Malacca and Singapore to build modern service and manufacturing facilities and attract foreign capital to build industries demanding and relying on an educated, skilled population. (The Ford Foundation had already undertaken a long-term commitment to upgrade a technological institute into what became a premier school of engineering technology. It also supported the development of the law faculty at the University of Singapore, which subsequently turned out some of the few brave voices of protest against Lee's jailing of political opponents. It also sponsored projects in family planning and English-language training.)

The prime minister deputed a young senior civil servant (in this brand new country all the civil servants were young) to show me around. He showed me some new public housing, and then we went to the highest point on the island, about forty feet or so, where the civil servant swept his arm from the northeast through one hundred fifty degrees to the south to delineate the uninspiring vista of the Jurong swamps, where these modern industries were to rise to form the base of Singapore's prosperity. Having heard similar puffery in many parts of the world before, I thought to myself, "That will be the day." Some years later, I drove out to exactly the same spot. The landscape was covered with bright, modern, functioning industrial plants and shipping facilities. Singapore workers not only found well-paying jobs, but the city-state's public housing program, in which workers became owners of their apartments, was possibly the most successful in the world. Thanks to the government's very tough anti-corruption policies, built on the premise that civil servants should be well paid and absolutely clean handed, the island became a favorite investment spot for Western capital and such a totally modern city that the government eventually found it necessary to create a Disney-like quarter to try to re-create the lively street life, the small houses, and crowded streets of the old Chinese city (if not its smells). The accompanying costs of prosperity Lee Kuan Yew-style were not inconsiderable: one-party domination of the political process, an annoying insistence on controlling public morality (banning spitting, littering, and male long hair), incessant meddling in people's private lives (perhaps best typified by the government's position that poor women should breed less, higher-class women more), a small but not insignificant and implacable tradition of locking up political opponents, and a general dullness of civic life.

Next door, the Malay elites were constructing their own vision of a multiethnic modern society, in this case with the majority Malays (58 percent of the population) employing the power of the state to reduce the economic dominance of the Chinese (about a quarter of the population) and to improve the economic status of the poor Malay peasantry (along with the large numbers of already well-to-do Malays as well). There was a sizable (8 percent) but not politically significant ethnic Indian population as well. This was a typical case of perceived injustice dating from the colonial period: the British were said to have favored the Chinese in colonial administration and trade over the indigenous Malays, who were viewed as hopelessly ignorant rice paddy laborers. The great rallying cry of the Malay population was rights for the *bumiputra*, the Malay sons of the soil. MIT scholar Lucian Pye observes that the two cultures "present numerous points of conflict that make Chinese and Malays scornful of each other. The Chinese are urban people, interested in money and market activities, and they are committed to self-improvement and have strong family ties. The Malays are rural, are contemptuous of merchants, prefer service careers in the army and police, are more easygoing in social relations, and are tolerant of divorce...With respect to religion and customs, the two rub each other the wrong way: Malays practice Islam in varying degrees, but they universally abhor the pig; Chinese have vaguer religious identities and are fond of eating pork."

Long before the Europeans came, the traditional rulers of the Malay peninsula, the vast Indonesian archipelago, and the few, tiny settlements on the coastal plains of the huge, wild island of Borneo (where in Sarawak in the mid-nineteenth century a British adventurer named James Brook, called the "white raja," founded a dynasty that lasted until the Second World War) were ethnic Malay sultans who embraced Islam in the fifteenth century. In most cases, the British colonialists provided political advisers but left the sultans on their thrones to deal with local administrative and ceremonial matters (a policy first practiced in India with maharajas and princes), while they concentrated on the really important business of extracting enormous profits from rubber plantations and tin mines. Deeming indigenous Malay labor to be unsatisfactory, the British brought in indentured Chinese laborers and, in lesser numbers, Indians from the subcontinent, and thereby laid the tinder for Malaysia's post-independence political struggles. The Malay sultans tolerated and profited from the activities of the Chinese trading families who, migrating from South China over many centuries, dominated import, export, and internal commerce. With the traditional Chinese dedication to hard work and family improvement, many of the sons of these overseas Chinese communities became educated and took senior jobs in the British administrative services. Some of their sons also became leaders of the Communist Party of Malaya, whose membership was predominantly Chinese and which led the resistance to the Japanese occupiers during the Second World War. In 1948, the Malay Communist Party began a now mostly forgotten, intense, bloody rebellion against the British that lasted twelve years (during which period the British High Commissioner and commander, Sir Gerald Templer, invented some of the basic strategies of modern counterinsurgency operations). In 1957, the British negotiated independence with a coalition of parties representing Malay nationalists and wealthy Chinese businessmen headed by Tunku (Prince) Abdul Rahman, the English-educated son of the twenty-fourth sultan of Kedah. Part of the agreement established a rotating kingship among nine sultans, who every five years choose one of their members to serve as king, a position primarily representing national solidarity and defense of the Islamic faith. As in the case of mother England, true political power resides in the parliament and prime minister, but Malaysia to this day accords the regional sultans a considerable degree of regional authority and prestige.

This potentially enormously prosperous country—valuable mines, productive rubber plantations, tropical hardwoods, and oil and gas, all to be developed and managed by a relatively small population of twenty million people, the majority of whom were Malay—was obsessed with the Chinese question: how to get economic power out of the hands of the Chinese and into those of the Malays. There could not have been a more sensitive issue for the foundation to get involved in, but in 1963, in response to a request from then-Deputy Prime Minister Tun Abdul Razak, who became Malaysia's second prime minister in 1970, the foundation agreed to support the development of research capacity and training of staff in the Economic Planning Unit and a new Development Administration Unit attached to the primer minister's office.

Razak was the development brain of the government, having served as both deputy prime minister and minister for rural development. He was a bright, charming man who probably understood both the inherent difficulties of raising the economic status of the rural Malays and the political dangers of inaction better than any other politician. The situation was indeed becoming explosive. In 1969, a rising young Malay politician, Dr. Mahathir bin Mohamad, published an angry book called *The Malay Dilemma*, arguing that the Malays had been second-class citizens throughout the colonial period in large part because of their own apathy, and that they needed to get tough about taking over their rightfully dominant position in society. In the same year, Malay-led, anti-Chinese riots broke out in Kuala Lumpur that killed at least two hundred people, mostly Chinese (some observers thought the toll was much larger), sparked by the prospect that political parties representing a Chinese-Indian coalition of interests might take over power from the Malay-dominated coalition that had governed Malaysia since independence. The government declared an emergency, suspended parliamentary rule, and expelled Mahathir from the ranks of the ruling party. It amended the constitution to establish Malay as the official language, codify the special rights of ethnic Malays, and guarantee the traditional rights of the Malay sultans.

As concerned economic policy, helping the Malaysian government figure out how to plot the course for possibly the most ambitious and sweeping "affirmative action" program any non-communist, post-World War II Asian government ever undertook became the primary task of the Economic Planning Unit, whose Harvard-supplied Western advisers, funded by Ford, were a group of five American and Western economists headed by a tough, smart, engaging Norwegian chief adviser named Just Faaland. The chief of the Economic Planning Unit was an ethnic Chinese civil servant, Thong Yow Hong. In the late 1950s, Thong had spent a year as a Ford-funded fellow studying economic development at Harvard and was primarily responsible for bringing the Harvard group to Malaysia. The Chinese everywhere in Malaysia were in a difficult position in the wake of the Kuala Lumpur riots and the incessant political agitation for more of everything immediately for the Malays. I became a good friend of a distinguished, ethnic Chinese professor of economics at the University of Malaya, where the ethnic Malay vice chancellor had launched a crash program requiring Malay language fluency for all staff members, the use of Malay as the language of instruction (virtually all instruction had been in English), and expedited, preferential admission of students of Malay origin (all of which soon became government policy). When my professor friend and I talked, it reminded me of conversations in my old days in the Soviet Union—the professor would lower his voice and look over his shoulder to see who might be listening.

In the months immediately following the riots, Just Faaland, the chief adviser, whom a subsequent project evaluator hired by the foundation described as "in his bones a Scandinavian socialist," became convinced, as the evaluation put it, "of the need for a dramatic shift to a radically interventionist program of racial redress." Finding that the Economic Planning Unit was being frozen out of high-level decision-making (and that several of his colleagues in the EPU did not support his views), Faaland took his case to senior Malays he knew in and out of the government. A Faaland paper, which he identified as personal and not official, in support of his arguments, was immediately followed by a counter-paper, written at Thong's request by another Harvard economist, Henry Bruton, which also recommended immediate changes to address the status of Malays but argued that the government's development goals must combine both equity and economic growth. Faaland and Harvard—and the foundation—eventually parted company. Both his emphasis on the urgency of redress, and Bruton's emphasis on economic growth became reflected in subsequent policies.

In 1971, Tun Razak announced a "New Economic Policy" (in no sense a copy of Lenin's famous New Economic Policy of the 1920s) that set forth two goals: "To reduce and eventually eradicate poverty, and to accelerate the process of restructuring Malaysian society to correct economic imbalance, so as to reduce and eventually eliminate the identification of race with economic function." The essence of the NEP remains at the heart of Malaysian economic and social policy today. In a 1990 research paper, published two decades after the NEP was launched, Harvard economist Donald Snodgrass, who had worked years earlier as an adviser in Kuala Lumpur, analyzed the results of the program. As concerns its goals, employment was to be restructured by sector and occupation, eliminating the "ethnic division of labor" that had been created in colonial times and remained quite evident in 1970. The ownership and control of wealth were to be restructured; specifically, Malays were to hold 30 percent of corporate-sector assets by 1990, compared to their share then of 2 percent; Chinese and Indian Malaysians were to hold 40 percent (which was actually a few points above their share then), while the foreign (mostly British) share was to plummet from 65 percent to 30 percent. The overriding goal was national unity. Snodgrass concludes that on balance this unprecedented affirmative-action program was a success. Poverty eradication was a clear-cut, impressive success. Poverty in rural, mostly Malay, households declined from nearly 50 percent in 1970 to 15 percent in 1990. Employment restructuring succeeded: the number of Malays working in the increasingly modern, medium-and high-technology industrial sector soared from one hundred seventy three thousand in 1970 to almost one million in 1990. Malay employment in the service sector rose from two hundred thousand to over a million. Malays are now slightly over-represented in professional and technical and in-service occupations—thanks, no doubt, to government employment, Snodgrass notes. As concerned probably the most difficult single task, the restructuring of corporate ownership and wealth, Malay ownership of corporate wealth is estimated to have risen from 2-plus percent in 1970 to more than 20 percent in 1990, and foreign (mostly British) ownership declined from 60-plus percent to about 25 percent in 1990. While the vast majority of the Malay community is much better off, the Chinese community has not ceased to prosper, although, as Snodgrass notes, it was "often frustrated by its inability to influence policy through political action." Chinese emigration was surprisingly limited.

The foundation ceased its support of the Economic Planning Unit in 1976 after a ten-year investment of almost three and a half million dollars in advisers and training fellowships (forty-eight Malaysian officials were trained), although the unit continued to receive assistance from other external funding agencies for several years. All the plans since 1976 have been prepared entirely by Malaysian staff. Mahathir, the radically nationalist Malay politician, was elected prime minister in 1981 and has been Malaysia's political master ever since, re-elected regularly. Increasingly authoritarian and grandiose in his vision, Mahathir presided over the construction of the world's tallest building in Kuala Lumpur to show what Malays could do. He brooked no opposition in the ruling Malay party and eventually threw his rising and increasingly popular deputy prime minister in jail on sex-crime charges—a case many human rights activists have charged was trumped up. Mahathir loves to twit the West about its decadence and coming decline. He has consistently opposed the efforts of the international financial institutions to impose their policy views on the Malaysian economy—most notably in the great crash of the Southeast and East Asian economies in the early nineties when he mandated restrictions on short-term movements of foreign capital. This proved to be an absolutely sound decision that protected Malaysia from the damages suffered by those of its neighbors who followed Western policy recommendations. Mahathir has been an irritating, heavy-handed, and generally effective leader.

In the early 1970s, as my feisty young staff and I sized up the region and the development problems in which Ford assistance could be helpful, we agreed on several points. If history could be said to pause—which, of course, it never really does—we were at such a moment. The first generation of the founding fathers of Southeast Asian independence was passing from the stage. The early institution building work the foundation had undertaken was either completed or in final stages. In Thailand, for example, the National Institute of Development Administration (NIDA), strongly supported by the government, was beginning to produce highly qualified graduates for both government and private-sector management positions. Major institution building grants at the University of the Philippines and the Asian Institute of Management in Manila were virtually finished. The foundation's long commitment to economic planning in Malaysia was winding down. On the other hand, there was still much to do in agricultural research and experimentation with new concepts in multi-cropping systems based on rice and with small-scale irrigation systems, and population and family planning programs continued to be generally under-funded and only sporadically effective.

A second conclusion was that no one was adequately addressing a number of important issues. The plundering and misuse of the natural resources of water, forests, and fisheries throughout Southeast Asia had gone very far. The great teak forests of Northern Thailand were receding year after year because of the slash-and-burn farming practices of the rapidly growing population of poor farmers and unchecked illegal logging that turned many bureaucrats and generals into millionaires. On the big island of Mindanao in the southern Philippines, the tropical hardwood forests were virtually disappearing before one's eyes as you flew over the jungle. We recruited an imaginative young scientist, Jeff Romm, trained at the University of California in Berkeley with degrees in forestry and economics, to work on these problems and equipped him with what the foundation called in its internal jargon a "Delegated Authority Project," essentially a small, designated pot of money for exploring a new subject with small grants, consultants, small-scale research, and conferences. Romm brought a British scientist and ecologist, Gordon Conway (who later became the president of the Rockefeller Foundation), to the region to work with him, and they began to lay the foundations of what became a Southeast Asia-wide movement to improve the conservation and management of natural resources, involving both governments and local populations.

We decided to expand the small-scale work the foundation had undertaken in arts and archaeology, making, for example, small grants to support private groups like the Siam Society in Bangkok and to establish a new Council of Living Traditions in the Philippines, an organization of Filipino humanists dedicated to the preservation and public understanding of the Filipino cultural heritage. We would continue to support agricultural research and add a series of small, experimental grants in rural development (local-level, citizen's group management of small irrigation systems, for example). In education, we agreed to strengthen the non-economic social sciences throughout the region, and, where the opportunity existed, to use research and training to highlight and deal with specific problems in public education. A case in point was northeast Thailand, which in spite of its political sensitivity was at the bottom of the barrel of Thai public education. A young staff member, Bill Fuller (subsequently president of the Asia Foundation), an economist and a specialist in education, went to work with a small, enthusiastic group of young Thai economists and educators whose published work unequivocally demonstrated the gap between budget-planning figures and funds actually allocated and proved to be the catalyst that finally began to upgrade the northeastern Thai school systems.

Our riskiest decision, in political if not financial terms, was to open a small grant-making office in Vietnam. This proved to be an enterprise of truly quixotic proportions but one that none of us ever regretted. The foundation had never had a presence in Vietnam. The Ford decision-makers of the 1950s and 1960s thought the foundation's basic, long-term, institution-building strategy would not work in a country essentially in a state of civil war. By the late 1960s, the U.S. official presence dominated and overwhelmed the country, not only in its military and intelligence embodiment but also through the world's largest-ever U.S. Agency for International Development assistance program and office. But the Paris peace accords of January 1973 terminated American military intervention and held out the possibility that, in the quasi-peace that characterized the scene, Vietnam could begin to develop along peaceful lines. While I was still managing the Asia program in the New York headquarters of the foundation in March 1973, the trustees authorized an exploration of grant-making needs and opportunities in Vietnam, with special attention to cultural factors, namely language, history, humanities, art, and archaeology, on the assumption that these largely had been ignored while American official assistance concentrated on the economy and strengthening the bureaucracy. Our central argument was that Vietnam was one of the most important societies of Southeast Asia and that its development could contribute much to the achievement of a community of nations in the region. We thought that the foundation, as a private, independent funding agency, could play a role in encouraging some degree of pluralism in the intellectual life of South Vietnam. We did not want to get involved with supporting the government but thought we could usefully support individuals and selected institutions, such as universities, without identifying ourselves with the policies of a particular Vietnamese regime. We could manage a small exploratory program using the resources of the Bangkok regional office with only marginal additions to staff and management structure.

In undertaking the exploration, we took care to make it clear that as a private philanthropy we were prepared to support development activities in both the north and the south. We communicated this to Hanoi in a message through the North Vietnamese embassy in Laos, and I was invited to visit Hanoi in early 1973 but could not do so because of a locked-in prior commitment (and was never invited again). In the summer of 1973, we hired Charles Benoit to set up a small office in Saigon to support the exploratory activities. Over the next several months, the regional staff plus a number of outside consultants examined their fields of activities—agriculture, education including the arts and humanities, population, and management—and the overall political, economic, and social scene in the south. Benoit, a broad-shouldered hulk of a young man with an easy smile, was, I thought, a perfect fit for our needs. As a humanities student at Yale, he had been a second-string All-American blocking back on the football team. He went on to pursue a PhD in Vietnamese classical poetry at Harvard. He spoke fluent Vietnamese and Mandarin Chinese, had traveled throughout Vietnam as a student and as a stringer correspondent for CBS, and was the favorite American of every poor Vietnamese shoeshine boy on the teeming streets of Saigon.

When in the uneasy spring of 1974 we launched this limited program, we found—not entirely to our surprise—that the South Vietnamese government looked on us with mixed views. The Ministry of Foreign Affairs thought we should support only development programs it regarded as high priority and said flatly that culture and the humanities, although important, were luxuries secondary to other more pressing needs. The minister of education, on the other hand, praised our interest, saying that the years of warfare had left cultural areas neglected and underdeveloped. The government delayed the authorization of the "status agreement" required to allow us to begin our work officially until the fall of 1974, and, since we had been open in our intentions to try to be of assistance to the north as well, we were not considered to be part of American assistance but put into a category that included only the Quakers and the United Nations Children's Fund.

In the brief year of our work in Vietnam before the North Vietnamese swept down from the mountains and drove their tanks into the South Vietnamese presidential compound, while in scenes of panic and chaos Americans fled in helicopters from the American embassy roof, we achieved very little. After the Communist victory, in May 1975 the regional staff and I—we were about eight people—met in an off-season beach house in Pattaya on the Gulf of Thailand south of Bangkok for a weekend discussion of what we had tried to do and what we should do now. The weather was rainy and dismal, as was our mood. We all had grown to like and respect the Vietnamese we were working with, often in circumstances of personal or professional difficulty for them, and thought we were on the right track with our modest, non-official grant-making. Benoit and I then spent a few days in isolation in Baguio, the old hill resort in the highlands above Manila, to write a report and evaluation for the foundation's board of trustees back in New York. Benoit's report summed up: "Although promising beginnings were made, few projects had actually been completed, and after the tumultuous days of April, relatively little in terms of programs remains to be evaluated.... One could say...that the foundation had made a modest beginning toward identifying numbers of talented Vietnamese with whom to chart a future course." We had made, for example, four awards to scholars at Vietnamese universities. One was to assist young staff members at the University of Hue to complete their PhD training in Vietnamese history and linguistics at Saigon University. A second went to the University of Can Tho to expand a rare, local initiative in surveying socioeconomic indicators in the Mekong Delta. A third supported the expansion of a research and training program in economic geography at Saigon University that involved preparation and publication of provincial profiles, and a fourth was to Van Hanh University, a private Buddhist institution, to begin a program for training teachers of Vietnamese classical music. We had made a small grant to a leading Buddhist organization, the Vien Hoa Dao, for lectures and performances of Vietnamese classical arts at a national conference and a small award to the local Vietnamese chapter of the International Pen Club for research on traditional Vietnamese theater. We made a number of individual awards to Vietnamese scholars for support research on Vietnamese literature, history, and the arts, and small grants to the National Library to provide microfilm to supplicate the archives of the Nguyen dynasty and to the National Museum for a Filipino display specialist as a short-term consultant to improve its exhibits. We had begun to identify and place Vietnamese in a number of regional foundation fellowship programs, including population and archaeology. We were on the verge of launching a promising small program in agricultural research and rural development.

On the eve of the fall of Saigon, Benoit and our only other resident American, Jerry Silverman, left. The tiny Vietnamese staff chose to remain and to continue to report for work until ordered to stop by either the foundation or the Vietnamese authorities. From one report we heard, they were still appearing for work six weeks after the fall—we had left sufficient funds to cover salaries for a period of several months while we tried to establish new communications through the new regime—which proved to be impossible. Then all went silent. Almost immediately after the fall of Saigon, Benoit made one extremely risky trip back into South Vietnam to find and bring out his daughter, the issue of a love affair with a Vietnamese woman with whom he had parted company. In more recent years, he made a number of trips to the south trying to trace what happened to our staff and finally found out. The two senior Vietnamese men on the staff, both of whom before working for us had served as officers in the south's army, were arrested, sent to re-education (forced labor) camps, and eventually executed. Benoit is now a private businessman living and working in Shanghai. The foundation has a sizable grant program in Vietnam, headquartered in Hanoi.

What can one say about Vietnam that has not been said better by others? Neil Sheehan's *A Bright and Shining Lie* is a book for the centuries: an overwhelming, passionate portrayal of the war and the corruption of power of both Americans and Vietnamese. The American experience in Vietnam is widely and richly documented in fiction, film, and memoirs. With all the war's horrors and cruelties, I shared with Graham Greene, writing much earlier, and most of the war correspondents a fascination with the style, the smells, the taste, the self-contained and frequently gorgeous women of Saigon, and the uniquely Saigonese mixture of Vietnamese and French ways. The countryside, with both rice paddies and mountains, was poetically beautiful. Benoit, Charlotte, and I once drove in his old Citroën Deux Cheveux up to Dalat to spend a weekend in an old French-built resort hotel. After driving for hours through the hills on ominously empty roads—this was late in the war, and an empty road often meant trouble ahead in the neighborhood—we found the entire hotel empty and at our service with a French-trained chef who fed us veal that could not be surpassed in Paris and fine French wine. In 1974, Mac Bundy came to Vietnam for his first visit since he had left the Johnson White House. He was received in a far different style—this time, with a total absence of fanfare. Benoit and I introduced Bundy to some Vietnamese scholars in Saigon and drove him out to Can Tho to visit the agricultural university. On the way back to Saigon for Bundy to catch his flight out, we stopped for early supper with a Vietnamese farmer and village headman whom Benoit knew. Bundy and the headman argued for hours in French about history and politics until we had to leave; the headman thought the Americans had never understood the Vietnamese and should never have taken over the burden of the war from the South Vietnamese government. It was a conversation Bundy might have benefited from ten years earlier. Bundy and I had had our own arguments about the expansion of the war in the early days of the Johnson administration, which led to the swollen and ultimately ineffective U.S. presence in the south, although I did not essentially disagree with the original rationale for supporting the South Vietnamese in fighting the Communists—in essence the trite but persuasive metaphor of dominos falling throughout Asia in the case of a Communist victory.

I was wrong about Vietnam in one important regard in our post-program, postwar evaluation. In a paper I wrote for the senior officers of the foundation in the summer of 1975, I said:

> The unified Vietnam that will emerge, probably fairly soon, should be the most dynamic, and in many ways the most powerful, state in Southeast Asia. The combined Vietnam is rich in resources and relatively underdeveloped; militarily, the Vietnamese armed forces are the most powerful in Southeast Asia; the Vietnamese people are vigorous, well-educated (the spread of public education in the South during decades of war is a tribute both to the South Vietnamese, who managed this effort under the most difficult of circumstances, and to the U.S. Agency for International Development, which funded much of it), and they are, relative to other Southeast Asians, well-trained in modern and developmentally useful technologies. The infrastructure left in South Vietnam by the war is virtually intact; its airports, ports, harbors, and roads are among the best in Asia. In sum Vietnam will be a formidable, zealous and confident power. Reconstruction is likely to take only a few, rather than many, years.

In fact, having won an impressively led, truly historic victory, whose consequences influenced American foreign and military policy decision-making for twenty-five years, the aging ideologues in Hanoi locked the doors and devoted themselves to a prolonged, cruel period of internal revenge and re-education, trying to create a 1930s kind of model Marxist society (while the rest of the Marxist world crumbled around them). Only in the last few years, faced with the continuing poverty and underdevelopment of their population and resources and their inability to control their people's minds under the onslaught of modern communications, has the Vietnamese government begun to open its doors in a modest way to foreign investors and ideas. It is only now beginning to assume a regional role as one of the major powers of Southeast Asia. Its leadership faces the same implacable question as the Communists in Beijing: how can they become relevant?

In the waning months of 1975, Mac Bundy and David Bell asked me if I would like to move to New Delhi and take over the job of foundation representative for India, Nepal, and Sri Lanka. Ever since I first visited India ten years earlier, I had thought this must be the greatest job in the world. Charlotte had gone with me on numerous trips to India from New York and shared my fascination with India. But there were now serious health considerations attached to a move to India. Bangkok offered a number of world-class health facilities (clean blood was readily available for transfusions if necessary, for example), and Charlotte's chemotherapy treatments had gone generally well. International-quality health care was not the case in India in those days (most wealthy Indians and senior government officials flew out to London or New York when they got really sick). We made a weekend flight to New Delhi to look into the health-care question and finally decided that a small, private hospital and clinic managed by an Indian doctor, who had cared for a generation of foundation patients and had access to the capital's best specialists, would probably work.

In early 1976, we said good-bye to our Thai friends and the staff in Bangkok (two of whom later joined me in India), and flew off to New Delhi in the first-class cabin of Lufthansa, holding our two, Chinese-style dogs, Mii Noi and Bitsy, on our laps, which Lufthansa had said would be permissible. This was the first time either of them had ever been outside our large compound in Bangkok. En route to the airport, we stopped by the roadside for a final canine pee, and they were amazed by the slight incline of the roadside berm, having never seen anything remotely approaching a hill in their lives. On the flight, they handled themselves with dignity and composure with one exception, when for no visible reason (she had been lying peacefully on my lap) Bitsy emitted one single, sharp yip that elicited completely justifiable glances of disapproval from our Germanic fellow travelers. In Delhi, we met the foundation staff, many of whom I already knew, quickly settled into the furnished house provided for the representative, then left the dogs with the household staff (two men—a cook and a bearer), and flew on to New York for medical checks for Charlotte and consultations for me. I wanted to be sure we had a chance for at least a short period of Indian-language training.

The foundation's New York headquarters agreed that en route to New Delhi we could stop in England for two months of intensive Hindi-language training at the School of Oriental and African Languages at the University of London.

12

A Farm in the Punjab

For a while, before Charlotte died, we lived on a small farm in the Punjab, outside New Delhi along an old Mogul roadway lined with ruined red sandstone tombs, palaces, and minarets, past the Qutub Minar, the stone victory tower celebrating the triumph of the Muslim general Qutb-ud-Din Aibak over the Hindu prince Prithwi Raja in AD 1199, and finally into a quiet country lane, where one was far more likely to meet a camel or a herd of goats or water buffaloes than a car. The foundation's administrative officer, Mr. Bhambri, accustomed to producing miracles for his bosses (the boss is known in India as the *bara* [big] *sahib* [master or boss]), found the farm for me when Charlotte, who loved gardens and space, almost visibly began to wither in the confines of our city house in the artificial atmosphere of the diplomatic enclave of the capital.

I informed Charlotte of Bhambri's and my good deed in New York, where she was undergoing a round of medical examinations and starting on new anti-cancer drugs. As I showed her photographs, she expressed some doubts on such points as kitchen and bathroom facilities, which were admittedly somewhat primitive. On our return, she confirmed these doubts forcefully, looking at the farmhouse facilities with dismay. But with some rebuilding, the farmhouse became a comfortable, small jewel of a lodging, invisible from the sleepy side road in its garden of roses, bougainvillea, and mango trees, surrounded by six acres of heavenly smelling lemon and orange trees. I drove into the city six days a week to work. Charlotte came in to New Delhi several times a week, and from time to time we spent a night in a small apartment in the foundation guesthouse in the modern Chanakya Puri neighborhood of New Delhi, where most of the diplomats and well-to-do foreigners lived.

New Delhi is a great, dull regal city (a "hick, Punjabi town," an Indian friend, himself a Punjabi, once said). It is the eighth city recorded historically to be built on this favored, well-watered, crossroads site on the plain of the somewhat holy Jumna River, which empties not far downstream into the extremely holy Ganges.

The handsome bones of the seven earlier cities lie scattered around the landscape in all directions. The British moved the seat of empire to New Delhi very late in their imperial rule in 1913, when they gave up trying to rule India from Calcutta, that endlessly rebellious Bengali city in eastern India. Historically, the Mogul emperors, living in Lahore, Delhi, and Agra, sent nobles regarded as dispensable down the Ganges to serve as governors of Bengal, where within a short time they were usually murdered.

The capital's symbolic and political center is a splendid, Cecil de Mille-quality, set of pink sandstone palaces and government buildings looming above a vast mall and parade ground to embody and glorify the British imperial power that the architect, Sir Edwin Luytens, thought would never end. When the British left in 1947, the Indian politicians and top government bureaucrats settled promptly and comfortably into the British-built imperial buildings. Particularly prized are the plush, government-owned bungalows—roomy, elegant houses with servant quarters, large, green lawns, and rose gardens—for ministers, senior generals, and civil servants. For my own taste, the Afghan and Mogul buildings of the earlier empires like the Red Fort and the Great Mosque in Old Delhi are far more elegant and graceful than Luytens's ponderous giants, although Luytens did make an attempt to incorporate Mogul motifs in his work.

As in another capital city I knew well, Washington DC, politics and influence peddling were New Delhi's chief business. The elites of the city traded gossip and rumors about the ups and downs of important politicians' hearts, stomachs, and moods as addictively as any Washington beltway journalist or political hanger-on. As in Washington, the most rewarding people in New Delhi were usually not politicians but journalists, writers, artists, and men and women who represented private groups, profit and nonprofit, trying to move the beast of government in one direction or another. In at least one respect, Delhi is rather more interesting than Washington. Those coming in from the provinces to seek their fortunes, find a job, or cook up a political alliance are a much more diverse and colorful lot—all colors, indeed, and dozens of languages and styles of dress—than the more heterogeneous American boon-seekers in Washington. Like Washington, no matter how the provinces decay and are in anguish, New Delhi prospers. Old Delhi is another world. Population growth has joined the two sites awkwardly together. The markets of the old city still teem with gold merchants, jewelers, silk and cloth merchants, tinsmiths, carpenters, and snake charmers up and down the narrow, crowded medieval streets. The Red Fort, the spectacular Great Mosque, the thronged Hindu temples with their drums playing, their resident monkeys, and the holy men with foreheads painted white and red, and the decaying red stone and brick town houses of the once-great merchant families and courtiers, with their balconied facades and interior courtyards, offer evidence of Delhi's past splendors. If I had been alone, I might have wanted to live there.

To run the farm, I hired an enthusiastic, retired agronomist from the government agricultural service as manager. Mr. Ramanathan regarded me as heaven-sent, a male incarnation of Lakshmi, the goddess of wealth, and, in acknowledgement of the superior wisdom of the gods, left no rupee unspent in order for us to be able to boast of the best small farm in northern India. With the help of two taciturn, stick-thin Punjabi farm laborers, we planted wheat and potatoes, some of which we ate but most of which we sold, and cared for the lemon and orange grove, whose fruit was small and sweet and brought a good price in the market. I hired a night watchman, who, in the best tradition of Asian folk tales, mostly slept. For the weeding, we hired work gangs of tough, local farmwomen, who giggled when I put on running shorts and jogged around a perimeter trail the laborers built on my instruction. Many of the younger women were stunning—tan, rosy skin, aquiline noses, and ravishing dark eyes which they used to their best effect in the direct, proud gaze of Punjabi women. In spite of their strenuous manual labor, with childbearing and a diet of buffalo milk, wheat chapattis (flat, unleavened bread), and clarified butter, they became fat-haunched early on, which is what Punjabi men prefer. The Bengali writer Nirad Chaudhuri, an unerring observer of Indian taste and psychology, wrote that "the Punjabi feminine body is seen at its best from behind, and that is also how the Punjabi men love best to gape at their women. When they see one of them approaching from the front, a hard and tense stare appears in their eyes, and there is in it only an expectation and no enjoyment; but as soon as the woman has passed them and they have, according to their invariable habit, made a right-about turn to look at her from the back, the eyes soften and a soft sigh escapes from their bosom."

My first-hand dealings with the Indian land and its fauna and flora made me an insufferable instant expert in my work on economic development problems with my colleagues at the Ford Foundation and elsewhere in New Delhi, many of whom were economists or other social scientists and engineers, both Indian and Western. They lived in modern houses and walled compounds in the sprawling city, and only occasionally, if ever, heard the price of wheat and potatoes from their cooks. On the farm, on the other hand, from day to day we knew what bugs were eating the wheat, how an unexpected high wind shattered the grain, and how villainously low were the futures prices quoted by the itinerant commodity traders, who all across the subcontinent take to the side roads as the grain and fruit crops ripen. In northern India, the Sikhs and the Punjabis make money out of farming. I was neither. We spared no expense and produced India's highest-cost wheat and potatoes.

But I regarded us as fortunate. In India, land and water are life itself, and on this blessed little farm, even in the burning, pre-monsoon heat and drought days of May and June, when great flocks of swallows cascaded down the yellow sky over the mango groves, and the earth was faint, and slow, distant thunder growled over the distant plains, our small tube-well delivered torrents of marvelously cold, sweet water for drinking and irrigation. The flame trees were fire-bright in the pre-monsoon heat. In the monsoon rains, nature exploded into growth, plants almost visibly rising and burgeoning before your eyes. In the autumn, the scent of sun-warmed lemon and orange blossoms filled our days, and in the still, clear winter our roses were exquisite.

The plains pulsated with life. Tame little gray doves cooed in the fruit groves. Partridges scuttled in the bushes. A dozen peacocks nested in the neem trees that marked the border of our land, by night interrupting our sleep with their Macbethian wailings. By day, the enormous burnished birds, who wrought havoc in the vegetable garden (peacocks will eat virtually anything), nonchalantly defied my sporadic efforts to encourage them to move on—a direct hit with an air rifle produced a small plop against the thick layer of lustrous feathers, a slight hop of surprise, and then back to the business of feeding. One evening, to my amazement and dismay, I killed a peacock with the air rifle while aiming at a barely visible blob high in a tree against a darkening sky. I had fired and begun to walk on when suddenly an enormous object plummeted to the ground. I had hit a peahen in its eye. Killing peacocks is illegal in India, so I hauled the dead bird over to the fence and, looking around me guiltily, left it by the side of the road. The carcass was gone in the morning, probably carried away by semi-wild dogs. Green parrots shrieked their song of gluttony in my papaya trees, and sometimes when I dozed in a deck chair in the garden shade I was awakened by papaya pulp raining onto my hair. One day, we found an old cobra living in a deserted pump-house, coping not very well with its job of eating the constantly multiplying hordes of field rats that burrowed in the mud irrigation channels and sallied forth by night to feast on the ripening grain. The gardeners promptly dispatched him with a hoe. The rats got worse.

Once or twice a day, small caravans of camels ambled along the dirt road that led past the farm to the arid, low hills that comprise one of the ridges defining the Delhi basin of the Jumna River. The hard-faced, mustachioed drivers, slumping forward and backward in the immemorial rhythm of the camel walk, were commonly thought to be smugglers, although the prosaic truth was that they were simply transporters of produce and construction materials to and from the semi-desert outskirts to the suburban markets of the vast capital city. Our two little Chinese-style dogs, brought to this fierce northern land from our earlier residence in Thailand, where they lived in a compound surrounded by orchids and ponds full of bright-colored carp, greeted the sound of camel bells with hysterical barking. The proverb proved true. The dogs bark. The caravan moves on. Bitsy, the smaller and brighter of the two (they were both dimwitted), once actually saw a camel at a distance of one yard and failed to recognize it as anything at all.

(A few years later, on a weeklong camel safari in the Pakistan desert, the group I was with sallied forth early every morning like a tribal war party, the great beasts pacing and dancing, bells jingling, heads high surveying the trail ahead. Persian and Arabic poets wrote love poems about their favorite camels, which are responsive, reliable, passionate, and jealous animals. In the rutting season, the males slaver and bellow and are in a mood to kill. When they fight, male camels wrap their long necks around each other, biting and feinting and throwing their weight like sumo wrestlers to knock the opponent off his feet and to the ground where it can be killed by kneeling on its chest and neck. In their wrestling, the earth literally shakes.)

A half-mile down the road toward the desert past the irrigated farmland was a stone quarry, which served to remind me that this Indian paradise also included hell. The quarry was worked by a hundred or so indentured, low-caste laborers, all of them almost certainly in debt-slavery for life. The wraith-like men and women and their older children cut stone and carried backbreaking loads up to trucks from dawn to dusk in blazing sun, torrential rain, and freezing cold alike. The filthy, miserable, smaller children perched on the cliffs like small, sick birds. Child labor was not illegal in India. In 1981, according to the highly respected American political scientist Myron Weiner, the Indian census reported that 80 million of India's 158 million children between the ages of six and fourteen did not attend school. Weiner noted: "They stay at home to care for cattle, tend younger children, collect firewood, and work in the fields. They find employment in cottage industries, tea stalls, restaurants, or as household workers in middle-class homes. They become prostitutes or live as street children, begging or picking rags and bottles from trash for resale. Many are bonded laborers, tending cattle and working as agricultural laborers for local landowners."

Weiner's meticulously documented *The Child and the State in India* argues that:

India is a significant exception to the global trend toward the removal of children from the labor force and the establishment of compulsory, universal primary-school education. Poverty has not prevented governments of other developing countries from expanding mass education or making primary education compulsory....The central proposition of this study is that India's low per capita income and economic situation is less relevant as an explanation than the belief systems of the state bureaucracy, a set of beliefs that are widely shared by educators, social activists, trade unionists, academic researchers, and, more broadly, by members of the Indian middle class. These beliefs are held by those outside as well as those within government, by observant Hindus and by those who regard themselves as secular, and by leftists as well as by centrists and rightists. At the core of these beliefs are the Indian view of the social order, notions concerning the respective rules of upper and lower social strata, the role of education as a means of maintaining differentiations among social classes, and concerns that "excessive" and "inappropriate" education for the poor would disrupt existing social arrangements...These beliefs are closely tied to religious notions and to the premises that underlie India's hierarchical caste system...Those who control the education system are remarkably indifferent to the low enrollment and high dropout rate among the lowest social classes. The explanation for policy lies not in interest group politics nor state interests, but in the beliefs and values of elites that shape their political actions, that is, in India's political culture.

In Delhi in the cool winter afternoons, a faintly warm sun lying orange on the horizon, the princes, the landowners, and the army officers played polo, and at the Gymkhana Club, the British-era country club with squash and grass tennis courts, the old Delhi elites gathered at lawn parties to discuss marriages and politics. Occasionally, one might even comment that the nights were so chilly that, according to the newspapers, some dozens of poor people, wrapped in their cotton rags, froze to death. Heads would wag with disapproval. In earlier assignments in New York and Asia, I used to arrive in New Delhi on such winter afternoons, full of excitement about the dynamism and pace of development and social change in East and Southeast Asia. Eager to share my experiences, I invariably found India interested only in itself. "Where did you say you have been?" an Indian friend would ask when I started to talk about what Lee Kuan Yew was accomplishing in low-income public housing in Singapore, or the tough and effective rural and industrial development policies of the South Koreans, or the adaptability of the Thai economic system. "But those are small countries," the bored reply would be, "it is much easier to do things there than it is in India. This is a vast (frequently pronounced 'wast') country." Properly deflated and put in place, I would turn to local gossip.

There was, of course, a considerable grain of truth in this skeptical Indian view of the relevance of the experience of the rest of the world. The Indian subcontinent *is* enormous, tradition-bound, and geographically and linguistically almost ridiculously diverse. East, west, north and south Indians do not look alike and speak different languages. In the north, they eat wheat; in the south and east, rice; in the west, millet. Ainslee Embree, a Columbia University historian, wrote that the only system that unifies India is belief in, or at least acceptance of, what he calls "Brahmanic" ideology. This view of the world, based on the Hindu caste system, is like an internal gyroscope installed at birth controlling and directing the behavior of every Indian, not only the Hindu majority but the Muslims as well, along with the relatively few Christians and a tiny number of Buddhists, most of whose families originally were low-caste or untouchable Hindus and converted to try to escape the caste system. (The essence of the caste system, stripped to its barest bones, divides society into four castes, into which one is born: priests, warriors, merchants, and workers. Beyond the pale were the untouchables, who performed polluting labor. Over many millennia, each caste gave birth to a bewildering proliferation of sub-castes. Even untouchables in the villages, for example, divide into sub-castes—"left hand" untouchables, who clean out the village latrines, and "right hand" untouchables, who skin dead animals and tan leather.) The unique characteristic of the "Brahmanic" ideology is this mandated existence of separate group identities, and these traditional Hindu conceptions of man, society, and the universe are the antithesis of the liberal, universalizing Western view of the social psychology regarded as basic to economic modernization (as argued by such scholars as R. H. Tawney in his *Religion and the Rise of Capitalism* and Karl Marx). One's station in life is largely predetermined by the merit and destiny (*karma*) earned through the satisfactory performance of the duty (*dharma*) attached to one's position in previous lives. The important issues in life are not equality or a broad concern for one's fellow men, but rather the performance of one's own dharma within the hierarchical system that affects all. The rules of the game differ for each group. The biblical rule—do unto others as you would have done to you—is of no relevance. Each caste and sub-caste has its own laws, its own preordained duties and ethics.

The Indian poet, scholar and grammarian, the late A. K. Ramanujan, in a 1980 essay noted that: "One has only to read Manu after a bit of Kant to be struck by Manu's extraordinary lack of universality. He seems to have no clear notion of a universal human nature from which one can deduce ethical decrees like 'Man shall not kill,' or 'Man shall not tell an untruth.' One is aware of no notion of a 'state,' no unitary law of all men." Manu was the classic law-giver in the Hindu tradition, whose role in the Hindu world is in some regards comparable to that of Moses for the Jews, Muslims, and Christians. Ramanujan recalls an observation of Hegel more than a century ago: "While we say, 'Bravery is a virtue,' the Hindoos say, on the contrary, 'Bravery is a virtue of the Cshatriyas' (the warrior caste)." (In my own search for understanding, I once remarked to an Indian journalist friend that I thought I was beginning to understand India. "Aha!" he responded with delight. "But what are you going to do about it?")

"Even space and time, the universal contexts, the Kantian imperatives, are in India not uniform and neutral, but have properties, varying specific densities, that affect those who dwell in them," Ramanujan writes. Time, for example, moves in enormous cycles called *yugas*, each of which breeds certain kinds of maladies, politics, and religions. Ramanujan recalls a story about two men coming to Yudhisthira, the prince of a great clan and a central figure of the Mahabharata epic, with a dispute. "One had bought the other's land, and soon after found a crock of gold in it. He wanted to return it to the original owner of the land, who was arguing that it really belonged to the man who had now bought it. They had come to Yudhisthira to settle their virtuous dispute. Just then Yudhisthira was called away for a while. When he came back the two gentlemen were quarrelling furiously but each was claiming the treasure for himself this time: Yudhisthira realized at once that the age had changed, and Kaliyuga had begun."

Kaliyuga, the last of the four enormous periods of Vedic time, is the age we live in today. According to Hindu doctrine, it began five thousand years ago on the death of Krishna, the irresistible, handsome, blue-skinned god-man-prince-shepherd-flute-player-great-lover-of-milkmaids, whose life and adventures are celebrated in Indian poetry, dance, and painting. Kaliyuga will last four hundred and thirty-two thousand years. In case you hadn't noticed, it is an evil and troubling time. The Hindu poet and religious thinker, Sant Tulsidas, born in 1532, described Kaliyuga as "the hotbed of sin." He wrote: "Men and women are all steeped in unrighteousness. Whoever launches spurious undertakings and is given over to hypocrisy, him does everyone call a saint. He alone is clever who robs another of his wealth. They alone who are babblers in thought, word and deed are orators in the Kali age. In the Kali age there ensues a confusion of castes (due to promiscuous marriages) and everyone infringes the sacred laws. Men perpetrate sins and reap suffering, terror, disease, sorrow and desolation."

The majority of the population was in many respects better off before the British came. The long colonial period reduced living standards for many Indians. The forced import of English cotton goods from Manchester, for example, decimated the cottage Indian textile industry. Even so, many Indians enjoyed a good life within the traditional society, found peace in the rituals of religion and myths, and took rightful pride and joy in the beauty of the language, the art, the music, and the dance. Classical India produced world-class philosophers, mathematicians, and poets; some of the world's finest sculptures; unique traditions of architecture and painting; and music and dance of universal value. The web of culture and religion from which these achievements arose remains strong and pervasive throughout Indian society—and is an essential part of the heritage of the growing number of successful Indian professionals and entrepreneurs who have migrated to the United States in recent decades.

Classical India created a host of traditional institutions that could be used in development: village council systems, institutions for land and water management, and community and family-based systems of social conflict resolution. Mahatma Gandhi believed in the perfectibility of the Indian village and traditional ways and thought these institutions should become the basic building blocks for the new India. Gandhi wrote: "I will give you a talisman. When you are in doubt or the self becomes too much with you, apply the following test. Recall the face of the poorest and weakest man you have seen and ask yourself if the step you contemplate is going to be of any use to him. Will he gain anything by it? Will it restore him to a control over his own life and destiny? In other words, will it lead to Swaraj (freedom) for the hungry and spiritually starving millions? Then you will find your doubts and your self melting away."

Jawaharlal Nehru, who became India's first prime minister, was a modernist, with little sympathy for traditional village ways. In a famous exchange in 1945, Gandhi wrote Nehru: "I am convinced that if India is to attain true freedom, and through India the world also, then sooner or later the fact must be recognized that people will have to live in villages, not in towns; in huts, not in palaces. Crores (tens of millions) of people will never be able to live at peace with each other in towns and palaces. They will then have no recourse but to resort to both violence and untruth."

Nehru replied: "I do not understand why a village should necessarily embody truth and non-violence. A village, normally speaking, is backward economically and culturally and no progress can be made from a backward environment. Narrow minded people are much more likely to be untruthful and violent." On another occasion, Nehru wrote: "It can hardly be challenged that, in the context of the modern world, no country can be politically and economically independent unless it is highly industrialized and has developed its power resources to the utmost. Nor can it achieve or maintain high standards of living and liquidate poverty without the aid of modern technology in almost very sphere of life...If technology demands the big machine, as it does today in a large measure, then the big machine with all its implications and consequences must be accepted."

Nehru was unequivocally a socialist, albeit not of the authoritarian variety, which did not prevent him from being a devout Hindu. Nehru wrote that when he was in jail under British rule he kept his spirits up by reading the *Bhavagad-Gita* (the *Song of God*), the most beautiful and important of the ancient Indian myths, which contains the famous dialogue in which Lord Krishna counsels Prince Arjuna that he must carry out his fate—to do his duties—and take up arms against his cousins if that is what justice requires. The Soviet model of centralized economic planning fascinated Nehru, and he installed a version of it in the form of the National Planning Commission. Nehru admired Soviet accomplishments in state-managed heavy industrial development in a once-poor and backward peasant society, and his first Five-Year Plan said: "One comes inevitably to the conclusion that a rapid expansion of the economic and social responsibilities of the state will alone be capable of satisfying the legitimate expectations of the people. This need not involve complete nationalization of the means of production or elimination of private agencies in agriculture or business or industry. It does mean, however, a progressive widening of the public sector and a reorientation of the private sector to the needs of a planned economy." Nehru believed that public sector (state-run) corporations should become the "commanding heights" of the economy. The public sector was to become overwhelmingly dominant—and costly—in the decades to come.

The Nehruvian conviction that government should be the lead change agent dominated the entire early course of economic and social development in India. Douglas Ensminger, the foundation's first representative, who knew Nehru well and greatly admired him, wrote in his 1971 memoir:

> When I went to India in 1951, Nehru was India…Nehru told the people of India what he expected them to do, and the people looked to Nehru to tell them what he wanted them to do. When disputes between the states arose, Nehru called in the concerned Chief Ministers and settled their differences…Nehru had great faith in the people of India. He believed they had the capacity to work together to build a new India, as they had worked and sacrificed to gain independence. To me it was logical and a matter of common sense to accept the wisdom of the government of free India in early recognizing their need for developing, within the government, the needed infrastructure to involve the people in development and for the government to effectively serve the people…I saw the necessity of supporting a wide range of new innovative institutional infrastructures within the government of India.

So for two decades, the foundation's grants in India mostly supported government programs. Harry Wilhelm, my predecessor as representative, changed that policy, drastically reduced the foundation's large expatriate staff, and began to support a variety of institutions in higher education, particularly in the development of the social sciences. Throughout both periods, a constant stream of grant-making supported reform and modernization of the problem-beset agricultural sector, where the majority of the poor population lived, worked, and died.

When Charlotte and I arrived in Delhi in the early summer of 1976, fresh from our two-month crash course in Hindi, we landed in the midst of India's most serious crisis since independence. Prime Minister Indira Gandhi had declared a national emergency in 1975 to put an end to riots and protests against her rule and the possibility she might be forced from office because of electoral law violations in her campaign of 1971. It was the first (and to date only) interruption in democratic rule in India, and it was ironic that the daughter of the great Nehru, who embodied the concept of an independent, democratic India, should have been the one to break the mold.

Born in 1917, Indira was born to rule, it seemed. At the age of twelve, she organized a "Monkey Brigade" of fellow schoolgirls to circulate anti-British, pro-independence pamphlets. She was educated in India; in Switzerland, where she accompanied her mother, Kamala, for treatment of the tuberculosis that killed her at the age of thirty-seven; and at Oxford. Indira married Feroze Gandhi, a member of Kamala's entourage (unrelated to Mahatma Gandhi). They had two sons, Rajiv and Sanjay. In 1938, at twenty-one, Indira entered the ranks of the Indian National Congress (usually referred to simply as the Congress, or the Congress Party) as a political worker. On her mother's death, she became Nehru's hostess and confidante. Nehru was often in jail, and in 1942 the British jailed Indira as well for eight months on charges of carrying out prohibited political activities. After Nehru's death in 1964, she entered the cabinet of the new prime minister, Lal Bahadur Shastri, as the minister of information and broadcasting. In the Congress Party maneuvering after Shastri's death in 1967, Indira outwitted the old men who outranked her and won election as prime minister in 1971, campaigning on the slogan of "Garibi Hatao" (Abolish Poverty). She became enormously popular in the wake of India's triumph over Pakistan in the 1971 war, when Bangladesh split from Pakistan, and the explosion of an Indian nuclear device three years later added further to her popular image.

But poverty refused to go away, and the food situation worsened in the mid-1970s. In the countryside, villagers began to resist the vastly unpopular government effort to reduce the Indian birth rate through the male sterilization campaign led by Mrs. Gandhi's son, Sanjay, which, according to some estimates, eventually physically touched twenty million Indian men, almost all poor and rural. Most educated Indians and virtually all foreigners thought that in order to achieve overall national economic growth India must reduce the population growth rate of 2.5 percent annually, which promised to double India's population within twenty-five years. Several factors combined to make it so high. The first was the decline in mortality rates, beginning early in the nineteenth century, because of the reduction of death rates from mass killers like smallpox and malaria. The second, and economically the most important, was the need for a family, particularly a poor family, to have available the maximum number of hands required to bring in enough food and income for survival. The third was the powerful cultural preference for male children; the eldest son is a central figure in Hindu family ritual. The fourth was an almost universal lack of knowledge about, and access to, modern health and family planning facilities and technologies. (In the late 1970s when I lived in India, the population was 475.0 million. By 2000, the size of the Indian population was estimated to be 1.016 billion. China, then the world's largest nation, had a population of 1.275 billion. In the early years of the twenty-first century, India is about to surpass China and continues to grow more rapidly. By 2050, the demographic consensus is that the Indian population will reach 1.531 billion and that of China 1.395 billion. The total world population of 6.3 billion in 2003 is expected to reach 9.4 billion in 2050. One of every three people in the world will be either Indian or Chinese.)

The male sterilization campaign was carried out in part through enormous vasectomy camps organized by district officers in the countryside. Under enormous tents and with little privacy, doctors sterilized hundreds and on some occasions thousands of country men, brought in by busloads in a festive atmosphere. After the brief vasectomy operation, the men were rewarded with a small bag of goodies, which might include some new clothing or even a small battery-powered radio. Charlotte and I visited a model camp in Maharashtra State, where the district officer had become nationally famous because of his success in organizing and bringing rural men to the camps. A young, newly arrived American staff member, recently engaged to a lovely, blond young lady, accompanied us on his first trip to the countryside. In the almost unbearable heat and bustle of the enormous tent where hundreds of men lay on cots awaiting or recovering from the vasectomy procedure, our young colleague fainted. When he came to—a doctor was on the scene immediately—I said with glee, "Congratulations! They did the operation, and you're all right." The more common practice was for government sterilization teams simply to appear in a village without notice and round up the men for vasectomies. I witnessed the fear this caused graphically shortly after my arrival when, with two Ford Foundation staff members and several Indian irrigation engineers, we drove into a village near the Ganges southeast of Delhi and found it virtually deserted by the men, who thought our jeeps were from the government campaign and had taken to their heels in the fields. After the collapse of Mrs. Gandhi's government in 1977, male vasectomy virtually disappeared as a method of birth control, and female sterilization, the most brutally inefficient way to reduce fertility, took its place.

Indira's 1975 Emergency was in no way as cruel as, for example, the Communist takeovers in Eastern Europe. But it was no joke. The Gandhi regime jailed a hundred thousand or so dissenters, some of whom were tortured. Twenty or so political prisoners died in jail. The lively Indian press was harassed and censored. Some newspapers turned into propaganda organs of the government. In my earlier travels to India, I had gotten to know two of India's finest journalists, Romesh Thapar and Khushwant Singh. Thapar, a brown-skinned bear of a man, knew more about Indian politics than anyone I ever met. He kept a map of pre-British India on the wall of his office and would trace for you how centuries-old allegiances to the surviving maharajas and princes, and regional caste, language and religious groupings, dictated the course of modern elections. The sparkling, weekly journal of political commentary that Thapar and his wife, Raj, published was shut down, and the Thapars put under personal surveillance. Thapar and I met from time to time for lunch at a small hotel and chatted quietly while he periodically glanced over his shoulder. Singh, a devout Sikh, who wrote a fine book about his own religion and its saints, was a fearless and controversial editor, a frequently scandalous popular columnist, and an unabashed lecher who thought my daughter, Kathleen, visiting us in India, was luscious. One of India's most popular writers, his *Last Train to Pakistan*, is the finest single work of fiction about the bloody 1947 partition. Singh, like Thapar, knew Mrs. Gandhi well and also found himself at odds with the regime. Both men were gifted with the marvelous Indian sense of humor, wasp-tongued, subtle, and quick at perfectly catching the essence of the person or a human circumstance. The full flavor was on display at the intimate whiskey-drinking soirees when friends dropped by Singh's apartment (in a grand compound his grandfather, one of the Sikh contractors who built New Delhi for the British, helped to construct) to find out what was really going on and to enjoy the great man. In addition to anger and disgust over the Emergency, people like the Thapars and Singhs were concerned about the growing power of Indira's younger son, Sanjay, who was being groomed to take over the Nehru dynasty, had assumed the leadership of the youth wing of the

Congress Party, and clearly intended to transform it into a force that would finally eliminate any role for the party elders, who remained deeply hostile to Mrs. Gandhi. Sanjay not only designed and pushed the national vasectomy campaign but also took credit for a nationwide program of slum clearance, which many Muslims regarded as aimed primarily at them, and launched a troubled venture to create an Indian automobile manufacturing industry with Japanese collaboration. His motto for Indians: "Work harder. Talk less."

In the mid-1970s, the official relationship between the U.S. and Indian governments, never warm, had turned frigid. India could neither forget nor forgive Kissinger's threat to deploy American aircraft carriers in the Bay of Bengal in support of Pakistan during the 1971 war, when India's intervention in East Pakistan helped Bangladesh break out of a united Pakistan and become independent. That same year, the Nixon administration suspended American official development assistance to India (renewed at modest levels in 1978). The ties with the Soviet Union, in contrast, were warm and multifaceted. A large colony of Soviet officials lived unostentatiously in apartment blocks near the Soviet embassy to manage military and arms sales and a host of commercial and trade transactions. Not far away, the Chinese embassy building and grounds were locked and deserted except for a tiny staff and security guards. The once-large Ford Foundation presence—in the last days of the Ensminger *raj*, there were more than one hundred expatriate experts—was drastically reduced, and I cut it a bit further still to the point where the professional program staff, Indians and expatriates, numbered about ten persons. We were small potatoes as far as the Indian government was concerned.

That by no means meant we thought the foundation had ceased to be a potentially very useful actor in Indian development. The foundation disposed of considerable assets in its India program. The record of its twenty-five years of work was widely, and generally favorably, known. The program had been broad and persistent; the foundation by and large had avoided the squalls and reefs of the U.S.-Indian official relationship. It had worked on subjects of major importance to India after the only other large foundation with a staff resident in India, the Rockefeller Foundation, closed out its program and the official U.S. aid program was terminated. We were the most important private outside agency working in India with Indian individuals and institutions.

Because of the scope and continuity of the foundation's program, our multinational professional staff (we had a few Americans, a few Indians, and at various times a British soil physicist, a French economist, and an Argentine irrigation engineer) possessed a probably incomparable range of knowledge among the development groups at work in India. Our skills included economics, engineering, forestry, anthropology and history, Sanskrit literature and archives, archaeology, and demography. The staff had access to India's thinkers and doers across a wide range of disciplines and professions, and its talents qualified it to serve as a small, but unusually well-equipped, think tank not only for foundation programs but for other agencies concerned with development as well—Indian and foreign. Matthew Dagg, our in-house agricultural scientist, an intense, hard-working British soil physicist (who began his career as an astrophysicist), was, for example, the only non-Indian member of an Indian Council of Agricultural Research team charged with the design of a new rice research program in eastern India. Matt would disappear for days at a time and return dead tired after hundreds of miles of bumping along on bad country roads traveling with Indian colleagues in the notoriously uncomfortable Indian car, the Ambassador, and hours spent in the broiling sun talking with farmers in rice paddies. We organized the staff formally in four groups—agriculture, resources, and rural development; education, public affairs, and culture; planning, management, and economics; and population, health, and nutrition. But we frequently combined parts of the professional staff into task groups for particular problems and used the entire staff as a committee of the whole when important deliberations and decisions were to be undertaken. Working with this group, some of whom I inherited but most of whom I recruited, was one of the joys of my life.

We set out to tap into the deep reservoir of Indian talent and ideas outside the government to find reformers and activists working, frequently at great personal sacrifice, to alleviate the problems of poverty and caste and to change the seemingly immutable and labyrinthine ways of interaction between citizens, especially poor ones, and the bureaucracies. A report we prepared for the foundation trustees in 1978 said: "Among the few institutions in India consistently concerned about...have-nots and able, in a modest way, to demonstrate that their economic circumstances, their social political organization, their health, and their chance in life can be improved are the voluntary agencies...In spite of the growth in numbers...and the increasing professionalism and competence of a number of them, generally they remain a rather unknown and underutilized resource on the Indian scene." In a real way, we turned away from the Nehruvian model of development toward the Gandhian, although when we found government institutions to which our program was relevant and which were seriously interested in experimentation and change, we were, of course, prepared to support their agendas in our modest way. In the six years I spent in India, we committed the foundation to a course (which it continues today) of supporting nonprofit citizens' action groups and a small number of government programs that have bettered the lives of large numbers of poor and disadvantaged Indians.

Our first grants to non-governmental organizations (NGOs) in the late 1970s were designed to help community groups manage forest resources and to organize poor women for employment-generating activities. One of the earliest of these went to the Self Employed Women's Association (SEWA) in Ahmedabad, founded by a quietly revolutionary woman named Ela Bhatt, a professed Gandhian. Although, to its misfortune, Ahmedabad is mostly known in recent years as a center of Hindu-Muslim riots and slaughter, traditionally it was a great Gujarati merchant and trading town. An old quarter of the city contains a few remaining streets of beautiful, wooden town houses with fancifully carved balconies and quiet interior courtyards, where wealthy merchant families lived. (Farther to the west, deep in the Thar desert near the Pakistan border, past the site of the Indian nuclear testing program, the same style is duplicated in the seemingly impossibly fine stone filigreed facades of the fairyland merchant houses of the Gujarati and Rajastani traders of Jaisalmer.) Gujarati, like Hindi, is a Sanskrit-derived language, but the two idioms are not mutually intelligible. The Gujaratis are a numerous, sober, thrifty (some say grasping), hardworking people (recent Gujarati immigrants to the United States, for example, dominate the modest-priced motel business). In the late nineteenth and early twentieth centuries, Ahmedabad, in the Middle Ages a famous center of handloom and carpet weaving, became one of India's great textile manufacturing centers, with an industrial proletariat straight out of the pages of Engels and Marx.

It is a city that, in spite of its miserable history of inter-caste and communal violence, has produced a host of progressive institutions and national leaders. Gujarat's most famous son was Mahatma Gandhi. Gandhi's merchant-caste father served as prime minister in the courts of a number of insignificant minor maharajas in western India. The son, Mohandas Gandhi (Mahatma, meaning great, was an honorific acquired later in life), broke family tradition and incurred caste displeasure when he went off to study law in London. His fellow students snubbed him there because he was an Indian (and very possibly as well because he was quite a peculiar person). Gandhi practiced law briefly in London and India and then moved to South Africa, where he opened a law office and began to organize a non-violent struggle for the rights of "colored" people (essentially the large Indian population) in South Africa.

After returning to India in 1914, Gandhi established an ashram (a teaching and meditation center) in Ahmedabad. In 1918, he attracted national attention when he started a fast to support a textile workers' strike. After three days, the mill owners settled. It was from his Ahmedabad ashram, called Sabermati, that in 1920 Gandhi, accompanied by some eighty followers whose ranks included some untouchables and a convicted murderer, launched a two-hundred-mile "march to the sea" (the Arabian Sea) to protest the British tax on salt, the burden of which fell disproportionately on the poorest of the poor who worked in the hottest of weather and most needed salt. As part of his strategy of anti-British but peaceful protest, Gandhi had written a letter to inform the viceroy, Lord Irwin, addressing him as "Dear Friend," of his intentions. On arrival at the seashore, Gandhi and his followers symbolically picked up salt mud to be processed into salt, which was illegal. In the ensuing days, when Gandhi announced plans for a peaceful take-over of a large salt works, the British arrested and jailed him. Although the salt tax was never repealed and independence was not achieved for many years yet to come, Gandhi became India's most powerful voice for freedom. Churchill felt called upon to comment with disgust at "the nauseating and humiliating spectacle of this one time Inner Temple (the London law courts), now seditious fakir, striding half-naked up the steps of the Viceroy's palace there to parley on equal terms with the representative of the King-Emperor." Gandhi, of course, sought not only independence. He wanted to reform Indian society. He rejected the entire concept of untouchability—his newspaper was called *Harijan* (the *Untouchable*). His views on caste and his insistence that Hindus and Muslims must live together in peace were anathema to conservative Hindus. In January 1948, not long after Gandhi's exhausting and dangerous efforts to stop the tidal wave of communal riots that preceded and accompanied the 1947 partition of India failed, Gandhi was shot and killed by a right-wing Hindu fanatic as he walked to prayer in the garden of a house in New Delhi. His assassin, Naturam Godse, remains a hero to some in India today, including some supporters of the Hindu nationalist Bharatiya Janata Party (BJP).

Ahmedabad's prosperity supported a wealthy upper class of entrepreneurs and financiers who lived in great style, some of them relatively progressive in their views about the need to improve labor conditions and inter-caste relationships and some regarding themselves as Gandhians. One of these Ahmedabad clans, the Sarabhais, produced the physicist Vikram Sarabhai, a founder of India's efforts in space science and a distinguished philanthropist and patron of the arts who counted himself a Gandhian. Sarabhai had befriended the foundation's first representative, Douglas Ensminger, and from that friendship and collaboration emerged two path-breaking institutions: the Indian Institute of Management, developed with the help of the Harvard Business School over ten years, and the National Institute of Design, where the American designers Charles and Ray

Eames were early consultants and teachers. Sarabhai's wife, Mrinlini, was a fine classical dancer (as is her daughter, Malika), and the family founded possibly the world's most beautiful textile museum, filled with exquisite carpets, wall hangings, and articles of dress—saris, tunics, trousers, royal robes, dresses, veils, and shawls.

I first met Ela Bhatt and was introduced to her work with poor women by Kamla Chowdhry, a member of the foundation's program staff, a woman of much charm and wisdom who had worked with Vikram Sarabhai in Ahmedabad. Together, Chowdhry and Sarabhai had planned and launched the Indian Institute of Management with private, Indian government and Ford Foundation grant funds, and before she joined the foundation staff Chowdhry taught there. Born into a well-off Punjabi family, Chowdhry earned a degree in mathematics and philosophy at Calcutta University. She married a promising young Indian Administrative Service officer (the IAS is the small, elite civil service, originally created by the British, that commands the top jobs in the vast machinery of the Indian government). One torrid night, while the young couple slept on the rooftop of their house in Delhi (sleeping on the roof in hot weather is a common practice), Chowdhry's husband was murdered in a knife attack by a man seeking vengeance because of a legal judgment. When she emerged from a period of grief and shock, she persuaded her parents to allow her to travel to the United States to study at the University of Michigan, an amazing odyssey for a young, single Indian woman to embark on during the Second World War. In 1945 Chowdhry earned a doctorate in psychology at Michigan. The title of her thesis was "Leadership in Small Groups," and a leader in small groups was what she became. Chowdhry was responsible for the management portfolio on our staff, but she cast her net much more widely into women's development activities and environmental issues.

Chowdhry's friend Ela Bhatt was a Gujarati Brahmin, a non-violent but formidable lioness in a bird-sized body, who believed one should live by Gandhi's principles. As a young woman, Bhatt went to work in the women's division of the Textile Labor Association, the oldest textile workers trade union in India, but she broke with the union leadership when they refused to countenance the political consequences of her controversial organizing activities with female hawkers, street vendors, and laborers, because they led to clashes with the police and city authorities. These women laborers carried enormous head loads of cotton cloth from the wholesalers to retail markets, pulled carts with rags and cotton waste from the mills to street markets, and sold recycled goods and remade junk items from technically illegal street stalls. Bhatt took me along to visit some of the steaming hot, crowded, dirty marketplaces where city dwellers came to find cheap goods. Naked, potbellied children, in the absence of any kind of toilet facility, defecated in the gutters, while their mothers worked at the stalls. Bhatt's early work concentrated on protecting these women from police raids and from exploitation by rag and cloth merchants, who routinely cheated the women in the handling of recycled goods. She began to organize them into cooperatives and to introduce the principle of saving—a women's bank lending at reasonable rates was an early innovation—along with health services for maternity and child care. (The plight of poor, working women like these in India—and, with rare exceptions, all poor women work—remains one of the ugliest consequences of India's broad failure to deal with education, health, and poverty. Even today, more than 94 percent of working women in India are self-employed, according to the Indian writer Kalima Rose. They work as potters, cigarette [*bidi*] rollers, incense stick makers, street vendors, spinners, metalworkers, carpenters, head loaders, cart pullers, waste paper pickers, or as agricultural laborers.)

I accompanied Bhatt, whom I called Elaben (the Hindi suffix "ben," which means "sister," is applied affectionately to particularly respected women) to sit in on discussion groups with women who were emerging as leaders. I was invariably struck by their directness and sense of themselves, the liveliness of their exchanges, and the universal socializing qualities of female conversation and role playing in the ways they used humor, voice intonations, and gestures to make a point. They would have been immediately at home at a town meeting or a dinner party in New England or New York. With Ford help, Ela Bhatt extended her activities to rural women workers, and the grant cycle we began with SEWA continued long after my departure from India. SEWA now has a membership of two hundred thousand women. Bhatt has served in the Indian Cabinet as a member of the Planning Commission and is a highly respected figure in international development circles.

This pioneering work with street women in Ahmedabad was only part of a flowering of leadership in the Indian women's movement in the 1970s, and during my six years in India, the foundation became an important source of support for a number of bright, tough-minded, and passionate women who dedicated their lives to improving the lot of poor people, with an emphasis on the roles of women. In both the Hindu and Muslim cultures of the subcontinent, women traditionally occupied a role subordinate to men. The most telling evidence is the sex ratio. In most societies, the sex ratio slightly favors women (meaning that more women survive childhood and are alive as adults than men). In the United States, for example, the male-female sex ratio is 0.96; in Austria, as another example, 0.95. The Indian male-female ratio is 1.07, Pakistan 1.05, Bangladesh 1.05. (It is noteworthy that, after a half-century of totalitarian rule, China records the same phenomenon, with a male-female sex ratio of 1.06.) These ratios result not just from female infanticide, which is relatively rare in India and more widespread in China, but a host of cultural factors in nutrition and health that favor males over females. Hinduism requires a male son to carry out a host of family ceremonies (as does traditional Chinese society). In poor families, males are fed before females and are far more likely to receive scarce medical attention when ill. The male vasectomy campaign which Indira Gandhi and her son, Sanjay, pushed in the 1970s was long ago replaced by female sterilization, which is a far more difficult and dangerous medical procedure and, since it is frequently performed with poor women who already have given birth to several children, is not even a very sensible way to limit family size. India today also witnesses the increasingly widespread use by families that can afford it of the modern technology of prenatal ultrasound testing for the sex of a fetus, which frequently results in the abortion of a female fetus. Although child marriage has long been illegal, I more than once saw dazed, pre-teen children, splendidly if garishly attired in festival costumes and headdresses, being married in Rajasthani villages, their marriages to be consummated when they reach puberty.

Attitudes in the subcontinent in regard to women and their roles are complex. The Indian and Pakistani feminist movements are very different from the American model in their lack of hostility to men and their recognition of the importance of traditional roles for women. Women in India traditionally were able to accumulate much real power in large households as mothers-in-law and community leaders, and female politicians have been more successful in South Asia than in any other part of the world. All the major South Asian societies—India, Pakistan, Bangladesh, and Sri Lanka (Nepal, the miserably governed, poor mountain kingdom, is the one exception)—have elected women prime ministers (although all of these, it must be noted, came out of political dynasties first established by men). In Bangladesh, two women, one the daughter of a (male) prime minister and the second the widow of another, have dominated politics for the past twenty years. Sri Lanka has elected two female prime ministers since independence. Upper-class, upper-caste women (and in small, but increasing, numbers, lower-caste women as well) are widely accepted in the political arena. At the other, awful end of the spectrum, India continues to witness the shame of hundreds of "dowry deaths" every year, in which the greedy family of a bridegroom, dissatisfied with the dowry money and gifts a bride has brought to the ceremony, burns her alive with kerosene.

As concerned the rest of the foundation program, we continued the long trajectory of support for agricultural research and production programs, but began to concentrate on the special problems of rice as opposed to wheat, whose cultivation generally is less plagued by disease and pests than rice, which spends much of its growing life in warm water. We funded a special program of research and field trials managed by the Indian Council of Agricultural Research in eastern India, where rice is the food grain of choice for the enormous populations of the lower Gangetic basin in eastern Uttar Pradesh, Bihar, West Bengal, and Orissa. These are among the most backward parts of the subcontinent, plagued by poverty and caste hatreds which, for many years in parts of Bihar and West Bengal, have fueled an extremely cruel civil war between upper-caste landlords and landless low-caste laborers.

Paradoxically, in earlier ages eastern India was the region that witnessed the flowering of India's classical Buddhist and Hindu cultures. The echoes of that glorious, idealized past still resound in people's minds, and its archaeological bones lie strewn before the passerby in the middle of rice paddies, crowded cities, and on hilltops throughout the countryside. I once listened for an hour to a high-caste Hindu professor at Patna University, who also happened to be a rich landlord, expatiate on why Buddhism essentially disappeared from these lands, where Buddha was born and preached, while it took wings, spread, and burgeoned in Sri Lanka, Southeast Asia, China, and Japan. Most of classical India was once Buddhist. The most famous of the classical Indian emperors, Ashoka, born in the third century BC and raised in the Jain religion, which itself preaches non-violence, embraced Buddhism after announcing that he was sickened by the bloodshed and suffering he had caused in his conquests. It is a widely held scholarly view that, over a period of many centuries after Ashoka's death, Hinduism slowly revived and triumphed over Buddhism as the religion of the masses in India because of the superior political skills of the Brahmin priesthood in influencing kings and the popular appeal of the elaborate, colorful, and musical rituals of Hinduism. Not so, said my discussant. Hinduism defeated Buddhism basically because of the superiority of its logic, he said, as recorded in the philosophical debates of fifteen hundred years ago between Hindu and Buddhist priests (this kind of flat statement will not surprise anyone who has ever argued with a Hindu friend: Hinduism requires that there be an answer for everything). Lisa Lyons, who had come from Bangkok to Delhi to help put together a cultural grants program, and I once visited the fine, small museum in Mathura, southeast from Delhi down the Gangetic plain, to see a just-discovered, exquisite, totally undamaged, near-life-size stone statue of the Buddha just uncovered in excavations for a new housing development. Under the floodplain of the holy river, archaeologists continue to find the ruins of once-great cities. The earliest were mostly built of wood and have not survived the ravages of time. The surviving temples at places like Khajurao and in Orissa and the stone and brick ruins of Buddhist monasteries in eastern and north central India are breathtaking in the boldness of their conception and the high art of their sculpture.

We also began to move the foundation squarely into work on environmental problems. In addition to supporting training, research, and experimentation in water management and irrigation, we began to make experimental grants in non-commercial forestry to fund research on new varieties of potentially useful, fast-growing trees and new ideas in village-level wasteland management. The goal was to increase the economic resources available to poor villagers and simultaneously to protect the natural environment from overgrazing, over-cutting, and erosion. Traditionally, the forestry departments of the Indian states traced their origins back to the elite British colonial forestry service and saw their primary role as guardians of the forests. Villagers in and near the forests, usually tribal people, from time immemorial had enjoyed access to forest lands for their livelihood—grazing their livestock, collecting and selling valuable seeds and firewood, and a host of minor forestry products.

By the mid-1970s, the great Indian forests were simply disappearing under the unending pressure of the steadily increasing human and animal populations. There was too much legally authorized logging, in which corruption frequently was involved; a great deal of criminal, unauthorized logging; uncontrollable, illegal overgrazing by ever-larger herds of scrub cattle, and the cutting of firewood for cooking and household purposes by poor, often landless farmers. I could go out on tour with the forestry officers of Madhya Pradesh, the enormous central Indian state that once contained some of India's greatest forests, and drive for hours through barren landscapes legally classified as "forest," with forest guards, the lowest rank of employees working at the local level, standing at attention along the roadside at intervals of every twenty-five miles or so and saluting us as we whizzed by in our Indian Ambassador cars, sweating in the superheated, humid wind and looking forward to an evening of drinking cold beer at the Forestry Service guesthouse and listening to the senior officers spin yarns about their encounters with tigers in the forests of yore. (One of them described how he was bicycling on his rounds down a forest trail when he met a tiger head-on. He stopped. The tiger stopped. The forester slowly and carefully turned and began riding away. When he looked back, the great beast was trotting along, following at the same distance, and followed him all the way back to the forestry hut before disappearing in the underbrush.) We made an ultimately not very successful grant to the Madhya Pradesh forest department to establish a new social forestry wing to work with village councils on finding approaches to common problems. Although the leaders of the department agreed that something had to be done differently if the forests were not to disappear entirely, the resistance of the bureaucracy was formidable. The career officers had usually been trained at their universities in forestry botany and silviculture and, with rare exceptions, were uninterested in new varieties of fast-growing trees that might be better suited to village firewood and grazing needs than the great teak and sal forests that the departments traditionally managed. The hostility between forestry officers and villagers was deep (as was the case with irrigation officers and villagers). They came from different social and caste groups (in most cases, villagers in forest areas were tribal people, outside the Hindu caste system, or low-caste Hindus), and their goals were very different. The foresters wanted to control and conserve; the villagers had to survive.

I regarded the disappearance of the great Indian forests and the fabulous beasts that inhabited them as a national tragedy not only in environmental and economic terms but in the very roots of Indian spiritual life as well, specifically as concerned the relationship between nature and Hinduism. I had seen the forests shrinking throughout Asia with my own eyes. Starting in the mid-1960s on my first visit to India, I frequently flew from New Delhi east by southeast and then north to Kathmandu, the capital of Nepal, over the once heavily forested jungle plains and low foothills, full of tigers, deer, wild pigs, wild elephants, wild dogs, and clouds of malarial mosquitoes, and watched the forests slowly melt away under the onslaught of Sikh farmers from the Punjab seeking rich new lands to cultivate. When the trees went, so did the animals. In none of the world's great religions are animals, as carriers of the sacred spirit and both its healing and destroying powers, as important as in Hinduism. The great national epic, the Mahabharata, takes place in a magical forest. Millions of Hindus worship, with wild music and in clouds of incense, their version of the godhead at temples to Hanuman, the strong, devoted, brave monkey god, and no aspect of the godhead is more popular than Ganesha, the elephant god of success, wealth, and wisdom. I theorized that the loss of the forests and its wild beasts had to affect the very heart of Hinduism. India by now had reached the stage where most boys and girls growing up rarely, if ever, saw a wild animal—other than the monkeys who hang around virtually all temples. The marvelous experience of walking quietly along a jungle or forest trail, which people with money like me could still do at the few remaining enormous nature preserves and parks, and going out on an elephant with a forest guard and actually seeing wild tigers and wild elephants, has disappeared forever from most Indian lives.

By the late 1970s, environmental degradation was becoming a national political issue in India, and the roots of a national environmental movement began to emerge, in whose development the foundation played an important role. In the early 1980s, with help from foundation staff, a group of private citizens and public officials established the Society for Promotion of Wastelands Development to serve as a national information and clearing house for private and public efforts to restore degraded lands. Within a short time, the society established collaborative projects involving community-based organizations and public and private corporations in twelve Indian states carrying out community-level forestry and water management. In one district in West Bengal, after several years of community management, forest destruction came to a halt, and the forest cover increased from 11 to 20 percent of the land. Much more recently (in 1999), when my wife and I took a month-long flying and automobile tourist trip around India—my first visit to the Indian backcountry in ten years—I was impressed by three marks of progress. The first was the amount of extensive tree plantings on strips of waste and degraded land, some of it community managed but more frequently privately planted and managed by village entrepreneurs with no opposition from the forestry departments. The second sign of progress was the spread of telephone communications in the villages—a villager can now use ubiquitous satellite services to call anywhere in the world (unheard of thirty years ago, when many villages were miles from anything like a telephone). The third was the growth in the number of modern tube wells in the villages to provide clean drinking water, replacing the notoriously unsanitary old village stone and mud wells (the tube wells were introduced by UNICEF almost forty years ago).

Convincing the government bureaucracies of the importance of the participation of the people was never easy; it simply didn't fit into the traditional concepts of governor and governed, high caste and low caste, Brahmins and workers. One of our small grants for field research to the Central Soil and Water Conservation Research and Training Institute at Dehra Dun helped to fund a land-and-water-management project at a village called Sukhomajri, located in the Shivalik Hills in Haryana State. The Shivaliks are a long, relatively low range of badly degraded hills populated by poor villagers who earn their living from rain-fed agriculture and livestock grazing. Governmental efforts to control grazing on lands nominally under the control of the forestry were generally futile. The Dehra Dun institute and the Haryana Forestry Department discovered that small check dams built at the top of the watersheds at very low cost—usually about $10,000—produced astonishing results in controlling erosion. In addition, water impounded in the small reservoirs thus created could be used for both irrigation, which dramatically increased the agricultural production of the villagers, and village water supply. To obtain the full benefits of the water the villagers had to control livestock grazing in the watershed (this is known in the development business as "social fencing") to avoid excessive runoff, erosion, and siltation. Controlled grazing created new sources of fodder for village livestock. One of the innovations at Sukhomajri was the decision to give every village household a right and a share in the water, whether the family owned land or not. The success of a number of these first small-scale dam projects at Sukhomajri led the foundation to propose a next-stage, larger experiment. This would be managed by a voluntary agency, or group of agencies, which would supply technical help to villagers in designing, building, and maintaining the earthen check dams. The agency would also manage the watersheds and water distribution systems so that both equity and production goals could be met. A self-sustaining, self-financing, locally managed system covering a large number of village watersheds was the goal. A big, experienced Indian NGO, headed by Manibhai Desai, a well-known disciple of Mahatma Gandhi, organized a staff unit to undertake this task. The foundation and the U.S. Agency for International Development were prepared to finance the expanded phase. We discussed these plans for expanding the Sukhomajri experiment at various levels of the government. Eventually, a senior government informed me that the government would not approve major funding of any Indian NGO because it would raise "political problems" with other NGOs. In any case, the official said, if the "work is important the government must do it." (Some years later, running a vastly larger development aid program as the U.S. AID Mission Director in Pakistan, I heard exactly these same words when I proposed using AID money to expand the development outreach of a number of Pakistani NGOs.)

In 1977, the second year of our assignment in India, Mrs. Gandhi decided that the excellence of her rule in the national emergency had ended the disorders that caused her to proclaim it, and that the new ways of working harder and talking less (as propounded by her son, Sanjay) must be widely popular. She declared an end to the emergency, called for new elections, and was promptly voted out of office. Without exception, our Indian friends, who were mostly journalists, writers, and professors, rejoiced. Some of them thought Indian democracy was witnessing a rebirth and that India, with a new sense of national resolve, would finally begin to deal seriously with India's always tremendous problems of poverty, social justice, and modernization. But the major characteristic of the period that ensued was the unseemly fighting for power among the "old men," the senior ranks of the Congress Party leadership, who had watched Indira's rise to power with disapproval and each of whom desperately wanted finally to grasp the ultimate prize, the prime ministership. The winner was the octogenarian Morarji Desai, a Bombay Brahmin of the purest caste, and in his day a famous fighter for independence. Desai, a decent, highly opinionated and unbending gentleman, didn't last long. The coalition of old hands he put together bickered and back-stabbed and lasted only until 1979. In 1980, Mrs. Gandhi, a formidable and tire-less campaigner (on one memorable occasion Mrs. Gandhi walked and rode on an elephant several miles along flooded roads to reach a Bihar village where a number of untouchables were reported to have been burned alive in a dispute with higher-caste Hindu landowners), won the elections and swept back into power in a stunning reversal of political fortune. She immediately faced a grow-ing and troublesome Sikh independence movement in the state of Punjab, headed by a Sikh holy man who had once been a favorite in her personal entou-rage. After she sent troops into the famous Golden Temple at Amritsar in a bloody raid to end the Sikh occupation of the temple, Mrs. Gandhi was assassi-nated in 1984 by one of her elite Sikh bodyguards, setting off an anti-Sikh pogrom that killed thousands of Sikhs in New Delhi and northern India. Mrs. Gandhi's son, Rajiv, an airline pilot whom she dragooned into politics in 1980 after her younger son, Sanjay, died in an airplane crash while doing acrobatics over New Delhi in a specially designed stunt airplane, was then elected prime minister. Rajiv lost power in the 1989 elections and was assassinated by a Tamil terrorist in 1991 while campaigning to regain office. Christopher Marlowe could not have written a bloodier scenario than that of Mrs. Gandhi and her sons.

The much duller Morarji Desai, her replacement in 1977, lived to be ninety-nine (dying in 1995), attributing his health and longevity to adherence to Vedic practices, which in his case included eating the finest of cashew nuts and the freshest of yogurts and drinking a pint of his own urine every day. He dressed in fine homespun cotton and linen and affected the Congress Party workers' white fore-and-aft cap. I called on him once in the prime minister's office to request an appointment for McGeorge Bundy and Alexander Heard, the chairman of the board of trustees of the Ford Foundation, when the board was about to have its first-ever overseas meeting in India. Desai received me with great courtesy, and we talked far beyond our scheduled time while the prime minister told me how much he loved to play cricket when he was a schoolboy in Bombay. Heard asked me what the prime minister would wear when Heard, Bundy, and I called on him. We were in the midst of the hot season. I said Desai would be essentially wearing pajamas (a tunic and pajama-like trousers called *dhotis*) and that I planned to wear a sports shirt. Heard, a very formal man, was not amused. He wore a suit, Bundy a shirt and trousers, I a sports shirt and light khaki pants, and Desai his dhotis. Bundy, his wife, Mary, and I made a brief, enjoyable tour of foundation projects in South India, where he was garlanded in a welcoming ceremony by a temple elephant, who knocked his glasses off in the process, and Bundy, reluctantly and only at my insistence, drank most of a glass of fresh, warm milk when we met with the leaders of a dairy cooperative. On a second, short field trip in the Himalayan foothills with the director of the Sukhomajri project, a Brahmin, Bundy and the director, whose daughter was about to be married, compared notes about arranged marriages as practiced in modern, elite circles in both Boston and the subcontinent and agreed that they are not dissimilar.

When I was not on the road, Charlotte and I lived quietly on the farm with our Chinese style dogs, the peacocks, and the flights of green parrots. When she felt up to it, we traveled together to places like Udaipur to relax in the Lake Palace hotel or the enormous Jim Corbett tiger reserve in the Himalayan foothills, where we went out on elephant back and saw a tiger. We spent a magical week on an old houseboat on Dal Lake in Kashmir—long before the troubles started—watching jewel-like kingfishers from our porch, drinking Kashmiri tea, riding *shikaris* (small, gondola-like wooden boats) across the tranquil waters, having martinis and watching the sunsets on the hills, and shopping for shawls and jewelry in the markets. We shared the growing, implacable, unspoken certainty that a third presence, death, had taken up residence in our house. Often, coming home from work in New Delhi at dusk, I found Charlotte sitting in the bower in the garden, her hair now white from the effects of the disease, smoking a cigarette in the elegant gold clip holder she affected, drinking martinis, and talking endlessly and laughing with Lisa Lyons, whom she loved; and from time to time we gave some of Delhi's best small garden parties for our Indian friends. We went into the city for dinner with friends like Khushwant Singh or the Thapars or to listen to Indian music recitals by the great performers like Ravi Shankar and Bismallah Khan. Kathleen, our daughter, just starting her career as a painter, came out to help, spending her free hours drawing the old ruins around the Qutub Minar, where she had to put down her brushes every few hours to fight off Indian men who assumed any unaccompanied Western woman was an easy and available lay. Peter, our youngest son, who had dropped out of college to become a fisherman, flew out once with his cousin David to visit his mother. I met them at the airport, and we drove back to the farm along back roads in the early dawn half-light, where a procession of men was heading out from the small clusters of village houses to the fields, bearing small metal pots of water. "Look how hardworking they are," David commented. "They're going out to work and taking their provisions with them." I offered a first lesson in things Indian. "They're going out to have a poop," I said. "Those are pots of water to wash off their butts."

As Charlotte's chemotherapy faltered, it became necessary every few months to make the long, exhausting flight back to New York for crisis management and to try new combinations of therapies. With her health and life slipping away, Charlotte thought about suicide. When we still lived in Bangkok, a young American friend, desperately ill with a kidney disease, had suggested they both visit a famous faith healer in the Philippines, who would with his hands draw the sickness out of the affected organs, but she decided not to. Charlotte's mother was an ardent Theosophist, and in her childhood at home and at a Theosophist school (where she received an excellent general education), Charlotte had been exposed to that curious mixture of Hinduism, Buddhism, and spiritualism first propagated by the Russian-born Madame Helen Petrovna Blavatsky (1831–1891), about whom an American scholar, Mathew Mulligan Goldstein, wrote recently: "She remains for most critics and historians an obscure, if vaguely absurd, figure...Blavatsky and her followers did much to introduce the West to Eastern religion generally, and Hinduism and Buddhism in particular." In her Indian travels in the nineteenth century, Blavatsky befriended another notable European woman, Annie Besant, an English citizen who became one of the principal organizers of the Indian National Congress that eventually led India to independence.

But there was not much help or light in Blavatsky, who opposed suicide, and none at all from Charlotte's Theosophist mother, who in response to a series of letters from Charlotte describing her conditions and concerns, wrote back a single, curt note saying that since Charlotte's fate was already decided there was nothing she as a mother could do. After that, she never wrote or called again. Charlotte sought counseling from Buddhist priests in India, and at her request I talked with a greatly respected old Indian guru, who as a young, Sanskrit-trained, Vedic scholar, had been a spiritual adviser to Mahatma Gandhi. I had met the guru earlier through an Indian friend when I was seeking an explanation of the existence of evil in the world. (Evil is the passing away of light, the guru said, and the dominance of the dark side of mankind.) The old guru spoke careful, self-taught English, had a delightful sense of humor, and after a serious conversation loved nothing more than serving ice cold Indian beer to special guests at his ashram, a small house built by the side of a small river in a quiet town. I described

Charlotte's dilemma and her principal question: could she commit suicide rather than endure the long, slow process of dying from cancer. The guru said the Vedas did not approve of suicide, but that in extreme circumstances it is not prohibited to Hindus. Charlotte decided to endure.

In the spring of 1978, with Charlotte now traveling in a wheelchair, we flew back to New York for further consultations with the doctors at Sloan-Kettering. After a couple of weeks of tests, her specialist said there was really nothing more that could be done. We had once owned a small house on the unfashionable, Gardiner's Bay side of the Hamptons at the tip of Long Island, and Charlotte said she wanted to see the ocean mist once more. We picked out a fine misty day and drove out, but she was too weak to get out of the car. I rented a temporary apartment in the building where our oldest son, John, lived and hired a part-time nurse. The children and I worked out a schedule to help with her care. Charlotte slowly slipped away. She stopped breathing one night in my presence. As she wished, we cremated her remains and gave a small, memorial reception for friends and family at which a lot of gin was consumed. The three children, my nephew David, and I drove out to her favorite beach near our old house in the Hamptons, waded into the water, sifted her ashes into the sea, and strewed a dozen yellow roses on the water.

Charlotte left these lines by Christina Georgina Rossetti, which I found in a book in her effects, marked in the margin "for Rocky":

> Remember me when I am gone away,
> Gone far away into the silent land;
> When you can no more hold me by the hand,
> Nor I half turn to go, yet turning stay.
> Remember me when no more, day by day,
> You tell me of our future that you planned;
> Only remember me; you understand
> It will be late to counsel then or pray.
> Yet if you should forget me for a while
> And afterwards remember, do not grieve;
> For if the darkness and corruption leave
> A vestige of the thoughts that once I had,
> Better by far you should forget and smile
> Than that you should remember and be sad.

(She crossed out the article "the" in the third line above and substituted "my.")

I also found in her papers a typewritten scrap with some lines by the Latin writer Juvenal:

Pray for a brave heart, which does not fear death,
which places a long life last among the gifts of nature,
which has the power to endure any trials,
rejects anger, discards desire.

And a handwritten note with a quote from the Buddha: "Death is no evil in itself, many even desire it to escape from the vanities of life, but I shall take no steps either to hasten or to delay my departure."

The foundation, which had been unfailingly helpful through all this, said I could take as much time off as I needed before returning to the subcontinent. Kathleen and I drove up to a small camp on an island in the Saint Lawrence River as guests of Charles Benoit, our quondam man in Vietnam. For about a week, I swam, took walks in the woods, and sailed with Benoit in his Hobie Cat. One morning, I decided I must get back to India immediately and caught a flight the next day. I was being swept along in the currents of emotions of survivors of a loved one who dies early after much suffering: relief and a sense of release and freedom because the suffering of the body has finally ended; then loneliness; and then rage at the senseless end of a life with so much still to live in it. And then the delusions, as the heart tries to trick the mind. From time to time, I would see a woman who reminded me of Charlotte. Sometimes, in my travels, I would see a mist over the waters and think that Charlotte must be out there somewhere, or I would come down from the mountains in India, gazing out on the infinite, crowded plains, thinking Charlotte might be there somewhere in the anonymous multitudes. I walked deep in thought along the quiet, flower-scented, dirt roads around the farm in the Punjab, accompanied by little green bee-eater birds that flew along ahead of me and perched on fence posts to wait for me, and mused that Charlotte was talking to me in the form of a bird. I resolved to simplify my life and live a semi-ascetic existence, concentrating on work, reading and writing, and greatly limiting my social activities. I was fifty-six years old when Charlotte died in June 1978, and this seemed the sensible way to go.

None of my resolution lasted long, of course. I soon left the farm and took a small town house in New Delhi. I did live simply enough for a while. I arose at dawn and drove myself to the park surrounding Humayun's tomb, one of the most beautiful and peaceful spots in Delhi, or to the green, spacious Nehru park, and walked or jogged for a while and then ate a simple breakfast of *chapatis* (thin, unleavened wheat bread), *dal* (lentils), yogurt, and South Indian coffee. Ram Prakash, my driver, loyal friend, and invaluable assistant, and I made a long car tour around the small cities and back country of southern and central India, visiting old foundation grantees and performing the valuable task of filling up the few remaining holes in my personal knowledge of what historically worked in the foundation's program and what failed, and why. In the process, we saw some superb old small temples off the beaten path. Back in Delhi, at a party one night several months after Charlotte's death, I found myself in lively discourse with an attractive, married Indian woman I had known for years and realized that I quite urgently wanted to sleep with her (which I didn't, although, with typical male vanity, I thought I could have).

Within eighteen months of Charlotte's death, I met and married a striking young woman, Suzanne Fisher, a journalist just arrived from Hong Kong to run the United Press International regional news bureau in New Delhi. UPI was gearing up not only to cover the subcontinent but more importantly to get on top of the increasingly nasty and important events occurring in Afghanistan. It was the second marriage for both of us; Suzanne was recently divorced from her high school sweetheart. During the courtship, I proved the bona fides of my intentions by plying her with cold beer while she unpacked her household goods on a scorching summer day and then suggesting that I had a lot of champagne in storage that needed to be drunk before it went bad. Her Indian landlady wanted Suzanne to marry her son. But when the landlady consulted her astrologer, the stargazer said Suzanne was destined to marry an American boy. I certainly filled half of that bill of particulars.

Suzanne and I got married legally at a Delhi municipal office by a bureaucrat whose duties included supervision of venereal disease programs, enforcement of alcohol and drug laws, and marrying foreigners. Then we really got married before forty or so Indian and Western friends in an early morning ceremony in a pine grove at Nehru Park, with a flute player playing like Krishna in the background, and a wedding breakfast of *chapatis, dal,* yogurt, coffee, and champagne for the guests. Romesh Thapar discovered at the last minute that we didn't have a Brahmin priest to bless our wedding. Thapar disappeared momentarily and came back with a Brahmin dressed in white *dhotis* and a black frockcoat, who took his shoes off and chanted and read the relevant Sanskrit verses while the flute player played amidst the trees. Then we had a big reception at the house. An Indian folklorist, Rajeev Sethi, and my daughter, Kathleen (who applauded the idea of my marrying again), organized the party, with Rajasthani village women painting marriage designs on the flagstone floor of our courtyard, a *hendi-wallah* (hand painter) offering her services to decorate ladies' hands with henna designs, a gaily painted elephant garlanding arriving guests (and depositing a large mound of steaming elephant dung on the entrance to my neighbor's driveway), and a Punjabi band with *shenai* (Indian oboe) musicians, singers, and drummers providing music for dancing, which required a lot of jumping up and down.

The marriage brought me not only a new wife but a new circle of friends as well. These were the foreign correspondents of the world's great newspapers and news agencies—the frigate birds of war—gathering in New Delhi as the best regional center from which to cover the Afghanistan war. That small war which was to shake the world began in effect in 1973 when King Zahir Shah was overthrown by his cousin, Daoud Khan, and a group of ambitious military officers and tribal leaders. (This is the same Zahir Shah who, as an old man, returned to Kabul in 2002 after his long exile in Italy to help bring peace to his war-mangled land—and promptly dropped totally out of sight.) The talented, highly competitive, and obstreperous journalist crew included Stuart Auerbach of the *Washington Post,* Michael Kaufman of the *New York Times*, Tyler Marshall of the *Los Angeles Times,* and Marcia Gauger of *Time* magazine. Suzanne traveled frequently with one or another of them to Pakistan and Afghanistan to cover the unfolding of the Afghan tragedy. As I observed their comings and goings, I had not a clue that in the next two decades my own life would be swept into the tidal waves of this human-caused earthquake.

I knew Kabul and Afghanistan slightly from a couple of visits before Zahir Shah's overthrow in 1973. Afghanistan was an extraordinarily poetic landscape then: endless brown plains, far snow-covered mountains, green irrigated valleys, handsome, fierce-looking men and women. In those pre-Taliban days, girls were still being educated, and relatively few women in the city wore the full burqa and veil. The country was essentially at peace. You could drive in safely from the North-West Frontier Province of Pakistan through the Khyber Pass, or fly in on the dilapidated national Ariana Airlines. Commercial trucks drove all the way from Europe across the Middle East and through Iran into Afghanistan without undue concerns for banditry. The competitions of the Cold War were evident mostly in the roads, dams, and irrigation systems being built by the major powers—the Soviets, the Chinese, and the Americans—each of which for its own reasons found it important to play the latest version of the Great Game in this ancient buffer zone. Visiting Kabul was like going back to the Central Asian Middle Ages—markets full of carpet merchants, antique dealers selling Russian samovars, mutton kebab and tea shops, and, looming above all, the forbidding palace and fortress that played a central role in the defeat and rout of the British in the nineteenth century and served as a foul jail and torture headquarters for the Communists and the Taliban alike in the twenty-five years of destruction and anarchy that followed the Soviet invasion in 1979.

The early course of the Afghan war was dictated by the fighting between leaders who headed the two major factions of the Afghan Communist party, the Khalq and the Parcham. Dauod Khan lasted about a year and was overthrown and killed in a Communist coup in 1978 by Nur Muhammad Taraki. Taraki, in turn, was murdered in 1979 by Hafizullah Amin. (In good communist-style jargon, the *Kabul Times* reported that Taraki, who had been hailed as a "great teacher…great genius…great leader" died quietly of "serious illness, which he had been suffering for some time." A few months later, it was reported that Amin had in fact ordered the commander of the palace guard to execute Taraki, who was suffocated with a pillow over his head.) A friend of mine, American Ambassador Adolph "Spike" Dubs, with whom I had served in Moscow, was kidnapped by a rebel faction during that tumultuous year and shot to death in a hotel room in an ill-organized government attempt to rescue him. On December 24, 1979, the Soviet Army invaded across the Oxus River frontier. The Soviets executed Amin and installed Babrak Karmal as prime minister. Karmal lasted until 1986, when he was replaced by Najibullah. In the years of chaos following the Soviet defeat, Najibullah took refuge in 1992 with the UN humanitarian mission in Kabul. When the Taliban captured the city in 1996, one of its first acts was to seize, publicly brutalize, and execute Najibullah.

The ultimate failure of the Soviet invasion and occupation and the humiliating withdrawal of Soviet troops in 1989 were key events in the subsequent collapse of the Soviet empire. The American government was proud of its role in the CIA financing and arming of the Islamic mujahideen who defeated the Soviets (Saudi money played a major role as well). But American policy, which appeared so farsighted during the war, made a costly error almost immediately after the defeat of the Soviets when the United States cut off assistance and abandoned Pakistan and Afghanistan to their fates. From the ranks of the fighters we had trained, and the young men educated in fundamentalist Islam in the *madrassas* (schools) built with Saudi money in the North-West Frontier Province of Pakistan, arose the training camps for Al Qaeda and the Taliban. It is important to recognize that the immediate planners and operators of the September 11, 2001, attack on the World Trade Center in New York were Saudis and Middle Easterners. Their guiding spirit and adviser was Osama Bin Laden, a Saudi, who still lives on in the wild tribal areas of Pakistan's Northwest Frontier with Afghanistan, sheltered by true believers after five years of what we are told is relentless pursuit by the Americans and the Pakistanis. A fundamentalist victory in Pakistan, with its nuclear weapons and strategic location, would be the most important prize the jihadists could dream of winning.

But in the late 1970s my world was India, Nepal, and Sri Lanka, not Afghanistan. I was interested in the excited reports of the correspondents returning from Pakistan and Afghanistan, but I was, of course, far more deeply involved with planning and managing the foundation's program. It was, I thought, shaping up nicely. We had intensified and focused our support for biological and socioeconomic research on rice, primarily in eastern India. In the semi-arid plateau region of central and southern India, outside Hyderabad, the foundation, together with the Rockefeller Foundation, had launched a new International Center for Research in the semi-arid tropics to work on millets, sorghum, and beans—essential dry-land food crops not only in this vast region of India but in Africa, many parts of Asia, and Latin America as well. We began to help build institutional research and training capacity in the regional university at Hyderabad to work with and adapt the scientific findings of the new international center. We launched a number of NGO experiments in rural development, with emphasis on the economic roles of women. Work in natural resources—improving water use and management and projects in soil conservation and forestry—became the single largest component of our program. We remained a major benefactor of the national management institutes, whose graduates were to play important roles in the industrial management reforms and the coming information technology revolution, and continued our support of the Indian Council of Social Science Research and a number of economic research institutes. In the wake of the disaster that befell the national family planning program after Indira and Sanjay Gandhi's forced male sterilization campaign, it had become extremely difficult to find Indian leaders even interested in talking about new directions in population-related activities. We did, however, find one serious, important partner in J. R. D. Tata, the powerful head of the Tata industrial empire that produced steel and built trucks, and helped him launch the new Family Planning Foundation of India. We began to make small experimental grants in health and nutrition, which later, in concentrating on women and children, became essential components in a more comprehensive foundation approach to the issue of rapid population growth.

I found particular rewards in launching a new exploratory project in cultural programming, finding myself in the happy circumstances of a field officer carrying out the intent of a New York headquarters policy decision approving cultural activities overseas that I had myself propounded as the head of the Asia program.

After a lot of staff work and discussions with scholars and cultural leaders, we agreed to begin work selectively in three categories—archaeology, historical buildings, and artifacts; fine and performing arts; and manuscript preservation in classical and regional languages. Since government and private organizations were more active in some of these activities than in others, we did not expect an equal amount of work in each category. The Archaeological Survey of India, for example, which was responsible for excavations and the maintenance of major sites, believed itself to be adequately funded, although barely, and was reluctant to receive outside assistance. (We diplomatically offered to provide specialists to help train staff to improve the execrable presentation of the treasures at the National Museum in Delhi, including a proper catalog for visitors, but were told by the director, not very diplomatically, that no help was needed; I found out that his staff didn't agree with him.) The director did allow some of his senior staff to visit major field expeditions in West and Southeast Asia which utilized techniques and methodologies of classification not yet practiced in India. But there were large subjects in preservation that fell outside the purview of the survey. In Hyderabad, for example, we agreed with the municipal commissioner to fund a model project on how to combine public policy and private business interests to conserve, for their cultural and historical importance and as a tourist attraction, the old buildings and important houses and shops in the late medieval Muslim city that surrounded the great mosque and the chief marketplace. We funded a yearlong national survey of folk arts and artisans by a talented young Indian designer, Rajeev Sethi (who produced the Adithi exhibit of Indian folk art and culture that many Americans saw on its U.S. tour in the 1980s). We hired a distinguished Sanskrit-trained archivist and historian, V. C. Joshi, to manage a small-grants project in the preservation of premodern (meaning pre-British and for the most part non-official) manuscripts. With very few exceptions, the conditions under which temple, monastery, and private manuscripts were housed were miserable. The project installed reprographic facilities and management systems in three manuscript repositories selected on the basis of the richness of their collections, their experience in the filming of manuscripts, and their willingness to provide funds for additional staff and facilities necessary to house and manage the collections properly.

An Indian scholar called one day at the foundation to inquire whether we could consider support for training activities in the traditional Buddhist arts at Dharmsala, the headquarters of the Dalai Lama in the Himalayan foothills northwest of Delhi. The Dalai Lama was forced to flee for his life from Tibet in 1959 when the Chinese Communists crushed a revolt in Lhasa, killing an estimated one hundred thousand Tibetans. The Indian government gave him political asylum, and allowed him to establish a small government-in-exile at Dharmsala. Within three years, India and China, whom Nehru had wanted to be brothers, went to war over a vast area of remote, frozen, almost totally uninhabited land along their 2,200-mile frontier (a line of control was eventually established to end the fighting, but both sides continue today to press their claims). Dharmsala, a tiny hill station, became, in effect, the world center of Buddhism because of the powerful spiritual authority of the Dalai Lama himself. The Tibetan presence in India is a sensitive matter, and the Indian government had on a number of occasions made it clear that any kind of U.S. government interest would be most unwelcome. Before proceeding further, I told a senior civil servant about the request, making the obvious point that we were a private organization. He telephoned in a few weeks and said, without enthusiasm, that we could proceed.

I drove up to Dharmsala, which is just below where the high, snowy peaks begin. Its lanes were crowded with Tibetan traders, monks, and a sprinkling of Western hippies, and shops where one could buy homeopathic remedies (I particularly remember ground owl bone), Tibetan tea, and dumplings. I talked with the senior monk who supervised the training programs in traditional Tibetan Buddhist painting and Tibetan dance, and met the Dalai Lama. As his countless admirers know, in a modest and unassuming fashion the Dalai Lama radiates a sense of enormous, happy power, is extremely well informed about the world, has a quick sense of humor, and knows exactly what he is about—which is trying to hold together the Tibetan national soul. We made two small grants—less than fifty thousand dollars or so each—to improve the training facilities for both the school for young painters and the ballet troupe, which performed athletic, wildly beautiful dances about devils and death, and whose dancers later on international tours earned plaudits for their originality and skill. Over many years now, the Chinese have basically budged not an inch in their long occupation of Tibet. The early days were characterized by the wholesale destruction of monasteries and art objects and the torture and murder of monks. Those activities, so far as one knows, have ceased. But Tibet is becoming Sinicized by the officially sponsored, continuing Han Chinese immigration into the region. The Dalai Lama, now an old man, appears likely to go down in history as a magnificent failure in his determination to return to an independent, or at least culturally autonomous, Tibet.

I took pleasure in participating in Suzanne's India education. When she could get a break from her reporting duties, we traveled not just to the usual tourist places but some of the back-country temples and hill stations I had become so fond of. Suzanne was always interested in finding off-beat stories to cover. In a clockwork fashion, when politics, war, or the excesses of Mother Nature failed to produce anything of interest, newly arrived Western correspondents wrote virtually identical stories year after year about bride burning and dowry deaths, tiger preservation, the pollution of the Ganges, and the great camel fair at Pushkar in Rajasthan. Suzanne did her share of that, but she also found a few different ones. She spent some time, for example, at an Indian classical dancing school in Southern India, about which she ultimately wrote a book. One story she didn't write was about an evening we spent drinking *bhang* with two very proper, upper-caste Indian friends, an Indian political scientist and his musician wife, and Marcia Gauger, the *Time* magazine correspondent. *Bhang* is a traditional Indian narcotic made from the hemp plant. Mixed with yogurt and sweetened with honey, it is served ice cold like a milkshake. An evening with *bhang* and food is supposed to be gently relaxing and dreamy, and one becomes silly and laughs a lot. The evening started that way. But the mixture turned out to be super strong and possibly adulterated as well, to the post-event mortification of our host. We all suffered terrifying hallucinations. Suzanne thought she was dying and had to be put to bed at our host's house. When Ram Prakash drove us home, I was convinced that his benign face had turned into that of a murderer, and that he was deliberately taking wrong turns instead of taking us home. Neither Suzanne nor I could sleep; Suzanne still thought she was going to die. Finally, at midnight, I called Tyler Marshall, the *Los Angeles Times* correspondent. Tyler and his wife, Pearl, came over and called the U.S. embassy nurse, who appeared promptly. The nurse said we clearly had drunk some bad stuff, which the kids at the international, mostly American high school frequently did, gave us a sedative with tea, and told us to go to bed and stop worrying. We both felt high as kites for two days, as did our apologetic hosts. I had visions of newspaper headlines: "Ford Foundation chief and UPI chief correspondent hospitalized for narcotics abuse."

In 1979, the third year of my India assignment, the foundation's trustees said good-bye to McGeorge Bundy. Bundy had been president for thirteen years. Over the years, working in New York and traveling together in Europe and Asia, we had chewed on a lot of riddles and vagaries in the development of societies and human character, talking with statesmen, scientists, intellectuals, and a host of poor farmers. I admired his grasp of history and politics, which was both encyclopedic and thoughtful. We and our wives had become good friends socially—Mac's wife, Mary, who went back to school and became a social worker, was as smart as he was, although in different directions, and equally as charming. Bundy seemed to know everybody. He took me to lunch in New York one day with Isaiah Berlin, for example, whom I regarded as the world's finest thinker on Russian history and philosophy, and once, entering a hotel lobby in Leningrad, he was greeted with a cry of joy by Lillian Hellman, with whom we promptly had lunch. I joined him in working conversations with people like Franz Joseph Strauss, the Bavarian political king, and Roy Jenkins, the brightest of the British Labor Party leaders, and we had discussed the failures of American policy in Vietnam with a Vietnamese farmer in the delta. I thought his overall stewardship of the foundation had been courageous and innovative. Bundy deployed the foundation's funding power in a number of controversial issues—minority rights for blacks and Latinos, public-interest law for poor people and the environment, community development in the urban slums, the status of women, decentralization of the New York school system, and voter registration. He made some costly and highly publicized mistakes—the travel and study awards the foundation made to staffers of Bobby Kennedy after he was assassinated were a good example—and invariably he came across to Congressmen investigating foundations as haughty and arrogant. But most of the staff at Ford admired and liked him: he was always open to ideas, unfailingly courteous, and frequently funny. Not everyone thought he was great. Mac Lowry, who originally hired me and who served as chief executive officer in the hiatus between Bundy's acceptance of the presidency and his arrival in New York, disagreed with both Bundy's program directions and his operating style, and through a long and painful exit process agonized about what was happening to the institution he loved. After Bundy left Ford, he became a professor at New York University, wrote a fine book on the development and policy challenges of nuclear weapons, and became a senior wise man advising U.S. presidents on foreign policy crises.

The man the trustees chose to replace Bundy was a fellow board member, Franklin Thomas. Thomas came out of a very different background. He was the first African-American to assume the management of a powerful U.S. foundation, and clearly the board wanted to make a statement with his appointment. Publicly, that statement said unequivocally that Ford was putting its influence to work more directly on America's most explosive problems of race and poverty. Under the surface, if I interpreted it correctly, the board thought that the Bundy (and David Bell) administration suffered from the hubris of power. It was too much involved in national and international political issues and too much controversy, and in some ways it seemed to be run like a loose group of individual baronies. (Ironically, this was the same criticism some earlier board members had made of the Heald administration Bundy came aboard to replace.) The trustees wanted grants to produce immediate, visible, on-the-ground results, and to be less involved in policy matters. The crowning irony was that the prime movers of the drive to replace Bundy appeared to be the big business executives Bundy himself had recruited to the board to provide greater real-world experience and strength.)

Unlike Bundy, whose roots were in the great postwar institution building days of NATO and the Cold War, Thomas came out of the generation that reached adulthood in the social revolution of the Vietnam days. He studied law and played basketball at Columbia University, was briefly a navigator in the U.S. Air Force Strategic Air Command, and then served as an assistant U.S. attorney and deputy police commissioner in New York. In that capacity, he attracted the attention of New York Sen. Bobby Kennedy, who had made the urban crisis a central point in his political agenda. The cities were desperately seeking ways to deal with the multiple impacts of the civil rights revolution, urban poverty, dysfunctional education systems, and the rise of black power in the ghettos. In 1967, Thomas became the president and CEO of the Bedford-Stuyvesant Restoration Corporation in Brooklyn, one of the nation's first public/private partnerships aimed at the comprehensive development of one of the country's largest, distressed urban communities. Thomas served there for ten years, and Bed-Stuy, as some people called it, became a model for hundreds of similarly focused community-based development corporations throughout the country, its programs benefiting greatly from both ideas and money from the Ford Foundation, whose board Thomas joined when he left Bedford-Stuyvesant.

I first met Thomas, a tall, graceful, good-looking, soft-spoken man, when the trustees held their first overseas meeting in India in 1978. He asked some thoughtful questions about grants relating to women and poverty. To celebrate the trustee meeting in good Indian style, Rajeev Sethi and Elisa Scatena, my former administrative assistant in New York, who had come out to help handle the logistics of the meeting, organized—at very little cost—an outdoor picnic with Indian food, Rajasthani folk music, acrobatics, and dancing under multicolored tent on the foundation lawns. The performers came from a small group of low-caste Rajasthani villagers for whom Rajeev was trying, with modest help from the foundation, to obtain official title to the land they had squatted on for years in a semi-commercial section of the city. Without that land title, they were classified as beggars by the authorities and treated as such by the police. Men, women, and children, they put on a spectacular performance, and most of the trustees went out of their way to say how delighted they were. I heard later that a few of them thought the evening was lavish, although it was really just a great, mostly non-alcoholic, Indian-style party full of the color, sounds, and delights of village festivities.

Thomas took no major steps during the first months of his incumbency to modify the policies, programs, or personnel of the foundation's extensive international and overseas development programs. But starting in 1980, he launched a sweeping reorganization of the foundation, presumably reflecting his and the trustees' desire to reduce what they viewed as its overreach, hubris, and visibility as concerned international matters. Central to the reorganization was the across-the-board dismissal of most of the senior program staff (which became known—not very imaginatively—at least among those affected, as "the night of the long knives"). The reorganization eventually did away with a separate division for international programs and established "universal" program foci, on the theory that the foundation would learn and contribute more by working on identical problems—rural poverty, for example, or the status of women as concerns employment, nutrition, and health—whether these were to be found in the United States or overseas. Thomas promoted Susan Beresford, a young foundation staff member, to be the officer in charge of women's programs in 1980, and the following year he named her vice president for worldwide programming. Beresford (who, after Thomas's long, seventeen-year tenure as president, succeeded him in 1996) once visited India to look at our work in rural development and women's issues and rather contemptuously dismissed much of it as old men (in one particular case, a particularly distinguished old Gandhian) telling women what to do.

In 1980, I flew back to New York to talk with the new management about possible future assignments. I was not interested in another overseas job and told Thomas that I would like to be considered for the top position in the worldwide arts and culture program that was part of the reorganization plan. The answer was that this was an interesting but unlikely idea. It was agreed that I should leave India in 1981 to return to New York and talk further about what might be available. As time went on, it became clear that I would not be forced out of the foundation—unlike most of the senior staff who were simply terminated under quite generous terms. It was equally clear I would not find a job in the new organization that I would want to accept. (I found later that a group of trustees thought my services had been sufficiently valuable that termination was not desirable.) I said I needed to go back to India briefly to attend to a number of projects that needed to get off the ground without delays that would put the Indian participants in difficulty.

One of these was the expansion of support for non-formal, alternative approaches to education for urban slum dwellers and the rural poor being worked on at the Indian Institute of Education in Pune, Maharashtra, founded by two

Gandhian intellectuals, J. P. Naik and Chitra Naik, his wife, in Maharashtra State. Naik, a tiny man with a gray moustache, a bubbling sense of humor, and an exceptional grasp of politics and human nature, for decades had been an important leader in Indian education at the national level. He was the creator of the Indian Council of Social Science Research in New Delhi. I used to visit J. P. there—he lived in a small room, sleeping on a simple cot in the spartan dormitory, and presided over informal evening get-togethers with simple Indian food and soft drinks, at which one frequently found visitors like Gloria Steinem or an American university president. Chitra Naik had been a teacher and a state director of public education. They were about to undertake an ambitious, UNICEF-sponsored project for the universalization of primary education in a poor, rural district. Our grant supported an evaluative mechanism for the various reform efforts the institute was undertaking. (Long after my departure from India, I heard that the UNICEF project had not gone well, not because of its inability to attract and give a good education to poor village students, whose parents were paid a small stipend as long as the children attended classes, but because its improved systems of teaching and examination differed from those of the traditional schools. Many poor parents thought their children would suffer in the job market because their educational preparation had been different.)

A second new project I was particularly interested in was the launching of the Centre for Policy Research in New Delhi, India's first real political affairs think tank, the brainchild of Pai Panandikar, a Goan political scientist wise beyond his years. Panandikar had served in various capacities in the Indian government, including a period as a special assistant to Prime Minister Morarji Desai. He wanted to emulate in an Indian setting the policy-relevant work and style of the Brookings Institution in Washington, bringing together under one roof scholars, journalists, and men and women who have carried out important functions in or related to government to conduct research, write books, and organize conferences and seminars on policy issues. From its inception, the center became a useful forum for examining such topics as press freedom, which had been badly buffeted during Mrs. Gandhi's emergency, defense policy, economic policy, and planning. We set up a separate fellowship and seminar fund for scholars, journalists, and senior government officials on leave to study and discuss political processes, human rights, press freedom, and public-interest law.

The good-byes we said were moving: Indians are extremely gracious with friends, and I had a lot of them. I thought my staff, both Indian and Western, had been the best of all possible staffs (which is what I usually think, wherever I am, if I pick the staff myself). But one can never really say good-bye to India. In my case I returned almost immediately in a different capacity. UPI agreed to transfer Suzanne to the international news desk at UPI headquarters in New York. Until the day we left, she continued to travel to Pakistan and its North-West Frontier Province to cover the Soviet war and occupation that started in 1979 and the flood of refugees streaming across the international border with Afghanistan, which snaked over a thousand miles of desolate desert and mountain country.

A final task was to find a suitable home for Bitsy, the surviving female Chinese-style dog Charlotte and I brought to India from Bangkok. Our future in New York was uncertain. In any case, I doubted that Bitsy, whose health was not strong, would survive the trip. Mi Noi, her mate, had died earlier under somewhat mysterious circumstances when I was on a trip to the south, and my cook had buried him in the front yard of my house in New Delhi. Delhi was a tough town for dogs: virtually all Indian veterinaries in those days had learned their trade in the Indian cavalry treating horses, not dogs and cats. Kamla Chowdhry, a dear friend and staff colleague, suggested Bitsy might go live with a friend of hers, the hereditary reigning princess of a tiny state in the Himalayan foothills. The princess loved dogs and had recently lost a favorite. One day, I held Bitsy on my lap while Ram Prakash and I drove up to a hill town villa and formally presented Bitsy to this gracious lady, a handsome, gray-haired woman who clearly lived in considerable style. I got occasional reports about Bitsy's life and health over the next few years. Kamla reported once, for example, an encounter with the princess and Bitsy in the Delhi airport. A household servant was carrying Bitsy in a wicker basket with a red velvet cushion, a fitting denouement in the life of a noble dog.

Finally, a week or so before our departure, I drove alone out to the farm in the Punjab and peered in over the gated door at the house and garden. A servant came out to the gate to ask what I wanted. "Nothing," I said. "I used to live here."

13

Foggy Bottom

When I arrived back in New York to explore my uncertain fate with the Ford Foundation, it seemed likely that my fifteen-year-long love affair with Asia, at least in terms of my physical presence living there or working on Asian affairs in New York, had ended. The Asian half of the world would slowly drift away in my memory like some fabulous ship sailing off toward the horizon, its passengers in their rainbow-hued clothing; the saffron-clad, Thai Buddhist novitiates heading out barefoot in the early morning with their begging bowls; the Indian holy men, their foreheads smeared with white or red caste marks; the sacred cows and monkeys and tigers; the solitary Hindu and Buddhist temples in the jungles; the splendid spaces of the great mosques in the crowded cities; the pungent bazaars; and the passionate music of *sheenais* and drums and sitars—all the richness and awfulness of Asia fading with the years. Of course, the traces of Asia would be indelibly imbedded in my synapses. But my daily life would no longer center on Asia, and eventually its tastes and colors and sounds and smells would blend into the palimpsest of my memory. From much earlier years, for example, I was accustomed to my memory, for no obvious clue or reason, conjuring up the taste of a taco from a street-side stand in Mexico City, the face of a big-nosed, beautiful Mayan Indian, the feel of a calm morning on Lake Patzcuaro, or a waterfall of cherubs on the wall of a crazily beautiful baroque church. Or I would find myself in the reviewing stands in Red Square as the massed military bands blared out a march, the canon booming in salute, echoing around the square, and pigeons whirring upward in white swirls of fright. But it turned out Asia was not finished with me. Almost immediately, I undertook a new Asian assignment that was to last six more years, first in Washington and then back to the Islamic, Pakistani side of the subcontinent, where some of the most important, defining, late events of the Cold War were unfolding in Afghanistan and Pakistan.

Franklin Thomas politely made it clear the Ford Foundation had nothing to offer me in senior assignments, although he never suggested directly that I leave.

A nonprofit institution in New York specializing in Asian affairs and culture invited me to join its staff as a vice president. I respected the institution, whose work was well done and important. But I didn't want to spend my life raising money from rich socialites and investment bankers (I was thoroughly spoiled by giving money away rather than pursuing it). I thought briefly about testing myself in the private sector, where I had virtually no experience since my early newspaper days but a lot of knowledge and experience in how to get things done in Asia. I was just beginning to explore those options when, early after our return, I got a telephone call from a friend, Nyle Brady, a world-renowned soil physicist. I had worked with Nyle for many years in his career of scientific and educational work in Asia, first under a series of Ford grants to Cornell University and later in his role as director general of the International Rice Research Institute in the Philippines. Nyle said he heard I might be leaving Ford. He inquired if I might be interested in joining him in Washington, where he had been appointed assistant administrator of the Bureau for Science and Technology in the Agency for International Development (AID).

In the historical line of descent from the Marshall Plan and President Harry Truman's Point Four postwar program of technical cooperation with poorer nations, AID is the U.S. government's chief instrument for providing non-military assistance to developing countries around the world. A much-maligned, rarely praised but seemingly indestructible organization, in the early days of the Reagan presidency AID was enjoying relatively smooth sailing under the vigorous leadership of a former Peace Corps volunteer and Republican stalwart named Peter McPherson, in private life a successful tax lawyer. McPherson had served as a young man in the Peace Corps in the back-country of Peru. He was, at least in part because of this experience, that rare conservative Republican who actually believed in foreign aid. McPherson worked on James Baker's staff in the Reagan presidential campaign of 1980 and then in the White House personnel office before moving to the top AID job. McPherson got along well with Secretary of State George Schultz (AID was staffed and managed separately from State and managed its own budget; the State Department was supposed to set the overall policy framework within which AID programs operated overseas), and was a virtuoso reader of congressional moods.

I told Nyle Brady I would indeed be interested in talking further with him. By the time I got down to Washington for personal conversations, however, the scenario had changed direction. McPherson, it transpired, was deeply unhappy with the management of the Asia regional bureau in AID, then the largest geographic bureau in AID, responsible for about $3 billion of assistance per year in South and Southeast Asia. Brady had told McPherson about me, and McPherson wanted to talk about another possibility, which was to join AID as deputy assistant administrator of that bureau, working as the number two to a political appointee who was the assistant administrator. I met both McPherson and the political appointee who would be my boss, who seemed less enthusiastic than his own boss about the prospect of my joining his staff. I made no bones about the fact that I was not a Republican. McPherson said that was OK: he wanted me for what I knew about Asia, and he wanted me immediately. He did not regard this as a political appointment. I would be hired under a reserve appointment to the Senior Executive Corps (in fact, after a short time I was nominated by the secretary of state and reappointed by the president as a minister-counselor in the career Senior Foreign Service from which I had resigned in 1964). I said I could start work at AID in January. At the Ford Foundation, Frank Thomas wished me well, as did a host of subordinate staff—most of the senior staff I had known was gone or on their way out the door. A week before my departure for Washington, the executive secretary of AID, Jerry Pagano, a career civil servant whom I had gotten to know and like, called and said he wanted to give me a tip: "You're not supposed to know this yet, but I thought I should alert you to the fact that when you arrive you're going to be the acting assistant administrator, because Peter is in the process of firing your boss. And by the way, your first job after being sworn in will be to present the new Asia budget to Congress. Good luck!"

So, on a frigid morning in January 1982, having taken the train down to Washington the night before, I presented myself as the acting assistant administrator for Asia in a spacious, comfortable office on the fifth floor of the State Department building overlooking the Lincoln Memorial and the Potomac River. The first order of business was to meet my senior bureau staff in the Monday morning staff meeting that is standard procedure in virtually all Washington bureaucracies. I shook hands with each of the eight office directors of the bureau as they filed in. We sat down and looked at each other expectantly. I turned to Jim Norris, a regional office director, whom I had been told was the most senior of those present, and said, "Jim, I am here to listen and learn, and I will work very hard to do that as fast as I can. I would like you to run this meeting while I listen and ask questions. Let me know what's coming up and what's really important for me to do first." Norris, a thin, elegant man, who had an advanced degree in economics and whom I came to admire greatly in a number of capacities over the next decade, performed this task with dispatch.

The first item on my agenda, which was long, was the congressional hearings, just a week away, on the fiscal year 1983 AID budget request. The hearings required both written statements and oral presentations before the relevant congressional committees and subcommittees on AID objectives and financial requirements in the South and Southeast Asia region, where AID operated through missions in Dhaka, New Delhi, Kathmandu, Colombo, Bangkok, Manila, and Jakarta (the much earlier, large AID program on the ground in South Korea had long ended, and the once enormous AID program in Vietnam vanished with the fall of Saigon). A small mountain of written materials was stacked along one side of my room. I locked myself up day and night with this impressive pile of paper, consulting frequently with the staff. The agency's congressional liaison staff briefed me on the idiosyncrasies of the congressmen and senators who might question me—this one liked India because he had a small but well-to-do constituency of Indian immigrant professionals and businessmen, that one for religious reasons opposed any funds for family planning. For the South Asia part of the presentation, we appeared in conjunction with State's assistant secretary for the Middle East and South Asia, where I discovered my chief role was to sit and listen while congressmen competed in getting on the record with their enthusiastic support for large, totally untied assistance for Israel (Israel and the Middle East were not my responsibility, this belonging because of organizational quirks to another part of AID). I once watched a small parade of congressmen march into and then immediately out of a subcommittee hearing simply to go on the record as they read virtually identical, prepared statements in favor of aid for Israel. The Israeli lobby's clout was enormous—and still is.

In all AID's relationships with the Congress, I learned quickly, the real operators behind the elected representatives on Capitol Hill were the congressional staff assistants. The assistants kept track of the details, regarding themselves as a shadow government to the existing structures and senior officials of the administration in power (with whom they often traded places after elections). Each had his own pet theories about development. Each had a string of fall guys and favorites among the bureaucrats. I grew to respect and like several of them who took their work seriously and had a genuine interest in both policy and programs. A few were spoiled and arrogant. One, a senior aide to a conservative Southern senator, was a petty tyrant who lived to bully executive branch officials (as did his boss) and maintained a small network of informers in key spots in the bureaucracy. I survived these baptismal hearings relatively unscarred, largely because few senators or congressmen paid much attention to Asia after the fall of Saigon, although the Soviet invasion of Afghanistan was beginning to thrust Pakistan to the forefront of attention.

I then set down to a second gargantuan task of ingesting the contents of the AID handbooks, which I found regularly referred to in the course of discussing projects or policy questions. These handbooks covered every aspect of AID operations, addressing such questions as who plays what roles in the processes of project planning, contracting, and procurement. How must a project paper be prepared, and what is required for approval of a project paper? How does one organize overseas training programs, and what kinds of reports are required? What are the differences between a loan, a grant, and a cooperative agreement? What are the differences between ESF (Economic Support Funds), Development Assistance, and PL 480 (Public Law 480, which governs food and commodity aid) funds? When I asked my extremely able secretary, Delberta Daveler, to get me a set of handbooks for my office, she looked at me amusedly and said, "Are you sure? A whole set will take up a lot of space." She was right: they filled an entire, large bookshelf. I skimmed through all of them and began to concentrate on those that dealt with policy, programs, and financial controls, including the roles of comptrollers and inspectors. I also wanted to be sure I understood how to seek exceptions to handbook rules, some of which seemed ridiculously overwritten for the kind of world I knew overseas. The operational manuals were obviously necessary for an organization responsible for handling large amounts of government funds. But under the accumulating weight of the multitude of programmatic and administrative mandates, policies, and reporting requirements imposed by Congress on AID over the years, virtually none of which were ever removed even though the original rationale had become invalid or irrelevant, the handbooks had swollen into a hydra-headed bureaucratic system that hampered sensible programming and discouraged innovative thinking. Years after I left AID, I served briefly as the senior staff member of a presidential commission appointed to study AID management, a perennial sore spot with Congress. We identified nearly forty policy requirements AID was supposed to adhere to in the consideration of all projects. I knew officers who spent most of their time rather like Talmudic scholars quoting scripture (the handbooks) and saying, "No, you shall not do that."

I was able to find time for these extra hours of indoctrination, while also carrying out a full daily schedule of meetings, largely because Suzanne was still resident in our East Ninety-Fourth Street apartment in New York, working on the UPI foreign news desk and arranging a transfer to the UPI bureau in Washington, which was approved in early spring. I went to New York in April, and we drove down Interstate 95, bringing along the two bazaar-bred cats we had carried back from India, and moved into a charming small house on Sherrier Street in northwest Washington, a couple of blocks up from the C&O Canal and towpath and the Potomac River and within easy commuting distance of the State Department and downtown Washington, where the UPI office was located. Our Delhi-bred female cat, Chandi, soon went crazy, forcing the neutered male, Pumpkin, to lie on his side and submit to long bouts of suckling. Chandi then began peeing on Suzanne's clothes in her closet, so I finally took Chandi to the neighborhood vet for assistance in moving on to her next incarnation. Pumpkin, who had always been subdued, promptly blossomed when he ceased to serve as a mother to his sister. We bought an enthusiastic Labrador puppy whom Suzanne named "Bosun" (after Lord Byron's Labrador). I started traveling to Asia frequently once the congressional hearings were over, but when I was in Washington we jogged daily with Bosun on the towpath above the Potomac, which is one of the most beautiful walks in the world. We partied with a lively mixture of Foreign Service and journalist friends and spent weekends sailing on the Chesapeake Bay on a thirty-foot, French-built sloop I had bought after Charlotte's death. My son Peter, who had become a fisherman in Galilee, Rhode Island, married a beautiful Italian-American girl, Paula, from a large local clan, and we drove up to Narragansett for the great occasion. At the wedding party, which looked like a scene from *The Godfather*, the master of ceremonies, presenting the parents of the bride and groom, cried "Wow, what a mother!" to wild applause when Suzanne was introduced. My daughter, Kathleen, got married to a jazz musician in our backyard in Washington to the background music of popping champagne corks and jetliners roaring overhead on the western takeoff route from National Airport, effectively shutting out most of the spoken vows (the marriage eventually went on the rocks but not because of that).

I knew relatively little about AID internally as an organization, even though in my Ford Foundation work in Asia from time to time I shared ideas and information with AID officials and technical assistance experts where our interests coincided—as, for example, the ubiquitous challenges of agricultural and rural development. Both organizations supported the international agricultural research institutes originally established by the Ford and Rockefeller Foundations, and AID continued its critical, major support long after the Ford Foundation moved on to other priorities. But on the ground in a given country, AID and Ford Foundation approaches were usually quite different. The foundation in Asia, to a large extent in response to my direction, had turned almost entirely away from supporting government programs and was concentrating on non-governmental entities. AID was still mostly a government-to-government lending and granting institution. For a few favored countries, AID still could muster the financial resources necessary to make important investments in capital infrastructure projects—dams, roads, irrigation systems (although less so as the years went by and AID budgets began to shrink). Such projects were always far beyond the foundation's resources. AID increasingly focused on "policy" lending and granting, which in essence meant negotiating and supporting changes in economic policy on the part of a host government in return for financial support from AID. In earlier days, the Ford Foundation itself had provided considerable numbers of Western economic policy advisers and trained hundreds of Asian economists and other academic and governmental experts in subjects essential in national development. But the foundation's funds *per se* were far too limited to persuade any government to change a policy. The foundation was far more useful in employing its flexibility to support innovations in new important and neglected fields—forestry and natural resource conservation as an example—and to encouraging nongovernmental organizations in social and economic development, hoping to demonstrate the unique capabilities of such organizations and their need for local, indigenous support. The most visible difference between AID and the foundation was in the amounts of money at stake and the sizes of staff. Even a small AID overseas mission controlled $25 million or so in a variety of funding lines. Big ones managed programs of well up into the hundreds of millions of dollars. The largest AID overseas program, in Egypt, ran at a little less than a billion dollars a year plus, thanks to Henry Kissinger's open-ended commitment of U.S. taxpayer funds for Israel and Egypt dating back to the 1970s negotiations to establish peace in the Middle East. In Israel, there was not even a USAID Mission: the U.S. Treasury simply sent a $1 billion check annually, which the Israeli government always insisted on receiving on October 1, the first day of the U.S. government fiscal year. (In all other cases of assistance, the U.S. government pays out grant commitments in installments, so that the Treasury can earn interest on the funds by selling bonds.) In contrast, the Ford Foundation's largest overseas program in India in the 1980s commanded $5 million annually. Ford was effectively highly decentralized as concerned its overseas offices and their freedom of search and action, although that began to lessen after Bundy's departure. AID decision-making was more centralized and subject to Washington checks and authorization requirements—although we were to achieve a considerable degree of decentralization in Asia during my years in Washington. The most troublesome problem in AID was that its long-term policy and program planning were subject to frequently shifting political priorities and the latest development fads imposed on AID by both the administration and Congress. AID was in the midst of such a period of policy and priority changing when I joined its staff in 1982.

The new Reagan administration brought with it the central ideology that government was not the answer but the problem, and that the true magic of development lay in the market. Its intellectual guru was Frederick Hayek, the Austrian-born economist and political philosopher, whose most popular book, *The Road to Serfdom*, condemned central planning of the economy as a major step to totalitarianism. The new management of AID under Reagan also liked to quote such scholars as the British economist Peter Bauer, a Hayek devotee, who argued that too often foreign aid turned out to be "transferring money from poor people in rich countries to rich people in poor countries." The correct way to view foreign assistance, as set forth in a recent paper by a Bauer admirer, Richard Rahn of the Cato Institute, a conservative think tank in Washington, is, "A country that establishes the rule of law and largely eliminates corruption, allows free markets to operate, establishes free trade, maintains low taxation and government spending, does not excessively regulate, and establishes a stable currency will attract sufficient domestic and foreign investment to grow rapidly, without foreign aid." A number of young men expounded this gospel in the Reagan administration and went on later to occupy key positions in the second Bush administration. John Bolton, for example, a fiery, hardworking lawyer who had worked on Sen. Jesse Helms's staff and was the assistant administrator of AID for policy in the early 1980s, served as the under secretary of state in charge of arms control in the first term of George W. Bush's administration and then, after a series of angry Senate hearings, became Bush's ambassador to the United Nations under a recess appointment. Paul Wolfowitz, an assistant secretary of state for East Asia in the Reagan administration, under Bush number two became the deputy secretary of defense and the most ardent single advocate of the disastrous and incompetently led Iraq war. Wolfowitz's reward was to become president of the World Bank.

Only an extremely small number of human societies, if any, come close to meeting the purity of standards required by the disciples of Hayek and Bauer. The United States falls short on a number of counts, and most overseas societies are hopelessly delinquent—including many that the U.S. government, whether in a Democratic or Republican administration, finds desirable to support for foreign policy reasons. Any short list of these perennial unsatisfactory aid recipients must be headed by Egypt, which remains, after a quarter century of large-scale U.S. foreign aid, notoriously corrupt and bureaucratized. Shortly following on the list are El Salvador, Guatemala, and Pakistan, whose fortunes go up and down, depending on how politically useful a country appears to be at a given moment. Israel, for decades the single, largest U.S. aid recipient, is far more of a socialist, statist place than the norms of the Hayek/Bauer doctrines would permit.

For many years, the main political justification for giving assistance to unsavory or less than satisfactory governments that for one reason or another were regarded as strategic was that we had to keep them on our side in the Cold War against the Soviet Union. The Cold War is over, of course, and rapidly fading in our memories, but the Bush war on terror continues to provide a seemingly even more imperative justification. The most recent additions to the list of major U.S. foreign aid recipients under Bush are the new Central Asian states spawned by the collapse of the Soviet Union. Without exception, they are cruel, corrupt, and careless of law, but their friendship and cooperation are now considered essential in the war on terror. The main problem with the right-wing theory of development is that it downplays to the point of caricature the potentially positive role of governments in managing common natural resources and helping to build institutions, basic infrastructure, and public education. In our own American experience, government funds and agencies played a fundamental part in building the United States in the nineteenth century, and the Great Depression of the 1920s and 1930s required the imaginative use of government power as exercised by Roosevelt in the New Deal (and the great stimulus of World War II industrial production) to restore health to the American body politic.

In Washington in the 1980s, these early efforts to instill a new set of beliefs were visibly at odds with the AID culture of earlier years. The traditional AID culture prized and rewarded project and loan officers who excelled at planning and supervising projects to build power and irrigation dams and highways in places like Pakistan and Afghanistan, setting up and funding major public health institutions and campaigns, supporting essential national food production programs, and building local higher education institutions in technology and management. In the health field, for example, AID was almost single-handedly responsible for funding the worldwide war on malaria for many years; the incidence of malaria overseas rose and fell depending on the ups and downs of AID budgets for insecticides—primarily DDT—and vehicles and staff for mosquito eradication programs. Much of this earlier AID work had been well done, although usually at high cost, because the primary contractors were always American engineering and consulting firms. Almost all of it, one way or another, amounted to government-to-government support. The new recipe for development was to persuade the recipient governments to get the economic policy right, as perceived by the followers of Hayek and Bauer—low taxation, little to zero corruption, low tariffs, free markets, and easy access for and unlimited movement of foreign capital. AID should deploy its funds, both grant and loan, to help willing governments to change their economic policies. In virtual lockstep with the

U.S. government, the World Bank and the International Monetary Fund began to change their lending policies as well.

The more adaptable of the AID Foreign and Civil Service officers embraced these new requirements quickly and imaginatively, and "policy dialogue" became an integral part of AID programming everywhere. (At a somewhat later period, I was reminded of this when in post-Soviet Russia I would meet Russian economists who had printed new business cards reading "Market Economist.") It was, of course, desirable and sensible to try to move recipient countries toward more efficient economic and legal systems. Many Third World economic development policies were destructive. Rampant and growing corruption constituted the main obstacle to development in most of the new nations, and it flourished in the bureaucratic jungles of licensing, regulation, and reliance on state corporations that characterized the economic development policies of postwar leaders like Nehru (who wanted the state and its public corporations to control "the commanding heights" of the Indian economy), Indonesia's Sukarno, and Ghana's Kwame Nkrumah. The challenge was to locate and put into practice the correct balance between a blind commitment to the magic of the marketplace, which had become a quasi-religious conviction on the part of some Western intellectuals and politicians, and tackling the social and economic problems that require government power and intervention. I was impressed at AID in the early 1980s when John Bolton's policy office published a series of development policy manuals that, in a common sense way, both preached the economic gospel on such topics as agricultural credit, energy pricing, nutrition, and public finance and taxation but also recognized that a process of give and take and adjustment must take place in a developing society as it seeks social justice as well as economic growth.

The real world is, of course, full of examples of different ways to achieve growth and widely shared prosperity. Mahathir's Malaysia, for example, achieved both under a not very benevolent authoritarianism. It was far from a free-market model but attracted impressive amounts of foreign investment and raised the living standards of an entire population. Cutting through the monstrous edifices of government controls and regulations *is* essential and does produce results. India's breakout from economic stagnation—what its economists used to call the "Hindu rate of growth"—began only when a reform-minded finance minister, Manmohan Singh, in the 1980s started to dismantle the Nehruvian edifice of state socialism and bureaucratic controls. The large, growing, and increasingly prosperous Indian middle class is the result, and Manmohan Singh deservedly, and fortunately for India, is now prime minister of India.

Working inside these intersecting matrixes of policy issues, bureaucratic cultures, and personal relationships was rather like swimming around inside the body of a whale and observing the functioning of its various organs and life fluids. The new, junior interns and officers coming into AID were lively and smart, I thought, much more at home with the anthropological and cultural dimensions of development than their seniors. But I also respected the wisdom of a good many of the more senior officers, not because of their command or knowledge of the culture and politics of a given country or region, which in at least some cases was superficial, but in their understanding of the forces and dynamics of the bureaucracy. AID was staffed both by technically trained people—public health, agronomy, educationists, population experts, agricultural economists—and by project managers and generalists, an increasing number of whom had some training in business management. Nyle Brady's Bureau of Science and Technology had the largest concentration of technically trained staff; the program (regional) bureaus tended to be staffed by managers and generalists, although they also had a number of staff people with technical backgrounds. AID always employed a fair number of professional economists, many trained to the PhD level and some doing interesting analytical and policy-related work. Others were doomed to work in the bowels of the organization on project analysis and cost-benefit questions. By and large, whether one was in a technical or regional program bureau, the day at AID was filled with project-and program-management chores. I spent hours daily in meetings inside the AID bureaucracy and in interagency forums expounding and defending positions, and I learned early on that time invested on the Hill keeping congressional staffers up to date with what was going on in Asia was essential.

The rewards for a bureaucrat are in the moment of triumph when one has successfully manipulated the system to produce the approval of a policy, program, or project that he believes sound and desirable, that satisfies both his own knowledge and the best social science findings, and that can survive relatively unscathed as it passes through the multiple requirements of all the bureaucracies he must deal with. On substantive matters concerning Asia, people in AID and State tended to listen to me because of my unusual, fourteen years of on-the-ground experience in Asian development matters with the Ford Foundation in New York, Bangkok, and New Delhi, which was, of course, why Peter McPherson hired me. My foundation background led me from time to time to respond with mild irritation to the not infrequent comment by AID staff members that the agency didn't have the staff time to waste on a "small" project of two or three million dollars, at which point I would usually observe that at Ford we thought we could change the world with grants that had some number of zeros subtracted from the tail end of the average AID grant figure, and that quality of ideas and the brains and promise of a grantee or loan recipient, rather than quantity, was what counted. I benefited greatly from an intensive, crash education from Fred Shieck, who preceded me in the Asia bureau deputy position. Shieck was thoughtful, engaging, and polite, one of the most respected and productive senior officers in AID, and usually won his arguments without offending anyone. He guided me for months on the bristly issues of the day and the idiosyncrasies of the key players and threw in such useful information as how to navigate swiftly through the back staircases and lesser-known corridors and byways in the State Department building so as to arrive promptly at the administrator's office, which was at the other end of the building, in response to an urgent call, or how to decide which senior officers in the Asia bureau should receive one of the prized, limited parking spaces in the State Department basement garage, a Solomonic task that became part of my job.

Because of my own experience, I firmly believed that field officers knew more than anyone in Washington about what was going on in their bailiwicks and was determined to be very supportive of the overseas field offices. But occasionally I had to take decisions that contradicted the overseas mission director's position because I thought the politics of Washington demanded it. Shortly after I joined AID, for example, I attended the swearing-in ceremony in the administrator's office of the new mission director in Pakistan, Donor Lion (whose name always struck me as marvelously appropriate for a person who made his living giving away large sums of money). Lion was indeed somewhat of a lion in AID. He was handsome in a Clark Gable kind of way, dressed in pinstripe suits, smoked cigars, and spoke in a growl. He had a PhD in economics from Harvard and had acquired a reputation for being a tough but successful operator in a variety of senior overseas assignments. Lion was an obvious choice to head the recently revived Pakistan USAID mission and to put together the major new development program that would support Pakistan while Pakistan in turn facilitated the U.S. overt and clandestine efforts to defeat the Soviets in Afghanistan. Over the first several months of his incumbency, Lion and his colleagues traced out and got Washington approval for a fairly traditional kind of AID field program: grants (because of the political situation, Pakistan was deemed to be an all-grant program) in agricultural research and commodities, on-farm water and large-scale irrigation management improvements, the improvement of Pakistan's ragtag power sector, including better coal technology and a large project for improving the efficiency of the power system; primary health care, malaria control, and population and family planning; and a series of projects in the strategic North-West Frontier Province (NWFP) and Baluchistan bordering Afghanistan. These included back-country road and primary school construction plus a sizable university building project at the University of Peshawar. Conspicuously absent was any AID effort in the narcotics field, which had become a virtual congressional commandment for AID overseas programs in areas where narcotic materials—coca leaves and opium poppies—could be produced. Because of the growing demand for heroin in the United States and Europe, opium poppy cultivation was increasing in Pakistan's border areas with Afghanistan, where Pushtoon or Baluch tribal law prevailed, and government access at best was limited and dangerous. Donor Lion had seen narcotics eradication programs at work in Latin America and took an extremely dim view of their benefit. He said flatly he would not recommend a project. "All we would do, in the unlikely event that a poppy eradication project works, is push cultivation further north and west to the next valleys," he said. I thought he was right. But the word on the Hill was that, in spite of Pakistan's high political priority because of the Afghanistan war and U.S. security interests, the Pakistan budget would take a sizable whack unless a narcotics project joined the program mix. I told Lion to prepare and send in a project for the NWFP. He did so reluctantly but faithfully, we approved it, and over the next several months Lion and his staff organized and launched the project, which involved "promoting development and eradicating opium producing by fostering viable economic systems in poppy cultivation areas." Its premise was simple: eradicate poppy cultivation, mostly through aerial spraying, and convince farmers to substitute other crops. The flaw in all such projects, of course, is that on poor soils no other crop is as easy to grow and as profitable as poppy. With a lot of concentration on the chosen northern valleys and after years of eradication efforts and never very successful experiments in crop substitution, poppy production slowed to a trickle in the chosen areas. But Lion, of course, was right: poppy production simply moved further north and west to virtually unreachable areas on and across the Afghanistan border. Today, twenty years later, Afghanistan is the world's largest producer of opium poppy. Pakistani production, after falling markedly, is now on the rise again in the troubled border provinces and Pakistan remains the major transit route for heroin from Southwest Asia destined for the insatiable appetites of Europe and the United States.

In the spring of 1983, I got a new boss when Charles Greenleaf moved over to AID from James Baker's staff in the White House to become counselor to Peter McPherson. After Greenleaf served a few months in the front office, McPherson named him as the new assistant administrator for Asia. Greenleaf was a genuine intellectual, fascinated by the processes and complexities of nation building and widely read in politics and history. He came from a well-to-do family in Indiana, went to school at Princeton, and in various periods of his life had traveled extensively abroad on his own to investigate questions of particular interest, which in recent years had included the riddle of development in the Indian subcontinent. At another level, he was a skillful and extremely well-informed and connected Republican political operator, who would sit in his office with his executive assistant, also a political appointee, late at night after the workday ended and analyze such esoterica as county-level trends across the country in local elections. I could not have asked for a better office chief and working partner, and our working relationship and friendship were to extend far into the future beyond AID. Greenleaf generally handled the high-level external relations within AID and State and on the Hill; I mostly ran the day-to-day operations of the bureau. But Greenleaf always stayed involved in the substance of our programs, and from time to time at Greenleaf's request I took on some of the senior-level representational responsibilities.

This became the case, for example, with the Asia bureau's participation in the annual World Bank-chaired economic consortium meetings convened to discuss development assistance plans and budgets in the several Asian nations for which donor consortia had been created. These included India, Pakistan, Nepal, Sri Lanka, Indonesia, and the Philippines. The consortia meetings took place in May and June in Europe, usually at the World Bank building in Paris, but in the case of the Indonesia consortium in Amsterdam, because of the historical role of the Dutch in that country. The United States was represented by a small delegation, headed by a senior AID officer and including officers from State, commerce and agriculture plus the AID mission director and the embassy economic counselor from the country concerned. The various European donors were represented by roughly comparable delegations. The country whose finances and development policies and planning were under discussion was usually represented by its finance minister and a bevy of senior officials and economists. The World Bank vice president for Asia, a Canadian economist named David Hopper (who had in his early career worked for Douglas Ensminger on the Ford Foundation India staff), presided over the meetings. Hopper knew Asia and the senior development figures in each country extremely well. Although his private comments about the quality of performance on the part of the recipient countries could be acid, publicly around the table there was never any doubt that the main purpose of the meetings was to marshal as many financial resources as the donors could put together. Charlie Greenleaf early and correctly decided that these meetings were exercises in international boredom. Thus the springtime visits to Paris and Amsterdam generally fell to me, effectively interrupting my cherished spring sailing plans on the Chesapeake Bay and invariably causing me to miss the annual miracle of the azalea blossom season in Washington. "I don't want to go to Paris in the springtime," I would say to my friends. "What a tough job you've got," they would respond. "Why don't you just shut up?" But it wasn't play-acting on my part. In fact, although I understood the original rationale for the consortia and the annual meetings as an attempt by the World Bank, the biggest donor of them all, to achieve some degree of common understanding and maybe even cooperation about development priorities, I began to believe that these annual conventions of the international development bureaucracies in their full panoply represented development politics at its worst. Consistent failures in promised performance were rarely, if ever, punished by the reduction or withholding of funds, and the symbiotic (some might say incestuous) relationship between big donors and recipients was painfully obvious.

Even with Paris, I liked my job. Charlie Greenleaf and Peter McPherson, my chiefs, seemed pleased with my work. I assumed I would stay with AID in Washington until 1987 when I became sixty-five, at which point I wanted to retire to read, sail, and enjoy living in the United States after spending so much of my life—two decades of it—living abroad. Suzanne was happy, although she didn't much like her job in the UPI Washington bureau, where she did more editing than the reporting on foreign affairs that she wanted to do. She had become somewhat of a protégé of the redoubtable Helen Thomas, the perennial thorn in the side of American presidents, and enjoyed that friendship a great deal. Early in 1985, though, McPherson and Greenleaf asked me if I would replace Donor Lion as the USAID mission director in Islamabad, Pakistan. Lion had done a sterling job launching the new AID program in Pakistan, which had become the most important single strategic outpost in the United States' proxy war against the Soviets in Afghanistan, but after three years he wanted out for family reasons. I would have preferred to stay in Washington, but AID had been good to me, and I was certainly a logical choice for the Islamabad assignment. I had lived six years in the Indian subcontinent. I had a limited command of Hindi that could be easily converted to an equally limited Urdu, the common language of Pakistan. (Hindi and Urdu are closely related offshoots of the historic lingua franca of the subcontinent, Hindustani, under both the Mogul and British empires: Hindi seeks to incorporate Sanskrit words; while Urdu looks to Persian and Arabic.) In my earlier years as the head of the Ford Foundation Asia office in New York, I had invested a lot of time traveling in Pakistan and studying its development.

Plus which, after three years, I knew my way around the Washington bureaucracies and the Hill, and that would be a great advantage in representing Pakistan's case.

Suzanne was enthusiastic. When we lived in New Delhi, she covered the Afghanistan story through frequent visits to Islamabad and Peshawar before Soviet troops finally occupied Afghanistan in December 1979. UPI did not have a bureau in Islamabad; like most of the news organizations covering the Afghanistan war, UPI sent staffers over as required from regional bases in New Delhi or Hong Kong. In any case, Suzanne increasingly wanted to try her hand at freelance writing. This would be a marvelous opportunity to get started. So she said good-bye to UPI, we packed up, not taking much with us since the government provided furnished housing in Islamabad, and sold our house. With the proceeds, we bought a romantically beautiful old waterfront farm on the Eastern Shore of the Chesapeake Bay in Northampton County, Virginia, where we expected to return when I eventually retired, and in late spring flew off to the pre-monsoon heat of Islamabad and the war zone that started seventy-five miles northwest of the capital.

14

The Great Game: An American Chapter

A not inaccurate way to think of Pakistan is as a faraway part of Asia where men have always gone to find excitement, danger, and glory. The tribal people of the Northwest Frontier, who fight for and against the Americans today, have bloodied all comers since time immemorial. Some of the men one meets on the frontier, blue-eyed and all carrying guns, bear the genes of the Greek warriors of Alexander the Great, who led his weary, homesick veterans across the Indus River in 324 BC to conquer the Indian empire and then died on his way back home to Macedonia.

In the heyday of the British Empire, a twenty-three-year-old, Sandhurst-trained cavalry officer, wearying of the polo playing, tiger shooting, and social routine of imperial cavalry service in Bangalore, heard reports in 1897 that war was brewing with the tribes in the Northwest. He pulled strings in London and got himself ordered to the Northwest Frontier as a war correspondent on leave from his cavalry regiment. "Campaigning on the Indian frontier is an experience by itself," Winston Churchill wrote in his autobiography, *An Early Life*. "Neither the landscape nor the people find their counterparts in any other portion of the globe. Valley walls rise steeply five or six thousand feet on every side. The (British) columns crawl through a maze of giant corridors down which fierce snow-fed torrents foam under skies of brass. Amid these scenes of savage brilliancy there dwells a race whose qualities seem to harmonize with their environment...Every man is a warrior, a politician, and a theologian...Every family cultivates its vendetta; every clan, its feud. Nothing is ever forgotten, and very few deaths are left unpaid. For the purposes of social life...a most elaborate code of honor has been established and is on the whole faithfully observed...The life of the Pathan is thus full of interest." Churchill found his excitement and glory: he shot, and got shot at, sent some highly praised dispatches off to the *Daily Telegraph*, and wrote a book, *The Malakand Field Force*, that caused a favorable stir among the London governing elites. Churchill's "picket," a possibly apocryphal observation post perched on a rocky ridge overlooking the fertile valley of the Kingdom of Swat, is still there. With a bit of imagination, one can hear the call of bugles, the sound of rifle fire, and the shouts and screams of battle. The British left none of their wounded alive on the field. The Pathans have the custom of cutting off their fallen foes' genitals and stuffing them into their mouths.

Another way to look at Pakistan is as possibly the single most consequential failure of the Islamic world's dream of building modern states in the post-World War II period when colonialism ended. Pakistan ("pure place") was born in much hope in the blood and ashes of the 1947 partition of the subcontinent. Its creation fulfilled the dream for a homeland for the Muslims of undivided India (although very sizable numbers remained in India). Its founders, principal among them Mohammad Ali Jinnah, represented, as Akbar Ahmed, a Pakistani anthropologist, writes, a "synthesis between South Asian and British culture...In European terminology, Jinnah was an English liberal. Trained as a lawyer in London, he possessed a superb command of English in which he spoke and thought. His almost English aloofness and bearing—elegant suit, spats, hat, watch-chain and cigar—appeared to confirm his reputation as a person of impeccable integrity and with high notions of just and what was right...On the surface an unlikely Muslim hero, he was to stir the Muslims of South Asia as no leader has done before or since. For those in Pakistan he would be Quaid-e-Azam, the Great Leader." (An excellent biography of Jinnah by Stanley Wolpert notes that Jinnah also enjoyed English-style sausage, which was sufficient to get the book banned in Pakistan.)

Pakistan came to nationhood with all the accoutrements of the modern state: a president, prime minister, legislature, and Western-style courts. But with the exception of the wealthy and long-settled province of Punjab in the east, which has historically dominated Pakistani politics and the economy, Pakistan was a far wilder and less settled country than India, where parliamentary democracy by and large has worked. Almost immediately, Pakistan began to run aground on the rocks of corruption and tribalism. Military coups arrived with depressing regularity. Its most promising years in terms of economic development came under the leadership of Gen. Ayub Khan, an ethnic Pathan, who seized power from a faltering civilian government in 1958 and for a decade ruled as a mostly benevolent dictator preaching what he called "guided democracy." Ayub Khan, to quote Akbar Ahmed, "never quite managed to shake off the values and change the behavioral patterns he acquired at the Royal Military Academy, Sandhurst, and in the Indian Army. His impressive physical bearing, clipped mustache and haircut, and his pastimes—shooting grouse on the demesnes of Scottish lords, the golf course, whisky in the evening—reflected an Anglicized lifestyle and social values." Most Westerners were charmed, and the general, who eventually promoted himself to the rank of field marshal, became the darling of Western development agencies. Ayub's model of "guided democracy," with village councils and a strong hand at the top, was thought to be the way the Muslim world ought to go. Ayub encouraged industrialization, tackled land reform—unsuccessfully—and launched various efforts in education reform. He also moved the capital from Karachi to Islamabad, in the foothills of the Himalayas and near to his home in the Northwest Frontier, to symbolize the new, pure spirit of Pakistan. But the Indo-Pakistani 1965 war greatly weakened the Pakistani economy, never strong at its best, and in early 1969, after nationwide riots and demonstrations, Ayub resigned and turned over power to Gen. Yahya Khan. Yahya Khan turned out to be a ruler of staggering incompetence, in 1971 presiding over the twin disasters of the successful rebellion of the Bengali Muslims in East Pakistan and the war with India. (Before he fell from power, Yahya Khan served as the intermediary for President Nixon in the ultra-secret negotiations with Peking for Nixon's pathbreaking visit to China in 1972. Henry Kissinger, whose 1971 secret flight to Peking took off from Pakistan, said in a July 19, 1971, White House conversation with Nixon, the transcript of which the National Security Archive, a private organization, recently obtained and posted on its website: "The cloak-and-dagger exercise in Pakistan arranging the trip was fascinating. Yahya hasn't had such fun since the last Hindu massacre.")

For a student of nation building, Pakistan is a case study in the often dubious benefits of allying one's self with the United States. In its early years—the 1950s and '60s—Pakistan enjoyed high priority in receiving U.S. economic and military aid because it was seen as a counterweight to India, which was deemed to be leaning toward the Soviet Union. Pakistan signed a Mutual Defense Agreement with the United States and at Washington's insistence joined two regional security alliances. It also provided air base facilities to the United States near Peshawar to fly military reconnaissance flights over the Soviet Union (Gary Powers's U-2 spy plane, shot down over the Soviet Union in 1960, took off from Peshawar). But by the 1970s, after Pakistan split into two countries and lost a war with India, Pakistan became somewhat of a pariah, and the United States greatly reduced its assistance. In 1974, after India successfully tested a nuclear device, Pakistan's prime minister, Zulfikar Ali Bhutto, reacted strongly and said Pakistan must develop its own "Islamic bomb." In 1979, President Jimmy Carter cut off all but humanitarian food aid because of the latest version of the Symington amendment (Sen. Stuart Symington, Democrat, Missouri) to the foreign aid bill that aimed to prevent non-nuclear states from acquiring uranium-enrichment technology.

In 1981, following the Soviet invasion of Afghanistan, Pakistan again became an American ally. Its cooperation was absolutely vital in defeating the Soviet Army in Afghanistan, and the United States agreed to provide Pakistan $3.2 billion, equally divided between economic and military assistance, over six years (which was renewed in 1986 with $4 billion over a further period of six years). To do so, the administration waived various congressional requirements requiring certification that Pakistan did not possess nuclear weapons. But as soon as the Soviet Union withdrew its defeated army from Afghanistan in 1989, the roller coaster headed precipitously down. The United States once again chose to take a hard line on the nuclear issue. In 1990 President George H. W. Bush refused to make the certification required under the Pressler (Sen. Larry Pressler, Republican, South Dakota) amendment, which singled out Pakistan among the growing numbers of powers seeking nuclear arms, whose numbers included India, China, and Israel, for particular punitive attention. As a result, the U.S. government terminated assistance to Pakistan (and Afghanistan) precisely at the point when the seeds of Al Qaeda and the Taliban were germinating in the post-Soviet war soil of Pakistan and Afghanistan. Saudi money was already pouring large amounts of money into the establishment of hundreds of fundamentalist *madrassas* in the North-West Frontier in Pakistan, whose graduates constitute one of the world's largest pools of men deliberately taught to hate America. The United States thus essentially opted out of any role in encouraging the peaceful development of Pakistani society until the World Trade Center attack on September 11, 2001, changed all equations. Today, once again, the nuclear objection has conveniently been pushed into the background, and Pakistan, because of the war on terror, is a very large recipient of American overt economic and military and covert intelligence assistance. A quarter of a century ago, it was still a reasonably moderate state. Today, it runs the danger of becoming a failing state, its Muslim populace increasingly fundamentalist, and potentially far more explosive and dangerous than Iraq. Unlike Iraq, Pakistan *has* nuclear weapons.

I found Pakistan a challenging and rewarding place. Although I had traveled there on both Ford Foundation and AID assignments, as I acquired a good number of Pakistani friends I realized that in many respects I had tended to see Pakistan through the eyes of India—the other side of the looking glass, as it were—and regarded it in some respects as a lesser version of the great civilization. Pakistan *is* part of Indian history, of course, and cannot escape that history in such matters as the concept of caste, which below the surface survives in large parts of Pakistan even though caste presumably cannot exist in Islam. I grew to appreciate the strengths and humanity of Pakistanis in their own right and in their differences from Indian culture, which are many and significant and are growing as the older generations, whose elites on both sides were often educated in the same institutions, pass away. In its northwestern desert and mountain reaches, Pakistan is Central Asian and in every important respect un-Indian. Along the Makran coast of the Arabian Sea and in the hot, sprawling, uncontrollable metropolis of Karachi, it is heavily influenced by the Middle East (the Makran once belonged to the Sultan of Oman, who still recruits his palace guards there). The parts of Pakistan truly reminiscent of India are the rich, irrigated plains of the five rivers of the Punjab and the great Punjabi city of Lahore, from which seat the Mogul emperors ruled their empire for many years. In the north, a concentration of some of the highest mountain peaks in the world jut upward in a spectacular display along the Chinese border, just a few hours drive from Islamabad up the frightening Karakorum highway carved out of the gorge of the Indus river (an old Silk Road branch route to the sea). The mountain tribes never formed part of imperial India in any significant fashion, either under the Moguls or the British.

Most of Pakistan's one hundred fifty million people are Sunni Muslims. Possibly 20 percent are Shias, and there are tiny Hindu, Sikh, and Christian groups as well. In their practice of Islam, both the Sunnis and the Shias of Pakistan traditionally followed a moderate approach to everyday life and their relationships with other peoples and countries (with the exception of India, which was always complicated). But a once small, indigenous stream of fundamentalist Islam existed in the subcontinent long before independence. The Deobandis are named after the Indian town of Deoband, ninety miles northeast of New Delhi. There, in 1886, a decade after the British suppressed the Sepoy Mutiny, deposed the last Muslim emperor in India, and shut down Muslim schools, a Muslim religious leader, Mohammed Quasim Nanotyi, founded a school known as Darul Uloom ("House of Knowledge"). The original purpose was to reform and unite Muslims as they were forced to live under a colonial, non-Muslim power. Deobandi schools teach reading and recitation of religious texts, mathematics, and logic. They hold that men are more intelligent than women; girls are not to be educated past eight years of age. Although the Deobandi school of Islam was less harsh than the Wahabi tradition that the Saudis have propagated and funded so widely throughout the Islamic world in recent years, the mixture of the two traditions increasingly affects political life in Pakistan and Afghanistan. The Taliban movement in Afghanistan started with a radically anti-modern interpretation of Deobandi doctrine as its inspiration. Gen. Zia ul Huq, the Pakistani president and dictator during the Afghanistan war, was a Deobandi, and Deobandi *madrassas* were being built in Pakistan long before Saudi money began to flow in. But in the late 1980s, both the Deobandi and Wahabi movements still were very much a minority, and most of the Pakistanis I knew still defined themselves as moderate Muslims in their personal and professional relationships and modern in their outlook. A central element of the creed, beyond the faith that there is one God, Allah, and that Mohammed is his prophet, is its egalitarianism, at least in theory and frequently in practice. The most powerful must respect and help the lowest. Islam was the central glue holding together a Pakistani society that at its moderate best functioned rather well, although it never did much in economic terms for its poor people. In its fundamentalist modes, Islam impeded progress and social justice—at least from a Western point of view.

After being invited to a great festival in her village, I once asked a good friend, who happens to be a Shia Muslim, her views about family and society in Pakistan and how Pakistan has changed since independence. Abida Hussain is a Punjabi aristocrat, a politician, and a great landowner who in her clan is regarded as a hereditary saint (Hussain served as Pakistan's ambassador to Washington in the early 1990s, has been a cabinet minister on various occasions, and currently is president of the Muslim League, a major, traditional Muslim political party). Hussain told me:

> In South Asia a person identifies himself first by religion, then clan, then region. I am a Musulman, a Jat (in both Pakistan and India, the Jats are a large, farming community primarily resident in the Punjab), and am from Sialkot. The family is still viewed as the parents, siblings, grandparents, aunts, uncles, first cousins. Because of intermarriage frequently you share grandparents. Clans may separate physically because of the requirements of modern living. But they always come together for great rites. The most powerful person becomes the clan head although weight is always given to the more senior. The Shah Jeevna clan (Abida's clan, named for the village) currently has no head because of political disagreements. The Bokharis (Bokhari trace their family lines back to Bukhara in Central Asia; they also call themselves Sayeeds—upper-class Muslims claiming descent from the family of the prophet; Abida is one) in the neighborhood number three or four thousand. The service classes or castes are much larger—twelve to fifteen thousand. Altogether, the groups comprise maybe one hundred thousand people living in a sixty-square-mile area, all working in agriculture or connected pursuits and services.

All the social systems were greatly affected by living with Hindus (before partition). Shah Jeevna was a self-sufficient village when I was a child. There were all kinds of service groups. Do's and don'ts were very specific. The cobbler's daughter would not marry the potter's son. But all kids played together. At puberty, separation by sex took place, but girls would still play with girls and boys with boys. In early adulthood, social and clan distinctions became powerful. But in joy or bereavement the hierarchies would break down, and the village community would come together. Everyone lived in mud homes (Abida's was much bigger), and you didn't travel much. Religion was central, and rituals and celebration very important—Moharram, Eids, deaths of saints and luminaries. The Hindu festivals were not formally observed but certainly remembered. Today, there is much more mobility, TV and VCRs. But religion remains crucial. Purdah was observed then, and is now, among land-owning families. The village is sex-segregated for all rituals. There is a sense of loss now over the village of yore. But there is also grudging respect for those who go out and make it in the big world. There is a very visible desire on the part of the young to urbanize and travel. Very few children see any future in the village.

Another Shia Muslim I knew, a politician and editor of an influential newspaper, took a much more conservative position. He said that "eighty-plus percent of the population still adheres to strict Islamic family value systems. The Westernized elites are out of touch and will eventually be swept away." He regards Iran as a great model of what should happen. "The consumption society is bad," he said. "The purpose of life is not fun, and in this sense the Americans are completely disoriented. Life is work, serious business. The way to serve God is to develop your faculties. The prayer of a person who has worked hard and developed his understanding is worth one hundred times that of an ignorant or lazy person. The West has lost its way in pursuing fun—drugs, sex, entertainment. Woman is the critical point. Woman must be in the home. She can be educated to some degree. But her role in family life and in the home is central."

Encompassing as it does a spectrum of beliefs and value systems ranging from the elites who move with ease in cosmopolitan circles in New York and London to anti-Western, anti-modern fundamentalists, Pakistan under the best of circumstances would be difficult to govern. When one adds to that the impact of the three million Pathan refugees from the Soviet war (some portion of whom have returned to Afghanistan), the flooding of the country with arms and ammunition from the war, and the growing violence and corruption caused by the narcotics trade, it is rather a miracle that any government can function at all. A Pakistani scholar once remarked to me: "Pakistan is simply appearing in its true colors. It is a feudal, violent society...This is a society in which when you want something of a *pir* (a holy man) or a *zamindar* (a big landlord) you make him a gift. It is probably not accurate to call this 'corruption' as it exists in the bureaucratic and modern world of Pakistan. It is simply the way the society works. Western institutions are bound to be used for traditional purposes. Similarly, in Pakistan powerful people traditionally have surrounded themselves with armed men, and that is what is happening today." A Baluch prince I knew said once: "What really counts is how many armed men you can assemble. I can produce ten thousand within twenty-four hours."

Of course, the most powerful single group of armed men in Pakistan is the army, and, as so often was the case in Pakistan, the army was in charge when I took over the management of the USAID mission in Islamabad in 1985. Gen. Zia ul Huq had seized power from Zulfikar Ali Bhutto in 1977. The scion of a powerful Sindhi landowning family and a Berkeley and Oxford-educated protégé of Ayub Khan, Bhutto founded the Peoples Party of Pakistan which, with a strong base in the industrial proletariat and the urban population, became West Pakistan's most popular political party in the late 1960s. His inability to come to an agreement as to how to form a national government with Sheik Mujibur Rahman of East Pakistan, whose party had assumed a comparable role in East Pakistan, was a direct factor in the collapse of a united Pakistan. Bhutto assumed power after the fall of Yahya Khan's regime and the loss of East Pakistan (now Bangladesh) during the 1971 rebellion and the war with India. (During those events, Bhutto had served as Yahya Khan's foreign minister, skillfully arguing Pakistan's case against the Indian intervention in East Bengal at the United Nations in New York. I watched a live television broadcast of this debate from my Ford Foundation office in New York: Bhutto spoke passionately and persuasively, without notes, for more than an hour, at one point driving home the argument that it would be a most dangerous policy for the new, developing nations to tolerate or approve outside interventions to assist ethnic or linguistic minorities that might claim the right of self-determination). As prime minister, Bhutto proceeded to lead the newly truncated Pakistan away from its Western alliances and to attempt to turn Pakistan into the leader of the Islamic nations. He made it clear, following India's explosion of a nuclear device in 1974, that this new policy would include the development of a nuclear weapon. In the midst of an election crisis in 1977, Zia ul Huq, whom Bhutto had elevated to the post of chief of army staff, seized power and put Bhutto under house arrest. In 1979, a court heavily influenced by Zia convicted Bhutto on charges of murdering the father of a dissident Peoples Party's politician. Zia hanged him.

This was not the end of the Bhutto story. South Asian dynastic tales go on for generations (as witness the Gandhis in India and the dynastic political successions in both Sri Lanka and Bangladesh and more recently even in Indonesia). Benazir Bhutto, his striking, passionate daughter, dedicated to reclaiming her father's reputation, returned to Pakistan in 1986 and launched a campaign in opposition to Zia's rule. When Zia was killed in a November 1988 military airplane crash (along with my good friends and colleagues, Arnold Raphel, the American ambassador, and Brig. Gen. Herbert Wassom, the U.S. Army military attaché), Benazir's alliance won a popular election, and she became the first female prime minister of a Muslim nation. She proved to be both incompetent as a leader and corrupt in the best tribal fashion, appointing her husband, Asif Ali Zadari, to the cabinet, where he happily set to work to enrich the family. Voted out of office in 1990, Benazir returned in 1993 until her government was again dismissed. She currently lives in exile.

General Zia had never been regarded as the most capable or promising of the Pakistan army's senior officers. When Bhutto surprisingly appointed him as chief of army staff, Zia superseded five more senior generals. He was born in the Indian Punjab in 1924, son of a teacher employed by the British army. Zia graduated from St. Stephen College, Delhi, entered the British army as a commissioned officer, and served in Burma, Malaya, and Indonesia during World War II. In the postwar Pakistani army, he was regarded as an unusually devout, polite, and modest Muslim, much dedicated to his family. His great outside passion was golf. But after wrenching power from Bhutto, Zia proved to be a formidable player in the world of power politics, his hand enormously strengthened by the Soviet invasion of Afghanistan in 1979. It seems apparent today that the United States failed to recognize Zia's long-term intentions to build a fundamentalist Islamic Afghanistan state under Pakistani tutelage as a strategic reserve to fall back on in its great, unending struggle with India. In 1979, following the Soviet invasion to the north, President Jimmy Carter, who had just finished cutting off all U.S. economic assistance as required by the Symington amendment, promptly offered Pakistan a new package of $400 million. Zia, who did not want Pakistan to be regarded as a client state of the United States, derided the offer as "peanuts." In 1981, Zia got a much more acceptable offer: Ronald Reagan's incoming administration agreed to provide Pakistan a six-year, $3.2 billion package divided equally between economic and military aid. With his position as Pakistan's leader reinforced as he furnished the United States the ideal platform for fighting a proxy war against the Soviet Union across the border in Afghanistan, domestically Zia began slowly but consistently to dismantle Western-style institutions in Pakistan and to install Islamic law.

The USAID mission I headed was one of the three major pillars of the U.S. assistance package, overt and covert, in Pakistan. The large, overt AID program (about $350 million in grants per year) aimed to invigorate Pakistan directly by infrastructure development and policy reforms. The U.S. military aid program, which strengthened Zia's position with the Pakistani military establishment, provided F-16 aircraft, M-48 tanks, naval missiles, helicopters, and artillery. The third pillar, a very large, covert CIA program, managed with great effectiveness by two senior CIA officers, William Piekney succeeded in 1986 by Milton Bearden, supported the mujahideen fighters in Afghanistan who were bloodying the Soviet army. The CIA worked with and through the notorious Pakistani Directorate for Inter-Services Intelligence (ISI), which after the U.S. departure from the scene in 1990 promptly turned into the major source of support for the Taliban. The key points for cross-border operations were Peshawar in the North-West Frontier Province and Quetta in Baluchistan, which dominated—to the extent that anyone ever controls this frontier—the mountain passes in and out of Afghanistan. (The ISI collects both foreign and domestic intelligence, carries out surveillance of foreigners, the media, and politically active persons and groups in Pakistan, intercepts and monitors communications, and carries out covert offensive operations, of which the most important have been Afghanistan and Kashmir. Its size has been estimated at around ten thousand officers and staff. It is reported to have trained more than eighty thousand Afghan mujahideen between 1983 and 1997.)

Presiding over this American imperial establishment when I arrived was one of the Foreign Service's most competent diplomats, Deane Hinton, a smart, cocky, elegantly tailored, poker-playing career officer with a long record of accomplishment and good luck behind him. Hinton had studied economics at both Tufts and Harvard and was one of the few State Department officers who understood much about the subject. He had spent two tours as an AID mission director (in Guatemala and Santiago from 1967 to 1971, while serving simultaneously as economic counselor in the embassies), and thus possessed a rare and useful understanding of AID's bureaucratic culture. He worked hard at maintaining excellent contacts on the Hill and at the Pentagon. As the American ambassador to Salvador from 1981 to 1983, Hinton distinguished himself by trying to balance the ferocious, U.S.-backed civil war against Marxist insurgents with honest reporting about civil rights and humanitarian abuses by the government and right-wing forces—and some thought that his assignment was cut short because of that position. Hinton recognized his own abilities, was pleased by them, and could be merciless in his criticism of subordinates. Generally, he left me to run the AID mission as I saw fit, and we became good friends.

The development challenge in Pakistan was, to say the least, daunting. Military expenditures, always justified by the need to compete with the military behemoth across the border in India, consumed an inordinate amount of the national income, and an unknown amount of money clearly was going into the development of nuclear capabilities. What the economists call "domestic resource mobilization" traditionally was weak. Tax evasion and corruption were widespread, and a potentially significant part of national income from agriculture remained completely untaxed because of the political power of large landlords. Government corporations were large, corrupt, and inefficient. The educational, health, and nutritional status of poor Pakistani citizens in general was bad, that of females particularly so. Only one quarter of the Pakistani population knew how to read and write. Female literacy rates in the rural areas were estimated at from 4 to 6 percent, and only half the country's primary school age children even started school. The most positive development of recent years was the inflow of hard currency from the tens of thousands of Pakistani workers in the Gulf States, which entering the country outside any official government channels invigorated the small towns and rural communities most of the workers came from.

The USAID mission staff was large. When I arrived, the first question I asked my administrative officer, Stan Hunsaker, a wily old-timer, was exactly how many people worked for me. He grinned and said, "Which number do you want?" Stan was not simply being facetious: the number of people who one way or another worked for the USAID mission included not only American and Pakistani direct-hire employees but a host of contractor personnel and consultants who reported directly to AID, plus large numbers of Pakistani maintenance and security people, all of them under contract arrangements. Some thirty or so AID Foreign Service officers planned the overall program and managed the projects. American citizen project contractors—in agriculture, energy, health and population, narcotics, and university development—added another fifty or sixty. Pakistani direct-hire employees, a few of whom had survived for many years the ups and downs of the overall AID relationship and were, of course, essential in getting things done with the Pakistani bureaucracies, numbered a few dozen. When one added the large numbers of contractual service and security staff people, the total number throughout the country, including sub-offices in Lahore, Karachi, and Peshawar, topped five hundred.

The AID program negotiated with the Pakistan government when major U.S. assistance was resumed in 1982 after the Soviet invasion of Afghanistan was a conservative package, reflecting mostly what the Pakistanis wanted in terms of development of important economic institutions. The AID staff my predecessor, Donor Lion, had brought in to plan and manage the package, reflected the way AID had done business for many years. Officers were taught to think in terms of projects. Large projects, very specific in their planning outlines and expected results, were preferred. With rare exceptions, projects required consultants and contractors. This meant that much of the AID money went into American contractor and consultant salaries. Although I did not participate in the negotiation of the original pact, which began before my arrival on the Washington scene, Pakistan undoubtedly would have preferred a simple outright annual grant of $375 million. But that was a precedent available only to Israel, and Washington insisted that the major part of the program be tied to specific development projects (as historically has been the case in the even larger Egypt program), believing that this would produce more results and less corruption. The project approach, we would see, was not a guarantee of results.

One of the priority projects launched by the time of my arrival, for example, was a large-scale effort to rehabilitate irrigation and on-farm management in the enormous gravity-flow systems supporting wheat, rice, and cotton cultivation in the Punjab and Sindh. The British originally engineered and dug these canals, which utilize the waters of the five rivers of the Punjab (the Jhelum, the Chenab, the Ravi, the Sutlej, and the Beas) as they flow down from the Himalayas through thirty-five-thousand miles of major and minor canals and farmers' field channels. The original purpose of the system, when the British started building canals in the mid-nineteenth century, was to avert the famines that periodically swept British India. The central planning policy was thus "protective"; that is, to give each of a maximum number of farmers a little bit of water. The irrigated region produces the overwhelming portion of the basic cereal grain, wheat, consumed by the Pakistani population, and it formed the base of the economic and political power that has enabled the Punjabis to dominate Pakistani political life.

The systems have grossly deteriorated since independence. The provincial Irrigation Departments long ago fell into corrupt ways. It became common practice for senior officials to auction off particularly profitable field assignments as district engineers in locations where large bribes are customary. In alliance with large farmers, some department engineers openly provided far more water than necessary to what are known as "headenders," while "tailenders" at the far end of the thousands of miles of canals, channels, and field ditches received little or no water. Maintenance, once rigorously carried out both at the heavy earthmoving and construction level by the departments and at the farm field level by "peons," who prevented grazing livestock from breaking through the embankments to drink and bathe and repaired canal roads so that unobstructed passage was available for inspection, had become almost a joke. The rewards of the system were such that one of the components of the AID grant for rehabilitation and modernization, a special MA-level fellowship program in select American universities in irrigation engineering, found virtually no takers because engineers made so much money in bribe-producing assignments that they could not afford to leave for training abroad. The AID funds also provided a large amount of new dredging and earth-moving equipment on the basis of a governmental commitment to redesign parts of the system and to enforce canal and equipment maintenance standards. Shortly after my arrival, a Pakistani friend drove me out into the back-country of south Punjab to show me a graveyard of earlier equipment provided by both AID and the World Bank, much of it in not bad or irretrievable shape but simply parked out of sight, because it was deemed easier to get new equipment through foreign assistance than to maintain and repair older equipment. Although the AID program did carry out some useful canal cleaning and rehabilitation projects and the on-farm field channel program established important precedents as to how to fight evaporation and deterioration of field channels, the Punjab Irrigation Department at its most senior levels clearly was not really interested in serious reform, and after two years I decided that AID should withdraw from its partnership with the World Bank, which I thought was far too easy on the Pakistanis in insisting on change, and spend no more on irrigation. We were simply replicating work AID, the World Bank, and others had done twenty years before (and would doubtless be asked to repeat twenty years later). This unexpected display of common sense bestirred both the World Bank and the senior bureaucrats in Islamabad to exert their serious muscle on the provincial Irrigation Department's senior officials, who agreed to take immediate steps to improve inventory controls of tool and equipment storage, modernize the monitoring of performance in the delivery of water, and to carry out the training programs previously agreed to. We reluctantly agreed to continue.

Other major parts of the program faced similar problems. A combined effort to modernize the old coal fields at Lakhra and improve the efficiency of the national power system, which relied on a mix of hydro, gas, coal, and oil-fired generation, and to encourage conservation on the part of industrial users was moderately successful. We began to discuss with our Pakistani counterparts the need to reorganize and privatize at least parts of the large (one hundred thousand employees), inefficient, and corrupt Water and Power Development Authority (WAPDA). Electric power was an old subject for AID: in the earliest days of independence, AID was a very large donor and planner in the power field, particularly in the design and construction of the country's largest hydroelectric dam at Tarbela on the Indus River northwest of Islamabad.

Probably the most cost-effective use of funds took place through a number of small Pakistani non-governmental organizations, frequently headed by progressive Pakistani women, to whom the Pakistani government gratefully left the unpopular tasks of population and family planning. Health and family planning were the only parts of the AID program in which NGOs participated. The career Pakistani bureaucrats who managed finance and development in Islamabad and had negotiated the AID agreement regarded NGOs with little favor and much suspicion. Their attitude, as the most senior and powerful Pakistani civil servant once put it to me after expressing astonishment at my suggestion that AID might consider a major investment in NGO development, was, "If it's important, the government must do it." The more I looked at Pakistani development, the more I became convinced that our program lacked balance, and that NGOs should be much more involved.

This doubtless reflected my biases from years of Ford Foundation work in Asia. While I worked in the Asia program in New York, I came to know well a Pakistani who was one of the greatest of the early generation of Asian NGO leaders. Akhtar Hameed Khan was a tall, handsome Pathan aristocrat who started his career in the 1930s as a member of the elite Indian Civil Service. He resigned in 1945 in frustration because of its inability to deal seriously with the problems of poverty and underdevelopment. Akhtar Hameed Khan was a Sunni Muslim, immersed like many Pakistanis in the Sufi traditions of poetry and philosophy that for many centuries have played an integral part in the lives of many of the Muslims of the subcontinent (and are antithetical to the harsh vision of the Deobandis and Wahabis). He also read Tolstoy, like Gandhi wore *khadi* (homespun cloth), meditated daily, and recited Buddhist sutras. After leaving the elite civil service, he worked as a locksmith and a teacher. Following the partition of India, in 1951 Khan became principal of a small college in a rural town, Comilla, located in the Gangetic flood plain of what was then East Pakistan. A few years later, the government asked him to serve as the first administrator of what was called the Village-Aid program, an early effort in rural development funded by AID, and he was subsequently appointed to direct a new Academy for Rural Development at Comilla, where he and his colleagues conceived and tried out many of the concepts that have become standard practice among development agencies around the world. These included female education, village-level-run health and family planning programs, and cooperative lending programs for villagers and slum dwellers. When I visited Khan in the modest Comilla academy headquarters, we would arise early to go out into the rice paddies and villages to look at work supported with foundation funds and talk with villagers. I commented one morning that the calm paddies, with their bright green shoots of new rice and the early sun shimmering on the water in the fields, looked like a vision of paradise. Khan looked down his long Pathan nose at me and said, "It's not. It's hell on earth." If I asked him if he slept well, he would say, "I recited sutras last night and got up early this morning to meditate. I feel great. How are you?" I said, "As a good Westerner, I slept badly and had bad dreams but I feel great too." Having fought our cultural skirmish, we would go off happily for a day of work in the steamy heat of either earthly peace or hell, depending on how one defines it.

Akhtar Hameed Khan left East Pakistan after it became Bangladesh (the Comilla Academy became the Bangladesh Institute of Rural Development) and returned to Pakistan. In 1980, at the invitation of a local bank, he began to organize the Orangi Pilot Project in one of Karachi's biggest slums (in the enormous sprawl of Karachi, filled to bursting with refugees from India, Bangladesh, and Afghanistan, Orangi occupies an area about the size of the city of Amsterdam). I went down early in my assignment as USAID mission director to pay a call on him. As in East Pakistan, he worked very long hours well into the night, surrounded by a small, enthusiastic young staff, many of them female. (Akhtar Hameed believed women generally to be more honest than men; all credit disbursements and repayments were handled by women.) The lack of sanitation and drinking water was the first problem the project tackled. An engineer worked with the small staff and residents to design technologies for toilets and latrine and sewer systems that Orangi inhabitants could build and install themselves—at a cost of about one-tenth that of commercial devices. Each neighborhood within the slum elected a manager to oversee the work of building sewerage lines, secondary drains, and latrines. Akhtar Hameed and his senior deputy took on the task of arguing with the municipal public works bureaucracy about permits and licenses. Using their own funds, residents eventually constructed over five thousand sewerage lines, some eighty thousand latrines, seven hundred fifty schools, and six hundred-plus health clinics. Infant mortality fell dramatically. Property prices rose. A project-run lending program relying on local references and recommendations achieved a repayment rate of 95 percent. Akhtar Hameed was glad to see me, but he needed nothing from AID (although he had excellent memories of earlier support from AID and the Ford Foundation in East Pakistan).

Then I flew up to Gilgit and Hunza in the high northern valleys of the Himalayas to look at the work of another group of advanced thinkers and doers. In 1982, the Aga Khan Foundation's Rural Support Program began to promote sustainable living in the villages and settlements clinging to the tiny, cultivable shelves that almost literally hang from the sides of the precipitous gorge of the Indus River as the great river grinds and growls down beneath snow-clad peaks from the Chinese border to the plains and the Arabian Sea. The population of these communities is almost entirely Ismaili Muslim (sometimes called Aga Khanis). The Ismailis are Shia Muslims, residing in more than twenty-five countries including Pakistan, India, Iran, Afghanistan, Syria, Kenya, Uganda, Tanzania, Canada, the United States, the United Kingdom and other parts of Europe, and in parts of China and Tajikistan. They are regarded by most other Shias and virtually all Sunnis as heretical because they trace their line of descent from Ismail, the oldest son of the sixth Imam (the spiritual leader) descended from Ali, the prophet's son-in-law, who was rejected by many other Muslims in a personal and religious dispute. The current Imam, his Highness Prince Karim Aga Khan, is the forty-ninth Imam of the Ismailis. His grandfather, Sir Sultan Mahomed Shah Aga Khan, was a famous playboy and bon vivant who lived in India and Europe and loved race horses and beautiful women (his son, Ali, an even greater admirer of women, became famous for marrying Rita Hayworth). Karim Aga Khan lives in Geneva and, with the help of a staff that includes several executives who learned their trade in the Ford Foundation, manages a multinational set of business and nonprofit enterprises that include education, culture, rural development, health, and housing. The Aga Khan's philanthropic activities are unique and admirable and there is, regrettably, nothing else like it in the Islamic world at large.

In these distant northern valleys, a separate Aga Khan education program had already successfully organized schools for girls. The new rural development was under the direction of a former elite civil servant, Shoaib Sultan Khan, a protégé of Akhtar Hameed Khan in his Comilla days, who, like Akhtar Hameed Khan, had left the bureaucracy to test his own ideas about development in a more congenial environment. The essence of the Aga Khan approach was to organize village communities around a physical infrastructure project that the majority of the villagers agreed to be the most important for improving their welfare. That could mean improving an irrigation system, for example, or building a farm-to-market road, or a school. Once the project was approved for funding, the program made a small grant for the requisite amount to the community and required villagers to work on its implementation, paying them at the going rate. When the project was successfully completed, the loan was forgiven, and the proceeds became capital for further projects. The work I saw in a village near Hunza, a tiny town built on a shelf of cultivable land below a spectacular peak, involved repairing and extending a small, community-built and managed irrigation system whose channels were carved out of solid rock, hundreds of feet above the valley along the canyon walls to the water source high on the side of the great peaks. These high-altitude irrigation systems (the Hunza valley is seven thousand feet high) water the apricot orchards for which the Hunza/Gilgit valley is famous (the apricots are thought to produce long life and vigor), and provide water for both villagers and their herds of goats, whose wool is highly prized. Hunza town is crowned by a forbidding castle and fortress, from whose roof the local *mir* (king) used to throw captives into the gorge below, which the descendant of the former *mir*'s prime minister described for us with considerable animation. The villagers and tourist agents will tell you that this is the model of the Shangri La that James Hilton wrote about and Hollywood portrayed in movies. Indeed, in the springtime when the apricot and cherry trees are in blossom, few places in the world can equal the spectacular beauty of these high Indus valleys. The village council I visited had just completed an irrigation improvement project and was about to launch a new, risky endeavor in establishing their own marketing system for their agricultural produce in the large towns and cities of the plains below. By 2003, the Aga Khan Rural Support Program reported that in these mountain communities some two thousand village organizations and fourteen hundred women's organizations were actively at work, whose members came from 85 percent of the total households in the region. Another source reported female school attendance at near 100 percent. The Hunza project needed no help from AID, but the director, Shoaib Sultan Khan, was eager to try the same techniques working with the culturally different, unruly Pathan tribesmen of the North-West Frontier where he had spent much of his early career. Unlike the mountain peoples, who had long ago learned to cooperate to survive, the Pathans generally could agree on nothing. After a long discussion with the government, which was skeptical, AID made a small grant for a pilot project in the Frontier, which to almost everyone's surprise, has prospered to this day.

An important part of the AID toolbox of funding instruments was "policy reform" grant making, in which the local government would receive a cash grant in return for carrying out policy reform activities that the two sides agreed would produce positive, long-term benefits. Usually, these were directed at economic or financial policies covering such topics as removal of subsidies in government-sponsored programs or tax policy reform. After a good deal of staff investigation of the Pakistani NGO scene, it became apparent that, in addition to the more visible groups like the Orangi project in Karachi and the Aga Khan work in the northern regions, far more small activities were under way than anyone suspected, most of them not only under-funded but badly needing guidance and training in how to raise funds and organize communities. There was nothing like a national clearinghouse where like-minded activists could get information and compare approaches. Working with Pakistani NGO leaders, we set out to see if something like a clearinghouse might be established. In 1987, after getting Washington's approval of this somewhat unusual definition of economic policy reform, we negotiated a cash grant of $30 million to the government of Pakistan for balance of payments support in return for its agreement to establish a Trust for Voluntary Organizations (TVO) to provide financial support. The government set up a fund in Pakistani rupees for an equivalent amount, the invested proceeds of which would provide basic funding, and authorized further tax-free contributions to the trust for its work from private sector and governmental sources, including foreign countries. A thirteen-member governing board that included ten private citizens and three government officials was named to manage the trust, whose income was generally not to be used for project grants (although that changed later on) but rather for grants for technical assistance to professionalize the indigenous NGO community and to improve its capacity to provide services on a self-sustaining basis. It was expected to emphasize community-based development programs like women's health and education centers, construction of rural roads, provision of potable drinking water, and basic sanitation services. Cynics, Pakistani and American, expected the whole effort to fall apart because of government domination at the board level. In fact, this did not happen, and several years after I left Pakistan I received a detailed report from a European development expert I knew who had just visited Pakistan and found the trust alive and well and performing good works. At about the same time, a Pakistani woman, who knew all about the trust, told me at a conference at Columbia University in New York, where I was teaching a seminar on Asian development as an adjunct professor, that the NGO movement had grown rapidly, and that NGO voices were now listened to in Islamabad policy circles. The trust publishes a site on the Internet, listing twelve offices throughout Pakistan to serve NGOs in a wide variety of programs including education, micro-credit systems, environment, health, women's activities, and food production, with a common theme of poverty alleviation.

We clearly succeeded in putting AID on the map as a source of funding for unusual ideas. Shortly before my tour ended, a prominent Pakistani lawyer from Karachi, recommended by a friend, called on me at my Islamabad office. The lawyer was a *pro bono* adviser to Abdul Sattar Edhi. In 1948, after migrating from India as a bazaar merchant of extremely modest means, Edhi became deeply concerned with the plight of the Karachi poor. He set out to organize a service using volunteer taxi drivers to transport injured or seriously ill poor people to hospitals and to deliver the bodies of people who died in the slums, whose families lacked means to carry out the ceremonial washing of the dead required by Islam, to suitable facilities so that their corpses could be washed and properly interred. Out of these beginnings grew a host of health-related activities including a private, citywide ambulance service for poor people. Edhi wanted to expand the ambulance facility to cover the entire region of the Sindh and Baluchistan provinces, and he and his advisers believed the only way this could be done was by helicopter. The overall program was generously supported by Karachi business and professional men. But a helicopter was beyond their means. After our staff gave a favorable verdict on the operations and management of the Edhi program, we agreed to provide $1 million of AID funds to buy a surplus U.S. military helicopter. The Pakistani Air Force offered free maintenance, and a private American oil company guaranteed free gas and oil. The Edhi Foundation is now the largest social welfare organization in Pakistan (it operates a fleet of one helicopter and three small ambulance aircraft), providing free medical services, homes for runaway or abandoned girls and women, infant clinics, adoption programs, drug rehabilitation, and prisoners' aid. Its advice and services are available outside Pakistan as well through offices in five other countries. The Edhi International Foundation, for example, recently purchased a four-acre plot in the suburbs of New York as a graveyard for Muslims and has begun a service of bathing and burying Muslim bodies.

I overemphasize the amount of time and money AID spent on assisting nonprofit groups, which in the larger picture wasn't much. But the involvement thoroughly convinced me what a powerful force Islam can be in inspiring private, benevolent, and socially useful activities. It can also be the case, of course, in Muslim societies—Palestine is an example—that private benevolent groups like Hezbollah not only organize and support activities in education, health, and social welfare but become deeply involved in politics and violence as well: Islamic fundamentalism, like the extremes of Christianity and Judaism, combines both benevolence and violence in its nature. The fundamentalist *madrassas* built by the

Saudis and the Deobandis in Pakistan taught both charity and violence and a very narrow view of Islam.

Far more of my working time went into managing the staff, meetings with senior officials in Islamabad and the provinces about program problems, and planning for the future. At the end of 1985, we began preliminary discussions with the Pakistan government about a second, $2.28 billion, five-year economic assistance agreement to begin in 1988 (with a comparably sized military assistance agreement to go into effect at the same time), and in 1986 that new agreement was signed.

I refused to become desk-bound in Islamabad, though, and made it a point to travel frequently to stay on top of project work throughout the country, including the difficult provinces of the North-West Frontier (NWFP) and Baluchistan. Usually in both the NWFP and Baluchistan, we traveled with an armed guard, frontier scouts selected from the local tribes riding along in pickup trucks in the clouds of dust behind our jeep or off-road vehicle and carrying a motley collection of arms. When I stopped to have a pee at the edge of a cliff or near a rare tree, they spread out very professionally and guarded me carefully. In the NWFP, AID was building market access roads and primary schools in some of the tribal districts deemed to be safe. Dating back to British days, there were traditionally two classes of tribal areas: one was totally off limits for outsiders—including Pakistanis—except for an occasional visit by a government political agent arranged with tribal leaders; in a second category, a government political agent was resident, and certain activities acceptable to the tribal leaders could be carried out. AID also launched a university institution-building project with a contract group of professors from the University of Illinois resident at Peshawar University (in the most recent chapter in the on-and-off again marriage of convenience between Pakistan and the United States, the University of Illinois is now back at work in Peshawar).

In those earlier days of the alliance of the Americans and Pakistanis against the godless Russians, Peshawar was relatively safe for Americans, even hospitable, and always marvelously intriguing in its bazaar life, carpet shops, and tea houses. Violence was never far from the surface. Every man, and many boys, carried a gun. Every woman wore a veil. AID leased and maintained a small, quiet, walled compound with a garden and a dilapidated grass tennis court where one could play a hilarious, Alice in Wonderland kind of tennis, with balls bouncing backwards and players tumbling into hidden ditches, and then have a delicious supper cooked by an Uzbek from northern Afghanistan. Presiding over the small office and guesthouse was Bob Traister, our man in Peshawar who, in addition to supervising the NWFP projects and the big narcotics project, managed our affairs in the vast, scarcely populated, wastelands of Baluchistan to the south and east. Traister began his overseas career as a Peace Corps volunteer in Thailand, then joined AID as a district development officer in bloody Vietnam, and came to Pakistan from assignments in Africa. Once a good-looking blond youth (judging by old photographs), Traister was now a tough, pudgy, balding, cigar-smoking master of the art of how to get things done in the boondocks. He was a bachelor, devoted to his aging mother, who lived in Florida until eventually, long after I departed the scene, she moved to Peshawar, of all places, to live with him. Traister was unflappable in his dealings with provincial bureaucrats and tribal chieftains alike, and I never saw a logistics problem he could not resolve. If I were to say, "Tomorrow we've got to go to the South Pole," Traister would probably ask, "Are you sure?" Then he would say, "OK, I'd better start getting things ready."

Development work was tough sledding in both the NWFP and Baluchistan. From time immemorial, the tribal leaders took the position that if an outside agency wanted to do anything in the tribal areas, whether this was building a school or a road, it should be prepared to pay for this privilege. That was not considered corruption. It was simply the way it always had been. This was the way the British had done it, and doubtless Alexander the Great carried a treasury with him for just such purposes. It was not, of course, AID policy, and so we had an immediate conflict. Most tribal leaders had a very different view of the benefits of public education, particularly for women (although the leaders at the very top generally saw to it that their sons got a good, Western-style education). Roads in limited amounts and to certain points were all right, particularly if they served the immediate interest of tribal seniors. But even road construction went slowly: local engineering and construction skills were limited; bureaucratic, tribal and security problems delayed progress; and projects stretched out far beyond their estimated dates of completion. Once roads and schools were finally completed, though, the demand and usage were immediately evident. Traister and I attended the inauguration of a twenty-mile stretch of gravel road up to a tribal village southwest of Peshawar that sounded like the beginning of World War III with men and boys of all sizes and ages firing rifles, Kalashnikovs, and even an old fifty-caliber machine gun in celebration while sheep roasted on the spits in the square. Within a matter of weeks, Toyota pickup trucks, the modern camel of the deserts and mountains of Pakistan and Afghanistan, were plying the road with people and goods in both directions. Schools sometimes had to be rebuilt two or three times during construction because of shoddy materials and workmanship.

When they finally opened, the local children did go to school, although in the few cases where girls were allowed they attended in separate, segregated buildings. I asked a young boy once what he liked in his education. He said, "I like learning to read so that I can study the Koran." When I asked him what he wanted to be, he said, "I want to be a truck driver." The trucks in his life were the heavy, gaily painted vehicles that carry freight to and from the Frontier to the entrepot of Karachi. They were a major channel for moving narcotics and guns in addition to more conventional produce. The truck trade had largely been captured by the three million Afghan Pathan refugees who flooded into the Frontier and Baluchistan to escape the death and destruction across the border. The refugee camps were miserable places at best, in spite of all of the efforts of Pakistan and many international agencies: there was simply no way this flood of millions of men, women, and children could be housed, fed, and kept healthy adequately. The camps were a major source of recruiting and organization for cross-border fighting, and after the Soviet defeat they turned into a prime recruitment and indoctrination center for the Taliban.

On my swings around the Frontier, we once took a jeep north up into the distant valley of Chitral to look at a proposed major construction project to rebuild the highway tunnel through the Lowari pass that provides the major connection between the valley and the rest of Pakistan. The tunnel had collapsed years before, thereby cutting Chitrali villages off from travel outside the valley during the winter snows. At a government guesthouse where we stopped to spend the night, we heard that the world's highest known polo match was about to take place still farther north at the eleven-thousand-foot high Shandur pass that connects the valleys of Chitral and Gilgit. This event first took place in the 1920s during British days, but it had not been played for many years, and President Zia was reported to be flying up by helicopter to attend. A few quick telephone calls to Islamabad and Peshawar suggested that if we showed up for the match we would be welcome. We drove up one of the most frightening one-way roads I had ever seen, literally hanging on the stone faces of the mountains, and reached the Shandur pass in low, near freezing clouds. Since we had not planned to go so high, we had not taken heavy jackets and were on the point of freezing. A Pakistani army officer took pity on us and produced four army jackets for our party. The match was a wild affair, played on a small, narrow rectangular field surrounded by a low stone wall. The ponies were small, tough animals bred from Punjabi and Afghan stock, ridden by the best riders and polo players in the two valleys. Zia flew in an hour before the match began. The daring and physical courage, not to say recklessness of the riders, were notable, but I was most impressed by the small, heated guesthouse with a Western-style toilet that the Pakistani army had built virtually overnight for Zia's visit. The Chitral team won. We never did rebuild the Lowari Pass—no one could produce a cost benefit analysis that would justify it. It has not been rebuilt to this day.

Islamabad, the new capital Ayub Khan caused to be built in the foothills of the Himalayas, was designed by Greek architect Constantinos Doxiades, who fancied himself a philosopher as well. In his heyday, Doxiades organized cultural cruises for clients and big thinkers on his private yacht in the Mediterranean. George Gant, who brought me into the Asia program at the Ford Foundation, had been invited on one of these cruises and was an admirer of Doxiades. Doxiades called his architectural philosophy "ekistics." Its central idea, stemming from classical Greece, was that all citizens in the city should be able to walk to a marketplace and a park. Islamabad was thus studded with small, green parks, which tended to become unkempt, and small markets and shopping centers, which were in fact very convenient. Its public buildings tended toward the grandiose, built on higher ground and dominating the residential quarters, which were characterized by large houses with gardens and walls built by generals and senior civil servants who received preferential treatment in buying lots when the new capital was erected. A few of the retired generals and civil servants lived in their houses, but in many cases they were rented out to diplomats.

The great flaw of architect-designed capital cities is that entertainment and commerce generally get short shrift in the designs, as witness Washington, New Delhi, Brasilia, and Chandigarh in the Punjab, Le Courbusier's white elephant. Islamabad's essential dullness as a city whose residents were predominantly bureaucrats, politicians, and diplomats was unmistakable. Gossip about who was conspiring to do what to whom constituted the daily fare of most bureaucratic and diplomatic life. Islam dominated the calendar of the day and the year. Loudspeakers called the faithful to prayer five times a day, and on the great religious festival of Eid ul Fitr, after the month-long fasting period of Ramadan, sheep, goats, and a few strings of camels (far more expensive than sheep or goats) were led into the city to be slaughtered for the great feast celebrating the revelation of the Koran to the Prophet Muhammad. Most diplomats entertained a lot, and were entertained by senior Pakistani government officials and other diplomats, and on cool, clear evenings nothing could be more pleasant than a roast lamb dinner on an Islamabad roof garden, while the coyotes howled in the foothills above. The Pakistani elites are sophisticated, hospitality at all levels of society is the national and cultural tradition, and the wives of the elites play an essential role in all family affairs—including the entertainment of foreigners. Our good friends included Abida Hussain, the Punjabi politician, landowner, and diplomat, and her husband, Faqr Imam, a progressive man who became minister of education in the Zia government (an essentially thankless job since no serious funds ever became available for education), and Jafar Leghari, a Baluch noble who lived part time in a family mansion in Lahore and part time in the family compound in a southern Punjabi village, where he arose every morning and in the reception hall of the family palace, usually dressed in his pajamas, presided over the tribal court, passing down decisions on disputes among members of the Leghari tribe (a Punjabi proverb holds that all strife originates in three subjects: *zar* [gold], *zamin* [land], and *zunt* [women]). Leghari's social circle included Mick Jagger, international cricket stars, and a number of minor Western movie actresses and models (he preferred blondes). He was, at the same time, as a tribal leader and big farmer, a very serious man engaged in the rehabilitation of a large, traditional hillside water conservation and irrigation system that served farmers in his tribe.

Lahore is a once magnificent old imperial Mogul city, famous in united India for its glittering Hira Mandi, the quarter of the courtesans—dancers, singers, and prostitutes. In a fine autobiography, *Punjabi Century*, the Indian writer Prakash Tandon, who went to school in Lahore in undivided India before partition, recalls that "after the sun went down it (the quarter) came into a dazzling and brilliant life." In cold weather the best houses served "the amber-colored Rajput-Mogul liqueur," made from saffron, pigeon and partridge blood, and a variety of spices. "A few drops were enough to produce a wonderful feeling of warmth which spread through the body and made one feel hot on the coldest night." Without Lahore's dancing girls, Tandon believes, "North Indian dancing might have perished as an art." Even today, stripped of its Hindu population and with a much-reduced Hira Mandi, the Lahore bazaars are worth a prowl, the Mogul forts and palaces are silently magnificent, and Kim's cannon, Zam Zammah, where Rudyard Kipling's most popular book begins, still stands in the plaza in front of the Lahore museum. South of Lahore, the desert takes over the landscape. Suzanne and I took a weeklong camel safari in the desert near the Indo-Pakistan border. Fascinated by the life of the tribal women who live in the sun-bedazzled villages of the region, she went back on her own a number of times and eventually wrote a best-selling young-adult novel, *Shabanu, Daughter of the Wind*, about the life of a desert girl whose family was persecuted by a cruel landowner.

Sufi traditions of mysticism remain strong in Pakistan, in spite of the inroads of the Saudi-sponsored Wahabism and the more extreme form of the Deobandi school of Islam, whose followers reject the worship of saints, music, and poetry. Sufism, as the Islamic scholar Kabir Edmund Helminski has observed, "is less a doctrine or a belief system than an experience and way of life." It has been part of Islam since its earliest days, arising in the deserts of North Africa and Arabia as the personal search for spiritual reunion with one's maker. Sufis practice poverty and meditation and turn to poetry, music, and dance in their search. Love for one's self and fellow men and tolerance are essential. There is a famous verse from the thirteenth-century Sufi poet Rumi: "Come, come, whoever you are. Worshiper, Wanderer, Lover of Leaving; ours is not a caravan of despair. Though you have broken your vows a thousand times…Come, come again, Come." I occasionally came across young Westerners who experimented with what they called "going Sufi," which usually meant that they lived for a while in a religious community in the boondocks, in many cases enjoying the easily available hashish and the singing and dancing that formed an integral part of the life of these communities. A Pakistani woman friend, widow of a prominent lawyer and politician, invited us to visit a traditional Sufi village in the Sindh and to meet the *pir*, the presiding holy man, who in his earlier life had been a successful Western-trained, Karachi physician. On the death of his uncle who had presided over the establishment, the doctor moved to the village and became the head of the community, taking an oath never to leave it. The village shrine and the reputation of the *pir* attract devotees from all over Pakistan, who are fed and housed in a large, medieval-style caravanserai. We talked with the *pir* briefly—our hostess had family problems to take up with him—and stayed long into the night watching throngs of male devotees, a few dressed as women, whirling to the beat of an enormous, military kettle drum in the great courtyard of the caravanserai. One night, at a rare recital in Islamabad, we heard the great Sufi singer Nusrat Fateh Ali Khan and his Qawwali group, whose ecstatic singing lit up the soundtrack of the movie *Dead Man Walking*. They sang wildly beautiful music (the medieval Sufi poet and musician Amir Khusrau said that music was the fire that burnt heart and soul), but it failed to rouse the staid Islamabad audience of civil servants and diplomats; most of them would have been afraid to lose their cool in public. Khan and his group, of course, routinely sang all night long at festivals and religious observances and generated rock-star style emotional reactions with dancing in the aisles, but in Islamabad they closed up shop early on a chilly night. Many of the elites privately practice Sufism in one form or another, and I knew numbers of Pakistanis who regularly consulted their "Sufi," a wise person frequently not connected with any formal religious organization, about problems in their personal lives.

From time to time, in the occasional absence on official duty or leave of the deputy chief of mission, Ambassador Hinton asked me to serve as the acting deputy chief. On one such occasion, September 5, 1986, a group of four Pakistani terrorists, disguised as security guards, hijacked Pan American flight 73 in Karachi with three hundred seventy-nine passengers aboard, including eighty-nine Americans, as it was about to take off for Frankfurt and New York. The terrorists seized the airplane at 6:00 AM. We got word of the hijacking shortly thereafter in a call from the Karachi consul general relayed to me by the Foreign Service duty officer, and while the ambassador got on a classified line with Washington from his residence, I set up and organized the operations of the command post at the embassy, first establishing a direct line of open, commercial communications with the State Department to back up the various classified channels of communication as necessary. My most useful action doubtless was instructing the embassy snack bar staff to set up emergency food and drink services at the command post. After sixteen hours, during which period the hijackers executed two American citizens, the Pakistani security services turned off the lights and ventilation to the aircraft, preparing to take it by storm. When the lights flickered off, the terrorists fired automatic rifles and threw hand grenades into the helpless passengers, slaughtering twenty-one more people including a number of crew members. The Pakistani security troops then stormed the plane, arresting all four of the hijackers. The leader of the hijackers, a Jordanian citizen named Zayd Hassann Abd Latif Safarini, was extradited to the United States for trial by the Department of Justice when he was released from a Pakistani prison in late 2001, and on December 16, 2003, was sentenced to serve three consecutive life terms plus twenty-five years. Safarini and his colleagues were members of Abu Nidal, protesting the plight of the Palestinians.

On another occasion, the ambassador asked me to accompany him to take notes on the business at hand at a private dinner and meeting with President Zia at his working office and residence, a former brewery. The business turned out to be the status of Pakistan's nuclear program. As I listened and took notes, it was obvious this was an old topic for the president and the ambassador. Ambassador Hinton pressed Zia politely and firmly on the limits of activities that the U.S. government could accept before cutting off military and economic aid. Zia would not admit that Pakistan was developing a bomb. He said he was very aware of American concerns, but that Pakistan must continue its research to protect itself against India. At the small dinner, attended by a few senior civil servants, Zia, who was an attentive host, turned to talk with me about the assistance program. He thought it was generally useful but pressed me to consider AID funding for a modern hospital in Islamabad, a project dear to his heart. I said as gracefully as possible that we thought modernizing the feeble public health clinic system was a far more productive investment of AID funds, and that in general the Pakistani government's under-funding and low priority for public health and primary education were, as they had been for many years, the most significant of Pakistan's development problems. I met Zia personally once more before we departed Pakistan, when he decorated me in a ceremony at the presidential palace with the Sitar Quaid e Azam (the Sword of the Leader) for services to Pakistani development (though we never funded the hospital project).

During my last year in Pakistan, Hinton was succeeded by another Foreign Service star, Arnold Raphel, who had not only risen to the top of the ranks of American diplomats in a relatively short time but actually spoke fluent Urdu, learned in an earlier assignment to the subcontinent, and had known Zia for many years. The two men were very different. Hinton seldom had doubts and could be rough on his staff. Raphel often agonized and was gentle. They shared an impressive ability to define and reach objectives. Raphel's new wife, Nancy Ely, who had been a senior lawyer in the State Department, took on an assignment in the AID legal office, where she played an important part in pushing through the grant to establish the trust fund (TVO) for the development of Pakistani NGOs. Much of Raphel's career had been spent in politico-military assignments in Washington and abroad, and he operated in the culture of the Pentagon almost as well as he did in that of the State Department—a great advantage in managing the three-ring circus of American political, economic, and military activities in Pakistan and Afghanistan. Raphel brought with him a well-deserved reputation for working with younger officers to develop their skills in reporting and negotiation, and for years after his unfortunate death with Zia in the 1988 crash of a Pakistani military aircraft I met younger Foreign Service officers who mourned his death as though Raphel had been a member of their family. To honor his memory, the State Department created the highly prized Arnold Raphel award presented annually to a Foreign Service officer chosen each year for leadership, motivation, and mentoring.

I greatly enjoyed working with both Arnie Raphel and Nancy Ely. If possible, Raphel gave me even more freedom in running the assistance program than had Dean Hinton, and the Raphels and Suzanne and I became good friends. But in 1988, I would celebrate, if that is the word, my sixty-sixth birthday, and I thought it was time to get on with my life. I wanted to return to the States to begin to enjoy our old farmhouse on the Chesapeake and to write a book about how Asia could modernize and still remain Asian. Suzanne had her own writing agenda to pursue; it was to become very successful. The AID mission and program were in good shape—my replacement was to be none other than the supremely competent James Norris, who had first welcomed me to the Asia Bureau in Washington six years earlier. The signing of the new, multiyear assistance package for Pakistan and subsequent negotiations had produced a program that was starting to move in what I thought were the right directions. For the first time, for example, it committed AID to work in educational reform in a project aiming to establish centers of excellence that would complement a large, new World Bank project in primary education. In 1985, Zia had made a trip to South Korea at the urging of Mahbub ul Huq, the finance minister, to look at the positive economic results of investments in first-rate public education systems. The notion was to show that you can have both guns and butter. Zia was properly impressed, and the government was slowly increasing education allocations in its budget planning.

In 1988, my last year in Islamabad, in an internal AID five-year strategy planning document that was subsequently leaked and widely quoted in the Pakistani press, I wrote a frank appraisal of Pakistan's situation, with particular emphasis on weaknesses in education and health. It began as follows:

> Pakistan's founder, Jinnah, dedicated his life to establishing a state that would unite Islam and his Westminsterian vision of democracy: yet Pakistan has suffered greatly from both religious discord and martial law. The official Islamic ideology, as expressed at high levels of government and by a host of *mullahs*, is conservative and ascetic. At the same time, much of the Pakistani society today is as consumption-oriented as an American shopping mall…The economy, fueled by (Arabian) Gulf remittances, smuggling, heroin, and the Afghanistan war, has boomed for eight years. The government meanwhile cannot mobilize money enough to remedy crippling inadequacies in education, health, family planning services, and infrastructure. The potential is equally clear. Underlying the contradictions is a fierce drive for self-betterment by most elements of the society. The Pakistani workers in the Gulf, who over the past thirteen years have sent tens of billions of dollars home to their mostly poor and rural household, are tough, hardworking, and self-sacrificing. The trading and industrial classes display tenacity and imagination in money making. The Pakistani civilian and military bureaucracies at their best are impressive. Throughout the society there exists a widespread, if frequently unsophisticated, yearning for democracy and justice and a far deeper devotion to the idea of Pakistan than the cacophony of national ethnic politics might suggest. The national endowment in land, water, and minerals is fragile but of enormous value if properly managed.

In a press conference before my departure, asked if I thought serious reforms could actually take place, I replied that this would depend on the Pakistanis. The national leadership appeared to be committed. A journalist then asked if the United States would turn its back on Pakistan, as it had on previous occasions, when the political situation changed, and the Soviets were finally defeated in Afghanistan. I said I did not believe that would happen, that our alliance was important, and that Pakistan's development would be in the long-term interests of the United States long after the fighting ended in Afghanistan.

Plans, hopes, and dreams are one thing. Life is another. Two months after my departure in the late spring of 1988, Arnie Raphel was killed with Zia in a military transport airplane crash. In 1989, the Soviets withdrew their troops from Afghanistan. In 1990, the U.S. government cut off assistance to Pakistan because of Pakistan's continuing development of a nuclear weapons capability. With the Soviets out of Afghanistan, neither President George H. W. Bush nor leaders in Congress made any serious effort to resolve the stark dilemma between U.S. interest in restraining Pakistan's nuclear ambitions and the need to preserve an uncomfortable alliance in this strategic corner of the world. The young mujahideen emerging from the *madrassas* of the North-West Frontier Province began to turn their eyes to new enemies, foremost among them as their *mullahs* taught, the Great Satan, the United States. At the same time, far away in the halcyon airs and bucolic beauty of the Eastern Shore of Virginia, my marriage slowly began to turn into an often angry, distant kind of affair, and in 1990 Suzanne and I separated, went our own ways, and were then divorced.

15

Interlude with Crab Cakes and Grits

Northampton County, at the southern tip of the long, narrow peninsula of Virginia's Eastern Shore, where Suzanne and I lived for two years before heading our separate ways, is a sparsely populated, sleepy, poetically beautiful land of big farms, small towns, pine forests, ferocious biting bugs, and shallow creeks running into the Chesapeake Bay. Just fifteen miles to the east on the Atlantic Ocean side of the peninsula are lonely ocean barrier islands and magnificent, deserted beaches. It was settled early by British colonists, and some of our friends traced their ancestry and their land back to those early years. Then history passed it by, leaving a few plantation houses, the big farms, and a landowning aristocracy who, like the Whigs of the Old Country, lived on their land but knew and enjoyed the delights of the great world outside. Paris and New York were regular ports of call for our neighbors, and the good lawyers graduated either from Harvard Law or the University of Virginia. A black laboring population of unbelievable poverty, on which neither emancipation nor the civil rights revolution had made much of a dent, lived in ramshackle houses, usually without indoor plumbing, built on low-lying, swampy land, and spoke a version of English that I found hard to understand.

Our house was originally built in the early nineteenth century as a combination general store, residence, and post office, added on to, with varying degrees of success, by later owners. It stood on a low rise of about six acres of land overlooking Nassawadox Creek, a half-mile or so before the creek's broad waters debouched into the Chesapeake Bay. We had a dock on the water, where at various times we kept a small outboard motor boat and a twenty-three-foot sailboat with a kick-up centerboard designed for shallow waters. In the creeks and shoals of the Eastern Shore, the centerboard kicked up a lot. I soon concluded, as any really experienced Bay sailor could have told me, that the southern reaches of the

Bay are a challenging and rather lonely place to sail, full of shoals, hot as sin in the summer, and characterized by constantly changing shallow channels into its relatively few interesting harbors and port towns (the northern Bay, from Annapolis to St. Michael's, is far better for sailing and sightseeing). Just below our dock was a small, commercial crabbers' wharf and packing facility where the local crabbers landed their catch of the famous Chesapeake blue crabs, and one could buy, dirt cheap, the world's tastiest fresh crabmeat. The crabbers took all the catch the law allowed, and in the fall and early winter hunted deer, wild geese, and ducks and drank bourbon. Our house had a name, Foxcroft, which sounded vaguely like something out of Daphne du Maurier or Margaret Mitchell. Local legend had it that one of the early owners converted it from a general store and a post office into a proper, gentry-style house to please his new wife, whose maiden name was Fox. The legend further reports that she was never happy there, and as proof that myth and legend have special powers in romantic places like the Eastern Shore, this held true in Suzanne's and my case as well. Our much-traveled Labrador, Bosun, after his confined life in Pakistan, where nobody liked dogs and he was once poisoned by meat thrown over the wall of our compound, must have thought he had died and gone to Labrador heaven. In Northampton County, everybody loved Labradors. Bosun would leap joyously off our dock to retrieve a stick thrown into the warm waters of the creek. He loved to roll around in the occasional dead fish kill on the beach and similar organic lotions encountered on the back roads along which we took long runs every day through the pine forests and soybean fields.

Our immediate neighbors were two first cousins from an old Eastern Shore family and their wives, Linwood and Caroline Walker and Mapp and Thady Walker. Linwood had been an architect, Caroline a teacher, and Linwood had designed and built their house. Mapp was a Dupont environmental engineer in Tennessee who came back to restore and retire in the lovely old family house where he had spent much of his childhood; his wife, Thady, had been a successful businesswoman. Both couples took deserved pride in their elegant houses and gardens and set forth to introduce us to local society. We became good friends of Russell and Carolyn Jones, the biggest farmers in the neighborhood, and Jack and Susan Wescoat. Jack was a landowner and a lawyer. Susan had just organized a group called Citizens for a Better Eastern Shore to fight the haphazard development of condominiums and golf courses and proposals for large-scale dumping of chemical waste and garbage from industrialized states to the north, and to take on the challenge of low-cost housing for poor blacks and whites. The Eastern Shore depended for its potable and irrigation water on a fragile aquifer whose origin was on the other side of the Bay; long-term conservation of underground water was essential to life on the narrow peninsula, and there was growing concern about agricultural chemical runoff into the waters of the Bay and its effects on the crab and fish populations.

Our property came with an extra small house that we set up as an office with separate work-stations for each of us. We were both working on ideas for books. Suzanne had made notes in Pakistan about her observations and conversations with women, young and old, in the desert tribes of the lower Punjab and Sindh, and she began to write a fictional life of a poor desert girl and her family who incur the wrath of a powerful local magnate. To resolve the family's difficulties, the girl, Shabanu, must agree to marry a rich, much older landlord and tribal leader, Rehim. The story, told simply and full of the color of desert life, with a major role played by Shabanu's powerful, faithful camel, was to become a best-selling, young-adult novel, still selling well in a paperback version after almost twenty years in print. My grandchildren read it in middle school in Rhode Island. Suzanne confessed to me once that the character of Rehim might be partly modeled after me.

I had brought along into retirement a couple of boxes of not very well-organized notes about Asia, accumulated in twenty years of working on and in Asia with the Ford Foundation and the U.S. government. I decided, incorrectly as it turned out, that the world badly needed a non-fiction book about how Asia could modernize without becoming Western. When I sat down to contemplate an outline, two facts became apparent. The first was that my old notes and papers were full of gaps and information about dates and persons. I needed access to a good library collection on Asian affairs. (This was long before Google.com arrived on the scene.) The second truth, which sank in only slowly, was that since I first started years ago trumpeting the news that Japan, South Korea, Singapore, Hong Kong, and increasingly Malaysia (and even China) were demonstrating that modernization did not require westernization—that Asians could be both modern and still preserve their Asian souls—the idea had ceased to be very original.

The best Asian collection within reasonable access was at Columbia University in New York, a half-day away by car and train. I called Ainslie Embree, the eminent historian of India at Columbia and a friend for many years, to ask if he could arrange for access to these unparalleled libraries. Embree said that would be difficult; one must have an official connection with the university to be able to use its libraries. But he could arrange that easily, he said slyly, if I were to agree to teach a graduate seminar on Asian development as an adjunct professor in the School of International Affairs. As I learned in the next few years, senior managers at American universities score points by being alert to new and different course offerings that may attract sizable numbers of students. Embree, in addition to being a history professor, was the director of the Southern Asian Institute. He had been looking for a qualified person to teach a seminar in South Asian economic and social development, and I met his requirements nicely. My unusual range of practical experience more than compensated for my lack of any serious academic qualifications. I had enough wit to insist that, in addition to gaining access to the libraries, I be paid the slave labor rate that adjunct faculty members receive in the American academic universe, particularly since it would cost a good deal to travel back and forth from the Eastern Shore to New York. When I started preparing materials for the seminar and then began to teach once a week, I easily convinced myself that my new academic career required a New York pied-a-terre to be used two or three days a week during the academic year for quick access to Columbia. It would also balance our country living with New York's incomparable cultural life. Suzanne thought this a great idea. We bought a comfortable studio cooperative apartment at Seventy-First Street and West End Avenue, a block west of the Broadway line subway that runs directly up to Columbia University at 116th Street, a short walk to three of the world's finest food stores and delicatessens and seven minutes from Lincoln Center and its opera, ballet, music, and theater. The commute from the Eastern Shore to New York was long but bearable, driving up Route 13 to Wilmington, Delaware, and then parking the car at the Amtrak station and taking the train to Penn Station. I had forgotten how much I loved New York.

I assumed teaching would be easy work. I knew so much about Asia that I expected that I could simply open my mouth before the eager class, and words of wisdom would fly out. I found, to the contrary, that I had greatly underestimated the amount of time and concentration it takes to teach a seminar: the preparation of important and interesting reading lists, specific topics for each meeting, time to prepare remarks, and time to talk with students about their questions and problems. Phil Oldenburg, a young political scientist, expert on Indian politics, and one of the most popular teachers at the School of International Affairs, opened up his own personal library collection and served as my mentor to help me organize the seminar. (Oldenburg never got tenure at Columbia, because the political science department grandees thought his specialization in India was beneath their dignity as they tried to move the department toward a more mathematical and presumably scientific approach to the analysis of politics. This was a flagrant, but not untypical, example of the disregard of the university system for professors who excel at teaching. In this case, Oldenburg was not only a thoughtful and popular teacher, his research on Indian politics and voting patterns was very solid, and his publishing record more than adequate.) My seminar proved to be popular over the next three years with an enrollment of fifteen or so graduate students, almost all of them MA candidates in various disciplines. Somewhat to my surprise, about half were from the Asian subcontinent—mostly Indian with a few Pakistanis, Nepalese, and Sri Lankans. They signed up not so much because they thought the course would be easy, since they were from the region, but because neither in the subcontinent nor in their stateside education had they been exposed to a systematic discussion of the politics and dynamics of poverty and development in South Asia. For reading materials, I used the writings of Asian leaders and thinkers (the Nehru–Gandhi exchanges about how to develop India, for example), policy documents from Asian planning commissions and think tanks, and a collection of Ford Foundation and World Bank policy papers, essays, and evaluations. We talked about the positive and negative roles of government, with a particular emphasis on why governments and the elites of the region have failed in public education and health, and the relationship between underpaid bureaucracies, excessive regulation and licensing, and corruption. I emphasized the importance of understanding cultural and religious traditions as these affect development, and we spent a good deal of time talking about the growing importance of non-governmental organizations throughout the subcontinent. I invited distinguished outside speakers, mostly from Asia, from time to time. In the first year of the seminar, I tried occasionally to have a student organize and lead the discussion in specific sessions, but this caused considerable unhappiness. "We pay good money to hear someone talk who's supposed to know what he is talking about, not another student," a young Indian commented. I found that most of the participants shared his view.

The Columbia libraries were, as expected, a treasure house, but the Asian collections were so large that it was difficult to know where to start. As inevitably happens to me in libraries, I found myself easily distracted by interesting books that I wanted to read that had no direct relationship to the task at hand, which was to write a book about Asian development. So my book writing went slowly. I finally produced an outline and a draft chapter and talked to an agent and an editor, who thought it interesting but possibly too grand a project, and not one many people would be interested in anyway. Slowly I drifted away from it, and then, a year or so later, wrote a different book entirely.

This new chapter of our life, centered on the Eastern Shore with frequent interludes in New York, seemed to be off to a good start. Thanks to the hospitality of our neighbors, we began to develop a small circle of friends deeply rooted in the land and traditions of the Shore. I would stop when I was out on my daily runs with Bosun, for example, to talk farming with Russell Jones who, with his wife Carolyn, a former beauty queen who could drive a combine as well as any man, ran a several-hundred-acre farm producing fruits and vegetables for the big-city markets to the north and soybean for the world market. They faced all the usual challenges of farming—excess or lack of rain, bugs, unpredictable market prices—plus the headaches of running a migrant labor camp to the satisfaction of the Department of Agriculture for the dozens of Latino field hands, mostly Mexican, who came up to the Shore in the harvest season to work in the fields and the packing plant. There were also big tomato farms on the Shore and large nurseries that specialized in growing ornamental trees and shrubs for export outside the country.

Many of our friends, whether they were farmers, preachers, or lawyers, regarded themselves as very much a part of the world outside, kept up with the Broadway theater, and vacationed in Paris and Rome. They entertained in style at candlelight dinners, almost invariably with crab cakes and Virginia ham and delicious homemade cakes and pies and much vin rosé, locally called "blush" (pronounced by lingering on the vowel). People liked to dress formally on occasion. Suzanne and I threw a great, small New Year's black-tie dinner and dancing party at Foxcroft that lasted till dawn. When conversations turned serious, a frequent topic was how to preserve the good life on the Shore in the face of the growing pressures for different uses of land for large-scale development. There was little social or economic integration of the white and black populations (as is true throughout most of the United States), but Susan Wescoat's new Citizens for a Better Eastern Shore had made a beginning in bringing a few black leaders, mostly preachers, together with establishment whites to talk about the extremely serious problems of the community in education and health. The public schools were deeply troubled, and drugs were becoming an epidemic, particularly among young black men, thanks to the well-organized networks of dealers up and down the eastern corridors of communication from Miami to New York. Wescoat's pioneering work was far from universally appreciated. A mutual friend commented, "She was educated up North, and I understand she went with black men when she was a student."

Beneath the surface of our marriage, things were not going well. From time to time, Suzanne would be seized with rage over something I had done or not done that I usually found difficult to understand. Usually, these tempests passed, and she would say that they weren't my fault. One morning, she asked me to sit down on the porch for a talk, the birds singing joyously in the trees, and told me she had decided she must establish her independence, and that she wanted a separation. We talked for a long time. At one point, I said that I had been very supportive of her new career as a writer, both in Pakistan and back in the States, but that seemed only to prove that to some degree she was not really independent. Suzanne said she had begun to see a counselor, a woman in New York (who had counseled Suzanne in her first divorce, which took place after ten years of marriage—about the same amount of time our marriage lasted). She did not want to consider joint counseling. I finally agreed that a separation might be desirable but said I hoped we could work out our problems, although I was still not really sure what they were. An old friend of Suzanne's, who knew her very well from her first marriage and divorce in Hong Kong days, said that "when the magic goes, that's it." My ultimate conclusion was that she simply did not want to be tied to a much older man who was settling down in retirement. Within a few days, Suzanne left to stay temporarily with a woman in New Jersey whom she had known since high school. Shortly after, she said she wanted a divorce. Before we finally parted, we agreed that, as a courtesy to our neighbors, the Walkers, who had been extremely kind to us, we should tell them personally what was going on. We went across the road to Mapp and Thady Walker's house and, to their obvious consternation, gave them our news. At one point Suzanne laughed nervously, and in my mind's eye there flashed an image of our two bodies lying on the floor while the real Suzanne shot at them. Divorce is, indeed, a death in the family, and I went through my own small version of the psychological results of the survivor—elation at the new freedom, anger, loneliness, and then a brand new life.

As part of the amicable divorce settlement, Suzanne received the studio apartment, although so far as I know she rented it out and never lived in New York. I did not want to remain in Foxcroft alone; New York was far more suitable for a newly divorced, aging white male. Within a few months, I sold Foxcroft and moved into a comfortable, quiet, two-bedroom apartment at Seventy-Third and West End Avenue, having decided that this neighborhood in the cultural heart of Manhattan was where I wanted to spend the rest of my life. Bosun stayed on the Shore with a family that loved Labradors. They had a big yard, children to play with, another dog, and a reputation for feeding well. I don't think Bosun missed us for a moment.

I never went back to the Eastern Shore and those days seem like another life. When I do think about them, it is like the opening scenes in that marvelous movie Alfred Hitchcock made from Daphne de Maurier's novel, *Rebecca*, with the camera slowly moving through the overgrown entrance road into the estate where the great house of Manderley stood. Only in my version, the house I picture is the low, white wooden house of Foxcroft on its broad lawn, surrounded by flowers, the pine grove down by the water, and, in the distance, the broad expanse of the creek, sparkling in the sun. Like Manderley, it turned out not to be a paradise at all.

16

The Rubble of Empire

A bachelor's freedom has its delights, I discovered as I settled down—briefly, it turned out—in Manhattan. For the first time in years, I bought some shirts and a suit strictly on my own and, indulging a long-suppressed desire, acquired and started lounging luxuriously in an enormous leather recliner from Bloomingdale's. Having some doubts as to my tastes in interior decoration, I consulted both my daughter, Kathleen, and Mary Bundy, who kindly came over from the Bundys' East Side apartment, dressed, as always, simply but elegantly and wearing cotton gloves, to help poke around and measure in my apartment and to recommend colors and brands of paints and lighting options. My somewhat tattered collection of old rugs and semi-antique art objects from Latin America, Russia, and Asia fit into the simple design and colors Kathleen and Mary recommended.

I was ready to launch my new self into the New York social whirl. I went out with a former Pan American stewardess whom I met through my old friend from exhibit days in Moscow, Jack Masey, who now ran a design firm in New York. She did not find me very exciting, probably at least in part because I insisted on taking her to classical music concerts. I talked philosophy and art with a young Asian-American artist from Florida, a friend of my daughter's, whose miniskirted entry down the orchestra aisles at Avery Fisher Hall turned every male head in the house, and I befriended a young Mongolian, Soviet-trained physician who was studying to pass the New York State medical board examinations. The doctor, Marina Malakshanova, hailed from Irkutsk. She had served a brief mandatory period in the Soviet army reserve and had a charming photograph of that period showing her in her lieutenant's uniform holding a Kalashnikov. We took picnic lunches to Central Park, went to the Metropolitan Museum of Art, and talked Russian. I was not without female companionship. But I was certainly no Donald Trump.

An important part of my life revolved around the School for International Affairs at Columbia University. I continued to teach the graduate seminar on

South Asian economic and social development and had been invited to sit on the Southern Asian Institute's advisory council, where it was thought my knowledge of the government and foundation worlds might be useful in raising money. There were some exceptional people in this group: the late Barbara Stoler Miller, America's leading Sanskrit scholar, who was working on a film version of the Hindu epic poem, the "Mahabharata"; Robert Thurman, the scholar of Tibetan Buddhism who more than any single person introduced the Dalai Lama to America and helped make Americans aware of Buddhism as a way of life; and, of course, Ainslie Embree, the doyen of Indian historical studies. In addition to their scholarly and personal qualities, they were all far better fund-raisers than I was but always polite in listening to my infrequent advice.

I was also working hard at finishing a small book. In 1991, the Ford Foundation asked me if I would write a report for publication about the history of its grant-making in India, to be released the following year as part of the celebration of the fortieth anniversary of the opening of the foundation's office in India. I said I would be delighted, but that I would do the project only if there was no editorial review on the part of the foundation. I would take complete responsibility for the contents. I would need access to the foundation's archives and files, both in India and New York, and it would be necessary to travel for a few weeks in India to interview former grantees and others with relevant views about the foundation's work. I worked on research and early drafting and traveled in India in the summer and early fall of 1991 and finished writing and editing the manuscript that winter in the study of my second-story West End Avenue apartment. In its infinite wisdom, the city decided at precisely that moment to rebuild the underground pipe systems of the sidewalk and street immediately outside my window, so I had excavator operators peering in my window and the machine-gun sound of jackhammers rat-tat-tatting away as I toiled. The book, *Forty Years; A Learning Curve*, was published by the foundation in 1992 and is a useful piece of political and economic development history.

When I left the Foreign Service, I swore that I would not fall into the common retiree trap of continuing to try to live an inside-the-beltway kind of life by seeking consultant work. Now, in my new, post-Eastern Shore of Virginia life, it seemed not a bad idea to do a consultancy from time to time, if I found the subject particularly interesting. In that spirit, I spent a few weeks in Haiti in late 1990 as a member of a three-person team looking at long-term AID development strategy. I had never visited Haiti but had been intrigued by the fact that it was the single Caribbean society with a genuinely powerful and unique indigenous cultural tradition and yet was unable to break out of its historical pattern of political repression and deep poverty. I found it a sad, scary place, little changed from the society Graham Greene described in his novel *The Comedians*, set in the Haiti of Francois "Papa Doc" Duvalier and his Tonton Macoutes police force. When I was there, the hope of the nation was Father Jean-Bertrand Aristide, a poor, politically active priest, who for years had risked his life leading protest movements of the poor and slum dwellers. Aristide eventually became president, but very little changed.

I took another assignment to look at the possibility of turning the relatively small USAID program in Thailand into a government-funded version of a privately managed economic development foundation, an idea popular in Washington during the first Bush administration. My colleagues and I thought this would make a lot of sense, but nothing came of it. A government-funded foundation would require longer political horizons and less political interference than an officially run development program, and no one was ready to fight for this.

In late 1991, I was asked to serve as a senior analyst on the staff of a presidential commission on AID management, put together at the request of Sen. Patrick Leahy (Democrat, Vermont), to survey and make recommendations to improve the unwieldy functioning of the foreign aid machinery. President Bush appointed five commission members, headed by a Republican businessman named George M. Ferris Jr. The executive director was Frank Kimball, a recently retired, senior AID Foreign Service officer whom I had known well in Washington and Cairo, where he ran AID's largest overseas program. Kimball was canny, politically sensitive, experienced, and realistic, and an excellent staff chief. Over a period of a few months, the commission organized public hearings and discussions with officials and private citizens, and the members and the staff interviewed a long list of officials and experts with particular knowledge of AID's history and operations. The commission report pointed out the unique nature of many of AID's management problems. AID was burdened by a ridiculously unworkable number of objectives and earmarks imposed by both the executive branch and Congress—thirty-nine by our count. It was spread far too thin, with offices in too many countries, and trying to carry out too many programs. Its career staff numbers had gone down in the last decade or so, while its project management burdens had increased. The commission recommended that: 1) The administration and Congress define and limit the mission and objectives of foreign assistance and enact a new foreign-assistance law. AID should become fully integrated into the State Department to meet the requirements of the rapidly changing, post-Cold War world; 2) The agency must reduce the number of Washington program and organizational elements, standardize procedures from strategic planning to information and contract management, and designate the deputy administrator as the chief operating officer; 3) AID should revamp its workforce planning, including recruitment and training, and impose higher foreign language requirements on its staff; and 4) A performance management system linking agency objectives, annual employee work plans or "contracts," and employee evaluations should be established. Internal financial controls needed to be strengthened throughout the agency. As is the case with most presidential commissions, a few of the recommendations were adopted; the most meaningful and difficult one—that AID be fully incorporated into the State Department to reflect the political challenges of the new world the United States faced after the fall of the Soviet Union—was not (although in early 2006 Secretary of State Condoleezza Rice announced a reorganization of the Department and the Foreign Service that moved in this direction).

We were still in the final stages of writing the commission report in early 1992 when I got a telephone call from Charlie Greenleaf, my old boss and good friend in AID from 1982 to 1985, when I served as his deputy assistant administrator in the Asia Bureau. Greenleaf, who left the government in 1987, had just returned to Washington after a private trip to Russia. The Soviet Union finally and irrevocably collapsed when the Supreme Soviet officially dissolved the Union of Soviet Socialist Republics on December 31, 1991, and Greenleaf was bubbling over with impressions, ideas, and questions about this event of truly historic proportions. He had reported his observations to various people at the State Department, in particular to James Baker, the secretary of state under President George H. W. Bush, for whom Greenleaf had worked in the Reagan White House. His main recommendation, which Baker liked, was that the State Department create a government-funded, privately managed foundation that could set up and manage a rapidly responding small-grant program in the former Soviet republics to assist economic reform and democratization. When we sat down to talk, Greenleaf recalled that I had spent five years of my earlier career on Soviet Union affairs, including three years in the Moscow embassy, that I spoke fluent Russian, and that I had extensive private foundation experience with the Ford Foundation in both New York and overseas. He thought I could be a big help in creating this new foundation. State, he said, had no higher priority than helping the new republics emerging from the rubble of the former Soviet Union to begin to build the new institutions of democracy, including a private, entrepreneurial sector totally absent in the long Soviet period. (The new republics were Russia, Ukraine, Belarus, Moldova, Georgia, Armenia, Azerbaijan, Turkmenistan, Uzbekistan, Kazakhstan, Kyrgyzstan, and Tajikistan. In the bureaucratic jargon, they promptly became known as the New Independent States, the NIS. This definition did not include the three Baltic states of Latvia, Lithuania, and Estonia, which had been annexed to the Soviet Union later and had declared their freedom earlier. The former Communist countries of Eastern Europe were classified separately.)

Virtually every dreamer and schemer worth his salt was busy suggesting ideas and projects for NIS assistance. State had established a senior-level coordinator of assistance to screen ideas and implementing agencies and to establish priorities, a post soon to be occupied by the redoubtable Richard Armitage, who knew little about the former Soviet Union except in military and political terms but brought a well-deserved reputation for getting things done. State wanted to keep AID out of the action as much as possible. AID, justly or not, suffered from a reputation for numbingly slow bureaucratic processes and a lack of vision. In addition, AID lacked career Foreign Service officers with language and area knowledge of the region and had never run an assistance program in a formerly Communist country. (Neither had anyone else for that matter. State could muster a small number of Russian-speaking officers, but virtually none of these brought any background or interest in assistance work.) While criticized by all, AID possessed one unbeatable advantage for staying in the game: it was the already-established agency for channeling funds approved by Congress into assistance programs, and no one else wanted to undertake this thankless role. Since time was of the essence, it was finally deemed necessary that AID must play this role in the NIS case as well, in the first instance by funding projects proposed by other agencies and institutions, public and private. But State would control policy and priorities. The development of full-fledged AID programs on the ground in the former Soviet republics took a few more years of persistence on the part of AID to achieve.

Greenleaf's idea about creating a foundation found support at State from a paper written by John Stremlau of the policy planning staff. Stremlau, a former Rockefeller Foundation program officer, had proposed the establishment of a small, privately managed foundation modeled after the Asia Foundation, whose work I knew well from my years in Asia with the Ford Foundation and AID. Originally set up by the CIA in the post-Korean War period to support small-scale, nation-building projects in Asia, the Asia Foundation survived the public outing of its CIA origins in the 1960s and continued to perform useful work, primarily relying on U.S. government funds now openly appropriated and channeled through the State Department. But we were under no instructions to copy the Asia Foundation. The design of the new foundation to work in the NIS was wide open, from its very name to the size and qualifications of its staff, and the size and nature of its grant program. It existed in State and AID planning documents only as a potential assistance project under the title "The Foundation." I thought this a once-in-a-lifetime opportunity and committed myself to stay on in Washington for a few months longer to work full time with Greenleaf. The third member of our planning group was a young, Harvard-trained, Russian speaking MD, Jim Cashel, whom Greenleaf had recently met at Cambridge where Cashel was working on an economic development project in the Ukraine (and also thinking about the utility of a foundation-like device for assistance). A young graduate student, Sara Rakita, joined us to work as Greenleaf's assistant and to handle the administrative side of the group's endeavors. Greenleaf arranged for the group to start work immediately as consultants to plan the new foundation, housed temporarily at the K Street offices of the Citizens Democracy Corps (CDC), a Washington NGO created by the Bush administration a few years earlier to provide volunteer help in start-up businesses and civil society groups in Eastern Europe. We had nothing to do with CDC's program, simply availing ourselves of its generously provided administrative services.

Our crew plunged into planning work with a sense of great excitement and adventure. Greenleaf was the leader of the group. Although he was primarily responsible for high-level negotiations at State and the outside-the-beltway world and, as necessary, on the Hill, he was also keenly interested in the program concentrations and priorities. Given my foundation experience, I gave particular attention to the design of the governance and structure of the organization—how decisions would be reached and at what levels—and the subject matter of the program and the staffing required to carry it out. As our ideas began to take shape, I conducted most of the discussions and negotiations with AID and occasionally at State at both senior and working levels. In my six years with AID in the 1980s, I had come to know and in some cases worked closely with a number of the middle-level and senior AID officers now assigned to the newly created NIS Bureau. Cashel concentrated on program and operating procedures and creating the machinery of actual grant-making. We functioned as a committee of the whole, sharing information and ideas and working together as circumstances required. We were determined to produce an organization that would be characterized by simplicity, speed of response, willingness to take risks, and low administrative costs. We felt great pressure to get the foundation established and visibly working on the ground in the former Soviet republics. As it turned out, we were embarking on an adventure in politics and bureaucracy worthy of comparison with the old movie serial, *The Perils of Pauline*.

Staples Bangkok residence, an old Chinese merchant's house with lotus pond.

Our farmhouse outside Delhi.

Punjab, India, 1975.
Looking at Goats. Author is fourth from left. John J. McCloy, Chairman of the Board,
Ford Foundation, is to author's left.

Left to right: Lisa Lyons and Charlotte Staples at a picnic outside Buddhist temple.

Left to right: author and Ram Prakash at Pushkar camel fair, Rajasthan, 1977.

McGeorge Bundy and author drink milk (reluctantly) with dairy co-op farmers. South India, 1978

Author feeding peacocks at dawn in courtyard of Maharajah's Palace hotel, Bikaner, Rajasthan, 1979.

Author with frontier guard escort, Jhil Jhao, Baluchistan, January, 1984.

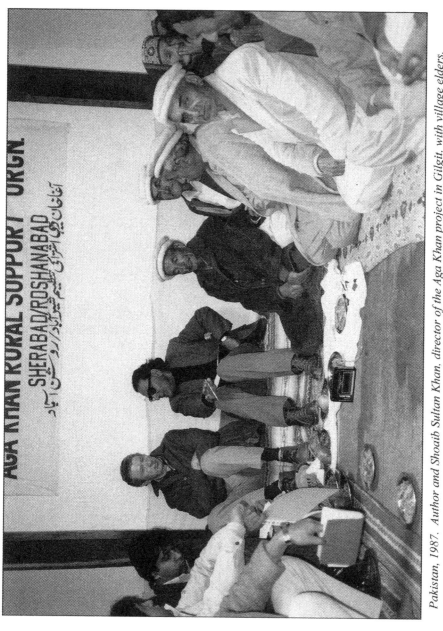

Pakistan, 1987. Author and Shoaib Sultan Khan, director of the Aga Khan project in Gilgit, with village elders.

Baltit, Pakistan, 1986. Author and Shoaib Sultan Khan on roof of the former palace of the Emir. Condemned prisoners were tossed into the gorge below.

Judy Reynolds and Eugene Staples after their wedding, Nantucket, October, 1993.

Author in Suzdal monastery compound at Eurasia Foundation conference, 1994.

Author and Eurasia Foundation Representative, Horton Beebe-Center,
Samarkand, Uzbekistan, 1994.

Author and Igor Bobrowsky, Eurasia Foundation Representative, Saratov, in Moscow, 1995.

Judy and Rocky Staples at riverside tea stall. Tashkent.

Marine Fighter Squadron VMF 452 reunion. Orlando, FL, March 2005. Left to right: Former Lieutenants Fletcher, Rogalski, Warren, Schaefer, Guetzloe and the author. Airplane is WWII Navy advanced trainer SNJ.

Author playing the violin, New York.

A number of issues demanded immediate attention. The first was the nature of the board of trustees. We took the position that for the foundation to have the maximum freedom of action all the trustees should be private citizens. In its startup phase, it was agreed that Greenleaf would prepare a list of possible trustees to be discussed with the secretary of state. Once the foundation was legally incorporated, which required only Greenleaf's signature as incorporator plus those of our two contract lawyers, Greenleaf would invite, from the list vetted by State, up to twelve distinguished private citizens to constitute the board. In subsequent years, trustees would be self-electing with no reference to any government agency. They would be appointed into three classes whose terms would expire by turn on a rolling, three-year calendar, with re-election or the election of new trustees as each class term expired. Incorporation required a legal name. After a short, spirited debate among ourselves and with State and AID we agreed to call the new organization the Eurasia Foundation, reflecting the European and Asian peoples and geography we would be dealing with. (There was some minor scholarly grumbling over the term "Eurasia," as bearing unfortunate overtones from its use in Hitlerian geopolitics, and there were a number of other suggestions, including the Foundation for the New States.) On April 29, 1992, the foundation was duly incorporated in the District of Columbia by Greenleaf and our two lawyers as trustees. The two lawyers then resigned and Greenleaf immediately invited Max Kampelman, a prestigious Washington lawyer, a Democrat, and a former arms negotiator with the Soviet Union, and William Frenzel, a respected former Republican congressman from Minnesota, now a senior fellow at the Brookings Institution, to become the first two board members.

Then the State Department committed a serious tactical error. After much consultation, Greenleaf sent to State for informal vetting a list of distinguished private citizens, after which process Greenleaf proposed to invite those approved to consider joining the board. But Deputy Secretary of State Lawrence Eagleburger's office (Eagleburger was about to become acting secretary of state and then secretary), now the controlling point at State, was unwilling to assume the responsibility of final, informal approval and sent the list to National Security Adviser Brent Scowcroft, who passed it on to the personnel office at the White House. Greenleaf, who had served in that office in the Reagan administration, groaned and said, "This is bad news." And it certainly was, on two counts. First, it was as though the list had been dropped into a hole. Week after week dragged by, with no word as to what was happening. Finally, in mid-summer, the list came back from the White House with some of Greenleaf's recommendations removed and two or three highly controversial names added, including one well-known Far Right religious leader. At this point, with only months remaining before the November 1992 presidential elections, the Democratic staffers of the House Appropriations Committee (the Democrats controlled both houses of Congress), which would have to approve the funds for the new foundation project to become a reality, became aware of the White House list and said flatly there was no way they would support a new organization using U.S. government funds with such a board.

A second crisis blew up. As we analyzed the new foundation's program priorities in this virtually unknown landscape, we argued strongly to our sponsors at State that it would be unwise at the outset to think narrowly. Within the broad categories of economic and administrative reform and civil society, we must have the freedom to explore and innovate since no one really knew very much about what was happening on the ground in the new republics. Flexibility was the essence of the idea of the foundation. But as our work proceeded, State informed Greenleaf that, in early discussions within the government about the foundation idea, Eagleburger had agreed with the deputy secretary of the treasury, John Robson, a former business school dean at Emory University, that one-third of the new institution's funds must be earmarked for business management training. Greenleaf and I reacted the same way: in the uncertain circumstances in which we would launch the foundation's programs, this was a nutty requirement. Almost certainly, from what we did know about the needs of the new republics, we would commit a good portion of foundation resources to business management training—very possibly more than one-third—but an earmark was the wrong way to start. It could be wasteful and prevent us from seizing valuable opportunities in other subjects. After arguing this position unsuccessfully in discussions at various levels in State, Greenleaf sent a letter to Eagleburger that strongly reiterated the case for flexibility while also underlining the foundation's expectation that business management training would constitute an important part of its programming. Eagleburger rejected Greenleaf's argument, confirmed his commitment to Robson, and said the earmark must remain. Greenleaf then resigned as the foundation's first president, sending a minor wave of incredulity through a tiny corner of the cynical world of Washington bureaucracy. In Washington, resigning over principle is about as rare as meeting a living saint.

Greenleaf's departure was a great blow. He worked very hard, had both exceptional vision and an uncommon fund of common sense, listened well, had good connections, and our tiny staff liked and admired him personally. We all considered leaving as well. I had certainly agreed with and reinforced Greenleaf's view that an earmark would be crippling. But Greenleaf argued strongly that we should stay: the idea of the foundation, which had begun to acquire the outlines of a program and a staff, was too important to abandon. State told us they would have a new president identified and in place within a matter of weeks. So Cashel and I agreed to stay to continue to work on program and organizational questions, leaving the question of earmarks to be decided at the board level when the board was finally constituted. In about three weeks, State informed us that it had found a new president, William Bader, a former Foreign Service officer, whom Eagleburger, himself a career FSO, had known in earlier Foreign Service days. Bader was an experienced and successful Washington operator. He had earned a PhD in history from Princeton, spent several years in the career Foreign Service, worked briefly as a program officer in the Ford Foundation in the 1970s, serving for a period as the foundation's representative in its Paris office for Europe, and then spent several years as the staff director of the Senate Foreign Relations Committee. Most recently he had been a senior vice president of the Stanford Research Institute, which he left after a major reorganization. Bader and I had known each other, although not well, at the Ford Foundation.

Bader settled in quickly and comfortably. He understood the politics of Washington and made it clear that he regarded his major role as attending to our high-level external relationships with State and the rest of the government, including Congress, and the outside world as appropriate. Cashel and I should continue to concentrate on program and management questions. That sounded fine to us. Working on the basic ideas we had agreed to with Greenleaf in the early months, by late summer we produced a set of draft papers on the policies, program priorities, and staffing and administrative requirements recommended for the new foundation. These were ready for formal discussion with State and AID and with new trustees as these were brought aboard. Briefly, we recommended the following:

> 1. The foundation would be privately managed by its board of trustees. Its grant-making processes must be made as simple and speedy as possible given the political importance of launching visible reform activities on the ground as soon as possible. We kept before us in our planning the admirable example established by the Eastern European foundations set up by George Soros in the 1980s, in which openness to grant seekers and speed of decision-making were essential. Our goal was to reach grant decisions and notify the grant seeker in less than thirty days. Achieving these goals of speed and simplicity would require a large degree of downward delegation of authority for grant approvals from the board to the staff, and, as field offices were established, from Washington headquarters to the field. The bylaws would establish the role of the board as the primary instrument for governing the affairs of the

foundation but provide that when the board was not in session an executive committee would act on its behalf. The full board of fifteen members (initially) would meet twice a year. The executive committee, composed of the chairman, a vice chairman, the president of the foundation (ex officio), and three additional trustees, would meet once a month or more often if necessary to provide policy, program, and management guidance and decisions and would report its activities to the full board.

2.   After getting up to speed and with a fully trained staff and administrative procedures in place, the foundation should aim to operate at an annual level of $20 million. Primarily it would make small grants although in a limited number of cases the board might wish to approve larger commitments. An annual budget much larger than $20 million would be unrealistic and difficult to manage, at least in early years, given the chaotic circumstances existing in the former Soviet republics and our own lack of experience; a budget much smaller would produce an insignificant program. Initial program priorities should include business education and management training, economics education, NGO development, improvement of the regional press, electronic communications, and local-level public administration.

3.   The foundation would maintain a lean administrative profile. At the outset, the headquarters staff, including both program officers and administrative staff, should number no more than twelve to fifteen persons (we actually started with about a half-dozen). Although we wanted to maintain a tight rein on administrative costs, we must, given the circumstances in which we would be operating and our responsibilities for U.S. government funds, build in solid financial reporting and controls, including regular audits of our records. We would establish small field offices in the new republics starting immediately, each to be run in the early years by a Russian-speaking American specialist with a small local support staff. Russian-language competence (even in the non-Russian republics, Russian would serve as the lingua franca for many years to come) would be required for all program staff members in both Washington and the field. The salary scale should be set at about the mid-level of comparable NGO institutions carrying out overseas activities.

4.   The foundation should plan at least a ten-year lifespan. It must rely heavily in the early years on U.S. government funds but would actively seek funds from private and non-U.S. government sources as its programs developed.

As the fall of 1992 arrived, official Washington gave itself over entirely to the November elections in which President Bush would be pitted against the Democratic candidate, William Clinton. Any hopes of getting the Eurasia Foundation launched before the elections vanished. Before the new institution could begin its grant-making business, we must sign a basic project agreement with AID as the funding agency and AID, in turn, had to be sure that the appropriate congressional appropriations committees were on board with the new project. In the two or three months before the elections, although we were more than ready to launch, the makeup of the new Congress was impossible to forecast. I took some time off and returned to New York, with an agreement to return to Washington after the elections if the atmosphere appeared appropriate. We already had achieved a basic agreement with AID on the outlines of the project paper authorizing our startup funding. The drafter and principal negotiator at AID was Laurie Mailloux, a talented, young AID Foreign Service officer in the new NIS Bureau, who had worked as a project officer at the USAID mission in Pakistan when I served there. Clinton, of course, won the election, the Democrats retained control of Congress (for the first term only), and Warren Christopher became secretary of state (and the old argument over the one-third earmark for management training vanished). But not until after the formal accession of the Clinton administration in January 1993 were we able to engage State and AID again in final negotiations.

In the midst of those uncertain days, in December to be precise, love, as the old song says, walked right in (to our K Street office) and brought my sunniest day. I was standing at the door to my office when Laura Guimond, who was working with our small group in the start-up phase, brought a new CDC employee around to meet the Eurasia Foundation staff. Her name was Judith Reynolds. I responded to her green-eyed, Irish beauty immediately the way men instinctively do in the presence of real beauty, a magical smile, a sense of mystery and elegance, and a graceful way of walking. It was certainly not, on the spot, reciprocal; as Judith describes her own recollections of that fateful moment, she remembered nothing at all. In the ensuing days, I pursued her whenever it was not too obvious, which it soon became, into the tiny kitchen that served as a snack bar to have a cup of coffee and tell her about life according to Rocky. Totally bewitched, I asked her out—unsuccessfully for a while—for dinner or a concert. Finally, she relented, and on Valentine's Day we went for supper to Dominique's, a great old restaurant on Pennsylvania Avenue, and then to the symphony at Kennedy Center—Judy had once been an usher there and had tickets. In the ensuing weeks, she taught me how to make angels in freshly fallen snow, fed me delicious homemade soup and chili in her Georgetown apartment, watched with delight as I taught her timid cat, Sam, who had been roughly treated in his youth as a street fighter before Judy adopted him, to roll over on command (having learned, Sam would roll over for guests at the slightest provo-

cation), and unveiled an endlessly fascinating personality, which included stop-
ping suddenly while walking down the street and doing a handstand against a
building because she felt like it, or pulling a guitar out from under the bed and
singing a love song in Portuguese, or unexpectedly kissing me on the street. Judy
was born in Mexico City, one of five children of a career CIA officer and his wife.
She grew up in Bolivia, Argentina, Brazil, and Washington, lived and studied in
Spain, and spoke virtually perfect Spanish and Portuguese. In Washington, she
worked as a translator at the Spanish embassy and more recently as a project
officer and assistant to the director of the Spain 92 foundation, celebrating the
quincentennial of Columbus's discovery of America. As spring came to Washington, I got to know Judy's parents, who were about my age, and by summer had
asked her to marry me. In October, we eloped to Nantucket and were married
(after Judy got her parents' blessing) by the town clerk on a sunny day in a garden
redolent of late summer flowers and buzzing with hungry mosquitoes, Judy
resplendent in a wedding gown purchased that morning in a town store.

Along with its azaleas and my own happiness, the Washington spring finally
brought the long-delayed launching of the Eurasia Foundation. We signed a
project agreement with AID granting the foundation $80 million for its first four
years of operations, with our commitment to raise additional funds from other
sources as our program got under way. Bader asked me to stay on for a while as
vice president for program and to help hire and train staff. Cashel agreed to stay
as the first program officer. Shortly thereafter, we hired Kathryn Wittneben, a
smart, hard-driving economist, to manage our business and economic development activities while Cashel concentrated on public administration, NGOs, electronic communications, and the regional press. Beverly Pheto, a young but
widely experienced and respected career government manager, read our advertisement for manager of administration and joined us because she thought our institution and our work were going to be exciting. The ranks of the board of trustees
began to be filled out with a number of distinguished private citizens. One of
them was Frank Press, the just-retired president of the National Academy of Sciences, whose name I had suggested because of his experience in scientific
exchanges with the Soviet Union and a reputation for good management.

The first full meeting of the board almost derailed the program-management
structure we had so carefully planned. From the earliest days of designing the
foundation with Greenleaf, the staff had concluded that the only way to achieve
the speed, numbers, and efficiency of small grant-making that our sponsors at
State and AID expected, and we believed necessary, was through a significant delegation of authority to the president or his designee to approve and sign off on

grant requests. This delegation, at much lower levels, would be extended to the new representatives in the field offices as they and their local program staffs were hired, trained, and acquired experience. I thought it was blindingly obvious that the full board of trustees, all of whom were prominent, busy men and women, would never be able to commit the time and study required to judge each of the hundreds and eventually thousands of small-grant requests the foundation was designed to consider. We estimated that the average grant amount would be less than $25,000 (indeed, in the early years it averaged around $17,000). We thus recommended a delegation of approval of grants up to $250,000 for the president's signature and up to $25,000 to field representatives, after a trial period during which each office's staff capabilities and procedures were examined in Washington headquarters. The executive committee of the board would meet monthly to review all grant decisions and other business as appropriate.

When the delegation question came up at the first, full board meeting, one of the trustees, with whom we had discussed the proposal, expressed great concern over the risks involved in making grants in the new republics and argued that the full board should approve each individual grant. I replied that this seemed to me unworkable—if we were to carry out our agreed mission of moving rapidly with large numbers of small grants. I noted that many foundations (including both the Ford and Asia Foundations) carry out their grant-making business with significant delegations of authority to operating officers and staff. For the foundation to achieve its goals, we saw no way to operate other than through a process of delegations of authority. The first-round count of hands when the board voted on the issue would have resulted in a one-vote margin opposing the delegations. At that point, before the count was finally confirmed, Frank Press intervened to ask me to say directly whether I was absolutely convinced that the lack of delegations of authority would make it impossible for the foundation to carry out its work. I said I had no doubt whatsoever. Press then proposed a second count, and the delegation authority was approved. In practice, it worked smoothly and brought the foundation an early reputation for its promptness in response and willingness to innovate. In large part, this was due to the management skills and wisdom of the executive committee, which has overseen the ongoing business of the foundation from the start. Sarah Carey, a top Washington lawyer who speaks Russian and manages the legal affairs of an important stable of business clients investing and working in Russia, and William Frenzel have alternated as board chairman and vice chairman. (Thirty years earlier, Carey worked for me as a spunky young exhibit guide on the staff of the first traveling exhibition in the Soviet Union.)

We began interviewing staff candidates immediately. We required all program staff members and field representatives to speak and read Russian fluently. We looked primarily for young men and women with an MA plus at least two or three years work experience, preferably in some relevant aspect of Russian or Soviet affairs. They also had to be tough and self-starting. Opening an office anywhere in the former Soviet republics was uncharted territory. The old service infrastructure had collapsed, banks for all practical purposes didn't exist, almost all financial transactions involved cash, the legal status of virtually anything was unclear, and our representatives would have to scramble, scheme and negotiate with frequently unfriendly former Soviet bureaucrats to find and set up adequate working space.

It was a tribute to the value of the Russian language and area training programs of the American universities (most of them funded in their early days by the Ford Foundation) that we got a flood of applications from extremely talented and well-qualified men and women. Horton Beebe-Center, who opened our Moscow office, a professional "tall ship" sailing captain, spoke virtually flawless Russian that he learned first in college and then perfected while living and working as a fish buyer with the American and Soviet trawler fleets in the Bering Sea. (A fine example of Beebe-Center's negotiating ability was the office space he found for us in the Soviet Academy of Sciences building, an old palace near the Kremlin originally built for Catherine the Great by one of her lovers so that she would not have to endure the smells that descended on the Kremlin from a pig farm when the wind blew from the west.) When we needed a tough, independent person to open our office in Saratov, historically an important trading center on the Volga where as a young, dissolute nobleman, fed up with gambling and womanizing in Moscow, Leo Tolstoy disembarked en route to the Caucasus to fight in the campaign against the Chechen and Dagestani rebellion, and, as it resulted, to begin his writing career, we hired Igor Bobrowsky, an ethnic Kuban Cossack and fluent speaker of both Russian and Ukrainian. Bobrowsky was a decorated Vietnam veteran who had organized exchange activities between American Vietnam War veterans and Soviet veterans of the Afghanistan war. Greta Bull, an intense, young scholar, opened our Ukraine office in Kiev. Our first representative in the Caucasus, Laurens Ayvazian, spoke not only fluent Russian but Armenian as well. When a bit later we felt sufficiently confident of our wares to launch an office in the Russian Far East, our first representative was Glen Lockwood, an intrepid young man with near perfect Russian who had already spent a year in Eastern Siberia organizing adventure tours in the Far East and Sakhalin, one of the world's last great unexplored regions. Fred Smith, who spoke English with his native Kentucky accent but virtually unaccented Russian, took on the Herculean task of setting up our operations in Central Asia, putting aside his work toward a doctorate in Russian literature because the foundation was more exciting.

It is hard to exaggerate the desolation of the physical and psychological worlds in which the foundation's representatives went to work. As I traveled across the vastness of the former empire, working with the field staff in setting up the foundation's programs, the physical evidence of defeat and despair was tumbled about the landscape in every direction: enormous industrial centers and entire cities and regions completely idle and eerily silent; the *kolkhoz* (collective farm) fields unplanted and untended (Moscow was living on mostly imported food); transportation systems in shambles; the centralized light and heating systems of all Soviet cities and towns almost entirely dysfunctional in the frigid grip of winter; clinics and hospitals in chaos; and thousands of once-comfortable, now-bankrupt citizens standing on street corners and in crowded informal bazaars selling any trinket or household treasure or piece of clothing that might yield enough money to buy food. In Vladivostok, which was a tightly closed city, impossible to visit when I served in the American embassy in Moscow in the 1960s, I climbed a hill above the harbor to see the once-mighty Soviet Pacific battle fleet lying at anchor slowly rusting away; there wasn't enough fuel for it to leave the harbor. In the old Soviet days, there was always too much heat indoors. Now, I almost froze to death in winter visits to places like Yerevan and Kiev. One night in Kiev at thirty degrees below zero, in the absence of taxis I had to walk a mile or so home from the opera, still heroically functioning in a collapsed economy, to a temporary apartment to sleep fully clothed and shivering under a pile of blankets and quilts. The ruble and its equivalent in the non-Russian republics were virtually worthless, and people lined up to trade rubles and dollars in portable vans guarded by Kalashnikov-bearing security guards. Old people and pensioners, many of them veterans and heroes of the Great Patriotic War, were starving.

The psychic effects were possibly even more difficult to deal with. Foremost among these emotions and feelings, even among the many former Soviet citizens who had concluded that Communism was a system doomed to failure and who welcomed the new freedoms, were wounded pride, shame, humiliation, and a pervasive sense of great loss. The Soviet Union had been both a great empire and a superpower, competing worldwide for global domination with the Americans. Now the Russians were unwelcome even in Ukraine or the republics of the Black Sea, whose beaches they loved, and under pressure to get out of the Central Asian republics, even though they might have been born there. The job security that the Communist system provided, even though it rested on a crazy perception of economics that ignored any kind of rationality and ultimately failed completely, had meant a great deal in the lives of many citizens and there was no assurance whatsoever that the new economic and political freedoms would ever produce that kind of security for the masses. The crime and brutality that festered under the surface of the Soviet system was now out in the open, visible to all in the flaunting of the power and riches of the new robber barons and the thugs: their Mercedes cars, the convoys of American SUVs with tinted windows, their young, beautiful blond whores, and a fierceness and cruelty that made La Cosa Nostra look like an old-fashioned picnic and soon vaulted Russian and Ukrainian gangsters to the top of the list of international criminal gangs in Europe and the United States. I sat one fine afternoon at an open-air café on the banks of the Neva in Saint Petersburg, across the water from the south bank where the old World War I cruiser *Aurora* is still anchored in front of the Smolny Institute and the Naval Academy. In Soviet days and Communist history this was a hallowed place. The *Aurora*'s enlisted men fought in the October Revolution and fired the big guns of the *Aurora* (the shots turned out to be blanks) to support the Bolshevik fighters taking over the Winter Palace. I drank an imported German beer and idly watched a pair of fat German businessmen making out with two pretty, young Russian girls. At a nearby table sat a group of muscular young thugs, shirts open to their chests and bedecked with gold chains, drinking and chatting on their cell phones about plans for the evening, while big black BMWs came and went at the curb with new companions. I thought to myself, "If Lenin could only see what he has wrought."

There was no lack of advice from the outside as to what the Russians should do. The Americans were peddling the magic of the marketplace and our own kind of judicial reforms, but for every American adviser and consultant there was a matching crew from Western Europe. Since Americans and Europeans do not agree on many political and economic issues, the resulting babble frequently produced only confusion. A decade later, both the Russians and their neighbors and the now much thinner throngs of American and Western advisers, consultants, and do-gooders realize that there are no easy answers. Privatization the way the Russians did it with American advice and financial support was brutally effective in terms of transferring the control of wealth out of state hands, for example, but whether it was the right way in a society where no real rule of law existed to protect the rights of the less powerful and less well connected is open to question. Institution building of any sort was particularly difficult in the ex-Soviet Union because it was singularly bereft of any indigenous models. In its final years, the people of the Soviet Union, unlike the countries of Eastern Europe or Communist China, lacked any historical reference points. Even its oldest living citizens had never known any way of life other than Communism. In China, by contrast, when Mao's successors discarded the totally failed commune system of agricultural production, many older Chinese peasants still remembered a tradition of private farming and free markets and knew not only how to survive but how to prosper as well. The painful and unjust privatization of Soviet natural resource industries that resulted from the direct translation of Western concepts into Russian theory and practice will bedevil Russian politics for generations to come.

The Eurasia Foundation avoided most of those pitfalls. It was not a policy advice kind of organization, although its trustees and staff believed in a democratic polity and a free economic system. Our challenge was to find groups of former Soviet citizens with their own good ideas and proposals as to how to develop new institutions that would work in the new order of things and to put quite small amounts of money into their hands to test the strength of their concepts. In the early years, we used a number of techniques for finding people with ideas and vision who might make good potential grantees. Cashel suggested that we concentrate at the start on making grants in provincial cities and regions, particularly in Russia, on the theory that since political power resided in the capitals those cities would tend to attract assistance anyway. The Peace Corps had begun to establish a somewhat precarious presence on the ground outside Moscow, and one of our early strategies in seeking grantees with ideas and ability was to build on the knowledge and contacts Peace Corps volunteers had begun to accumulate. Cashel saw our early representatives in the provinces as Johnny Appleseeds using very small amounts of money to sow good works. As we developed our knowledge of subjects and regions, the foundation began to publicize and sponsor competitions for local institutions seeking grant assistance. We funded the first major grant competition in Russia, for example, designed exclusively for new, indigenous non-governmental organizations seeking to improve their management and outreach activities and, in its early years, the foundation was for a time the single-largest international donor supporting women's NGOs in the NIS to train women entrepreneurs and women political candidates and to examine health and economic issues of concern to women. We used small-grant competitions offering funds for computers and staff training to encourage new ideas and excellence in the regional communications media, starting with newspapers and extending the idea later to radio and television stations. Our representatives and their local staffs traveled widely to meet with potential grant seekers, and we maintained an open-door policy that encouraged grant seekers to visit our offices, a practice successfully pioneered by the Soros foundations in Eastern Europe.

They were exhilarating times. The men and women we met were determined to build a new, better society, and many of them and their new institutions succeeded, judging by the results on the ground as seen ten years later. I admired them all. As the officer primarily responsible for the foundation's program, I lived in a state of creative tension between the management of the board, which invariably wanted more focus in the program, and my own strong conviction of the desirability of experimentation. Once in the early days, Horton Beebe-Center in Moscow took me to meet a skinny, harried-looking Russian who was dedicating his life to trying to improve the horrendous lot of prisoners (he had been a political prisoner under the Soviets). He had created a radio program designed to help prison inmates in the Moscow region receive messages from their families and to inform prisoners of their rights and legislation affecting prison administration and, improbably, had convinced the prison administration to allow it to be broadcast in most jails. Our friend's request was for a grant of $5,000 to add staff and rent one more room—he and his staff (consisting of two women) were working in a room far smaller than my hotel bedroom and piled high with papers. I told Beebe-Center that if, after checking out the request, he decided to go ahead, that would be fine with me. Reform of the dreadful prison system the Russians inherited from the Soviets fit into my definition of building a civil society. Beebe-Center went ahead, and some trustees thought this was a terrible grant. It was maybe my all-time favorite.

Overall, the foundation's takeoff and early growth were surprisingly smooth and accident free, thanks to the quality of the staff overall and particularly the field representatives, who were bright, dedicated, and worked their tails off. The indigenous local staffs they hired and trained, with rare exceptions, turned out to be an equally competent group. We found ourselves after a year or so with a high percentage of well-educated, English-speaking local female employees in both the Russian and the non-Russian republics (at one point in Saratov on the Volga, all three of the senior local staff members were women, all of them named Irina, and in Tashkent the senior local staff without exception was female). This trend marked the second round of field representative appointments as well: Beebe-Center, who wanted to go back to law school, was replaced in Moscow by Melanie Peyser, a creative, thoughtful lawyer; and in Saratov, Shawna Wilson, a young African-American who had begun her Eurasia Foundation career as a receptionist and then demonstrated exceptional management abilities, took over as representative from Igor Bobrowsky. With never a sputter although plenty of disagreements with me from time to time over program content, the executive committee system for overall foundation management worked smoothly, as did the system of delegations of authority for grant approvals.

My original commitment to Bader and the board was to stay for a year to hire and train the field staff and get operations started. But I found it difficult to disengage from the foundation. My personal relationship with the field and program staffs, all of whom I had recruited, seemed particularly important at this stage of the institution's development. I was the most useful single liaison with AID on budget matters and the integrity and management of our field programs, at least in part because, as AID opened and expanded its own offices throughout the NIS, I knew a majority of both the senior Washington AID staff and the new AID mission directors. So I stayed on for five years, far longer than I originally intended, serving in the last year as the foundation's president and, after retirement, continuing on the board of trustees for another three years. My successor, who has skillfully guided the foundation's further growth, was Charles "Bill" Maynes, a wise former career diplomat and foreign affairs expert who had served in Moscow in earlier years, spoke Russian, and had a distinguished career as editor of *Foreign Policy* magazine.

All of us took great pride in what we had built. Out of its modest and adventurous beginnings in 1992, the Eurasia Foundation grew into an innovative and dynamic institution that contributed a lot to the processes of democratic and economic reform in the former Soviet republics. From its inception in 1993 to 2005, the Eurasia Foundation made more than seven thousand grants in the twelve republics for a total of $140 million, 80 percent of these executed by the field offices with an average grant size of $20,000. In the limited number of cases in which the foundation chose to commit larger sums of money, working in cooperation with other donors, it helped create a number of business-management training institutes of international quality; a world-quality, graduate-level training and research program in economics; and a media-development alliance that strengthened a number of important newspapers, radio stations, and television broadcasters in Russia. It was a major mover in the spread of the information technology revolution in Russia, and a pioneer in small-business lending programs in Ukraine and Armenia. The foundation also has proved to be by far AID's most effective grantee in raising additional resources to forward its program goals, to date generating nearly $60 million dollars in support of its programs from a broad spectrum of non-U.S. government sources including private corporations, private foundations, European governments, international institutions like the World Bank and the European Union, and from NIS sources as well. One silent measure of its success is that AID, the World Bank, and other assistance agencies now widely incorporate the foundation's small-grant philosophy and techniques into their own grant programs. With private Russian support and major commitments from European foundations, the Eurasia Foundation in 2004 helped launch a promising indigenous Russian foundation, appropriately called the New Eurasia Foundation, headed by a prestigious scholar and public affairs leader, Andrei Kortunov, dedicated to carrying out a program of grants in economic and civic reform. In the wake of the Yushchenko democratic revolution in Ukraine that same year, the Eurasia Foundation was widely credited for its work in building democracy through its years of grant support for projects in civic education and the conduct of elections.

The current wisdom in the administration in power in Washington today (2005, the fifth year of the Bush administration) is that it is now time largely to disengage from Russia as far as assistance programs are concerned. Russia is certainly much stronger in gross economic terms, and its politics, if not satisfactory, are at least stable, fulfilling my early prediction to friends when Putin appeared on the scene that most Russians would prefer a strong hand in regard to law and order to the near chaos of the last Yeltsin years. U.S. government funds for Russian assistance are now to be much reduced, largely siphoned off to meet the new and insatiable appetite for funds in Iraq and the Middle East. The United States is increasing assistance funds in Central Asia and the Caucasus for security reasons related to the new American military presence in Central Asia near the flashpoints of Afghanistan, Pakistan, Iran, and the Middle East. It will be unwise for the United States to carry its disengagement from Russia too far. The task of building democratic and modern economic institutions is barely started in Russia, although the context and specific challenges have changed in many ways over the last decade. The West, particularly the United States, still has much to offer and to gain—or to lose—in that regard. Russia will remain the world's second-largest nuclear power for as far ahead as one can see. Its capacity for good or evil is very large. It will seek in every possible way to reestablish its place in the world as a great power, and its culture, history, and resources suggest that this will again be the case.

When Judy and I said good-bye to Washington in 1997 to settle down in our New York apartment on Manhattan's West Side, I left a part of my heart with my friends and co-workers in the Eurasia Foundation and made a commitment to stay connected to its work as a member of an international advisory council. I shed no tears on leaving the national capital itself. I had first known Washington a half-century earlier in the sordid, scary times of Sen. Joseph McCarthy. The politics of the 1990s in Washington, it seemed to me, were becoming equally as nasty, personalized, and even more dogmatic. The new era of the neo-conservative think tanks was in full cry. The Heritage Foundation, the Cato Institute, the American Enterprise Institute, all funded by wealthy Far Right donors (Richard Mellon Scaife alone contributed $345 million to such organizations, according to the *Washington Post*), churned out a river of position papers on every conceivable topic about organizing and running the world according to the gospels of Leo Strauss and Frederik Hayek. Meanwhile, although most of them never heard of either Strauss or Hayek, a nationwide flock of right-wing flacks—the Rupert Murdoch empire and the echo chamber of conservative radio and television talk shows—parroted the party line, regardless of the topic. Questioning an opponent's patriotism, McCarthy's favorite gambit, became routine practice. The "center" of politics, as defined by the new breed of Republicans, was shifting to what Republicans I knew in Washington a half-century earlier would have classified as "Far Right." The Democrats under Clinton and then John Kerry fell into this semantic trap and ever deeper confusion as they sought to locate and occupy the elusive and constantly receding "center."

Having witnessed first-hand the catastrophic effects of ideology in the Soviet Union, I regarded the growth of real ideology in my own country, to define the term in its pejorative, European kind of way as meaning a system of total, unquestioning belief, as deplorable. The New Right truly believes that it has the policy answer to any problem and the candidate with the ideologically correct doctrine for any job. Its win-at-any-cost stance reminds me of a quote from Lenin's seminal essay on how to organize the Bolshevik party to take over power in Russia, "What Is to Be Done." "We are marching in a compact group along a precipitous and difficult path, firmly holding each other by the hand," Lenin wrote. "We are surrounded on all sides by enemies, and we have to advance almost constantly under their fire. We have combined, by a freely adopted decision, for the purpose of fighting the enemy, and not of retreating into the neighboring marsh, the inhabitants of which, from the very outset, have reproached us with having separated ourselves into an exclusive group and with having chosen the path of struggle instead of the path of conciliation."

This kind of a rigid world-view is a poor paradigm for running the affairs of America and the world. Perhaps the most disastrous example is the Iraq war of 2003, the intellectual authors of which were a small group of "true believers" headed by Paul Wolfowitz and Richard Perle, under the enthusiastic leadership of President Bush, who believed that 9/11 afforded the United States not only an unparalleled opportunity but virtually a duty to use its military might to straighten out the affairs of the long-troubled Islamic world. The poorly conceived, incompetently conducted war, originally sold on the premise that Saddam Hussein's regime constituted an imminent nuclear, biological and chemical warfare threat to the United States, and then, when that proved to be false, justified as a war for freedom and against tyranny, continues to cost Iraqis and Americans dearly in blood, suffering, and treasure. (In early 2006, the Nobel prize-winning economist, Joseph Stiglitz, and Linda Bilmes, a former assistant secretary of Commerce, delivered a paper at the annual meeting of the American Economic Association that estimated the final bill for the Iraq war will likely be between $1 *trillion* and $2 *trillion,* rather than the $60 billion originally predicted by the President's budget office. Their paper notes that one trillion dollars would have fixed Social Security for the next seventy-five years twice over.) The war's most likely results, after who knows how many more years of Iraqi and American bloodshed, are a civil war between Shias, Sunnis, and Kurds, or an anti-American, Shia-dominated government, with close ties to Iran, that will establish Sharia law as the writ of the land. That will mean, for example, that Iraqi women, who long ago had achieved legal equality with men in the secular Baathist regime, will become legally worth half that. The war and the torture scandals of Abu Ghraib, Guantanamo, and Bagram cost Americans the respect and support of most of the rest of the world (which, of course, will endlessly complicate prosecution of the poorly named "war on terrorism"). The war strengthened the hand of fundamentalists throughout the Muslim world population, and by inspiring and training new generations of jihadists ensures that our future will be less safe. The respected London-based International Institute for Strategic Studies (IISS) said in a May 2004 assessment that "a rump leadership (of Al Qaeda) is still intact and over eighteen thousand potential terrorists are at large with recruitment accelerating on account of Iraq." Michael Scheuer, a former CIA official, in the 2004 book titled *Imperial Hubris: Why the West is Losing the War on Terror,* writes: "U.S. forces and policies are completing the radicalization of the Islamic world...There is nothing bin Laden could have hoped for more than the American invasion and occupation of Iraq."

17

Getting It Right

As a new century uneasily begins, Americans find themselves masters of a new world empire—or something like that—without ever having really voted on that matter. Our legions are everywhere. According to Global Security, a Washington-based, nonprofit organization, in 2004, not counting the one hundred thousand military personnel in the old bases in Germany, Italy, the United Kingdom, and Japan, the United States had two hundred and fifty thousand soldiers, sailors, airmen, Marines, and Coast Guardsmen deployed in nearly one hundred thirty countries in support of combat, peacekeeping, and deterrence operations. We add new bases as the circumstances dictate: Eastern Europe, the Caucasus, Uzbekistan, and Tajikistan. We run a worldwide network of military and intelligence prisons and interrogation centers. In ways unimaginable to the great empire builders of the past—the ancient Romans, the Ottoman Turks, or the British—Americans can obliterate militarily and with extreme force any society on the face of the earth (imagine what Nero would have done with nuclear bombs or the pilotless Predator spy plane/bomber).

But what do we do now? We are enormously, frighteningly powerful, yet at the same time perilously friendless and vulnerable. We concentrate on the power to wage war but have neglected our statecraft: the policymaking, planning, and negotiation functions of the State Department; the public diplomacy tasks of information and cultural programming overseas; and the nation and institution-building capacities of our development assistance programs. We thus appear in much of the world like some unpredictable giant with one mighty forearm and fist raised while its other, helping arm and hand hang thin, wasted, and ineffectual. The giant's once-strong and seductive voice now mostly utters harsh threats and war cries. There are some obvious reforms we can make in the machinery of foreign policy that can improve the current unsatisfactory performance. But fundamentally we must create a different conception of foreign policy in which strident unilateralism gives way to a lasting concern for international cooperation and the opinions of the rest of the world.

It is not that we don't know how to do things better. The record of American diplomacy and institution building overseas since World War II offers some formidable successes, beginning with the Marshall Plan in Europe and the building of democratic institutions in Japan. There are many others less well known. The green revolution of the 1960s, which transformed wheat and rice production in an Asia traditionally never far from famine, was led by American scientists originally funded by two great American foundations, Rockefeller and Ford, where patience, money, and knowledge of the terrain were taken for granted as necessary ingredients. When I worked at the Ford Foundation and the U.S. Agency for International Development, a ten-year-plus timeline for supporting the founding and nurture of institutions overseas was house doctrine. The payoffs can be spectacular. The current information technology revolution in India is directly descended, for example, from the Indian Institutes of Technology and the Indian Institutes of Management that Ford, the U.S. Agency for International Development, and European donors supported in their early institution-building stages. Similarly, the slow but crucial improvement in the status of women in South Asia owes much to the support of institutions like the Ford Foundation. The government-funded Fulbright program of educational and scientific exchanges, originally proposed by Sen. William J. Fulbright in 1945, made enormous contributions to both new knowledge and mutual understanding between the United States and the societies around the world, from which a quarter of a million students and scientists have come to study and work in our country. The role of foreign-born scientists and engineers, many of whom came to this country as exchange students, is indispensable today in American research and education.

Faced with the challenges of a perilous new century, it behooves us to mine this rich lode of experience. Some of our more thoughtful minds are doing this. It is moderately encouraging to observe, as the Iraq war drags on and deficits mount at home, some signs of a renaissance of pragmatism and moderation and a new willingness, apparent on both the conservative and liberal side of the political spectrum, to learn from our experience.

My own foreign policy agenda is brief:

1. Putting our domestic house in order.

Without a politically and economically healthy homeland, no foreign policy will long prosper. The American capitalist system is seriously out of kilter, a view shared by a growing number of conservative intellectuals and politicians. The challenge in the new century is to ensure that future growth, not only economically but in terms of social justice, will at least emulate, if not surpass, the record of past achievement. The most accurate measuring device I know for judging the likely health and progress of societies is the connection between elites and the mass of the population, first described by a distinguished anthropologist, Clifford Geertz, writing four decades ago in his studies of developing nations. When elites see that their own continuing well-being is organically connected to the well-being of the masses, Geertz predicted accurately that this society overall is likely to progress. For most of America's national life, with some important exceptions (particularly as concerned race), American society has generally measured up well using those calipers. Today, that measurement reveals an increasingly ugly picture.

The *New York Times* conservative Republican columnist David Brooks observed recently: "There are now few ideological checks on the corporate community's desire to use government to stifle competition. Now it is conservatives who often embrace special tax breaks, special subsidies, special regulatory sinecures. This is a cancer on modern conservatism, and most every conservative in his or her heart knows it." Management fraud and executive greed in the American corporate world are unparalleled in our history. The administration of the second George Bush rewrote tax policy to favor the richest Americans, who control an increasing share of our national wealth. The most graphic evidence of greed is the ratio between the overall compensation of senior management executives and employee salaries. In its issue of April 9, 2001, *Business Week* reported under the headline, "We're Back to Serfs and Royalty," that the average pay of CEOs at more than three hundred of the largest companies averaged 531 times that of their average employees. Comparable ratios are twenty-one to one for Germany and sixteen to one for Japan. Meanwhile, the number of Americans with no health insurance rose to forty-five million in 2003, according to a Census Bureau 2004 report, while thirteen million children live below the poverty line (with rates in some American cities as high as 35 percent).

Whether progressive conservatives (as Brooks hopes) or pragmatic liberals eventually invent and carry out reform is essentially immaterial. The current trends in the American political economy simply must be reversed if America is to progress as a land of economic opportunity and social justice. An added benefit will be an improvement in the attractiveness of the American model of democracy to increasingly skeptical societies overseas. A major reason the United States won the Cold War against the Soviet Union was because the majority of the people of the world believed that America was a land of hope, opportunity, and justice.

Part of the challenge in putting the American house in order to deal with the new century is strengthening our productivity in education, health, science, and technology. Public education and health care for the poor and minorities are mostly bad. Many scientists believe that our scientific and technological superiority, on which our military and economic power rests, may slowly be eroding. The Bush administration established the very bad practice of questioning and refusing to support scientific research that arrived at conclusions unpalatable to its political agenda, most notably in the fields of environment and biology. And, as it becomes increasingly difficult for security reasons for many foreign students and researchers to obtain access to the United States, an increasing number of overseas institutions are moving to establish leadership in critical fields of research, as is the case with stem-cell research.

The widespread anti-Americanism caused by the invasion of Iraq plus troubling visa and security concerns decreased the attractiveness for many foreign scientists of spending a considerable part of a career in the United States, and in the competitive worlds of science and technology American institutions are heavily dependent on foreign-born, U.S.-trained scientists, engineers, and foreign-born graduate teaching assistants. According to Adam Segal, writing in *Foreign Affairs*, 38 percent of the PhDs currently working in American science and engineering were born abroad, while from 1985 to 2000 more than half of all American doctoral degrees in science and engineering were awarded to students from China, India, South Korea, and Taiwan. The Council of Graduate Schools reports that international applications to U.S. graduate schools dropped 32 percent from 2003 to 2004. Professor Joseph Nye of Harvard writing in *Foreign Affairs* deplores the decline in the annual number of academic and cultural exchanges from 45,000 in 1995 to 29,000 in 2001. In Indonesia, to choose an example, only 1,333 students received visas to attend American schools in 2003 as compared to 6,250 in 2000.

2. Repairing and reinvigorating American diplomacy, particularly the public diplomatic functions of information and cultural exchange.

Americans who believe it generally best to deal with the world through means other than military have always had to combat the strong streak of isolationism that runs through the society. Americans must now find anew the stomach, wisdom, and patience required for the tasks of public diplomacy and institution building overseas, and that consensus must eventually be reflected in a bipartisan understanding among the leaders of our two major political parties. That was how we reconstructed Germany and Japan. That is how we won the Cold War. That is how to survive and prosper in the new century.

Much, of course, has changed since the days of the Cold War. Today, ideas about America arrive overseas almost entirely through private instrumentalities, notably the popular media. "Baywatch," CNN, and Arnold Schwarzenegger movies are popular around the world, and the Internet is an unprecedented universal web of largely uncensored information. As private communications have exploded in recent decades, government capabilities have weakened. Professor Nye, who served in the Clinton administration as an assistant secretary of defense, deplores what he calls the decline of America's "soft power," which he defines as the ability to attract others by the legitimacy of U.S. policies and the values that underlie them. He notes wryly that the United States, the world's only superpower and the leader in the information technology revolution, "is all too frequently outgunned in the propaganda war by fundamentalists hiding in caves." Nye writes: "The United States' most striking failure is the low priority and paucity of resources it has devoted to producing soft power. The combined cost of the State Department's public diplomacy programs and U.S. international broadcasting is just over a billion dollars, about four percent of the nation's international affairs budget. That total is about three percent of what the United States spends on intelligence and a quarter of one percent of its military budget."

Restructuring official radio and television broadcasting, information centers, and American libraries overseas, and cultural, educational, and scientific exchange programs will be far more difficult today than it was fifty years ago. Funding for these programs was slashed for budgetary reasons during the 1990s, when it appeared that Cold War requirements no longer dictated a high priority. Today, security concerns in most overseas societies increasingly limit free access to any kind of American official installation, and anti-Americanism is at historically high levels. In Islamabad, the capital of Pakistan, for example, the American cultural center and its public reading rooms are closed, and the number of young Pakistanis seeking advanced education in the United States has plummeted. But information, cultural programming, and propaganda are essential subjects in national security, and policymakers need to put their brains to work to develop new approaches and to reverse the downward trends in budget and staffing. At the start, that would mean a return to a policy of serious and aggressive federal government investment in difficult foreign languages and foreign area studies for American students like those who as graduates staffed both our public information and intelligence efforts of the Cold War years. Our failures in intelligence and public diplomacy this past two decades are in considerable part traceable to our ignorance of foreign languages and cultures.

Information, exchange, and cultural activities overseas functioned best during the Cold War years when the U.S. Information Agency (USIA) operated semi-independently from the State Department. In 1999, at the insistence of former Sen. Jesse Helms (Republican, North Carolina), most of these programs were unceremoniously dumped into the lap of the State Department, which did not want them, and where traditionally they were regarded as work for second raters (the opinion of most State Department career officers might be described as "real diplomats do policy," not information or culture). International broadcasting was separated out earlier and since 1994 has been under the supervision of a separate federal entity, a nine-member, bipartisan Broadcasting Board of Governors, which provides administrative and engineering support to five government-supported regional radio and television stations through an International Broadcasting Bureau. Not many people listen to them overseas. In Pakistan, a recent *Los Angeles Times* article reported that Voice of America Urdu-language broadcasting reaches only about 1 percent of Pakistan's 160 million people. The USIA model itself may not, of course, be appropriate for the current circumstances, although it is hard to conceive of a worse approach than the existing pattern of activities. A recent Council of Foreign Relations task force recommended the creation of a White House Public Diplomacy Coordinating Structure, led by a presidential appointee, and a nonprofit Corporation for Public Diplomacy to help mobilize the private sector. The final form of a revamped public diplomacy effort is less important than the brainpower, leadership, and money devoted to it. Its success will ultimately depend on the commitment and the policy leadership it gets from the president. Absent that, the inevitable congressional coalitions of know-nothings and isolationists will eventually cripple it.

3. Understanding nation building and practicing it better.

President George W. Bush and his advisers disdained nation building as a concept before they came to power, then adopted it almost as an afterthought to the military conquest of Iraq. They subsequently practiced it with breathtaking incompetence during the occupation period. The subject deserves better than that. America's past experience in nation building overseas is broad and frequently has been successful.

The first lesson is that the building process is long. Nations are built by inventing and painstakingly adapting indigenous and foreign ideas and institutional models (the United States of 1776 is itself a prime example), not imposing rigid paradigms. The time horizon required is decades, not a few years. The second lesson is that both public and private institutions must be built and strengthened. In recent decades, the theoreticians of the magic of the marketplace have

ruled the debate about nation building with the argument that if only free markets and free movement of capital can be established, economic development will
largely take care of itself. Indeed, that was the primary supposition of the early
occupation period in Iraq. In many respects, this worldwide emphasis on free
markets was a desirable correction to the earlier emphasis in the development theory of the 1950s and early 1960s on strengthening government institutions.

We see now, however, that the institutions of law and order are fundamental
to all others. The constitution, the executive arm, the legislature, the military,
and the police—all are of necessity government functions. To quote David
Brooks, the conservative writer, again:

> We need to strengthen nation-states. The great menace of the twentieth cen-
> tury was overbearing and tyrannical governments. The great menace of the
> twenty-first century will be failed governments, because those are the places
> where our enemies will be able to harbor and thrive, where violence can nur-
> ture and grow, where life is nasty, brutish and short. We are going to have to
> construct a multilateral nation-building apparatus so that each time a nation-
> building moment comes along, we don't have to patch one together ad hoc.
> Now we know that law and order is the first thing they need. We are going to
> have to construct new institutions to help nations develop rule of law within
> their boundaries, for if that is not accomplished, all the economic develop-
> ment in the world will not help.

Law and order in the order of priority of fundamental institutions must be
closely followed by public education and public health. Our most costly development assistance failures in the Islamic world occurred in those fields in Pakistan
and Afghanistan where, after the Soviet defeat in Afghanistan in 1989, we had
the opportunity but failed to stay the course and invest our wealth and experience
in long-term institution building.

Afghanistan and Iraq also teach us that soldiers should be expected to be soldiers and not nation builders. In spite of the admirable civic affairs work of many
officers and soldiers, the Pentagon made a mess of the immediate, postwar reconstruction and development work in both Afghanistan and Iraq. The experience of
the British empire is instructive. The Colonial Office and the colonial civil services were as important as the British army in imperial planning. The military
was expected to fight, not develop political and social institutions. The colonial
civil service was designed and organized to move in immediately with trained
cadres to undertake reconstruction and institution building. If we are to fight and
then build nations overseas, something resembling that model would be far more

serviceable than the Pentagon-driven model of control of the early phases of reconstruction and development that we witnessed in Afghanistan and Iraq. A logical organizing point could be a specialized service, possibly within the State Department, drawing on the department's regional experts and the trained disaster and development staff of the U.S. Agency for International Development, working in close cooperation with and support from the Pentagon. It would need to recruit and deploy far stronger language, area, and cultural competence in its ranks and leadership than anything currently on the scene. (As of late 2004, the State Department announced the formation of a new Office of Reconstruction and Stabilization, headed by Ambassador Carlos Pascual, a career Foreign Service officer who came up through the AID ranks. The new office is charged by the National Security Council with "leading, coordinating and institutionalizing U.S. civilian government capacity to prepare for post-conflict reconstruction and stabilization efforts." Assigned to the office are thirty staff members from the departments of State, Defense, the Treasury, the CIS, AID, and the Army Corps of Engineers. It is *not* active in Iraq or Afghanistan, and it is not clear how much clout the new office will be able to muster for the almost certainly coming bureaucratic wars.) It would be wise to provide extra pay and benefits to those officers prepared to devote a significant part of their lives to long and difficult assignments in the risky but vital tasks of nation building.

Improving nation building and development assistance also needs to include a major effort to de-bureaucratize the machinery. William Easterly, a respected economist specializing in overseas development, writing in the July/August 2002 issue of *Foreign Policy*, charges that the global foreign aid bureaucracy "has run amok in recent years" in a foreign aid cartel of donor nations and organizations that includes the World Bank, AID, the International Monetary Fund, the regional international development banks, the United Nations, and the major European aid agencies. Easterly writes, "The typical aid agency requires governments seeking its money to work exclusively with that agency's own bureaucracy," and the aid organizations "mindlessly duplicate services for the world's poor." As an example, Easterly writes, "A team from the U.S. Agency for International Development produced a report on corruption in Uganda in 2001, unaware that British analysts had produced a report on the same topic six months earlier." Easterly cites the case of Tanzania, where, "the government churns out more than twenty-four-hundred reports annually for its various donors, who send the poor country some one thousand missions each year."

The current ways of doing foreign aid not only needlessly add to the work load of recipients in preparing work plans and funding requests but then, more often than not, run aground when Congress fails to provide the promised funding levels. For example, two years ago President Bush, with great fanfare, called for "a new compact for global development" using the mechanism of a "Millennium Challenge Account" in which development assistance would be provided to poor countries that "rule justly, invest in their people, and encourage economic freedom." Congress authorized a new Millennium Challenge Corporation (MCC), a publicly funded but privately governed institution, to manage the program and gave it $1 billion in initial funding for fiscal year 2004. As the corporation's staff identified recipient countries, made the first of continuing rounds of staff visits to them, which presumably took a lot of the scarce time of national leaders, and began to develop long-term plans, the president requested $2.5 billion for fiscal year 2005. Congress promptly cut this by half to $1.25 billion. As of early 2005, the outlook for the new program remained uncertain.

American assistance needs to be both highly selective and occasionally universal in its scope and targets. Most of the staggering problems of the poor majority of the world's people, as the world population balloons from today's three-plus billion to a projected nine billion mark around mid-century (after which it is expected to begin to decline), are already far past the reach of any traditional outside assistance. Mike Davis, in a *Harper's Magazine* report titled "Planet of Slums," writes that "ninety percent of this final buildup of humanity will occur in the urban areas of developing countries," and that the "most celebrated result will be the burgeoning of new megacities with populations in excess of eight million, and even more spectacularly, hypercities with more than twenty million inhabitants." He notes that half of today's worldwide slum population is under the age of twenty-five. In Africa, "Lagos is simply the biggest node in the shantytown corridor of seventy million people that stretches from Abidjan to Ibadan, probably the biggest continuous footprint of urban poverty on earth."

Direct development assistance can do little to alleviate this kind of stark poverty in the poor nations, although public-health assistance will be extremely important both to indigenous populations and, in keeping plagues under observation and control, to the American population itself. In economic terms, a liberal trade policy, with increasing access to American markets, is in many cases the most effective single action we can take—and reducing tariffs is always controversial at home. As important as Pakistan is to the United States in the war on terror, for example, the White House has consistently rejected President Musharraf's plea to lower U.S. import duties on Pakistani textiles—primarily underwear and shirts. Reducing duties is the single most important step the United States could take to improve the Pakistani economy, where 45 percent of manufacturing jobs are found in the textile industry, and help Musharraf survive against Al Qaeda, the Taliban, and homegrown fundamentalists.

We certainly need to explore new concepts of assistance. Davis points out that true political power and the effective governance of much of the world's new urban poor, which decades ago would have been a target for Marxist political parties, now lie in the hands of populist Islamic organizations throughout the Muslim world and Pentecostal Christianity in sub-Saharan Africa and much of Latin America. The power of these indigenous populist groups grows out of their commitment to addressing the social and economic needs of the poor, whether those be legal aid, the organization of night schools, or the provision of medical assistance and burying the dead. In some countries—the luckier ones—these populist groups will assuredly take over and exercise national power peacefully, as has been the case with the ruling Justice and Development Party under the leadership of Prime Minister Erdoğan in Turkey (Indonesia eventually may follow the same path). Occasionally, such groups combine good works with terrorist activities—as is the case with Hamas in Palestine and Syria. Americans are not without experience in working in such environments. In Gaza and the West Bank, for example, non-governmental organizations like Save the Children and the YMCA have used AID funds for many years to create jobs and expand economic opportunities.

Indeed, over the past half-century American NGOs have grown to be major participants in international development work, using both private and U.S. government funds. They are bound to grow further in their importance as scouts and partners with indigenous, grass-roots institutions. In its early years, AID was suspicious of NGOs, believing that heavy lifting could be carried out only by formal, large-scale AID projects. It now lists more than three hundred NGOs with whom it cooperates and provides funds. The Eurasia Foundation is a good example of the changing government approach to assistance. The foundation is mostly government funded, although it also marshals significant funding from a long list of non-U.S. government sources. It is privately managed, comparatively quick and flexible in its decision-making processes, and able to move much faster than a formal government agency in identifying opportunities and local leadership in economic reform and democratization. In the war-ravaged, wild, and dangerous environments of Afghanistan and Iraq, hundreds of U.S., international, and local NGOs are major actors in efforts to build new institutions. In the immediate post-invasion period in Iraq before the insurgency caught fire, for example, my old boss from Eurasia Foundation days, Charlie Greenleaf, utilizing an Iraqi NGO, launched a promising micro-credit program that reached thousands of new, small-scale Iraqi entrepreneurs. NGOs cannot be the ultimate tool of development, of course. They cannot establish law and order or carry out a host of critical governmental functions like public health and primary education, and as they grow in the size and scope of their programs they run into the dangers of bureaucratization and becoming less responsive to the changing dynamics of on-the-ground problems.

It has been argued that AID itself should be transformed into a central, foundation-like institution, funding NGOs and private business and educational groups for specific tasks in overseas assistance. Congress resisted this idea in the past, and it is unlikely that any central development assistance agency can—or should—escape direct congressional oversight and approval of appropriations. A central agency will continue to be a necessary element in dealing with truly worldwide challenges. Probably the best example is the health problems of poor populations everywhere in the world, which intimately concern all of us. In earlier days, Americans took pride in supporting humanitarian efforts to improve the health of poor populations overseas. In those good old days, the problems—smallpox, malaria, river blindness, the guinea worm—conveniently remained overseas with the poor people while, through AID and support for United Nations programs, we played an honorable role in their eradication or containment. Plagues today respect no frontiers, and Americans as a matter of direct self-interest must support funding for research and the prevention and control of plagues like HIV, tuberculosis, and the new diseases of poor and overcrowded societies (SARS is the latest example, and avian flu may be the next) that, thanks to modern travel and migration patterns, will sweep through the twenty-first-century world. The Bush administration deserves applause for committing important resources to the worldwide war on HIV (although the effectiveness of these funds is limited by prohibitions on sex education), and even more so does the new generation of big American philanthropists like Bill Gates of Microsoft as they step up to the plate to fight disease and improve public health in the developing world.

What AID needs most of all in order to do a better job is for Congress to remove the policy and bureaucratic incrustations it has imposed on the agency over many years (thirty-nine earmarks and objectives at last count). That will never occur without presidential leadership and a lasting bipartisan commitment to the essential role of foreign assistance in the post 9/11 world. AID's strongest case for receiving this kind of support lies in its dedicated core staff of career Foreign Service officers, with a cumulative vast body of knowledge of what works and doesn't work in building institutions and nations overseas. In addition to strengthening its staff by greatly improving its language and area competence, AID must lengthen their overseas assignments, which still generally follow the State Department practice of moving Foreign Service officers every two to four years. (Because of security and health problems overseas, the State Department is actually *reducing* the length of Foreign Service overseas assignments—in some cases to one year!) Given the institution-building nature of AID's work, a four-year, extendable assignment to the majority of overseas posts (unless extreme hardship or danger prevails at the post) should become policy.

Having belatedly embraced the concept of nation building, the Bush administration also deserves credit for increasing development assistance spending overseas, although the levels on a dollar equivalent analysis still lag far behind those of the Cold War years. The fiscal year 2006 foreign aid budget requested an increase from $10 billion to $15 billion, including new funds for the already under-funded Millennium Challenge account. In the vast U.S. economy and federal budget, this amount constitutes only moderate spending on an increasingly important component of foreign policy. Official development assistance stimulates and supplements a much larger private effort on the part of American foundations, NGOs, corporations, universities, and religious groups, estimated by AID at about $34 billion. As a reference point in this Washington dance of the billions, Department of Defense spending is currently projected at $401.3 billion, a figure supplemented by perhaps as much as 50 percent more, some analysts claim, with defense-related spending included in other departmental budgets (as, for example, $4 billion in foreign military assistance traditionally included in the international affairs account managed by the State Department and the Pentagon.)

Statecraft, foreign aid, and propaganda are far less exciting subjects than war. But the military option is deceptively two-edged, as we see in Iraq. America must strengthen its diplomacy, its once-strong information and cultural activities, and its once widespread and successful commitment to helping build basic institutions in the strategically important regions of the world. Absent this, all the military might in the world will not suffice to protect us. It's time to make love and friendship, not war.

18
My America

In the waning years of the magnificent and terrible twentieth century, Judy and I settled down in our New York apartment on Manhattan's Upper West Side. New York is a city made for an old wanderer like me. In a five-minute walk to Broadway and the grocery store, we encounter a dozen specimens of our common humanity—squat, big-nosed Mayan Indians looking like a carving from Monte Alban; Pakistani and Sikh cab drivers; towering African princes managing the food market checkout lines; hard-faced Korean deli owners; Polish plumbers; Russian hardware store owners; and a still sizable but declining population of WASPs like me and Upper West Side Jews. The languages of the street carry the lilts and rhythms of every continent. The city's residents walk fast, talk loudly and a lot, and think big. Beneath it all, in education, business, music, dance, and theater, is a world of quiet hard work, discipline, talent, pride, enterprise, and risk taking. Nowhere else are the power, magic, and variety of the human spirit so generously on display.

We also own a small house in Rhode Island, overlooking an inlet of the Atlantic Ocean, not far from where my sea captain son, Peter, and his family live. We watch the gulls fishing the waters of the inlet, listen to the songbirds, smell the beach roses, and swim in the chilly ocean. Like a kid in a candy shop, I treasure the time to read and to enjoy music. Five years ago, I resurrected the old violin of my childhood days, which lay stowed away and untouched for a half-century under various beds and in closets and storage bins, got it repaired by a violin shop near Carnegie Hall, found a teacher to help reinstall my technique, and now play Bach and Schubert for an hour or so daily.

My generation quietly exits from the stage, of course, like the musicians in Haydn's farewell symphony. We have probably had our last World War II Marine Corps fighter squadron reunion of the surviving pilots. But age, like youth and maturity, has its rewards. If you are fortunate, chief among these is memory. In his late eighties, Czeslaw Milosz wrote: "I felt a door opening in me and I entered the clarity of early morning. One after another my former lives were departing, like ships, together with their sorrow. And the countries, cities, gardens, the bays of seas assigned to my brush came closer, ready now to be described better than they were before."

Not long ago, my cousin and friend of my youth, Marvin Stanley, died. My brother, Murray, Judy, and I flew out to the rolling fields and broad, fertile river bottomlands of northern Missouri to visit his wife of sixty-plus years, Gladys. In the 1920s, when Marvin was a boy learning to be a farmer, horses and mules still pulled plows, cows were milked by hand, farmers butchered their own pigs, the country roads were dirt, you read at night by lamplight, heated water on a stove to take a bath once a week, and used chamber pots and outdoor privies. The great railroads, where my father and his brothers all worked, were the arteries along which American meat and grain, heavy freight, and coal and oil moved across the vast land. Robber barons lived fresh in the popular consciousness. The way many working-class people chose to fight them, as my father did, was by joining a union. Most Americans lived, loved, worked, and died on the farms and in the small towns where we were born. In spite of hard times, most Americans believed that the frontier was still out there somewhere, and that opportunities in America were endless if you worked hard and were lucky.

Marvin left Missouri only once, when he joined the Army and went off as an automatic rifleman to fight the Germans across Europe from the Normandy to the Elbe. When he returned, he never again left the farm, although the way Marvin farmed in his later years, with a lot of land, costly machines, and computerized business planning, bore scant resemblance to the farming practices of his youth. He was the only one of us to follow the farming and railroad traditions of our ancestors. In my immediate family, Murray and I both joined the Marine Corps to fight the Japanese in the Pacific. Neither of us ever lived in Missouri again. Murray devoted his life to the Marine Corps, fighting in two more wars, and then designing fighter aircraft as an aeronautical engineer. In the great migrations of the postwar years, I never went home, and traveled the world like a modern Sinbad as a journalist, diplomat, and foundation executive. What led us to follow such different paths? Hindu philosophy would probably say this is not a significant question. We each followed our *dharma*, our duty. No philosophy or religion tells us precisely how that is constituted: what part is willed and purposeful, what part predestination, what part luck. In my own life, certainly, a passion for questing led me to worlds beyond those of my birthplace. And if good health and a sanguine temperament are inheritable, then genetic predestination as well equipped me to follow the paths I chose. Beyond that, I was lucky to be born as an American in a society about to explode into a world of a thousand new opportunities.

Marvin is buried in a simple family plot in the churchyard of the old wooden Baptist church in Rothville, the tiny town where my mother was born. His grave looks out across the tree-lined channel of Yellow Creek to the fields that Marvin loved and cultivated until the day he died. Marvin's sister, Margaret, who lived with us in Kansas City when I was a boy, drove up to Rothville with us. Gladys cooked her standard Missouri working-farm lunch for us: beef brisket, chicken, scalloped potatoes (a great favorite of Marvin's, and mine as well), string beans, homemade rolls, three or four salads, and pie and cake for dessert. I said the usual words of consolation to Gladys when we went to the cemetery, and she wept. I asked if she remembered when we met, soon after she and Marvin were married. I had come back from someplace overseas and had driven up to spend a few days with Marvin and Gladys in the old farmhouse, now long since demolished, that originally belonged to my aunt and uncle, Amelia and Will Stanley.

I told Gladys that when I met her with Marvin I thought I had never seen a love as radiant and full of physical delight as theirs. They smiled every time they looked at each other. Gladys nodded her head and said, "Yes, yes." I then repeated the story, which of course she already knew, about Marvin, my brother, Murray, and me riding down to Yellow Creek in the sweltering afternoon days of August to swim in the brown, shady cool stream and throw rocks at turtles. She recited the names of the horses—Dandy, Nelly, and Charlie—and for a moment it was as though they were there with their liquid eyes, their smell of horse sweat, and their fat haunches, shaking their manes, stomping, and switching their tails against the big horseflies.

Index

A

Academic and cultural exchanges 357
Afghanistan war 252, 275, 278, 284, 306, 345
Aga Khan rural support program 295
Aircraft carrier *USS Franklin* 32-43
Al Qaeda xii, 200, 253, 282, 353, 363
Allen, George V. 83
Allende, Salvador 78, 80
American National Exhibition Sokolniki Park 97-108
American NGOs (non-governmental organizations) 363-365
Anti-Americanism 357-358
Aquino, Benigno 206
Arbenz, Jacobo 76
Armas, Castillo 76
Armitage, Richard 320
Asia 8, 55, 173-195 (Ford Foundation programs in Asia), 196-219 (Southeast Asia), 221-262 (Ford Foundation in India), 264-278 (AID programs in Asia), 279-307 (AID in Pakistan), 310-312 (teaching about Asia), 316, 317
Asia Foundation 214, 320, 344

B

Bader, William 340
Balanchine, George 121, 136, 137, 139, 158
Ban Chiang 202
Bangkok 171, 179, 182, 194-196, 198, 200-204, 214-216
Bearden, Milton 288
Beebe-Center, Horton 345, 349
Bell, David E. 166

Benoit, Charles 183, 215, 250
Benson, Charles 187
Bhatt, Ela 236, 238-239
Bhutto, Benazir 287
Bhutto, Zulfikar Ali 281, 286
Bobrowsky, Igor 345, 349
Bolton, John 270, 272
Borlaug, Norman 163, 179
Brahmanic ideology 227
Brady, Nyle 264, 273
Bresnan, Jack 179
Buddhism 198-199, 241, 248, 256, 317
Bull, Greta 345
Bundy, McGeorge 166, 175, 246, 257-258

C

Carey, Sarah 344
Cashel, James 321
Catherman, Terry 130
Chanute Daily Tribune 56
Chile 5, 75-80, 190
Chilean politics 77-78
Chowhdry, Kamla 238, 262
Chinese Confucian influence 199
Citizens Democracy Corps 321
civil rights revolution 163, 259
Civilian Pilot Training 21, 24
Cold War xi, 55, 69, 72-75, 82, 120, 157, 169-170, 175, 252, 259, 263, 271, 356-359, 365
Columbia University 193, 227, 259, 310-311, 316
Corsair fighter airplane 27
Cuban missile crisis 138, 152

D

Dalai Lama 255-256, 317
Deobandis 283, 292, 298
Desai, Morarji 246, 261

E

Eblen, Margaret 16, 19
Edhi Foundation 297
Edhi, Abdul Sattar 297
Edwards, Robert 191
Eisenhower, Dwight D. 82-83, 86, 97, 159
Ely, Nancy 305
Embree, Ainslie 310, 317
Ensminger, Douglas 160-162, 189, 230, 237, 276
Eurasia Foundation 319-321, 338-351, 363

F

Forty Years: A Learning Curve, book on India 317
Failures in intelligence and public diplomacy 358
Figes, Orlando 120
First Latin American Congress for Peace 69
Fisher, Suzanne 251
Ford Foundation 80, 139, 152-170, 175, 179-194, 196-198, 201, 202, 207, 210-220, 221, 223, 230-239, 241-247, 250-251, 254-261, 263, 265, 268, 269, 273, 277, 292, 317
Ford II, Henry 156, 159, 166
Ford, Henry 11, 156
Foreign policy agenda 355
Foreign Service xi, xii, 5, 70-76, 79-88, 100, 107, 108, 110, 121, 123, 127, 129, 152-154, 265, 288- 289, 304-305, 317-320, 361, 364-365
Foreign Service Institute 108, 110
Foxcroft 309, 313-315
Frei, Eduardo 78, 80-81
Frenzel, William 338, 344

Fulbright program 355
Fuller, Buckminster 101
Fuller, William 214

G

Gandhi, Indira 186, 188, 191, 231, 240
Gandhi, Mahatma 176, 229, 231, 236-237, 245, 248
Gant, George 169-170, 179, 194, 198, 301
Garmisch-Partenkirchen 112, 121
Global foreign aid bureaucracy 361
Goodman, Benny 14, 135-136
Greenleaf, Charles 275-277, 319-321, 338-340
Green revolution in wheat and rice 163
Guatemala 68, 76, 270, 288
Guimond, Laura 342

H

Hanson, Haldore 179
Harkness, Albert 79
Harrar, George 161, 163
Heald, Henry 158-159, 166, 190
Herron, Frank 74-75
Herzen, Alexander 109, 132
Hill, Francis "Frosty" 161, 163
Hindu caste system 227, 243
Hinton, Deane 288-289, 304-305
Huq, Zia ul 284, 286, 304-305

I

Ibañez del Campo, Carlos 78
India 148, 157, 160-163, 176, 221-262
International Institute of Applied Systems Research 170
Islam 116, 178, 200, 209, 253, 283-285, 297-298, 301, 303, 306
Islamabad 191, 277-278, 281, 283, 286, 291-292, 297-298, 301, 303, 305-306, 358

J

Jinnah, Mohammad Ali 280

K

Kaliyuga 228

Kansas City xi, 1, 7-22, 42, 55-57, 62, 72, 81, 136, 368

Kansas City Star 7, 42, 56

Kennan, George 122, 150

Kennedy assassination 150-152

Kennedy, John F. 86, 138, 167

Key, William 83

KGB 112, 114, 116, 122, 126-128, 131, 133-135, 141, 145, 149, 151-152

Khan, Akhtar Hameed 292-294

Khan, Ayub 188, 280, 301

Khan, Shoaib Sultan 294-295

Khrushchev, Nikita 97, 103-104, 128

Kiev 112-119, 345-346

Kimball, Frank 318

Kirstein, Lincoln 137, 152, 158, 172, 194

Kitchen Debate, The 104

Kittikachorn, Thanom 204

Kohler, Foy 151

Kukrit, Pramoj 205

L

Leghari, Jafar 302

Levi, Primo 150

Light cruiser USS *Santa Fe* 40, 41

Lion, Donor 274-275, 277, 290

Littell, Wallace 100

Lockwood, Glen 345

Lowry, W. McNeil 152, 154, 158, 166, 169

Lyons, Lisa 192, 202, 205, 241, 247

M

Madrassas 188, 253, 282, 284, 297, 307

Mahathir, Mohammad 188, 212

Mailloux, Laurie 342

Malakshanova, Marina 316

Marcos, Ferdinand 206

Marine Corps 18, 20, 23, 27, 30-31, 34-35, 43-44, 60-62, 366-367

Masey, Jack 100-102, 105, 107, 113, 134, 316

Mattsfield, Wallace 40, 43

Maynes, Charles Bill 350

McCarthyism 82

McClellan, Harold C. 98-103, 107

McCloy, John J. 156

McPherson, M. Peter 264-265

McSweeney, John 150

Messmore, Howard 98-99

Mexico 62-71, 81, 153, 157, 343

Mexico City College 62-63, 65

Mexico City Herald 63, 65

Miller, Frank 179

Mogul emperors 148, 222, 283

Mojave Marine Corps Air Station 27

Montevideo, Uruguay 73

Moos, Malcolm 159

Moscow correspondents 126

Moscow Embassy 100, 108, 112, 120, 127, 134, 319

N

Nassawadox Creek 308

nation building xi, xii, 157, 177, 276, 281, 359-361, 365

Naval Aviation Cadet training 20

Nehru, Jawaharlal 162, 176, 229

Nelson, George 100-102

Neo-conservative think tanks 352

New Asian States 177

New Delhi xi, 80, 160, 162, 219-224, 226, 233, 237, 246-247, 250-252, 261-262

New world empire 354

NIS (New Independent States) 320

Nixon, Richard 83-88

Northampton County, Virginia 278

O

Oldenburg, Phil 311
Oswald, Lee Harvey 124, 151-152

P

Pace, T.D. 29, 37-39, 43
Pacific war 18, 32, 36
Pakistan 73, 187-188, 253, 274, 277, 279-307, 358, 362
Panandikar, Pai 261
Pares, Bernard 117-118
Peaceful competition 97, 108, 112, 128
Pearl Harbor 18, 43
Peyser, Melanie 349
Piekney, William 288
Pipes, Richard 132
Presidential Commission on AID Management 318
Public diplomacy xii, 129, 354, 357-359

R

Radio Liberty 108, 131
Rogalski, William 40
Rakita, Sara 321
Raphel, Arnold 287, 305
Razak, Tun Abdul 210
Reagan administration 270, 338
Reynolds, Judith 342-343
Rockefeller Foundation 157, 161, 163, 174, 180, 197, 234, 254, 268
Roosevelt, Franklin D. 55
Rothweiler, Jack 58-62, 71
Russian language 108-112, 345
Russian winter 142

S

Santa Fe Railroad 1, 7, 10-11, 72
Santiago, Chile 76-77
Scatena, Elisa 259
Schaefer, Peter 38, 40

SEWA (Self-Employed Women's Association) 236
Shieck, Fred 274
Singh, Khushwant 233, 247
Sisco, Frank 129
Smith, Fred 345
Solzhenitsyn, Alexander 111, 133
Soros, George, Soros Foundations 340
Southeast Asia 174-180, 182-184, 194-219, 265-266
Soviet Union 11, 55, 59, 69, 70, 73, 98, 100, 108, 111-116, 120-153, 169-170, 234, 271, 319-320, 346-348, 352
Spanish conquest 67, 199
Stanley, Marvin 3-4, 367
Staples, Murray 3, 12, 36, 367
State Department 70, 79, 83, 85, 97, 108, 110, 111, 114, 123, 129, 144, 176, 264-265, 274, 288, 304, 305, 318-320, 338, 354, 358-359, 361, 365
Status of women in South Asia 355
Stern, Charlotte 64, 247-250
Stravinsky, Igor 122, 136
Stremlau, John 320
Sufism 303
Sukarno 175-176, 186, 205, 207, 272

T

Taliban 188, 252-253, 282-284, 288, 300, 363
Tartar yoke 118
Task Force 58 36
Thailand 196-220
Thapar, Romesh 233, 251
Theosophy 64, 248
Thomas, Franklin 258, 263
Thompson, Lewellyn 108, 123
Traister, Robert 298-299
Tremaine, Frank 65
Truman, Harry 12, 57, 59, 65, 82, 264
Trust for Voluntary Organizations (TVO) 296

U

U.S. Agency for International Development 166, 182, 190, 214, 218, 245, 264-278, 355, 361

Ulithi atoll 35

United Press 65, 70-71, 76, 84, 126, 251

United States Information Agency (USIA) 72, 79-88, 97-108

University of Missouri 16, 59-62, 160, 190

U.S. Army Russian Language school Oberammergau 111

U.S.-Soviet information and cultural exchanges 129

V

Vietnam 155, 167-168, 174, 177, 180-182, 199, 201, 204-205, 214-219, 266

Voice of America 82, 108, 131, 359

W

Warren, Joe 40

Washburn, Abbott 86, 97, 99

Wassom, Herb 287

Watts, Bill 130, 159, 163, 165, 169

Weiland, Pat 32

Wilhelm, Harry 190, 231

Wilson, Shawna 349

Woods, Rose Mary 83

World Bank 156, 163, 181, 187, 270, 272, 276-277, 291, 306, 312, 350, 361

Y

Yevtushenko, Yevgenniy 134

Yew, Lee Kuan 176, 189, 206-208

Ylvisaker, Paul 164, 168

Z

Zeidenstein, George 191

978-0-595-37662-9
0-595-37662-2

CPSIA information can be obtained
at www.ICGtesting.com
Printed in the USA
BVHW030038060821
613755BV00025B/33